VANCOUVER
BEST PLACES

Robert G. Gifford
1254 Alderside Road
Port Moody, B.C.
V3H 3A7

VANCOUVER BEST PLACES

The most discriminating guide to
Vancouver's restaurants, shops, hotels,
nightlife, arts, sights, and outings

Edited by Kasey Wilson
and Stephanie Irving

SASQUATCH BOOKS
SEATTLE

RAINCOAST BOOKS
VANCOUVER

First edition published in 1994.

Library of Congress Cataloging in Publication Data
Vancouver best places : the most discriminating guide to Vancouver's restaurants, shops, hotels, nightlife, arts, sights, and outings / edited by Kasey Wilson and Stephanie Irving.
p. cm.
Includes index.
ISBN 0-912365-96-X : $13.95
1. Vancouver (B.C.)—Guidebooks. I. Wilson, Kasey, 1944-.
II. Irving, Stephanie, 1962-.
F1089.5.V22V355 1994   917.11'33044—dc20
93-45944   CIP

Canadian Cataloguing in Publication Data
Wilson, Kasey
Vancouver best places
Includes index
ISBN 1-895714-37-0

1. Vancouver (B.C.)—Guidebooks. I. Title.
FC3847.18.W56 1994   917.11'33044   C93-091973-4
F1089.5.V22W54 1994

Cover illustration by Nick Gaetano
Cover design by Karen Schober
Interior illustrations by Jerry Nelson
Interior design by Lynne Faulk
Map by David Berger

The Best Places guidebooks have been published continuously since 1975. Books in the Best Places series read as personal guidebooks, but our evaluations are based on numerous reports from locals and travelling inspectors. Final judgements are made by the editor. Our inspectors never identify themselves (except over the phone) and never take free meals or other favours during reviews. Readers are advised that places listed in previous editions may have closed or changed management, or are no longer recommended by this series. In other words, if you have an old edition, you're on your own. The editors welcome information conveyed by users of this book, as long as they have no financial connection with the establishment concerned. A report form is provided at the end of the book. All Best Places guides are available at bulk discounts for corporate gifts, conventions, and fund-raising sales for clubs and organizations.

Published in the USA by:
Sasquatch Books
1008 Western Avenue, Suite 300
Seattle, Washington 98104
(206) 467-4300

Published in Canada by:
Raincoast Book Distribution Ltd.
112 East 3rd Avenue
Vancouver, BC V5T 1C8
(604) 873-6581

CONTENTS

Acknowledgements

The real people behind *Vancouver Best Places* are not only the lucky contributors who eat, shop, and travel—and get paid for it—but also all the unnamed inspectors who have alerted us to their favourite Vancouver finds. True, our inspectors (who always review anonymously and never accept any freebies) are the ones who decide what is best about our city, but not before taking into consideration comments from myriad regional spies and sources. As the most discriminating and evaluative guide to British Columbia's most dynamic metropolis heads to the printer, we'd like to thank everyone who ever wrote, called, or faxed us a suggestion.

In particular, we'd like to give an extra star to the seventeen intrepid reviewers who scoured Vancouver from top to bottom, ferreting out the best places for you to dine, sleep, shop, dance, explore, or just sip some tea with a good friend: Scott Barratt, Pat Fraser, Anne Garber, Anthony Gismondi, Elizabeth Grant, Jason Robert Jones, Eve Johnson, Mark Laba, Lynne MacNamara, Kerry McPhedran, Angela Murrills, Isabel Nanton, Ara Parker, Anne Tempelman-Kliut, Steven Threndyle, Gerry Wingenbach, and Stephen Wong.

But a book is not made by writers alone. Another round of applause is due for all the dedicated people who worked in the trenches: associate editor Nancy Leson, copy editor Nancy Flight, proofreader Robin Van Heck, cover designer Karen Schober, cover illustrator Nick Gaetano, interior designer Lynne Faulk, interior illustrator Jerry Nelson, and map maker David Berger.

—*The Editors*

Introduction

Vancouver is the best city in Canada and better by far than all the major cities of the United States that I have seen.

What, you got a problem with that? You wanna get quibbly? You want a punch between the horns?

Look, I've only been here since 1936, with a few middle years spent learning tea-drinking etiquette in Victoria, and I've never been tempted to leave. I got offers to move to bigger papers in bigger towns. Charlie, Charlie, I coulda been a contenda. I coulda been a somebody. Guys I worked with moved east and got the title shot. I held on to my one-way ticket to Palookaville.

I'm glad I did.

You have to understand what Vancouver is and that's a tough course. People who have never been here, or maybe just visited in 1986, our Expo year, sccm to think that Vancouver is a young megalopolis that sprawls from the Pacific Ocean halfway to Alberta. Wrong.

First of all, Vancouver doesn't sprawl. There's not enough room. The City of Vancouver is a peninsula, built up over the centuries from Fraser River sand. And it looks like we could use a few more truckloads of fill, the way new people are pouring in.

To put it more succinctly, the City of Vancouver is a tiny little living room, entirely surrounded by bedrooms. And you have to cross a bridge to get to most of the beds. That presents access problems, most of which become numbingly clear at 7:30am and 5pm. But somehow it works. It works because there are no uniformed cops, no flashing arrows to control the seven lanes of traffic that have to funnel into the two available lanes on the bridge. It works by courtesy. We merge by instinct and good manners and we always give a little wave to the guy or woman who lets us in.

I have this jewel-like memory of such a morning, when I eased back to let a lady in a red sports car pull ahead on my right. Her left arm came out of the window in a languid wave of thanks, and in her hand she held a long-stemmed red rose. I got a rose waved at me for yielding! I was on a high for the rest of the day.

You may have heard that we can ski within sight of downtown Vancouver and be on the water catching a spring salmon, all in the space of 30 minutes. It's true—as long as your skis have quick-release bindings. Otherwise, it might take up to 45 minutes.

The best day of my life in Vancouver began one New Year's morning. I had quit drinking several years earlier, so on this particular January 1, I woke up early, able to hold my head any way I wanted and still feel good. I drove up Seymour Mountain, above a rippled quilt of clouds that covered the city like the mashed potatoes on a shepherd's pie, and I watched the sun rise. Then I drove down to Dundarave Pier and talked to a 10-year-old boy about the perch he was going to catch with pile-worm bait. I drove out to Spanish Banks and saw people walking and watering their dogs. I drove to the Ho Inn in Chinatown and had beef and broccoli and steamed rice and two pots of gunpowder tea.

I remember all this in exquisite detail. But I can't remember who played in the Rose Bowl that day.

Don't get me started on Dundarave Pier. It's the best place in Vancouver to be by yourself. I think it's the place Leonard Cohen meant when he wrote in "Suzanne," "And Jesus was a sailor when he walked upon the water, and he spent a long time watching from his lonely wooden tower..."

On Dundarave Pier you can look along the sandy beach and see little kids exhuming bright stones and shells and sticks with the enchantment of archaeologists on an Egyptian dig. You can look out at English Bay and see empty-bellied freighters pulling on their anchor chains, swaying in unison like range cattle facing into a snowstorm. When the sun is going down, you can see the little tugs running to the harbor, heads up, bums down, like little boys hurrying to be home before dark.

You should also know that Vancouverites are a very different, a very specific kind of Canadian. In Toronto, for instance, they say Thank God It's Monday, because they can get back to work. We say Thank God It's Thursday, because we can spend the next morning making restaurant reservations and deciding between golf, wind-sailing, cross-country skiing, fishing, or taking the boat up to see Chatterbox Falls before booking off at noon.

Torontonians work hard to make enough to buy another blue suit. Vancouverites put in just enough hours to pay for an extension on the hot tub.

We eat the best in Canada. What's your pleasure? A perfect, formal, four-course meal winding up with port and Stilton in the clubby Chartwell in the Four Seasons Hotel? Heat-lacquered tandoori chicken out on Main Street? Potstickers and gailan at Hon's Noodle House? Italian sausage with fried peppers on Commercial Drive? A White Spot hamburger from a formula unchanged after 50 years? Homey spaghetti and no-nonsense meatballs at Nick's? Can you say eclectic? Tuck in and fill your boots because we've got a menu that doesn't quit.

We've got an awful lot of building going on downtown, but whatever old structures they knock down to make room for some new knock-ups, nobody—developer or demolitionist—touches my favorite downtown structure, the Marine Building. It was completed in 1930, the year I was born. I was six when we moved to Vancouver from a little copper-mining town called Anyox, BC. I had never seen a building higher than a townsite shack, never seen a light brighter than a light bulb. When I saw the white paint that still adorns the cornices at the top of the Marine Building, I thought it was snow, frozen there all year, same as on a mountain peak. The perfectly preserved and restored brass and glass and tiles in the Marine Building's art deco lobby are magnificent.

You should also realize that what we have right now is the second, or perhaps the third, coming of Vancouver. The first coming was a grubby little sawmill town. It burnt down all in one day: June 13, 1886. Next day, they put up tents and started over again.

The snowcapped (I still believe it) Marine Building and the zinc-roofed Hotel Vancouver, which anchors downtown, remain a lovely, visible part of the second phase of cityscape. But they are smaller now, dwarfed by new development: the pinkish Park Place office building; the gleamingly new, 38-storey Wall Centre, with 392 hotel rooms, built on the highest part of the downtown core and topped off with a lethal-looking steel spire; the year-old BC Hydro headquarters building, brightening the forlorn and almost-forgotten Victory Square neighborhood. And abutting the old Expo site between the Granville and Cambie bridges is a whole new, vertical-rise town called Yaletown. The soaring physical change of the last five years is breathtaking. In fact, in 1994, there is so much new building going on in the downtown peninsula that it's as if they just unrolled the blueprints on phase three. All over the cityscape the overhead cranes perch like huge insects, pulling buildings out of the ground like worms. There will be lovely new urban apartments and office space for all the newcomers, new shops, new restaurants, fresh capital, higher horizons, and new opportunities.

I'm not sure I like the pace of it. We're fast-tracking to the year 2000. If you are ever going to visit us, do it now, while we are in the transition between the old tent-town of 1886 and whatever we'll be in the uncomfortably close 21st century.

Denny Boyd

How to Use This Book

This is a rare city guidebook, as candid and frank as it is informative and trustworthy. It is written by and for locals, but visitors will find it just as valuable. *Best Places* reviewers accept no free meals or accommodations; our books have no sponsors or advertisers.

Stars We rate restaurants and lodgings on a scale of zero-to-four stars (with half stars in between), based on uniqueness, enjoyability, loyalty of local clientele, excellence of cooking, performance measured against the place's goals, cleanliness, and professionalism of service. All places in the book are recommended, even those with no stars.

★★★★	The very best in the region
★★★	Distinguished, many outstanding features
★★	Some wonderful qualities
★	A good place
(no stars)	Worth knowing about, if nearby

Price Range When prices range between two categories (for example, moderate to expensive), the lower one is given. Call ahead to verify. All prices are in Canadian dollars.

$$$	Expensive (more than $90 for dinner for two; more than $100 for lodgings for two)
$$	Moderate (between expensive and inexpensive)
$	Inexpensive (less than $35 for dinner for two; less than $60 for lodgings for two)

Cheques and Credit Cards Most establishments that accept cheques require a major credit card for identification. American Express is abbreviated as AE, Diners Club as DC, Discover as DIS, Enroute as E, Japanese Credit Card as JCV, MasterCard as MC, Visa as V.

Addresses All listings are in Vancouver unless indicated otherwise. *Vancouver Best Places* covers the North Shore to White Rock, the West Side to New Westminster.

Phone Numbers All calls are local from Vancouver (area code 604), except where indicated. Telephone numbers preceded by the area code are long distance from Vancouver.

KIDS and FREE We have provided [KIDS] and [FREE] labels throughout the book to indicate attractions and events that are especially suited to children or that are free of charge.

RESTAURANTS

Restaurant Index

★
Akbar's Own Dining Room
Aki
Al Ritrovo
Allium
Alma Street Cafe
Annapurna Vegetarian
    Cuisine of India
Bodhi Vegetarian
    Restaurant
Bo-Jik Vegetarian
    Restaurant
Bridges
Cafe Roma
Earl's
El Caravan
Grand View Restaurant
Hon's Wun Tun House
Isadora's
Japanese Deli House
Joe Fortes
Kilimanjaro
King's Fare Fish & Chips
Kitto Japanese Restaurant
Las Margaritas
Lok's Chinese Restaurant
Lorenzo's
Milestones

Moutai Mandarin
    Restaurant
Nazarre BBQ Chicken
Nonya Baba
Noor Mahal
Nyala Restaurant
O-Tooz The Energie Bar
Olympia Fish Market and
    Oyster Co.
Park Lock Seafood
    Restaurant
Persia Restaurant
Pho Hoang
Settobello
Shinla Korean Restaurant
Singapore Restaurant
The Sleighs
Stepho's Souvlakia
Steveston Seafood House
Sun Wong Kee
Surat Sweet
Szechuan Chongqing
Tang's Noodle House
Tio Pepe
The Tomahawk
Tomato Fresh Food Cafe
Tropika Malaysian Cuisine
Won More

[no stars]
Boss Bakery and
    Restaurant
Ezogiku Noodle Cafe
Hamburger Mary's
Ikea
Kam Gok Yuen
Major The Gourmet
Musashi Japanese
    Restaurant
Naam
Natraj
On Lock
The Only Seafood Cafe
Pepitas
Picasso Café
Sawasdee Thai Restaurant
Umberto Al Porto
Vanier Café
White Spot
Woodlands Natural Food
    Restaurant
Yaohan Supermarket and
    Shopping Centre

[unrated]
English Bay Cafe
Il Barino

LOCATION

Burnaby
The Bread Garden
Earl's
Horizons on Burnaby
    Mountain
Kamei Sushi
Milestones

Chinatown
Aki
Boss Bakery and
    Restaurant
Hon's Wun Tun House
Japanese Deli House
Kam Gok Yuen
Phnom Penh Restaurant
Pho Hoang

Downtown
The Alabaster Restaurant
Anderson's
Bacchus Ristorante (The
    Wedgewood Hotel)
Bandi's
Bianco Nero

The Bread Garden/
    Gallery Cafe
Cafe de Paris
Caffe de Medici
Chartwell (The Four
    Seasons)
Chez Thierry
Chili Club
Chiyoda
CinCin
The Clearwater Café
Da Pasta
Delilah's
Dynasty Restaurant
    (Vancouver Renaissance
    Hotel)
Earl's
El Caravan
English Bay Cafe
Ezogiku Noodle Cafe
The Fish House at Stanley
    Park
Five Sails (Pan Pacific
    Hotel)

Flying Wedge
Griffins
Hamburger Mary's
The Hermitage
Herons (Waterfront Centre
    Hotel)
Il Barino
Il Giardino di Umberto
Imperial Chinese Seafood
    Restaurant
Joe Fortes
Kamei Sushi
Kirin Mandarin Restaurant
Kitto Japanese Restaurant
Koji Japanese Restaurant
Le Club (Le Meridien
    Hotel)
Le Crocodile
Le Gavroche
Mescalero
Milestones
Monterey Lounge & Grill
    (Pacific Palisades Hotel)

Moutai Mandarin
  Restaurant
Musashi Japanese
  Restaurant
Nonya Baba
O-Tooz The Energie Bar
Olympia Fish Market and
  Oyster Co.
Pepitas
Persia Restaurant
Phnom Penh Restaurant
The Prow
Quilicum Restaurant
Raincity Grill
Raintree
Santa Fe Cafe
Settebello
Shabusen Yakiniku House
Stepho's Souvlakia
Tai Chi Hin
The Teahouse at Ferguson
  Point
Tropika Malaysian Cuisine
Villa del Lupo
White Spot
The William Tell (The
  Georgian Court Hotel)
Won More
Zefferelli's
Zuni Cafe

Eastside
Accord
Al Ritrovo
Allium
Ashiana Tandoori
Bodhi Vegetarian
  Restaurant
The Cannery
Cipriano's Ristorante &
  Pizzeria
Dario's La Piazza
  Ristorante
Floata ChiuChow
  Restaurant
La Villetta
Le Grec
Lok's Chinese Restaurant
Natraj
Nazarre BBQ Chicken
Noor Mahal
On Lock
The Only Seafood Cafe
Park Lock Seafood Cafe
Pho Hoang
The Pink Pearl
Rubina Tandoori

Sawasdee Thai Restaurant
Shanghai Garden
  Restaurant
Shinla Korean Restaurant
Spumante's Cafe Ristorante
Sun Sui Wah Seafood
  Restaurant
Sun Wong Kee
Surat Sweet
Szechuan Chongqing
Tak Sangka Indonesian
  Restaurant
Tandoori Taj
Tio Pepe
Vong's Kitchen
White Spot
Wonton Noodles

Gastown
Kilimanjaro
La Brochette
Le Railcar
Umberto Al Porto
Water Street Cafe

Granville Island
Bridges
Isadora's

Ladner
La Belle Auberge
Uncle Herbert's Fish &
  Chip Shop

North Shore
Beach Side Cafe
The Bread Garden
Cafe Norté
Cafe Roma
Capers
Corsi Trattoria
Earl's
King's Fare Fish & Chips
La Cucina Italiana
La Toque Blanche
Pepitas
Peppi's
The Salmon House on
  the Hill
Salute
The Tomahawk
White Spot

Richmond
The Bread Garden
Floata Chiuchow
  Restaurant
Ikea
Kamei Sushi

Maple Garden Restaurant
The Sleighs
Steveston Seafood House
Sun Sui Wah Seafood
  Restaurant
Top Gun Chinese Seafood
  Restaurant
Yaohan Supermarket and
  Shopping Centre

Surrey
Earl's
White Spot

West Side
Akbar's Own Dining Room
Alma Street Cafe
Annapurna Vegetarian
  Cuisine of India
Arirang House
The Avenue Grill
Bishop's
Bo-Jik Vegetarian
  Restaurant
The Bread Garden
Bridges
Capers
Earl's
Fiasco
Flying Wedge
Fortune House
Grand King Seafood
  Restaurant
Grand View Restaurant
Hung Fook Shanghai
  Restaurant
Kamei Sushi
King's Fare Fish & Chips
Kirin Seafood Restaurant
Landmark Hot Pot/
  Landmark Seafood
  Restaurant
Las Margaritas
Le Coq d'Or
Lok's Chinese Restaurant
Lorenzo's
Major The Gourmet
Milestones
Mocha Cafe
Montri's Thai Restaurant
Naam
Nyala Restaurant
Ouzeri
Passionate Pizza
Pepitas
Phnom Penh Restaurant
Picasso Café

Raku Kushiyaki
The Red Onion
Saltimbocca
Santa Fe Cafe
Sawasdee Thai Restaurant
Seasons in the Park
Shabusen Yakiniku House
Shijo Japanese Restaurant
Shiro
Singapore Restaurant

Sophie's Cosmic Cafe
Star Anise
Szechuan Chongqing
Tang's Noodle House
Tojo's
Tomato Fresh Food Cafe
Towkay Singapore Seafood
Vanier Café
Vassilis Taverna
White Spot

Won More
Woodlands Natural Food
  Restaurant
Zeppo's Trattoria

White Rock
Earl's
Giraffe
White Spot

FOOD AND OTHER FEATURES

African
Kilimanjaro
Nyala Restaurant

All Night
The Bread Garden
Naam

Bakery
The Bread Garden

Breakfast
Alma Street Cafe
The Avenue Grill
Bacchus Ristorante (The
  Wedgewood Hotel)
The Bread Garden
Capers
Griffins
Hamburger Mary's
Herons (Waterfront Centre
  Hotel)
Isadora's
Le Coq d'Or
Mocha Cafe
Monterey Lounge & Grill
  (Pacific Palisades Hotel)
Picasso Café
The Red Onion
The Tomahawk
Tomato Fresh Food Cafe
White Spot
The William Tell (The
  Georgian Coast Hotel)
Woodlands Natural Food
  Restaurant

Breakfast, All Day
The Tomahawk

Brunch
The Alabaster Restaurant
Anderson's
The Avenue Grill

Bacchus Ristorante (The
  Wedgewood Hotel)
Beach Side Cafe
Bridges
The Clearwater Café
English Bay Cafe
Fiasco
The Fish House at Stanley
  Park
Giraffe
Griffins
Herons (Waterfront Centre
  Hotel)
Horizons on Burnaby
  Mountain
Isadora's
Joe Fortes
Le Coq d'Or
Mescalero
Milestones
The Prow
Raincity Grill
The Salmon House on
  the Hill
Seasons in the Park
Sophie's Cosmic Cafe
Star Anise
The Teahouse at Ferguson
  Point
Tomato Fresh Food Cafe

Burgers
The Avenue Grill
Earl's
Griffins
Hamburger Mary's
Milestones
Mocha Cafe
Raincity Grill
The Red Onion
Sophie's Cosmic Cafe
The Tomahawk
White Spot

California Cuisine
The Avenue Grill
Giraffe
Monterey Lounge & Grill
  (Pacific Palisades Hotel)
Santa Fe Cafe
Zuni Cafe

Cambodian
Phnom Penh Restaurant

Caterers
Ashiana Tandoori
Beach Side Cafe
The Bread Garden
Bridges
Cafe Norté
Il Barino
Kilimanjaro
Kirin Mandarin
  Restaurant/Kirin Seafood
  Restaurant
La Toque Blanche
Major The Gourmet
Mescalero
Mocha Cafe
Montri's Thai Restaurant
The Pink Pearl
Raintree
The Red Onion
Rubina Tandoori
Shijo Japanese Restaurant
Tojo's
Tomato Fresh Food Cafe
Umberto Al Porto
Water Street Cafe
The William Tell

Children's Menu
Alma Street Cafe
Cafe Norté
Griffins

King's Fare Fish & Chips
Monterey Lounge & Grill
 (Pacific Palisades Hotel)
The Red Onion
Sophie's Cosmic Cafe
White Spot

Chinese
Accord
Dynasty Restaurant
 (Vancouver Renaissance
 Hotel)
Floata ChiuChow
 Restaurant
Fortune House
Grand King Seafood
 Restaurant
Grand View Restaurant
Hon's Wun Tun House
Hung Fook Shanghai
 Restaurant
Imperial Chinese Seafood
 Restaurant
Kam Gok Yuen
Kirin Mandarin
 Restaurant/Kirin Seafood
 Restaurant
Landmark Hot Pot
 House/Landmark
 Seafood Restaurant
Lok's Chinese Restaurant
Maple Garden Restaurant
Moutai Mandarin
 Restaurant
On Lock
Park Lock Seafood
 Restaurant
The Pink Pearl
Shanghai Garden
 Restaurant
Sun Sui Wah Seafood
 Restaurant
Sun Wong Kee
Szechuan Chongqing
Tai Chi Hin
Tang's Noodle House
Top Gun Chinese Seafood
 Restaurant
Vong's Kitchen
Won More
Wonton Noodles

Chinese Fine Dining
Dynasty Restaurant
 (Vancouver Renaissance
 Hotel)
Fortune House

Grand King Seafood
 Restaurant
Imperial Chinese Seafood
 Restaurant
Tai Chi Hin

Continental
Delilah's
English Bay Cafe
La Toque Blanche
The Prow
The William Tell (The
 Georgian Court Hotel)

Delivery
Grand View Restaurant
Passionate Pizza

Desserts: Excellent
Bacchus Ristorante (The
 Wedgewood Hotel)
Beach Side Cafe
Bishop's
The Bread Garden
Chartwell (The Four
 Seasons)
CinCin
Giraffe
La Toque Blanche
Le Club (Le Meridien
 Hotel)
Le Crocodile
Mocha Cafe
Raintree
The Red Onion
Star Anise
The William Tell (The
 Georgian Court Hotel)

Fireplace
Bacchus Ristorante (The
 Wedgewood Hotel)
Bandi's
Cafe Norté
The Cannery
Chartwell (The Four
 Seasons)
The Hermitage
La Toque Blanche
Le Gavroche
Monterey Lounge & Grill
 (Pacific Palisades Hotel)
Seasons in the Park
The Teahouse at Ferguson
 Point
Villa del Lupo
Water Street Cafe

Fish 'n' Chips
King's Fare Fish & Chips
Olympia Fish Market and
 Oyster Co.
The Only Seafood Cafe
Uncle Herbert's Fish &
 Chip Shop

French
Cafe de Paris
Chez Thierry
The Hermitage
Le Coq d'Or
Le Crocodile
Le Gavroche

Fusion
Herons (Waterfront
 Centre Hotel)
Mocha Cafe
Raku Kushiyaki
Saltimbocca
Zuni Cafe

Greek
Le Grec
Ouzeri
Stepho's Souvlakia
Vassilis Taverna

Health-Conscious
Allium
Alma Street Cafe
The Clearwater Café
Isadora's
Mescalero
O-Tooz The Energie Bar
Raintree
Tomato Fresh Food Cafe
Woodlands Natural Food
 Restaurant

Hungarian
Bandi's

Indian
Akbar's Own Dining Room
Annapurna Vegetarian
 Cuisine of India
Ashiana Tandoori
Natraj
Noor Mahal
Rubina Tandoori
Surat Sweet
Tandoori Taj

Indonesian
Tak Sangka Indonesian
 Restaurant

Italian
Al Ritrovo
The Alabaster Restaurant
Bacchus Ristorante
  (The Wedgewood Hotel)
Bianco Nero
Cafe Roma
Caffe de Medici
CinCin
Cipriano's Ristorante &
  Pizzeria
Corsi Trattoria
Da Pasta
Dario's La Piazza
  Ristorante
Fiasco
Il Barino
Il Giardino di Umberto
La Cucina Italiana
La Villetta
Peppi's
Salute
Settebello
Spumante's Cafe Ristorante
Umberto Al Porto
Villa del Lupo
Zefferelli's
Zeppo's Trattoria

Japanese
Aki
Chiyoda
Ezogiku Noodle Cafe
Japanese Deli House
Kamei Sushi
Kitto Japanese Restaurant
Koji Japanese Restaurant
Musashi Japanese
  Restaurant
Raku Kushiyaki
Shabusen Yakiniku House
Shijo Japanese Restaurant
Shiro
Tojo's
Yaohan Supermarket and
  Shopping Centre

Jazz
Alma Street Cafe

Kitsch
Al Ritrovo
Cipriano's Ristorante &
  Pizzeria
Sophie's Cosmic Cafe
The Tomahawk
Tomato Fresh Food Cafe

Korean
Arirang House
Shinla Korean Restaurant

Late Night
The Bread Garden
CinCin
Mescalero

Lebanese
El Caravan

Malaysian
Nonya Baba
Singapore Restaurant
Tropika Malaysian Cuisine

Mexican
Cafe Norté
Las Margaritas
Pepitas
Tio Pepe

Native Indian
Quilicum Restaurant

Non-Smoking
The Fish House at Stanley
  Park
O-Tooz The Energie Bar
The Salmon House on
  the Hill
Tomato Fresh Food Cafe

Outdoor Dining
Beach Side Cafe
The Bread Garden
Bridges
Cafe Norté
Caffe de Medici
The Cannery
Capers
Chez Thierry
Chili Club
CinCin
The Clearwater Café
Delilah's
Earl's
English Bay Cafe
Fiasco
The Fish House at Stanley
  Park
Giraffe
Hamburger Mary's
Horizons on Burnaby
  Mountain
Il Barino
Il Giardino di Umberto
Isadora's

Kilimanjaro
King's Fare Fish & Chips
La Belle Auberge
La Cucina Italiana
La Villetta
Las Margaritas
Le Coq d'Or
Le Crocodile
Le Gavroche
Mescalero
Milestones
Monterey Lounge & Grill
  (Pacific Palisades Hotel)
Naam
Ouzeri
Peppi's
The Prow
Raincity Grill
The Salmon House on
  the Hill
Saltimbocca
Seasons in the Park
Settebello
The Sleighs
Sophie's Cosmic Cafe
Tojo's
Umberto Al Porto
Vassilis Souvlaki
Water Street Cafe
Zeppo's Trattoria
Zuni Cafe

Persian
Persia Restaurant

Pizza
CinCin
Cipriano's Ristorante &
  Pizzeria
Earl's
Fiasco
Flying Wedge
Passionate Pizza
Settebello

Post-Theatre Menus
Alma Street Cafe
CinCin
Mescalero
Villa del Lupo

Pre-Theatre Menus
Bianco Nero
Bridges
Chartwell (The Four
  Seasons)
Mescalero
The William Tell (The
  Georgian Court Hotel)

Private Rooms & Parties

Bacchus Ristorante (The
  Wedgewood Hotel)
Cafe de Paris
Caffe de Medici
The Cannery
Chez Thierry
CinCin
English Bay Cafe
The Fish House at Stanley
  Park
Giraffe
Grand View Restaurant
Horizons on Burnaby
  Mountain
Il Giardino di Umberto
Kirin Mandarin
  Restaurant/Kirin Seafood
  Restaurant
La Belle Auberge
La Cucina Italiana
Le Club (Le Meridien
  Hotel)
Le Gavroche
Mescalero
Montri's Thai Restaurant
The Pink Pearl
The Prow
Quilicum Restaurant
Raintree
Rubina Tandoori
Seasons in the Park
Shijo Japanese Restaurant
Sophie's Cosmic Cafe
Umberto Al Porto
Villa del Lupo
Water Street Cafe
The William Tell (The
  Georgian Court Hotel)
Zuni Cafe

Romantic

The Alabaster Restaurant
Anderson's
Bacchus Ristorante (The
  Wedgewood Hotel)
Bandi's
Bishop's
Bridges
Cafe de Paris
Cafe Norté
Caffe de Medici
The Cannery
Chartwell (The Four
  Seasons)
Chez Thierry
CinCin

Delilah's
English Bay Cafe
The Fish House at Stanley
  Park
Five Sails (Pan Pacific
  Hotel)
Giraffe
Il Barino
Il Giardino di Umberto
La Belle Auberge
La Cucina Italiana
La Toque Blanche
La Villetta
Le Club (Le Meridien
  Hotel)
Le Coq d'Or
Le Crocodile
Le Gavroche
Mescalero
Monterey Lounge & Grill
  (Pacific Palisades Hotel)
Montri's Thai Restaurant
The Prow
Raintree
The Salmon House on
  the Hill
Saltimbocca
Salute
Seasons in the Park
Star Anise
Umberto Al Porto
Villa del Lupo
The William Tell (The
  Georgian Court Hotel)
Zefferelli's
Zeppo's Trattoria

Seafood
(See also Fish 'n' Chips)
Bishop's
The Cannery
CinCin
The Fish House at Stanley
  Park
Grand King Seafood
  Restaurant
Imperial Chinese Seafood
  Restaurant
Quilicum Restaurant
Raintree
The Salmon House on
  the Hill
Steveston Seafood House
Sun Sui Wah Seafood
  Restaurant
Tojo's

Singaporean

Nonya Baba
Singapore Restaurant
Towkay Singapore Seafood

Soup/Salad/Sandwich

Alma Street Cafe
The Bread Garden
Bridges
Earl's
Milestones
Mocha Cafe
Monterey Lounge & Grill
  (Pacific Palisades Hotel)
The Red Onion
Tomato Fresh Food Cafe

Southwestern

Mescalero
Santa Fe Cafe
Zuni Cafe

Spanish

The Sleighs

Sushi

Aki
Japanese Deli House
Kamei Sushi
Kitto Japanese Restaurant
Koji Japanese Restaurant
Musashi Japanese
  Restaurant
Raku Kushiyaki
Tojo's
Yaohan Supermarket and
  Shopping Centre

Swedish

Ikea

Swiss/French

The William Tell (The
  Georgian Court Hotel)

Takeout

Allium
The Bread Garden
Cafe Norté
Cipriano's Ristorante &
  Pizzeria
Flying Wedge
Grand View Restaurant
King's Fare Fish & Chips
Major The Gourmet
Montri's Thai Restaurant
Nazarre BBQ Chicken
Passionate Pizza
The Pink Pearl

The Red Onion
Rubina Tandoori
Sophie's Cosmic Cafe
Tojo's
Tomato Fresh Food Cafe
Vong's Kitchen
White Spot

Tapas
Mescalero
The Sleighs

Thai
Chili Club
Montri's Thai Restaurant
Sawasdee Thai Restaurant

Vegetarian
Akbar's Own Dining Room
Allium
Alma Street Cafe
Annapurna Vegetarian
  Cuisine of India
Bodhi Vegetarian
  Restaurant
Bo-Jik Vegetarian
  Restaurant
Capers
The Clearwater Café
Grand View Restaurant
Isadora's
Naam
Surat Sweet
Woodlands Natural Food
  Restaurant

Vietnamese
Phnom Penh Restaurant
Pho Hoang

View
Anderson's
Beach Side Cafe
Bridges
The Cannery
Chili Club
English Bay Cafe
Five Sails (Pan Pacific
  Hotel)
Giraffe
Herons (Waterfront Centre
  Hotel)
Horizons on Burnaby
  Mountain
Imperial Chinese Seafood
  Restaurant
Peppi's
The Prow
Raincity Grill

The Salmon House on
  the Hill
Seasons in the Park
The Teahouse at Ferguson
  Point

West Coast Cuisine
Beach Side Cafe
Bishop's
Capers
Chartwell (The Four
  Seasons)
Delilah's
English Bay Cafe
Five Sails (Pan Pacific
  Hotel)
Horizons on Burnaby
  Mountain
Joe Fortes
Mocha Cafe
Monterey Lounge & Grill
  (Pacific Palisades Hotel)
Raincity Grill
Raintree
Seasons in the Park
Star Anise

Wheelchair Access
Alma Street Cafe
Ashiana Tandoori
Beach Side Cafe
Bianco Nero
The Bread Garden
Bridges
Cafe de Paris
Cafe Norté
Caffe de Medici
Cipriano's Ristorante &
  Pizzeria
Corsi Trattoria
Giraffe
Grand View Restaurant
Horizons on Burnaby
  Mountain
Il Barino
Il Giardino di Umberto
Imperial Chinese Seafood
  Restaurant
Kilimanjaro
Kirin Seafood Restaurant
La Cucina Italiana
La Toque Blanche
Le Coq d'Or
Mescalero
Milestones
Montri's Thai Restaurant
Noor Mahal

Passionate Pizza
The Pink Pearl
Raintree
Raku Kushiyaki
The Red Onion
The Salmon House on
  the Hill
Salute
Santa Fe Cafe
Seasons in the Park
Sophie's Cosmic Cafe
Sun Sui Wah Seafood
  Restaurant
Szechuan Chongqing
The Teahouse at Ferguson
  Point
Tojo's
Umberto Al Porto

Restaurants

Accord ★★ Behind white venetian blinds, this restaurant serves excellent Cantonese seafood. Try the live spot prawns steamed in the shell and brought to the table with a serrano soy-based dipping sauce, or the beef tenderloin teppan with peppercorn sauce. The menu also includes a handful of Chiu-Chow specialties. Open till the wee hours—perfect for those late evenings when Chinese food is the only thing that will do. Ask for the midnight snack menu, which features smaller dishes ranging between $4 and $8 each. It's written only in Chinese, so you'll need to ask for recommendations or translations. ▪ *4298 Main St; 876-6110; $$; no alcohol; no credit cards; no cheques; dinner every day.*

Akbar's Own Dining Room ★ Sunset-pink walls, white wicker chairs, and antique fabric wall hangings provide an understated, elegant backdrop for Indian food in this West Side haven. The sophistication extends to the authentic Kashmiri and muglai cuisine, which delicately balances spices and flavours. Shrimp pakoras, zingy with ginger and green chiles, are crunchily wrapped in sesame seed batter. Lamb tikka has an equally surprising overcoat: a batter that hints at tandoori. Particularly good are the fiery prawn vindaloo, or the more subtle prawn Kashmiri, cooked with butter, tomatoes, apples, and cream. Try the felicitous combination of lamb—either ground or in meltingly tender chunks—and spinach, perfumed with fresh fenugreek. The biryanis, heady with saffron and shot through with your choice of chicken, lamb, prawns, or vegetables, are exceptional. Vegetarian dishes include the irresistible alu gobi—chopped cauliflower and potato. ▪ *3629 W*

Broadway; 739-8411; $$; full bar; AE, MC, V; no cheques; lunch Mon-Fri, dinner Mon-Sat.

Aki ★ A few steps from Vancouver's own Japantown (which centres on Oppenheimer Park) is the small, unpretentious Aki. With its screened rooms and tatami mats, this intimate Japanese restaurant was the place where more than a few locals were introduced in the '70s to the then-dubious joys of sushi and sashimi. Sophisticates that we are now, we still go back—for the same reasons we went in our student days: the food is good and the bill won't make a major dent in your pocketbook. The menu embraces all the favourites: teriyaki, sunumono, and those uniquely Japanese udon noodle dishes that manage to be both light and robust. A crisp and fragile batter lifts the tempura here far above the usual. Sushi choices let you stay with the tried and true or experiment with sea urchin or flying-fish roe. Service is concerned and consistently charming. ■ *374 Powell St; 682-4032; $$; full bar; AE, MC, V; no cheques; lunch Mon-Fri, dinner every day.*

Al Ritrovo ★ With its backlit paintings of moonlit piazzas; the odd string of fairy lights; Italian classics played on the accordion, guitar, and bass (on weekends); and couples of all ages taking to the floor, the ambience seems to come straight from the cover of a romance novel. The mainstream Italian menu occasionally plays second fiddle to the dancing, with service scheduled around the sambas and tangos. Expect solid Italian cuisine like Mamma used to make. Servings of lasagne or tagliatelle alla boscaiola—pasta laden with bacon, mushrooms, and cream—are robust. A flavourful veal saltimbocca is aromatic with fresh sage. For lovers of old-time dancing, this is the place. Pizzas after 10pm. Minimum of $15 per person after 9pm. ■ *2010 Franklin St; 255-0916; $$; full bar; AE, MC, V; local cheques only; lunch Tues-Fri, dinner Fri-Sun (closed in Aug).*

The Alabaster Restaurant ★★★ Central to the decor in this surpassingly elegant yet informal Yaletown spot is a thoughtful alabaster statue of Venus. It's as sensuous and cerebral as the food that Markus Wieland serves here. A young chef, Wieland has experience—stints in some of the city's best restaurants, a grand tour of Europe—that many chefs twice his age might envy. His European approach is implicit in everything from the *amuse-gueule* (literally a "tastebud tickler") that prefaces dinner to his much-lauded eggplant confit on toasted baguette, or the inspired pairing of a frozen walnut parfait with a fruit coulis. Whether you choose the Tuscan fish soup or the ambrosial risotto with mushrooms or the flawless saltimbocca, you can't go wrong here. Flavours perform solo before combining into memorable tastes. A starter of polenta is layered with mozzarella, tomatoes, and pesto. A seafood terrine comes with a feather-light sauce of crème fraîche and lime. Potato gnocchi ring a perfectly prepared beef tenderloin in a wine-dark sauce. Presentation is literally picture perfect. ■ *1168 Hamilton St; 687-1758; $$$; full bar; AE, MC, V; no cheques; lunch Mon-Fri, dinner Mon-Sat.*

Allium ★ Tucked away on one of Vancouver's more food-loving stradas is a pint-sized lunch place that has them lining up at the door. Credit owner/chef Anne Henry's shining credentials (former sous chef at the Pan Pacific Hotel), her commitment to quality, and a passion shared with her clientele for downright good value. Citrus-coloured walls provide a backdrop for chalkboard menus, and shelves stacked country-store style with preserves, salsas, and teas. Servers are friendly and knowledgeable about the scrupulously fresh ingredients that go into Allium's earthy, uncomplicated dishes. The daily soup might be a flavourful black bean spiked with orange, chile, and cumin or a jalapeño-fired corn chowder. Aficionados have been known to phone ahead to check the availability of the ultra-smooth, sage-scented parsnip soup. Big, bulging vegetarian sandwiches come with an exceptional house salad. Garlic is a constant. ■ *1885 Commercial Dr; 253-4224; $; no alcohol; V; cheques OK; lunch Mon-Sat.*

Alma Street Cafe ★ The Alma Street Cafe is something of an institution, one of the first to marry jazz and dining in Vancouver. The neighbourhood jazz-loving clientele includes a mix of gracefully aging hippies, new agers, and even a few undercover yuppies who come for the food as well as the music. On the culinary front, this is a cafe in the truest sense of the word, with a day-long operation that caters to every mood. The breakfast fare is healthy, and the menu acknowledges a sizable vegetarian clientele. A daily dinner sheet usually offers some eclectic spontaneity worth checking out, sometimes with mixed success. A generous Australian lamb leg steak may be accompanied by a delicious curried apple chutney. But yellowfin tuna can be concealed by an oddly bitter amalgam of lemon zest and black olives. Seating is tight, but thanks to pleasant (deflected) lighting and good acoustics, neighbours and their conversations are rarely intrusive. Service can be erratic, and the plates sometimes arrive warmer than the food. ■ *2505 Alma St; 222-2244; $$; full bar; AE, MC, V; no cheques; breakfast, lunch, dinner every day.*

Anderson's ★★ The great sweep of windows overlooking False Creek ensures that this waterside eatery is visited as much for its scenic as its edible pleasures. It's fascinating by day, as pleasure craft and ferryboats provide a constantly changing picture, and dazzling at night, as lights flicker like fireflies across the water. It's the place Vancouverites take pleasure- or business-bent out-of-towners to show off their scenery—and their seafood: delicate sole paupiette rolled with

▼

Top 175 Restaurants

▲

prawns and blanketed in a lobster sauce, prawns briskly sautéed with tomatoes and shallots and finished with garlic butter. Local salmon is served in the best way possible: simply cooked and drizzled with lemon butter. The fresh sheet offers such trans-Pacific fusions as shellfish in black bean sauce, or seaweed-wrapped fillets of halibut or salmon served with a decidedly Asian cilantro and ginger chile butter. ▪ *1661 Granville St; 684-8080; $$$; full bar; AE, DC, MC, V; no cheques; lunch Mon-Fri, dinner Mon-Sat, brunch Sun.*

Annapurna Vegetarian Cuisine of India ★

The Annapurna is the first in the Lower Mainland to tap into the most highly developed vegetarian cuisine in the world. Every vegetarian who's opened a menu at an Indian restaurant to see the same standard meatless dishes just one too many times is going to like Annapurna a lot. There are unfamiliar dishes to try, and some of them—like the lentil dumplings soaked in yogurt with chick-peas and chutney—are especially good. The service, however, is long on grand gestures and short on noticing when your water glass needs to be filled. And the small dining room, its ceiling covered with lanterns, has a ringside view of a busy intersection. ▪ *1812 W 4th Ave (near Burrard St); 736-5959; $; full bar; MC, V; no cheques; lunch, dinner every day.*

Arirang House ★★

Located at the south end of the Cambie Street Bridge, Arirang House, one of the city's first Korean restaurants, continues to be a popular venue for those who consider garlic a major food group. In the evenings, the restaurant serves a dish revealingly called Jumuluck Garlic Lovers. Combining marinated beef, lettuce leaves, and vast quantities of raw garlic, it's a cook-it-yourself variation of traditional Korean barbecue. Less daunting are bulgogi—marinated filet of beef—or bulgabi—ribs—or any of the other tabletop grill options. Sizzling and deeply flavoured hot pots, assorted seafood preparations, and savagely good kimchi (the incendiary Korean pickle) round out the menu. The lunchtime barbecue buffet is an exceptional value. ▪ *2211 Cambie St; 879-0990; $$; full bar; AE, MC, V; cheques OK; lunch, dinner every day.*

Ashiana Tandoori ★★

Ashiana moved from its decade-long, well-worn Victoria Drive location to emerge on Kingsway as the most upscale Indian restaurant in Vancouver. The new place features split-level seating divided into three rooms by unique mosque-shaped arches lushly decorated with brass wall platters and elaborate carvings. The owners spared no expense—this includes the confident cooking in the kitchen. The tandoori dishes come sizzling from the oven to the table on cast-iron platters. The Chicken Tikka is tasty and moist; the Lamb Tikka superb—tender, fragrant, and rich from its marinade of yogurt, ginger, garlic, and spices. Murg Makhani—one of eleven chicken curries—is luscious and sweet and delectable on paneer naan deftly flavoured with fresh coriander. Speaking of breads, the whole-wheat paratha with cheese is a must with the Channa Masala—chick-peas stewed with garam masala, onions, and tomatoes. This is food that makes you happy. ■ *1440 Kingsway; 874-5060; $$; full bar; AE, MC, V; no cheques; lunch, dinner every day.*

The Avenue Grill ★★ Locals call this California-type bistro "the Ave." Chef Dorothy Lilace has created a trendy menu with a fusion of Californian, French, Asian, and Italian influences. Very popular with the neighbourhood Kerrisdale crowd, and a fun place for weekend brunch. For dinner, try the superb pecan chicken with pommery mustard sauce or one of the imaginative daily salmon specials. There's also a good selection of wines by the glass. ■ *2114 W 41st Ave; 266-8183; $$; full bar; E, MC; cheques OK; breakfast Mon-Fri, lunch Mon-Sat, dinner every day.*

Bacchus Ristorante (The Wedgewood Hotel) ★★★ A glaring game of musical chefs went on for a few years until dedicated hotelier Eleni Skalbania discovered Alan Broom. The emergence of Executive Chef Broom as a first-rate talent has put Bacchus on the culinary map. Geographically speaking, the chef is decidedly British, but the climate is distinctly Northern Italian. Bacchus is an extraordinarily pretty place, with a striking open kitchen. You're relaxed, and you feel everyone in the kitchen is too: timing is superb. The moderate prices belie the high quality of the food. An appetizer special of raw Tofino oysters escorted by a papaya-lime salsa is outstanding. A light dinner can be made of a pasta and a salad. Try pairing ravioli stuffed with salmon and potato, scented with truffle oil, and topped with a lemon cilantro sauce with a salad composed of fresh figs, Asiago cheese, and baby lettuces. It is difficult to choose between the grilled salmon with citrus and cracked-pepper butter sauce and the tiger prawns with ginger cream sauce. A crisp, roasted free-range chicken with baked garlic and lemons served with a mountain of mashed potatoes and fresh greens competes with an exemplary osso buco. Surrender to a raspberry crème brulée, homey bread and butter pudding, or a frosty trio of sorbets served in a tulip shaped cookie. ■ *845 Hornby St; 689-7777; $$; full bar; AE, DC, MC, V; no cheques; breakfast, lunch, dinner every day, brunch Sun.*

Bandi's ★★ At Bandi's, chef/owner Bandi Rinkhy produces the robust country food of Hungary, with maître d' and co-owner Kader Karaa's sense of humour providing the dash of paprika. Start with an excellent sour-cherry soup and the dangerously addictive langos, a deep-fried peasant bread served with raw garlic (order one for your friends, one for yourself, and one to take home). Duck aficionados who haven't experienced Bandi's signature dish—crisp duck served with red cabbage braised in Tokay wine—should by all means do so. Goulash is presented in a little kettle set over a portable flame, and the paraszt sonka (smoked farmer's ham with fresh horseradish and green onions) is served in large, hearty portions. Uborkasalata (cucumber with sour cream dressing) may be the only concession to a timid palate. Desserts are mostly rich, sweet crêpes. A bottle of Badacsony off the good wine list is a decent value and is among Hungary's best white wines. You'll exit in a fog of garlic. ■ *1427 Howe St; 685-3391; $$; full bar; AE, MC, V; no cheques; lunch Mon-Fri, dinner every day.*

Beach Side Cafe ★★★ With their creative and varied approach to regional cuisine, owner Janet McGuire and chef Carol Chow have turned this little Ambleside haunt into one of the area's more serious kitchens. The surroundings are woodsy and the mood relaxed. The summertime deck rates among the city's best, with views of Stanley Park and Kitsilano across the water. Choices are plentiful, with emphasis on daily specials as well as a cutting-edge list of better West Coast wines. Well-informed staff members are happy to make recommendations. In season, look for steamed mussels and swimming scallops in a zesty garlic and wine sauce. Definitely order the goat cheese salad, with endive and a pungent sun-dried tomato vinaigrette. Dessert lovers swear by the crème brulée and the lemon meringue pie. ■ *1362 Marine Dr (between 14th St and 15th St), West Vancouver; 925-1945; $$; full bar; MC, V; no cheques; lunch Mon-Fri, dinner Mon-Sun, brunch Sat-Sun.*

Bianco Nero ★★½ Bianco Nero's bold black and white decor with splashes of colour never fails to impress, though, unfortunately, the service doesn't always live up to the surroundings. Attitude is always the unknown ingredient—sometimes warm and accommodating, at other times unfriendly and condescending. Luckily, the well-prepared food remains the most consistent factor. The kitchen has a healthy regard for garlic, onions, and olive oil (but a macho disregard for presentation). You may feel overwhelmed by all the choices; a sheet of daily specials is so crammed that they hardly seem special. Every Italian dish imaginable makes an appearance here, as do some surprises, such as sole in aquavit with Danish caviar, radicchio alla griglia (oven-broiled with garlic cloves and splashed with olive oil, lemon juice, and salt), tortellini alla nonna (in a delicate mustard cream sauce), and osso bucco. A recent penne with four kinds of mushroom was outstanding. This is the place for lovers of Italian wine, with one of the most comprehensive, sophisticated selections in Canada, including a full range of vintage Barolo. ■ *475 W Georgia St; 682-6376; $$$; full bar; AE, MC, V; no cheques; lunch Mon-Fri, dinner Mon-Sat.*

Bishop's ★★★★ The fashionable dining crowd may flirt with newer places, but in the end they remain faithful to Bishop's.

When the 1993 Summit came to Vancouver, the White House summoned John Bishop to create his wonderful grilled Pacific salmon fillet for presidents Clinton and Yeltsin (Bishop now has a standing invitation to the White House). Hollywood knows about Bishop's as well—Goldie Hawn, Richard Gere, and others have been spotted here. Bishop warmly greets his guests (celebrity and otherwise) and, assisted by the most professionally polished young staff in the city, proceeds to demonstrate that he understands the true art of hospitality. Attention to detail is important in this minimalist Kitsilano restaurant. Appetizers might include grilled baby calamari, fresh local clams or mussels, or a delicate wild mushroom soup with sage. Entrées are uncomplicated. Lamb is always tender and excellent, as is daily fish (recently, halibut roasted with strawberry mint salsa). We favour tandoori chicken marinated in yogurt and cumin, then oven-roasted and served with mango chutney, Marsala-soaked raisins, roasted tomatoes, and basmati rice—but you really can't go wrong here. Everything bears the Bishop trademark of light, subtly complex flavours and bright, graphic colour. Desserts too are not to be missed. Death by Chocolate is easily the most talked-about dessert in Vancouver, and if you want President Clinton's choice, order the blueberry tart with homemade maple syrup ice cream. Nothing comes closer to dining perfection than Bishop's. ■ *2183 W 4th Ave; 738-2025; $$$; full bar; AE, DC, MC, V; no cheques; lunch Mon-Fri, dinner every day.*

▼
Top 175
Restaurants
▲

Bodhi Vegetarian Restaurant ★ The takeout deli showcases "pork," "squid," and "braised beef," but the restaurant is 100 percent vegetarian. These terms are merely masks for the elaborate and ingenious simulations crafted out of soy products and wheat gluten. Each of the 130-plus dishes is excellent—and not just for the many Chinese Buddhists who frequent the Bodhi. Dumplings, steamed or Swatow style, and the fluffy lo-hon buns, are all regular dim sum items. For dinner, try vegetables with winter melon soup, mock abalone in black bean sauce, crisp vegetarian duck, and the unique salt and chile bean curd. An enlightening place. Check out the calligraphy adorning the walls—it's Buddhist riddles pointing the way to (vegetarian) nirvana. A must-try, even for carnivores. ■ *337 E Hastings St (at Main); 682-2666; $; no alcohol; MC, V; no cheques; lunch, dinner, Wed-Mon.*

Bo-Jik Vegetarian Restaurant ★ As part of a well-established Buddhist vegetarian tradition—there are hundreds of these restaurants in Hong Kong—Bo-Jik brings all the force of Chinese culinary tradition to bear on the problem of eating well without eating meat. Generally, you want to avoid the gluten dishes, which substitute textured soy protein for meat—though the barbecued satay delights and the basic gluten with chile black bean sauce isn't bad—and steer toward the vegetable dishes—the Bo-Jik veggie pancake, for example. It's a tangle of stir-fried vegetables, a generous stack of paper-thin Mandarin pancakes, and a hoisin sauce—altogether like mu-shu pork without the pork. Pair it with shiitake on vegetables, big fresh mushrooms on a bed of brilliant green sautéed gai lan, and you have, with a few bowls of rice and some tea, a splendid dinner for under $25. Portions are extremely large, and only two of Bo-Jik's 100-odd dishes cost more than $10. Service is friendly, if somewhat disorganized. Unfortunately, the restaurant is on one of the uglier stretches of West Broadway and has the lighting of a mall record store. ■ *820 W Broadway 872-5556; $; no alcohol; MC, V; no cheques; lunch, dinner every day.*

Boss Bakery and Restaurant The Boss is a slice of Hong Kong life transplanted intact from Asia's distant shores. Once beyond the sand-blasted glass door with its tongue-in-cheek silhouette of a man in a bowler smoking a pipe, you can easily imagine yourself transported across the Pacific. In one booth is a group of young teenagers reading to each other from their Chinese comics. In another, a businessman is taking lunch with an associate, next to three older men debating the prowess of their favourite racehorse of the day. The menu is uniquely and eclectically Hong Kong–style cafe—a strange hybrid of East and West. Spaghetti is topped with baked seafood; macaroni is served up in soup with crunchy Chinese meatballs or strips of ham. A recent $3.50 lunch included a flavourful crêpelike omelette with chicken, a croissant that tasted of Portuguese egg bread, and a stiff cup of Hong Kong–style coffee whitened with condensed milk. Chinese noodle dishes and congees are also offered. If you are visiting Chinatown, the Boss is a must for both taste and fauna. Besides, where else are you going to get Ovaltine served hot, iced, or with a raw egg? ■ *532 Main St; 683-3860; $; no alcohol; no credit cards; no cheques; lunch, dinner every day.*

The Bread Garden ■ Gallery Cafe ★¹/₂ The Bread Garden is Vancouver's original bakery-cafe, and still the most successful. Opened in 1981 as a croissant bakery, it quickly turned into an all-night coffee bar. Now there are five Bread Gardens, and all but the Park Royal branch are open 24 hours a day. As the Bread Gardens proliferate, the deli cases grow bigger and bigger. The First Avenue Bread Garden is still the scene for early weekday coffee and (much later) weekend brunch, but now, for under $25 for two, you can also eat a quick and entirely satisfying dinner: wholesome, homey food such as shepherd's pie, lasagne (vegetarian and meat), fruit salad, potato salad, or black bean and corn salad. Desserts are homey too, including cheesecakes, fruit crumbles, Rice Krispie squares, double-chocolate brownies, and bread pudding made from croissants. Similar in concept is the Gallery Cafe, a lively spot in the Vancouver Art Gallery. ■ *1880 W 1st Ave and branches; 738-6684; $; no alcohol; E, MC, V; no cheques; breakfast, lunch, dinner every day.* ᕫ ■ *750 Hornby St; 688-2233.*

Bridges ★ One of the city's most popular hangouts has a superb setting on Granville Island. On a warm summer's day, seats on the outdoor deck, with its sweeping views of downtown and the mountains, are at a premium. Bridges is actually three separate entities: a casual bistro, a pub, and a more formal upstairs dining room. The bistro's casual offerings are the best bet; upstairs, the seafood can be inconsistent. The pub, unfortunately, has a remarkably poor offering of beer on tap, even lacking a selection from the neighbouring highly successful Granville Island Brewery. ■ *1696 Duranleau St (across from Granville Island Market); 687-4400; $$; full bar; AE, MC, V; cheques OK; lunch, dinner every day, brunch Sun.*

Cafe de Paris ★★ Lace curtains at the window, paper covers on the table, a mirrored bar, and Piaf or Aznavour on the sound system: this is the bistro that takes you back to the Left Bank. Cafe de Paris's heart-of-the-West-End location draws locals and Francophiles alike. The frites—genuine french fries—have become a Vancouver legend; crisp and light, they accompany all entrées and have regulars begging for more. As in France, you can opt for the three-course table d'hôte menu or pick and choose from à la carte offerings. Among the latter: a savoury bouillabaisse dense with prawns, scallops, mussels, and monkfish, its broth infused with saffron and Pernod, and a deeply comforting cassoulet. Chef André Bernier also creates his own contemporary French cuisine: orange-glazed salmon slices perfumed with tarragon and flashed under a salamander; smoked rack of lamb. Table d'hôte offerings may include the leek and duck confit tarte, a satiny hot chicken parfait, or meltingly tender roast pork in a garlic cream sauce. Try this bistro for lunch or dinner, *naturellement*, but also for a glass of wine and a pâté or a crème caramel and coffee after the movie. Commendable wine list with several surprises. ■ *751 Denman St; 687-1418; $$$; full bar; AE, MC, V; no cheques; lunch Mon-Fri, dinner every day.*

Cafe Norté ★★ Tucked away in Edgemont Village, this friendly spot is just minutes away from the north end of Lions Gate Bridge. An extensive menu offers a wide cross-section of regional favourites. Peruse it while sampling the addictive house salsa and tortilla chips. There's a full range of serious nachos: warm black bean guacamole, chile con queso topped with chorizo, sweet pineapple with jalapeño, and more. Smooth, rich, cream of crab soup comes with a garnish of finely chopped red peppers and parsley. Fajitas arrive with tender pieces of still-sizzling chicken nudged up against onions and green peppers. San Pedro pizza and smoked turkey quesadillas are noteworthy. For diehard traditionalists, the refried beans are great and the margaritas perfectly slushy. Of the too few Mexican restaurants in Vancouver, Cafe Norté reigns supreme. ■ *3108 Edgemont Blvd, North Vancouver; 255-1188; $$; full bar; MC, V; no cheques; lunch Mon-Sat, dinner every day.*

Cafe Roma ★ Mario Corsi (also of the Park Royal Hotel and Corsi Trattoria) operates this friendly, casual room with a view. The food is good—and very Italian. Excellent focaccia bread appears at your elbow while you contemplate the menu. Some of the pasta dishes, like the ultra-spicy spaghetti trasteverini sauced with minced chicken, black beans, garlic, and pepperoncini, are rarely seen ouside the old country. There are several choices of pizza, as well as many nicely prepared fish and meat dishes. For lighter fare, choose the halibut cooked on a slate with fresh herbs and olive oil. For the undecided there are combinations offering a variety of samplings. The deck is superb in summer, with an impressive view of downtown. ■ *60 Semisch St (at Esplanade), North Vancouver; 984-0274; $$; full bar; AE, DC, E, MC, V; no cheques; lunch Mon-Fri, dinner every day.*

Caffe de Medici ★★½ As you enter Caffe de Medici, you are immediately made to feel like a favoured guest. The high moulded ceilings, serene portraits of members of the 15th-century Medici family, chairs and drapery in Renaissance green against crisp white table linen, and walls the colour of zabaglione create a slightly palatial feeling; diplomatic waiters seem pleased to be looking after your needs. Businesslike by day, romantic by night—the mood changes, but the quality of the Northern Italian food does not. Skip the soups and order the beautiful antipasto: a bright collage of marinated eggplant, artichoke hearts, peppers, olives, squid, and Italian cold meats. The bresaola della Valtellina (air-dried beef, thinly sliced and marinated in olive oil, lemon, and pepper) is lovely. Pasta dishes are flat-out *magnifico*—a slightly chewy plateful of tortellini alla panna comes so rich with cheese you'll never order any of the others. Although it's mostly a Florentine restaurant (with a knockout version of beefsteak marinated in red wine and olive oil), we've also sampled a fine Roman-style rack of lamb. ■ *1025 Robson St; 669-9322; $$$; full bar; AE, DC, DIS, JCV, MC, V; no cheques; lunch Mon-Fri, dinner every day.* &

The Cannery ★★ A Vancouver original, serving "salmon by the sea" for more than 20 years, though the building has been cleverly refurbished to look and feel even older than that. Salmon selections run the gamut, from house-smoked items to the restaurant's hallmark, salmon Wellington. Seared salmon fillet, infused with flavours imparted from a cedar plank, has a subtle quality; by contrast, a mesquite-grilled smoked fillet has a lovely, truly strong barbecued flavour. An award-winning wine list offers one of the city's best selections, but service can be rushed and inconsistent. ■ *2205 Commissioner St; 254-9606; $$$; full bar; AE, DC, DIS, MC, V; no cheques; lunch Mon-Fri, dinner every day.*

Capers ★★ Healthy, holistic, fresh, inventive—pick practically any current cuisine buzzword and Capers fits the bill. Two locations serve up West Coast cuisine, pure and simple, but what sets them apart from virtually any other restaurant in the city is that you can shop here too. Finds (and customers) crowd the country store settings: glorious produce, unusual condiments, and—these being the cocooning '90s—a broad assortment of takeout dishes. Less than a half hour from downtown, the Dundarave location wows with water and city views from the outdoor terrace. Generous helpings and low prices draw local residents, who come for the Mexical pita stuffed with guacamole and tomatoes or an organic roast beef sandwich. Noted chef Anne Milne dispenses stylish holistic food at the recently opened Kitsilano location. Expect to find local fresh seafood and chicken. Build your own pizzas—smoked chicken to totally vegetarian—and pastas, which include corn- and rice-based noodles and soba. Vegetarian emphasis translates into big-flavoured dishes like cornmeal pie with ratatouille. ■ *2496 Marine Dr, West Vancouver; 925-3316; ■ 2284 W 4th Ave; 739-6685; $; beer and wine; MC, V; local cheques only; breakfast, lunch, dinner Mon-Sat, breakfast, lunch Sun.*

Chartwell (The Four Seasons) ★★★★ This welcoming, classic restaurant is a mecca for lovers of food and wine. Chartwell, named after the famous abode of Sir Winston Churchill, evokes an upper-class English men's club atmosphere. Executive chef Wolfgang von Wieser has expanded the menu's horizons to include Pacific Northwest food graced with Chinese, Japanese, Thai, and Indian touches. Savour lightly smoked yellow snapper with garlic ravioli and chile orange oil, grilled organic beef fillet, or chardonnay steamed lobster—all lovely. From the city's most imaginative vegetarian menu come zucchini carpaccio with lemon-vegetable crudités, potato tart and Mediterranean vegetables with arugula oil, and spinach sautéed in garlic and seasoned with just the right amount of sugar. Dessert is brilliant; plans just to taste may be foiled when the apple tatin and cherry soufflé arrive. Master host Angelo Cecconi and his staff give Chartwell its distinctive stamp of personal service—warm, discreet, and attentive. A pretheatre dinner menu with valet parking is an outstanding value. ■ *791 W Georgia St; 689-9333; $$$; full bar; AE, DC, MC, V; no cheques; lunch Mon-Fri, dinner every day.* &

Chez Thierry ★★ Restaurateur Thierry Damilano shops at the market in the morning, goes off windsurfing, and later in the day comes back to roll out the red carpet for regulars. He presides over his cozy restaurant with sunny good nature and flirtatious (very French) charm. Chef François Launay leaves experimentation to the nouveaux chefs and instead prepares simple, traditional meals without a lot of ornamentation. The house pâté is good but not outstanding; try a watercress and smoked salmon salad instead, or the impossibly melting chicken mousse, served warm in port sauce. A find: fresh tuna grilled with artichoke, garlic, and fresh tomato. Chocolate desserts are rich and just bitter enough; the tarte Tatin is superb, served upside down and flamed with Calvados. The wine list is carefully chosen; some may even be stored under your seat. For an unusual show, order a bottle of champagne and ask Damilano to open it for you—his favourite party trick is slashing off corks with a military saber, decked out in his flashing Napoleonic uniform. ■ *1674 Robson St; 688-0919; $$; full bar; AE, DC, E, MC, V; no cheques; dinner every day.*

Chili Club ★★ Despite the name, with a few noteworthy exceptions, Chili Club's fare is not particularly hot. The staff members, however, are well informed and helpful, and if you want it spicy, they'll gladly oblige. We've enjoyed pork satay and Tom Yum Kung soup (prawns and mushrooms married in a good broth with hot spice and deep-scented lemon grass), and when giant smoked New Zealand mussels, stuffed with a mild, thick curry paste, are available, order them; the same goes for solidly spiced chicken curry, made with coconut milk and bite-size Thai eggplant. There's plenty from which to choose. Popular wines and beers are available at realistic prices. For the best view of False Creek, try the holding bar upstairs with ceiling-to-floor windows on all sides. Even when the food is fiery, the decor is rather cold. ■ *1000 Beach Ave (under the Burrard Street Bridge, near the water); 681-6000; $$; full bar; AE, MC, V; cheques OK; lunch, dinner every day.* ♿

▼

Top 175 Restaurants

▲

Chiyoda ★★ In a town full of sushi restaurants with robata grills on the side, Chiyoda is a robata restaurant with a sushi bar. Built on a generous scale, the robata bar was designed in Japan. Robata selections are arranged in wicker baskets on a layer of ice that separates the customer's side of the bar from the cook's side. Order from the simple menu; it lists a score of dishes, including snapper, squid, oysters, scallops, eggplant, and shiitake. The cook prepares your choices and hands you the finished dishes across the bar on the end of a long wooden paddle. Seafood is excellent, but don't miss a foray into the cross-cultural world of robata-cooked garlic, potatoes, and corn. A popular spot for downtown businesspeople, the Chiyoda also attracts Japanese visitors exhausted from shopping in the huge gift shop downstairs. ■ *1050 Alberni St; 688-5050; $$; full bar; AE, MC, V; no cheques; lunch Mon-Fri, dinner every day.* ⅋

CinCin ★★★ *Cin-cin* is a hearty Italian toast, a wish of health and good cheer, all of which is implied in this sunny Mediterranean place. The scent from wood-burning ovens, the warm surroundings—what more could one need? If you can, sit in the northeast corner by the window, where it's cozy and you can survey the entire room. CinCin's breadsticks and baked breads (vegetable-herb-seed and Tuscan) are irresistible, delivered with a spill of balsamic vinegar in a pool of olive oil. Launch your meal with a wonderful roasted red pepper, goat cheese, and sweet onion relish, or a carpaccio of lightly smoked beef. Name your noodle—it's made fresh daily and nicely sauced. Lasagne is layered with house-made sausage, fresh spinach, and mozzarella; linguine ribbons are laced with pesto or a mingling of sea creatures; and rotini is dotted with juicy morsels of roast chicken and porcini mushrooms. The well-crafted wine list is international in scope and uncompromising in quality, and markups on high-end wines are reasonable. Desserts are all homemade in the best sense of the word, including the inevitable tiramisu. A great place to sip wine with the gang in the lounge (food's served until 1am). ■ *1154 Robson St; 688-7338; $$$; full bar; AE, MC, V; no cheques; lunch Mon-Fri, dinner every day.*

Cipriano's Ristorante & Pizzeria ★★ This compact and friendly pasta-pizza house is approaching institution status for its basic and most plentiful (for some, too plentiful) portions. Strains of Tony Bennett and Frank Sinatra fill the air as straightforward Italian home cooking arrives at your table, preceded by great garlic bread, dripping with butter and deluged with Parmesan. The caesar salad, an exercise in excess, is garlic laden and crammed with croutons, and it comes in a giant bowl, which is, according to the menu, "Made to Share, Amore Style." Deep-dish pizza, pasta puttanesca, and chicken cacciatore are all worth your attention, though some sauces can be remarkably similar. Short routines from owner and onetime standup comedian Frank Cipriano punctuate the meal. For atmosphere and value, few places compare, and lots of folks think so—reservations are a must. ■ *3995 Main St; 879-0020; $$; full bar; V; no cheques; dinner Tues-Sun.*

The Clearwater Café ★★ Reminders that Vancouver is a health-conscious city abound, but nowhere more so than here, where you can watch the Spandex-clad denizens of the West End saunter by. Power-packed fresh juices, Einstein or Celebrator, are only one draw in this new age vegetarian venue. Bright faux-painted decor draws the sunshine in—even on rainy days—and the lineup of multicultural dishes is just as enlightening: tofu creole, tortilla or tamale pie, "won hoppers." Terrific salads, inventively dressed, are loaded with nutritionally correct ingredients. The flavourful Vancouver Club teams smoked wild coho salmon with lemon aioli, red onions, and cucumber. A taki roll-up crams sprouts, brown rice, sunflower seed pâté, and a spicy tomato sauce inside a chapati. Weekends, it's the place to go for brunch before (or after) a jog or stroll around the Stanley Park seawall. ■ *1020 Denman St; 688-6264; $; beer and wine; MC, V; no cheques; lunch, dinner every day, brunch Sat-Sun.*

Corsi Trattoria ★★ This little family-run trattoria makes a great excuse for a mini-cruise via the SeaBus. The Corsi family was here on the North Shore before the SeaBus terminal and Lonsdale Quay Public Market existed. The family ran a trattoria in Italy, and the old-country touches still show. Twenty-odd homemade pastas include the house specialty, rotolo—pasta tubes stuffed with veal, spinach, and ricotta and topped with cream and tomato sauces. Or try trenette al salmone affumicata—pasta with smoked salmon, cream, olives, and tomatoes. Adventurous eaters might try the Roman food orgy (served for a minimum of two big appetites): four pastas, mixed salad, a platter of lamb, veal, and prawns, followed by coffee and dessert. Those who can't resist a challenge should take on the spaghetti trasteverini, loaded with garlic, hot peppers, chicken, black beans, and olive oil. ■ *1 Lonsdale Ave (across from the Lonsdale Market), North Vancouver; 987-9910; $$; full bar; AE, DC, E, MC, V; no cheques; lunch Mon-Fri, dinner every day.*

Da Pasta ★★ The concept of mixing and matching pasta with sauce isn't a new one, but it works better here than most places. Aubergine-coloured walls, explosive artwork, and a kitchenside view of the action crank up the visual volume. The can't-miss location on Robson Street draws everyone from the Docs-and-jeans set to kids with their elderly aunts; the ebullient, pasta-literate servers make all feel welcome. The pastabilities are endless, with 8 different pastas and 15 assorted sauces adding up, theoretically, to 120 different dishes, but servers are strong at steering you to what best complements what. Perhaps they'll even suggest some intriguing fusions of West Coast produce and seafood with Asian ingredients: roasted chicken with shiitake mushrooms and fresh spinach or calamari with mushrooms and hoisin-pickled ginger are unlikely pairings that work. Good lunchtime deals on designer salad and pasta combos. ■ *1232 Robson St; 688-1288; $; full bar; AE, DC, MC, V; no cheques; lunch, dinner every day.*

Dario's La Piazza Ristorante ★★ Dario's is not an upstart trendy restaurant where one is assured of classical competence at every turn. The decor is simple and functional. A salad and antipasti station displays the day's offering and splits the room into sections for nonsmokers and for those otherwise inclined. Large tropical plants and floral displays complete the comfortable illusion of dining in a courtyard instead of alongside the industrial artery where the restaurant is located. The small bar extends into a floor-to-ceiling wall of wine racks, highlighting the restaurant's considerable inventory. Service is mature, understated, efficient, and seamlessly orchestrated—a pleasant change from the flamboyant casualness that seems to pervade the contemporary "concept" dining scene. The large menu at Dario's also bucks the trends and is full of familiar favourites now considered out of vogue: fettuccine alfredo; risotto al funghi; veal scalloppine with lemon and white wine. A glorious stracciatella soup of Parmesan, egg swirls, and spinach followed by a perfectly sauced plate of sundried-tomato and sausage penne makes a very satisfying lunch. ■ *3075 Slocan St (Italian Centre); 430-2195; $$; full bar; AE, MC, V; no cheques; lunch Mon-Fri, dinner Mon-Sat.*

Delilah's ★★ The unlamented three-martini lunch may be gone, but let's hear it for the one-martini cocktail hour with hors d'oeuvres at Delilah's. Start with valet parking (the quickest in town) and if you're early enough, grab a red plush banquette. People line up to get into Delilah's (if you'd rather not, arrive shortly after 6pm), and it really doesn't matter what you eat here—the place is a giggle. Food comes in small portions but is good and reasonably priced. Your menu is your bill; simply check off your selections and hand it to your waiter. The peanuty yam soup is a good choice, and so is the grilled beef tenderloin with mushrooms in a red wine demiglace. The house specialties are the 30-plus varieties of martinis, which you shake (or stir) yourself. Tucked away under the old Buchan Hotel, Delilah's is an intimate room with beautiful young things of every possible sex gathered at the bar under the frescoed ceilings. Reservations are accepted only for groups of six or more. ■ *1906 Haro St; 687-3424; $$; full bar; MC, V; no cheques; dinner every day.* &

Dynasty Restaurant (Vancouver Renaissance Hotel) ★★★
The masterful Lam Kam Shing has left our favourite Cantonese restaurant, and at press time the consensus on the effects of this change was still not in. Although recent visits have been reassuring, we'll withhold the fourth star until we can again attest that the Renaissance Hotel's restaurant is indeed unsurpassed by any other. The serene, white-walled room is beautiful, with etched glass and a myriad of visual details. The focus on freshness is also unchanged. Whole steamed rockfish with ginger and scallions scores top marks, as do the drunken prawns steamed tableside (the broth is carefully ladled into silver-lined bone china bowls and served as a second course). A recent dim sum lunch was unhurried and prepared to order—excellent

shark's fin soup, dumplings, and shrimp and mango rolls. The wine list remains the best in any Chinese restaurant in Vancouver. It seems that the efficient hotel-based management structure is not about to let this hard-earned success story slip into obscurity while waiting for chef Lam's replacement. ■ *1133 W Hastings St; 691-2788; $$$; full bar; AE, DC, MC, V; no cheques; lunch, dinner Tues-Sun.* &

Earl's ★ It's fast food and it isn't. Each pearl in Earl's chain has the same sassy style and emphasis on fresh-only ingredients, whether on pizzas, in pastas, or with burgers. Earl's follows food trends closely and trains its staff accordingly, once a year shipping the whole management team off to Tuscany (or wherever) to experience the cuisine firsthand. The menu caters to all tastes and ages, but you'll mostly find a younger crowd here. Open until midnight; some locations even later. ■ *303 Marine Dr, North Vancouver; 984-4341;* ■ *1185 Robson St; 669-0020;* ■ *901 W Broadway; 734-5995;* ■ *1601 W Broadway; 736-5663;* ■ *4361 Kingsway, Burnaby; 432-0840;* ■ *700-7380 King George Hwy, Surrey; 591-3500;* ■ *1767-152nd St, White Rock; 536-8700; $$; full bar; AE, MC, V; no cheques; open 11:30am-midnight (some locations later) every day.*

El Caravan ★ Make a note to visit this Lebanese restaurant the next time you're downtown shopping or taking in a little Mozart at the nearby Orpheum Theatre. Levis or black tie, you'll be equally at home in El Caravan's roomy interior, where peachy walls and vases of pampas plumes subtly allude to sunnier climes. Chef Leila Wehbe cooks the dishes she learned at her grandmother's elbow. Long on parsley, the tabouli is refreshing and clean to the taste buds. Partnering the usual Middle Eastern appetizers—hummus, baba ghanouj, and grape leaves—are her exceptionally spicy carrots. There are pita sandwiches filled with commendably good falafel and various souvlakia. All entrées—the prawns, lamb chops, chicken, spinach pie, moussaka, and souvlakia—come with the aforementioned spicy carrots, rice that's lightly tossed with vermicelli, and Leila's pickles. ■ *809 Seymour St; 682-7000; $$; full bar; AE, MC, V; no cheques; lunch, dinner every day.*

English Bay Cafe [unrated] At press time, this quintessential Vancouver restaurant was undergoing name and menu changes. But this casual bistro (downstairs) with a summertime deck is one of the city's favourite spots. The upstairs room has a comfortable, woodsy West Coast feel, with plenty of greenery and a view of English Bay. At last check, the kitchen is conservative, at times uninspired, but there are standouts in the diverse menu, including rack of lamb, filet mignon Oscar, and a combination of veal scalloppine and prawns. Brunches are still well attended, although the quality of the legendary fare that once made this one of the city's hottest brunch spots has waned. An award-winning wine list features a good selection of West Coast vintages. ▪ *1795 Beach Ave; 669-2225; $$; full bar; AE, DC, DIS, E, JCV, MC, V; no cheques; lunch Mon-Sat, dinner every day, brunch Sat-Sun.*

Ezogiku Noodle Cafe If it weren't for the word *noodle* in its name, one would expect to find a trendy espresso and pastry bar here; instead, ramen dishes are the order of the day. There are only 10 seats at the counter and 4 at the window. The menu offers ramen in regular (pork), miso, or soy broth, a fried rice dish, a fried noodle dish, a curried dish, and gyozas—and that's it. Ezogiku's size and focus are the secret to the large bowls of perfectly cooked chewy noodles in rich, steaming broth. Do what the old master in the movie *Tampopo* instructed: study, sniff, and savour. Lineups are common, but it's always worth the wait. A new, much larger location at 1329 Robson St (685-8606) now accommodates 70 noodle fanatics with equally focused food. Other branches are in Honolulu and Tokyo. ▪ *1684 Robson St; 687-7565; $; no alcohol; no credit cards; no cheques; lunch, dinner every day.*

Fiasco ★★ Eagerness to have their flagons filled and their palates sated is what draws a hip urban crowd to this easygoing West Side eatery. The only thing cooler is the decor, a light and lofty room that, come summer, spills out onto the sidewalk. The skylit bar has its own faithfuls who come to watch the game on TV and sip Rickard's draft or Granville Island beer. The menu feels more Californian than Tuscan, the pizzas more Puck-ish than most. In the open kitchen with its wood-fired brick oven, you can watch the cook making a Cajun shrimp version or one topped with smoked goose breast, grilled zucchini, bocconcini, and oyster mushrooms—or you can simply build your own. Eight variations on carpaccio highlight the appetizer listings. Pastas are esoteric: ravioli is filled with smoked chicken and corn in a yellow pepper salsa; tortellini are stuffed with salmon and Camembert. Live entertainment Thursday through Sunday. Bargain seekers should look for the weeknight specials. ▪ *2486 Bayswater St; 734-1325; $$; full bar; AE, MC, V; no cheques; lunch, dinner every day, brunch Sun.*

The Fish House at Stanley Park ★★ Located in the old Beach House Restaurant close by the tennis courts is high-profile restaurateur Bud Kanke's latest acquisition. This handsome eatery carries off a clubby feel with convivial booths and low lighting reminiscent of San Francisco's financial district. The menu is equally attractive, featuring 25 fresh seafood items, with daily changes to keep abreast of seasonal catches. The Pacific salmon steak is cooked on the same kind of cedar plank used by the early native people of the West Coast, infusing the fish with a natural wood fragrance. When it comes to shellfish, worry not; the extensive collection of fresh-shucked oysters is first-rate, as are the prawn and crab offerings. ■ *2099 Beach Ave (entrance to Stanley Park); 681-7275; $$; full bar; AE, DC, E, MC, V; no cheques; lunch Mon-Sat, dinner every day, brunch Sun.*

Five Sails (Pan Pacific Hotel) ★★★ From this restaurant's perch the view of the city is magic, gentled in the daylight, jewelled by nighttime. Facing the harbour from your table, you could be aboard a luxury liner sailing smoothly to Alaska. Loyal fans know what to expect in the serene and civilized world of chef Ernst Dorfler's domain—attentive service, spare luxury, and the joy of lots of space between tables. Dorfler's pièce de résistance, an appetizer of succulent warmed salmon gravlax delicately sandwiched between two crêpes, is evidence of his talents with seafood, as is a perfectly charbroiled fillet of salmon swimming in an orange and rosemary sauce, or a wonderful caramelized swordfish served with a Thai green curry hash. Desserts are not exceptionally creative, but you'll be more than pleased with the poached pear in puff pastry. ■ *999 Canada Pl; 662-8111; $$$; full bar; AE, DC, E, MC, V; no cheques; dinner every day.* ⚐

Floata ChiuChow Restaurant ★★ The Lam family has been in the restaurant business for generations, giving Vancouver its first ChiuChow restaurant, and, most recently, the Floata. Connie Lam, number one daughter and most amiable hostess, makes excellent recommendations from the menu. Traditional favourites such as double-boiled duck soup with dried lemons, and ChiuChow poached duck in five spices and soy, are once again true to form. Cold steamed Dungeness crab with vinegar dip offers a different take on our favourite regional crustacean, and sautéed satay beef served over sweet and crunchy gai lan (Chinese broccoli) can be most memorable. Another restaurant, open for dim sum and with a seafood focus, is located in Richmond. ■ *4316 Main St; 879-8118; $$; full bar; AE, V; no cheques; lunch (dim sum), dinner every day;* ■ *1425-4380 No. 3 Rd (Parker Place Shopping Centre); Richmond; 270-8889; $$; full bar; V; no cheques; lunch, dinner every day.* ⚐

Flying Wedge ★★¹/₂ Pizza is all they sell, but it's arguably the best in the city in two convenient locations. Join the lunchtime business crowd on Robson Street or the Kitsilano Beach bunch on Cornwall Avenue, just south of the Burrard Street Bridge. You'll find funky, Crayola-coloured surroundings in both venues, as well as generous wedges of thin-crusted pizza, served cafeteria style, for $3 a pop. They constantly change the menu, keeping old faves like Deep Purple, heady with marinated eggplant and a good spicy Szechuan chicken, and bringing in new tastes like spinach fettuccine or peaches and Black Forest ham. There is a wide choice of nonalcoholic drinks. Open till 3am on weekends. ■ *1937 Cornwall Ave; 732-8840;*

▼

Top 175 Restaurants

▲

■ *1175 Robson St; 681-1233; $; no alcohol; no credit cards; no cheques; lunch, dinner every day.*

Fortune House ★★½ This upscale restaurant undoubtedly benefits from its location in the busy Oakridge Shopping Centre, since parking spaces in the middle of one of the most affluent neighbourhoods in Vancouver can be difficult to find. Although the glass and brass interior of Fortune House borders on the generic, booth seating along one wall of the restaurant makes it quite comfortable and conducive to more intimate dining. The menu borrows from the diverse culinary regions of China with delectable and innovative results: the braised dishes in hot pots, eggplant in chile with minced pork, and seafood with hairy squash and vermicelli are excellent. The chef's masterful touch and the adaptability of Chinese cooking are well illustrated by the generally successful integration of typical local ingredients into the menu. For instance, salmon, a fish seldom used in Chinese restaurants, is deep-fried, then smartly dressed in salt and chiles. It turns up again succulent and delicious in black bean sauce served over chow mein. The sometimes mundane permutations of dim sum rise to new heights with wonderfully delicate items like tempura nori, tofu rolls, and scallop dumplings. ■ *5733 Cambie St; 266-7728; $$; full bar; AE, MC, V; no cheques; lunch, dinner every day.*

▼

Top 175
Restaurants

▲

Giraffe ★★ This delightful, elegant neighbourhood restaurant with a view of Semiahmoo Bay strongly believes in the three Gs of California-style cooking—garlic, goat cheese, and grilling. As you peruse the menu, a basket of crisp pappadums is delivered to the table. Nobody will rush you through luxurious appetizers of crispy wonton skins filled with fresh crab and served with honey mustard, or a layered torta basilica of cream cheese, pesto, pine nuts, and sun-dried tomatoes with garlic crostini. The lamb loin in mustard herb sauce with carmelized onions is outstanding—ditto the boneless chicken breast with mixed berries. Save room for "The Graze"—a desert sampler with an array of sweets that may include cheesecake, fruit and berry sorbets, or a rich chocolate cake. And owner/chef Corinne Poole constantly peeks out to ensure that everyone is finishing what's on their plates. ■ *15053 Marine Dr (across from the pier), White Rock; 538-6878; $$; full bar; MC, V; no cheques; dinner every day.*

Grand King Seafood Restaurant ★★★½ Local lovers of Chinese food let out a collective sigh of relief when they learned that chef Lam Kam Shing decided to stay in Vancouver. His celebrated stint at the Dynasty Restaurant in the Vancouver Renaissance Hotel earned him a reputation as one of the best chefs in Vancouver. Now, once again, an appreciative crowd is frequenting his new restaurant, located in the Holiday Inn on West Broadway. The decor here is no match for the elegant

Dynasty, but the service—led by the ever-courteous Simon Lee and affable Peter Ling—is correspondingly less formal, equally helpful, and somehow more comfortable. The menu is trademark Lam—a creative assimilation of his diverse experience in Chinese regional cuisines with innovative touches gleaned from Japanese and other Asian cooking styles. Local ingredients become new classics in dishes like poached geoduck and beef tenderloin with chile soya, and black cod smoked with essence of red wine. Above all, ideas both simple and complex are backed by thoughtful and impeccable execution in the kitchen. Examples are the steamed rock cod, barely off the bone and doused with Lam's secret blend of soya, and crispy roasted suckling pig trimmed to present just the right balance of skin, fat, and lean meat. The remarkably rich hot and sour seafood soup is now available in individual portions. The chef's special menu changes monthly, ensuring that the kitchen's creative juices continue to flow—and that you'll be coming back for more. ▪ *705 W Broadway; 876-7855; $$$; full bar; AE, MC, V; no cheques; lunch, dinner every day.*

Grand View Restaurant ★ In the rapidly changing Chinese restaurant scene in Vancouver, Grand View is almost like a granddaddy. It has been there—same owner, same crew—for well over 10 years, carrying on business with the serenity of an elder, quietly setting the trends. Grand View was among the first to introduce weekend Northern-style dim sum brunches serving steamed pork dumplings, robust beef noodle soups, and foot-long fried dough with soya milk—salted or sweetened for dunking. A separate "vegetarian delights" section on the menu includes meatless versions of the garlicky Sichuan eggplant, hot and sour soup, and the Mah Po bean curd. Departing from convention, the chefs quick-fry geoduck in a spicy garlic sauce and substitute squid for chicken in a Kung-Pao-style sauté. Lamb dishes and the Shanghai-style, white-cooked pork in garlic and chiles deserve kudos. To revisit Grand View is to wonder how we could have stayed away so long. ▪ *60 W Broadway; 879-8885; $; full bar; V; no cheques; lunch, dinner every day.*

Griffins ★★½ The eminently respectable Hotel Vancouver (one of the historic Canadian Pacific chateaus that dot Canada) houses a bright and lively bistro. With taxi cab–yellow walls, griffin-motif carpet, and a feeling of urban action, the place has energy to burn. Three meals a day (plus high tea) are served à la carte, but the buffet meals are the way to go for those who choose not to choose. The breakfast buffet lets you veer toward the healthy—muesli, fresh fruit compote, and such—or the hedonistic: carved Pepsi Cola–glazed ham or smoked chorizo. An Asian corner supplies early birds with, among other delicacies, a fix of grilled salmon and toasted nori. Make a dinner of smoked salmon or roasted peppers with basil at the appetizer bar, or work your way through entrées of silver-dollar scallops in garlic sauce, an exemplary steak, or a pasta dish, then take a run or three at the pastry bar. ■ *900 W Georgia St; 662-1900; $$; full bar; AE, DC, MC, V; no cheques; breakfast, lunch, dinner every day.*

Hamburger Mary's "Open 22 hours out of 24" says the sign, and in this neck of the woods the action lasts till the wee hours, when singles and couples wind up the night with a snack at good ole Mary's. It's the diner we all grew up with gone upscale, with groovy chrome 'n' glass-block decor and heartachey songs on the jukebox. A West End fixture since 1979, Hamburger Mary's has stayed open by racing apace of fickle appetites. Thus, starters are whatever's hip, be it potato skins, chicken strips with plum sauce, or potstickers. Big burgers are the major draw here: served with bacon, cheese, and just about any other combo that strikes your fancy—with the Works for the undecided, the double-size Banquet Burger for the ravenous, and fish and chicken burgers for the quasi-vegetarians. Not forgetting its diner roots, Hamburger Mary's also serves up chips with a side of mayo or gravy and humongous milkshakes in a chrome container, and genuine corned beef hash shows up occasionally as a special. ■ *1202 Davie St; 687-1293; $; full bar; AE, MC, V; no cheques; breakfast, lunch, dinner every day. Open till 4am.*

The Hermitage ★★ Owner-chef Herve Martin (who was once chef to the late King Leopold of Belgium) sticks strongly by his French roots, although a highly innovative menu includes a few items that are more local in flavour. Like their owner, the surroundings are quiet and unassuming. Martin's menu varies, although he often prepares special requests with sufficient notice. Highlights of one visit were a spinach salad, gently warmed, with a smooth, tongue-teasing tarragon vinaigrette, topped with pieces (not bits) of bacon; plump prawns with sweet and sour apples and a pomegranate sauce; and medallions of veal tenderloin, gently sautéed and served with a mild wild mushroom sauce and garden fresh vegetables on the side. For dessert: chocolate and pistachio pâté and a delightful combination of kiwi, papaya, and raspberry sorbets. The Hermitage is a reminder that good restaurants reflect the uniqueness and personality of their hosts. And while The Hermitage (as its name implies) may be hidden, it's well worth the looking. ■ *115-1025 Robson; 689-3237; $$; full bar; AE, DC, E, JCB, MC, V; no cheques; lunch Mon-Fri, dinner every day.*

Herons (Waterfront Centre Hotel) ★★½ Executive Chef Thomas Dietzel is up to the challenge of attracting diners' attention away from the panoramic harbour view and the hustle

▼

Top 175
Restaurants

▲

and bustle outside the Waterfront Centre Hotel. His globe-trotting menu and daily fresh sheet offer generous portions of seasonal dishes, conjuring up the flavours of Bangkok, Toyko, Beijing, or Bombay. For a taste of Dietzel's deft wizardry, don't miss the warm scallop sausage and mussel appetizer, and the outstanding grilled yellowfin tuna with a black sesame and wasabe butter. At lunch, have a caesar salad tossed with your choice of bacon, shrimp, or chicken, and you'll see just how good this ubiquitous salad can be—when it's tossed by the right hands. Desserts could be more inventive. ■ *900 Canada Pl; 691-1991; $$; full bar; AE, DC, E, JCV, MC, V; no cheques; breakfast, lunch, dinner every day, brunch Sun.*

Hon's Wun Tun House ★ Vancouverites have tracked the growth of Hon's from a diminutive space with windows that were continually steamed up by simmering stockpots to its present surroundings in one of Chinatown's newer retail spaces. The decor may now be urbanly chic, but the lineups, noise level, rock-bottom prices, and menu remain reassuringly the same. Soups are a major draw: basic won ton, pig's feet, fish ball, and 90-odd variations—all in a rich, life-affirming broth. Equally noteworthy are Hon's trademarked potstickers. Pan-fried or steamed, they come circled like wagons around a ginger-spiked dipping sauce. ■ *108-268 Keefer St; 688-0871; $; no alcohol; no credit cards; no cheques; lunch, dinner every day.*

Horizons on Burnaby Mountain ★★½ A drive to the top of Burnaby Mountain leads right to this spacious room, where its numerous windows command a spectacular view of the city, snug in Burrard Inlet far below. Increasing emphasis on local fare in the hands of chef Deb Connors has produced a menu with specialties such as alder-grilled BC salmon, a scallop and prawn risotto, and seafood bouillabaisse. Many BC wines are featured on the restaurant's extensive list. Watch for seasonal food and wine promotions. Thanks to Connors's efforts, quality, which has in the past been hit and miss, now seems to be more consistent. ■ *100 Centennial Way, Burnaby; 299-1155; $$; full bar; AE, E, MC, V; lunch, dinner every day, brunch Sun.*

Hung Fook Shanghai Restaurant ★★ Pristine surroundings, meticulously attentive service, and a fish tank at the end of the dining room: welcome to Vancouver's new breed of Chinese restaurant. Now that we've learned to appreciate the restaurant's focus on sublimely fresh ingredients prepared with utmost simplicity, Hung Fook is taking its place among our faves. Here the emphasis is on seafood. Choose a live crab, and within minutes it's back on your table, flash-cooked and sauced with green onion and ginger, black beans, soy, or curry. Steamed rock cod, like abalone, eel, and other denizens of the deep, is so perfectly cooked it needs little in the way of embellishment.

Uncomplicated but intriguing chicken, duck, and meat dishes are similarly flawless. It pays to talk to the servers, all of whom are delighted to translate the Chinese side of the menu. That's where you'll find interesting dishes like soyed spiced beef and jelly pork. ■ *3466 Cambie St; 876-4220; $$; beer and wine; MC, V; cheques OK; lunch, dinner every day.*

Ikea Why would we suggest a meal in a furniture store? Two reasons. One, if you've never wandered through this phenom-enally successful high-concept, low-priced, serve-yourself Swedish store, you're in for a treat. More to the point, it's the only place in and around Vancouver (20 minutes from down-town via the Knight Street Bridge) that serves Swedish food. It's also the only cafeteria—let alone furniture store—we know of that lets you sip a glass of wine with your meal. You'll find a variety of spiced or marinated pickled herring, liver pâtés, cu-cumber salad, and robust smoked or spiced sausages round-ing out the cold side of the buffet. Red cabbage and köttbullar (Swedish meatballs) are usually among the hot dishes offered. Open-face hoagies and children's box lunches are also avail-able. Nearby, you can gather an armload of such specialties as lingonberry preserves or Swedish flatbread to take home. ■ *3200 Sweden Way, Richmond; 273-2051; $; beer and wine; MC, V; cheques OK; lunch every day, dinner Wed-Fri.*

Top 175 Restaurants

Il Barino [unrated] Once the darling of the Armani set, this al-most too elegant Tuscan-style restaurant has certainly had its ups and downs, with five chef changes in three years. At press time another new chef is just settling in. Cute, sloganlike menu writing makes for tongue-in-cheek reading. The agnolotti with "Gorgonzola yield signs and interstate pepper purée" was de-void of the creative impact implied. A substantial portion of dill risotto with seafood was good but lacking texture. We are sit-ting on the fence on this one. ■ *1116 Mainland St (at Helm-cken St); 687-1116; $$; full bar; AE, DC, MC, V; no cheques; lunch Mon-Fri, dinner Mon-Sat.*

Il Giardino di Umberto ★★★ Stars, stargazers, and the movers and shakers come to Umberto Menghi's Il Giardino to mingle amid the Tuscan villa decor: high ceilings, tiled floors, winking candlelight, and a vine-draped terrace for dining al-fresco (no better place in summer). The emphasis is on pasta and game, with an Italian nuova elegance: farm-raised pheas-ant with roasted-pepper stuffing and port wine sauce, tender veal with a mélange of lightly grilled wild mushrooms. An ac-companying slice of pan-roasted polenta adds a comforting homey touch. Be warned: the prices on the specials are in their own category. For dessert, go for the tiramisu—the best ver-sion of this pick-me-up in town. ■ *1382 Hornby St; 669-2422; $$$; full bar; AE, DC, E, MC, V; no cheques; lunch Mon-Fri, dinner Mon-Sat.*

Imperial Chinese Seafood Restaurant ★★★ The Imperial may lay claim to being the most opulent Chinese dining room around. There's a feeling of being in a grand ballroom of eras past: a central staircase leads to the balustrade-lined mezzanine, diplomatic dignitaries and rock stars dine in luxurious private rooms, and windows two storeys high command views of Burrard Inlet and the North Shore mountains. The food can be equally polished, as in the superb pan-fried prawns in soy, addictive beef sautéed in chile with honey walnuts, and crunchy-sweet gai lan with garlic and bonito. Dim sum is consistently good. If it weren't for a bit of unevenness in the service, this could be a perfect restaurant. Reservations recommended on weekdays. ▪ *355 Burrard St; 688-8191; $$; full bar; AE, MC, V; no cheques; lunch, dinner every day.*

Isadora's ★ Parents with young children frequent Isadora's on Granville Island. Its children's menu (clown-faced pizzas and grilled cheese with potato chips), in-house play area, and tables next to the outdoor water park in summer make this a family favourite. Isadora's wholesome menu also features more grown-up items, such as smoked wild salmon sandwiches, organic salads, great nut burgers, and plenty of choices for vegetarians and vegans. Open at 7:30am weekdays for early-morning business meetings over the restaurant's own blend of organic coffee, Isadora's is busiest at Sunday brunch. Service is generally slow. ▪ *1540 Old Bridge St (Granville Island); 681-8816; $; full bar; MC, V; no cheques; breakfast, lunch, dinner every day, brunch Sat-Sun.* &

▼
Top 175
Restaurants
▲

Japanese Deli House ★ This is the bargain beauty of the sushi crowd, right in the middle of old Japantown's grocery and fish stores. The Deli is an old, high-ceilinged room with big windows, arborite-topped tables, and an all-you-can-eat philosophy applied to sushi most days and during special hours. Start with eight pieces of nigiri sushi, four pieces of maki, and soup for $8.95; if you can eat more than that, it's yours for free. Quality is surprisingly good, especially if you arrive early. There's a state-of-the-art takeout branch across the street specializing in sushi to go and bento boxes. ▪ *381 Powell St; 681-6484; $; beer only; no credit cards; cheques OK; lunch every day, dinner served till 8pm Tues-Sat, till 6pm Sun.*

Joe Fortes ★ You might be in New York or Boston: Joe Fortes —named for the city's best-loved lifeguard—has that kind of high-energy, uptown chophouse feel to it. "Joe's" is one of downtown's hippest watering holes, where Vancouver's glossiest young professionals flock after putting in a hard day at the stock exchange or ad agency. The draw is more than the big U-shaped bar where designer water and single-malt scotch are in equal demand. It's the oyster bar too, dispensing faultlessly fresh Quilchene or Malpeque or any of a dozen other varieties, all sold individually. Sipping, schmoozing, and sampling (inventive starters include oyster crostini and duck confit with mashed potato cake) often segue seamlessly into the dinner hour. The fresh fish is a constant lure, with 18 daily selections (staff simply tick off what's available). Dungeness crab is reliably good, as are the succulent, blackened snapper, mahi-mahi, and skate. ■ *777 Thurlow St; 669-1940; $$; full bar; AE, DC, MC, V; no cheques; lunch Mon-Fri, dinner every day, brunch Sat-Sun.*

Kam Gok Yuen If you're ravenous from souvenir shopping in Chinatown and can no longer resist the insistent beckoning of barbecued ducks hanging in food store windows, Kam Gok Yuen is the place for an affordable repast. Its famous barbecued meats are sold out every day, so a near-empty window is not suspect but is a sign that you should hurry and get in before the store runs out. Some of the best congee—rice porridge with meats or seafoods—in town are cooked to order over hissing burners in the open kitchen up front. Watch as wontons and noodles are tossed, caught, and transferred into awaiting bowls with a magical ease that borders on showmanship. Be sure to ask about specials posted on the walls in Chinese, since they can be some of the best. Brisk, no-nonsense service. ■ *142 E Pender St; 683-3822; $; no alcohol; no credit cards; no cheques; lunch, dinner every day.*

Kamei Sushi ★ ★ Kamei Sushi just keeps growing. Now at six locations, Kamei may no longer be the best Japanese restaurant in town, but its simple, Westernized dishes certainly make it one of the most popular. The original Thurlow Street location, though a bit dated, is still our favourite and is particularly lively at night when the theatres empty out. Try for a seat at the sushi bar so that you can watch the antics of the sushi chefs. Combination platters contain all the standards (tuna, salmon, octopus, abalone, salmon roe), or try the red snapper usuzukui, thinly sliced and fanned on the plate, accompanied by a citrus sauce. Robata dishes are the special focus at the Broadway Plaza location and can be very good. The luxury-class Kamei Royale on West Georgia Street seats over 300, with open and private tatami rooms. ■ *811 Thurlow St (and branches); 684-4823; $$; full bar; AE, DC, E, MC, V; no cheques; lunch Sun-Fri, dinner every day.*

Kilimanjaro ★ Like East Africa itself, Amyn and Nargis Sunderji's restaurant is an intriguing melting pot—visually, and culinarily. African masks and batiks mix with the deep pink walls, French provincial prints, and swirling ceiling fans to create the atmosphere of a chic Nairobi restaurant. Try the coconut fish soup, a recipe from Zanzibar of amazing complexity and depth; a Swahili specialty of curried goat; the prawns piri piri; or the uniquely African (specifically, Zairean) combination of chicken in ho-ho peppers, palm oil, and garlic. "Burning Spear"—lamb served flaming on a sword—is the house specialty. Desserts bring a fittingly exotic finale, from a tangerine cheesecake to a safari mango mousse. The Safari Bistro downstairs offers spicy ethnic fare as well as colonial indulgences like fish 'n' chips for lunch or a late-night snack. ■ *332 Water St (Gastown); 681-9913; $$; full bar; AE, DC, MC, V; no cheques; lunch Mon-Fri, dinner every day. (Bistro open daily for lunch.)*

King's Fare Fish & Chips ★ Walk into this (usually) busy, small restaurant and you'll immediately sense that this place means business. You'll probably have to wait, but not for very long, as things move along at an efficient pace. Just take in the bric-a-brac, which includes an intriguing miniature, old-fashioned gas-pump-turned-vinegar-dispenser. The menu is concerned totally with fish and chips in various combinations. The place is also as clean as a whistle, smoke-free, and grease-free too, because the fat's changed daily. While the staff hustle, they still find time to be polite, stopping to chat with the regulars, of whom there are plenty. Portions are more than generous, the food is hot and the batter is perfect: light but not greasy, crisp but not too much so. The fish, quite simply, is wonderful, cooked just to a turn. The potatoes come from Ladner and are chipped in the kitchen. Even the coleslaw is made from scratch, and served in portions that you don't mistake for the coffee cream. Decent ale on tap adds that little extra touch of authenticity. There's a second location at 235 15th Street, West Vancouver. ■ *1320 W 73rd Ave; 266-3474; $; wine and beer; E, MC, V; no cheques; lunch, dinner every day.*

Kirin Mandarin Restaurant ■ Kirin Seafood Restaurant ★★★ Kirin's postmodern decor—high ceilings, slate-green walls, black lacquer trim—is oriented around the two-storey–high mystical dragonlike creature that is the restaurant's namesake. The menu reads like a trilingual (Chinese, English, and Japanese) opus spanning the culinary capitals of China: Canton, Sichuan, Shanghai, and Beijing (live lobsters and crabs can be ordered in 11 different preparations). Remarkably, most of the vastly different regional cuisines are authentic and well executed, but the Northern Chinese specialties are the best. Peking duck is as good as it gets this side of China, and braised dishes such as sea cucumber with prawn roe sauce are "royal" treats. Atypical of Chinese restaurants, desserts can be excellent—try the red bean pie, a thin crêpe folded around a sweet bean filling and fried to a fluffy crisp. The Western-style service is attentive though sometimes a tad aggressive. Unless you are in the mood to splurge, stay away from the Cognac cart.

The second, equally fine outpost is in City Square, with a passable view of the city. It focuses more on seafood and has great dim sum (including a definitive hargou or shrimp dumpling). ■ *1166 Alberni St; 682-8833; $$$; full bar; AE, DC, E, JCV, V; cheques OK; lunch, dinner every day;* ■ *201-555 W 12th Ave; 879-8038; $$$; full bar; AE, DC, E, V; cheques OK; lunch, dinner every day.* ♿

Kitto Japanese Restaurant ★ Kitto opened to instant success in 1990 on the fashion strip on Robson Street. Now another one is thriving on theatre row on Granville Street. The reason for their success? Authentically flavoured, accessible Japanese food at rock-bottom prices—a '90s backlash against the trendy '80s gourmet mania. The high art of sushi and sashimi is not to be found here. Instead there are udons, ramens, sobas, and donburis—rice and noodle dishes that are fast and satisfying. Or try some robatas, including smoky yakitori chicken with green onions; fleshy, velvety fresh shiitake mushrooms; zucchini with dry bonito flakes; and an incredible dish of hamachi gill. Two or three with a bowl of rice make a wonderful meal, with dinner for two comfortably priced around $10 a person. It's not a place to linger and hold hands—even though the booth seats are private and comfortable enough—but it's a great place for before or after a movie. ■ *1212 Robson St; 662-3333;* ■ *833 Granville St; 687-6622; $; beer only; V; no cheques; lunch every day, dinner Mon-Sat.*

Koji Japanese Restaurant ★★ In our opinion, Koji has the most beautiful garden in a downtown Vancouver restaurant—an island of pine trees and river rocks on a patio above Hornby Street. The best seats are the nonsmoking ones by the windows looking out on the garden or at the sushi and robata bars. The rest of the restaurant is a crowded, smoky room often full of Japanese tourists. The sushi is not the best in town, but selections from the robata grill are dependable; grilled shiitake, topped with bonito flakes and tiny filaments of dry seaweed, are sublime. The Japanese boxed lunch might contain chicken kara-age, superb smoked black cod, prawn and vegetable tempura, two or three small salads, rice with black sesame seeds, pickled vegetables, miso soup, and fresh fruit—all for around $10. Finish with green tea ice cream. ■ *630 Hornby St; 685-7355; $$; full bar; AE, DC, MC, V; no cheques; breakfast, dinner every day, lunch Mon-Fri.* ♿

La Belle Auberge ★★ Thirty minutes from Vancouver, owner/chef Bruno Marti seeks to preserve and enshrine traditional French cuisine at this old Victorian manse in Ladner. Marti is well known to Vancouverites as a member of the gold-medal-winning team at the 1984 Culinary Olympics. The duckling in blueberry sauce is, deservedly, his most popular dish, on a predictable but superb menu offering rack of lamb, milk-fed veal, and some game dishes. ■ *4856 48th Ave (at 48A), Ladner; 946-7717; $$$; full bar; AE, MC, V; no cheques; dinner every day.*

La Brochette ★★★ The focus of this Gastown hideaway is a huge, antique Normandy *tourne-broche*, the granddaddy of modern rotisseries, and its practitioner, Dagobert Niemann, is a master of the art. A true *rotisseur*, Niemann uses hardwood chips to attain his unique flavour and works for three uninterrupted hours in front of his glowing fire. He stokes, turns, carves, sauces, tests, cuts, and grills, co-ordinating the arrangement and delivery of every order. His leg of lamb is minced with fresh herb and served with a pungent aioli, the strong, garlicky flavours of the creamy sauce combining with jus (replenished on cue to keep things hot) in an intense dose of flavour. Watch for roast half of duckling, which emerges from the rack with crisp skin and tender, moist flesh. Also from the grill come great vegetables—grilled baby asparagus in season, lightly buttered and salted, is an extra treat. Lead up to the main event, perhaps, with Brie en feuillette or with mussels in a light, creamy broth flavoured with Pineau des Charentes. The wine list is one of the city's more comprehensive and is well presented. After dinner, head downstairs to the fireplace with cozy wraparound seating. Reservations are a good idea. ■ *52 Alexander St; 684-0631; $$$; full bar; AE, V; no cheques; dinner Tues-Sat (may be closed in July and Aug).*

La Cucina Italiana ★★ Stuck rather incongruously in the middle of North Vancouver's strip of car dealerships and video shops, La Cucina's rustic character overcomes its surroundings. The attractive dining room has Italian opera playing at just the right volume. When it's available, try bresaola—air-dried beef from Switzerland—or the cold antipasto. Pastas range from traditional spaghetti with tomato and meat sauce to fettuccine with squid and sweet red peppers. Fish specials are usually good; or try pollo alla diavola, a grilled chicken breast with black-pepper-crusted skin. The house lasagne is outstanding. Don't leave without sampling the homemade ice cream. ■ *1509 Marine Dr (at McGowan Ave), North Vancouver; 986-1334; $$; full bar; AE, MC, V; no cheques; dinner Mon-Sat.*

La Toque Blanche ★★ This cozy, '70s retro-woodsy retreat tucked behind the Cypress Park Mohawk gas station is still West Vancouver's best-kept culinary secret. Underscoring owner Peter Wieser's European passion for detail are appetizers such as duck liver terrine with cassis coulis and filo-wrapped escargots served with a mild pepper salsa. Lobster bisque is wickedly rich and served piping hot. For entrées, try the breast of duckling glazed with Calvados or morsels of lamb cooked perfectly pink in a mustard sauce. A well-thought-out wine list complements the menu. Considering the quality, detail, and presentation, the meals are a bargain. ■ *4368 Marine Dr (next to the Cypress Park Market), West Vancouver; 926-1006; $$; full bar; AE, MC, V; no cheques; dinner Tues-Sun.*

La Villetta ★¹/₂ Inauspicious surroundings hide a romantic little Italian restaurant where first dates or flourishing relationships can find nourishment both on the menu and in the setting. In summer, the outdoor patio lures. Wintertime, habitués opt for the cozy, fireplaced dining room. The draw apart from the decor? Simple, basic Italian food, perfectly cooked by chef Aldo Zenone: golden roast chicken, its rosemary-and-oregano-flavoured pan juices poured over the top; clams in an herby tomato sauce; impeccably fresh mussels served with nothing but pepper, butter, parsley, and garlic. Zenone's pastas, including homemade seafood canneloni, crab ravioli, and rugged rotini matriciana, all have a staunch following. Specialties include a fish of the day (prawns if you're lucky), a quartet of veal dishes, a few chicken preparations, and rabbit, when available, simmered in herbs and wine. Don't miss the tiramisu. ■ *3916 E Hastings St; 299-3979; $$; full bar; MC, V; local cheques only; lunch Mon-Fri, dinner Tues-Sun.*

Landmark Hot Pot House ■ Landmark Seafood Restaurant

★★★ Hotpotting—traditionally for the warming of body and soul on long wintry nights—seems to have transcended its seasonal limits to emerge as a Chinese culinary trend. In the Landmark, the centre of each table is cut out for the built-in natural-gas stove and its settings, which include a personal strainer and chopsticks. The menus are simply lists of available ingredients and prices; the rest is up to you. We ordered the Duo Soup Base of satay and chicken broth and happily experimented with platters of fish, chicken, beef, dumplings, vegetables, and noodles. This is heartwarming, healthy food at its simplest, embellished only by the chef's exquisite knife work and perfect presentation.

For more conventional dining, try Landmark's sister restaurant, Landmark Seafood Restaurant at 3338 Cambie Street (873-3338). You can watch your excellent food being prepared in the glass-lined open kitchen. ■ *4023 Cambie St; 872-2868; $$; full bar; MC, V; no cheques; dinner every day.* &

Las Margaritas ★ *Olé!* Sombreros hanging from the ceiling, red-tiled floors, and white stuccoed archways all add up to quintessential Mexican restaurant decor in this lively Kitsilano cantina. The crowd changes with the hour. Early evenings, expect families (there's a good, inexpensive children's menu). Later, people come in for the margaritas: pick from three sizes, eight flavours. This is a popular hangout for couples or the gang from the office. A little nacho-noshing or a few dips into Mexican cheese fondue with optional chorizo takes the edge off the appetite while you mull the relative advantages of tacos and enchiladas. Chile rellenos, chimichangas, and flautas—you'll find all the standards here, including combination plates for ditherers who can't decide. Servings are *¡muy amable!* and the

▼

**Top 175
Restaurants**

▲

margarita pie ¡*muy bien!* ■ *1999 W 4th Ave; 734-7117; $$; full bar; AE, MC, V; no cheques; lunch, dinner every day.*

Le Club (Le Meridien Hotel) ★★½ Hidden just a few steps behind the bustling Gerard Lounge in Vancouver's venerable Le Meridien Hotel is this wonderfully romantic dining room with its salmon-coloured fabric walls, original artwork, and European furnishings. Although it's rather formal and old-fashioned looking, a hip, casually dressed crowd brings its appetites here. Stick to the $35 table d'hôte menu and you'll get a brilliant dinner at a reasonable price, orchestrated by new chef Christian Mamber. One recent offering included a complimentary *amuse-gueule* of smoky chicken with pecans; organic greens bathed in a vinaigrette and topped with grilled prawns and steamed oysters; sautéed halibut with yellow squash; and rare rack of lamb served with a lentil cream sauce. Anything from the dessert cart is worth saving room for. ■ *845 Burrard St; 682-5511; $$; full bar; AE, DC, E, MC, V; no cheques; dinner Mon-Sat.*

Le Coq d'Or ★★ Bruno Born's French bistro has a touch of urban chic, in a sunny room with tall windows and rich, mustard-coloured walls. Meals are simple and well executed—perhaps half a chicken roasted with fresh herbs, caramelized garlic, and lemon, or an extra-thick pork chop served with Le Coq's famous crisp pommes frites. Some specific dishes we'd return for: steak tartare, for example, and an eggplant and roasted red pepper appetizer baked with goat cheese. The wine list is fairly pricey; what you save on the reasonably priced food, you'll spend on the wine. Born's weekend brunch is one of the best in the city. Jazz piano happens on Friday and Saturday nights. ■ *3205 W Broadway; 733-0035; $$; full bar; MC, V; no cheques; breakfast, lunch Tues-Fri, dinner Tues-Sat, brunch Sat-Sun.* 占

Le Crocodile ★★★★ France without a passport—that's Le Crocodile. Chef and owner Michel Jacob named his bistro after his favourite restaurant in Strasbourg, his hometown, and his Franco-Germanic culinary heritage is obvious throughout the menu. He accompanies a wonderfully savoury onion tart with chilled Alsatian wine in green-stemmed glasses. Salmon tartare and sautéed scallops in an herb sauce are both showstoppers. Luscious Dover sole, duck (lacquer-crisp outside, moist inside) accompanied by a light orange sauce, calves' livers with spinach butter—it's a trauma to choose. The best desserts are the traditional ones, such as a tangy lemon tart, a soothing crème brulée, and, of course, a tarte Tatin. What with the well-thought-out wine list and the European atmosphere, a dinner at Le Crocodile is an affair to remember. The new location on a one-way street can be difficult to find. ■ *100-909 Burrard St (enter off Smithe St); 669-4298; $$$; full bar; AE, DC, MC, V; no cheques; lunch Mon-Fri, dinner Mon-Sat.* 占

Le Gavroche ★★★ Arguably the most romantic restaurant in
the city, Le Gavroche is perfect for a lingering lunch or special
dinner. In the charming dining room, complete with blazing
fire and glimpses of snowcapped mountains, your meal isn't so
much served as orchestrated, with subtle but attentive service.
The food tends to creative versions of the classics, though the
recent return of chef Scott Kidd possibly signals a shift toward
a more contemporary approach. À la carte selections include
an excellent house hot smoked salmon, homemade pâté, and
delicious salmon baked with goat cheese. Look for the lobster
bisque, fork-tender biftek entrecote in green peppercorn sauce,
and tender house-smoked pheasant breast. Thorough, indul-
gent, and still very French, with one of the city's better wine cellars, Le Gavroche is a delight. ▪ *1616 Alberni St; 685-3924;*
$$$; full bar; AE, DC, MC, V; no cheques; lunch Mon-Fri, din-
ner Mon-Sat.

Le Grec ★★ A hit from the moment it opened, Le Grec took
a gutsy stance in the heart of Vancouver's Little Italy by fo-
cusing purely and simply on mezéthes: Greek-style tapas. With
an ambience as cheerful as that of a Corfu taverna, big servings
of consistently good food, and low prices for food and booze,
this three-level restaurant is packed night after night with a
lively crowd. Owner/chef Manolis Daroukakis knows what ap-
peals. Kotopita encases rosemary-perfumed chicken in crackly
filo pastry. An assertive, tartly refreshing artichoke salad is
speckled with capers and sweet red pepper. Briam translates
as roasted vegetables in their own savoury juices. Portions are
generous and meant to be shared (really). Along with old
friends like moussaka and souvlakia, the menu provides in-
troductions to lesser-known dishes: skordalia, a rich, potato-
based dip that shrieks with garlic; polentalike bobota
simmered with tomatoes and feta; and the Greek version of salt
cod, bakaliaros. Fabulous not-too-sweet baklava rounds out the
meal. Treat yourself to an after-dinner glass of raisiny Mavro-
daphne. ▪ *1447 Commercial Dr; 253-1253; $; full bar; AE,*
MC, V; no cheques; lunch, dinner Mon-Sat.

Le Railcar ★★ Outside are the cobblestoned streets of Gas-
town. Inside, you could be aboard the Train Bleu en route to
adventure. Built in 1929 for the superintendent of the Canadian
Pacific Railway, and still standing on real railroad tracks, Le
Railcar is, no contest, as romantic as it gets. The mahogany
panelling is new, but the bar, the milk-glass lamps, and the
shiny brass fixtures are all original. Owner Daniel Thomas and
chef Brendon Cowell—who share a passion for quality—have
built a reputation for Old World service with New World cui-
sinc. But this is Vancouver, so Asian and Pacific Northwest in-
fluences do tend to creep in. Thus, the seasonal menu might,
in the warmer months, include salmon glazed with Indonesian

▼

**Top 175
Restaurants**

▲

condiment kecap manis, red snapper with spinach and co-conut, or scallops napped with cream, chardonnay, pickled ginger, and sea urchin, as well as traditional bistro fare. If it's listed, go for the simply grilled Italian sausage with a tomato and pepper sauce and big, chunky, sizzling hot frites on the side. In colder weather, the menu ventures into more robust cuisine, such as venison scalloppine or bastilla—a Middle Eastern filo-wrapped pie of chicken spiced with cinnamon and garlic. Desserts are *magnifique!* ■ *106 Carrall St; 669-5422; $$$; full bar; AE, DC, MC, V; no cheques; lunch and dinner Mon-Sat, daily during summer.*

Lok's Chinese Restaurant ★

This longtime neighbourhood favourite from the East Side of Vancouver is now winning converts at their second location at 2006 West Fourth Avenue. Their formula is: good simple food, hard work, and genuinely friendly, family-style service a cut above that of other restaurants of this class. Choose from great clay pot dishes; Cantonese satays and curries; fresh, well-prepared seafood dishes; wontons, noodles, and congee; and a solid repertoire of barbecued meats—all familiar and all reasonably priced. And if you don't feel like venturing out, delivery service is just a phone call away. ■ *4890 Victoria Dr; 439-1888; $; beer and wine; MC, V; no cheques; lunch, dinner every day.*

Lorenzo's ★

Operatic arias and walls resplendent with Old World prints help cozy-up this urban eatery, where classic Italian cuisine is the order of the day. Antipasto focuses on favourites: an impeccable carpaccio, melon with prosciutto, snails baked in garlic and white wine, and mussels marinara. The house special scampi is indecently good (try it for an appetizer if you don't believe us). Side by side with the traditional fettuccine al pesto and linguine with clams is the unexpected—a dish of duck-stuffed ravioli in an orange brandy sauce, or a dark and woodsy plateful of vermicelli graced with seasonal wild mushrooms. The veal's always dependable (especially when stuffed with oyster mushrooms in a baritone sauce of marsala and wine), as are the rack of lamb and chicken stuffed with an aromatic pairing of spinach and prosciutto. Unusual among Italian restaurants, for a few dollars more, Lorenzo's offers all entrées as a table d'hôte three-course dinner. ■ *3605 W 4th Ave; 731-2712; $$$; full bar; AE, MC, V; no cheques; lunch Mon-Fri, dinner every day.*

Major The Gourmet

Strictly speaking, this is not a restaurant but the perennially busy headquarters of caterer-about-town Nicky Major. No matter. Savvy Vancouverites know that this is the place—in fact, in this largely light industrial area, the only place within blocks—for a lunch that's as interesting as it is fast. Major spins the ingredients so that the menu is rarely the same. Grilled chicken might go on a daily pizza, be featured in a salad, or go mano a mano with Thai noodles. Locals know Thursday is burger day; other times, curried lamb may show up, or a chicken and broccoli pasta. Vegetarian and meat lasagnes, hearty pot pies, and shepherd's pie are staples. Desserts and soups change daily. Counter service year-round, with tables outside in warmer months. Jet-setters often pause here en route to the airport for takeout that's classier than Business Class. ▪ *102-8828 Heather St; 322-9211; $; no alcohol; MC, V; no cheques; breakfast, lunch Mon-Fri.*

Maple Garden Restaurant ★★½ The Maple Garden was well received by its Richmond audience when it rode in on the crest of the wave of Hong Kong–style, high-end Chinese restaurants that were opening in the Lower Mainland about five years ago; it quickly grew into a chain that occupies four locations. But like so many other establishments of its genre, the Maple Garden has not been immune to the downturn in the economy and the fiercely competitive restaurant business. The astonishing selection of prestigious and pricey dishes that once dominated the special feature menu—including exotic preparations of game and the classic quartet of Chinese culinary treasures, abalone, dried sea cucumber, shark's fin, and fish maw—has been replaced by more rustic selections: squid sautéed with preserved mustard greens; duck marinated and steamed with taro root; beef combined with braised eggplant; and sliced chicken with scallops in hot bean sauce. The result is, overall, much more accessible food highlighting the ever-steady hand in the kitchen. A takeout menu, with somewhat pedestrian, somewhat overpriced dishes, is also available. ▪ *145-4751 Garden City Rd, Richmond; 278-2323; $$; AE, MC, V; no cheques; every day.*

Mescalero ★★ The very good Mescalero has become a most popular hangout (especially on Thursday nights) for southwestern food and atmosphere. The rustic decor works well (though you may end up with some very authentic splinters). For best value, order from the tapas list; you can piece together a meal from spicy ceviche with marinated scallops, tuna, and jalapeños; roasted mussels in shellfish broth; and grilled eggplant salad with fresh spinach leaves and tangy blue cheese dressing, generously garnished with pine nuts—among others. A dark chocolate "pizza" with pistachios and walnuts in ginger and nutmeg chocolate sauce at the end of the meal will send you rolling out. Trendy and casual (though service may be a touch *too* casual). The wine list is made up of Chilean popular wines with more than half of them available by the glass. ▪ *1215 Bidwell St; 669-2399; $$$; full bar; AE, E, MC, V; no cheques; lunch Mon-Fri, dinner every day, brunch Sat-Sun.* ᕓ

Milestones ★ Mega-servings of food (and booze), priced cheap, are the draw at Milestones, which, despite being a chain, manages consistently to impress with its witty takes on West Coast food trends. Witness the appetizers (most big enough for a light lunch) and the southwestern chicken strips with ancho chile sauce and a cilantro-infused cream for dipping. Salads are generous: the caesar apparently uses an entire head of lettuce, and the seafood pasta salad is lavish with lobster, shrimp, and smoked salmon. Pastas range from the mundane to the unusual, such as a Mongolian chicken penne. A jet-setting menu swings from Sicilian meatloaf rife with fresh herbs to Sichuan peanut chicken and shrimp quesadillas. Try the trademarked Rollups, whole-wheat tortillas encasing everything from smoked chicken or spiced brisket to grilled eggplant. Fresh fruit martinis, frozen Bellinis, and sinfully good desserts. ■ *1210 Denman St; 662-3431;* ■ *2966 West 4th Ave; 734-8616;* ■ *1145 Robson St; 682-4477;* ■ *4420 Lougheed Hwy, Burnaby; 291-7393; $; full bar; AE, DC, MC, V; no cheques; brunch, lunch, dinner every day.*

Mocha Cafe ★★½

Lunch here is the way Vancouverites have liked it all along: muffins, soups, salads, and sandwiches. But at dinner, the Mocha goes a little wild. It's the home of—among other things—Vancouver's best oyster stew, served with cheddar cheese bread. Other items include a great designer pizza, lamb chops with blueberry sauce, and creamy agnolotti with chicken, rosemary, and mushrooms. Salads like Belgian endive, with impeccably fresh walnuts and blue cheese, make a statement. The wine list is a careful collection of moderately priced BC, Washington, and California wines; 10 or so are available by the glass. ■ *1521 W Broadway; 734-5274; $$; beer and wine; MC, V; no cheques; breakfast, lunch, dinner Mon-Fri.*

Monterey Lounge & Grill (Pacific Palisades Hotel) ★★

Rod Butters, former chef at Chateau Whistler, is stirring the pots at the Monterey Lounge & Grill. Butters is a skilled, creative devotee of regional farming and organic foodstuffs. His roasted pumpkin and smoked ham chowder, or arugula and grilled beet salad with duck and crackling, is exactly what you need before getting back to the sale racks on Robson Street. Don't skip dessert—especially if the divine double chocolate mashed brioche is on the menu. The restaurant itself is an odd space looking out over the hotel's courtyard. We prefer to dine in the comfortable lounge where jazz pianists tickle the ivories six nights a week. ■ *1277 Robson St (Pacific Palisades Hotel); 684-1277; $$; full bar; AE, DC, MC, V; no cheques; breakfast, lunch, dinner every day.*

Montri's Thai Restaurant ★★★

Top marks to Montri Rattanaraj for presenting an authentic cuisine not watered down for Vancouver tastes. Thai cuisine is a careful balancing act, based on six interconnecting concepts: bitter, salty, sweet, hot, herbaceous, and fragrant. The heat content is rated on a scale of one to five chile symbols, five being the level for masochists and

Thai nationals. What to order? Everything is good. Tom yum goong is Thailand's national soup, a lemony prawn broth, and it lives up to its name—yum. The tod mun fish cakes blended with prawns and chile curry are excellent, as is the salmon simmered in red curry and coconut sauce. Rattanaraj's Thai gai-yang, chicken marinated in coconut milk and broiled, is a close cousin to the chicken sold on the beach at Puhket. Have it with som-tam, a green papaya salad served with sticky rice and wedges of raw cabbage; the cabbage and the rice are coolants, and you *will* need them (Thailand's Singha beer also helps). ■ *2611 W 4th Ave; 738-9888; $$; full bar; AE, MC, V; no cheques; dinner every day.* &

Moutai Mandarin Restaurant ★ The menu at this tiny restaurant was modelled after the one at the well-patronized Szechuan Chongqing; now West Enders don't have to leave their territory to get good versions of Szechuan Chongqing favourites such as green beans with pork and plenty of chile pepper. We particularly like the specials: spicy clams in black bean sauce and the blistering stir-fry with tiger prawns known as dai ching. Moutai's acid-green tabletops and arborite trim in a pebble-pattern gray are miles removed from red-dragon tacky or Hong Kong slick, which seem to be the city's dominant Chinese restaurant styles. A tropical fish tank divides the room into two tiny sections (smoking and non). ■ *1710 Davie St; 681-2288; $; full bar; AE, MC, V; no cheques; dinner every day.* &

▼
**Top 175
Restaurants**
▲

Musashi Japanese Restaurant Sushi is high art in Japanese cooking, but for ordinary folks who have fallen in love with the stuff, a steady diet of it can prove costly. Not so at Musashi, where high art is offered nightly at low prices—usually to a packed house. You'll find no frills here. The decor is universal neigbourhood eatery, Japanese style. The view out the window is only interesting during rush hour—if you take perverse pleasure in watching those strange things that BMW and Benz drivers do when they are stuck in traffic and think no one's watching. Value is the story here, and a remarkable story it is too. Nigiri sushi—shrimp, tuna, geoduck, sea urchin, and more—starts at $1 a piece and tops at a whopping $1.50 for the deluxe Tsukimi ikura. Makis (rolled sushi), which yield four bite-size pieces, range from $2 to $4.50. A full range of soups, salads, appetizers, tempuras, rice and noodle dishes, and combination dinners are also available. ■ *780 Denman St; 687-0634; $; beer and wine; no credit cards; no cheques; dinner every day.*

Naam With its funky decor and friendly staff, Vancouver's oldest vegetarian restaurant is the last outpost of a time when West Fourth Avenue was hippie heaven. Lineups are common (maybe because the service is so slack).Summertime, we try to nab a seat in the tiny private garden patio. Winters, the candle-lit Naam is as cozy as a Gulf Islands cabin. You can still sip dandelion tea and nibble at a bee pollen cookie, but the menu has broadened considerably over the years. Habitués breakfast on a mishmash of eggs, cheese, tofu, mushrooms, and tomatoes on toast. The house salad—a toppling heap of red cabbage, shredded lettuce, thickly sliced tomato, and sunflower seeds—is humongous. The veggie burrito is the size of a neck pillow. The menu wanders lazily around the world, stopping for nachos, hummus and pita, Thai and caesar salads, sesame fries with miso gravy, and enormous pita pizzas. ■ *2724 W 4th Ave; 738-7151; $; beer and wine; MC, V; no cheques; breakfast, lunch, dinner every day. Open 24 hours.*

Natraj Natraj opened almost five years ago to rave reviews when Vancouver's food scene was in the grip of ethnic experimentation. As the nearby Punjabi Market at Main Street and 49th Avenue grew and prospered, Natraj continued to benfit from its proximity. The decor of the restaurant has always been spartan at best. Beer cases stacked up in full view in one corner next to a filing cabinet don't help. But look past the neglect of the premises and you'll find a competent kitchen skilled in the magical application of spices that characterize Indian cooking. The Chicken Shahjahni Biriyani is a fascinating mélange of flavours boasting the use of 21 exotic spices and served over aromatic basmati rice cooked with saffron. The mixed grill from the tandoor is a fine sampler of spicy beef Seekh Kabab, tender chunks of marinated chicken and lamb with sweet wilted onions and tomatoes. Complete the meal with buttery patties of potatoes, vegetables, and cheese, called Malai Kofta, and an order of the Special Nan KW: stuffed with nuts and bits of chicken. ■ *5656 Fraser St; 327-6141; $; full bar; MC, V; no cheques; dinner every day.*

Nazarre BBQ Chicken ★ There are rubber chickens on the turntables decorating the new storefront location, but only tender barbecued chicken finds its way onto your plate. French-born and Mexican-raised owner Gerry Moutal bastes the birds in a mixture of rum and spices in the rotisserie—the chickens drip their juices onto potatoes roasting and crackling below and are delivered with mild, hot, extra-hot, or hot garlic sauce. There are a few other goodies (vegetarian empanadas, tacos), but it's the chicken you've come here for. Eat in, at one of four tables, or take out. ■ *1859 Commercial Dr; 251-1844; $; no alcohol; no credit cards; no cheques; lunch, dinner every day.*

Nonya Baba ★ It's no secret that some of the best foods in Asia are found on the streets. The food tastes better, not only because of the smells and sights and sounds, but because the cooks are focused. They don't have the huge repertoire, the prestige, or the ego that restaurant chefs are burdened with.

Instead, they get to cook with their hearts. At Nonya Baba, that's the kind of food one gets—hawker's food, lovingly prepared for common folks who miss their homelands of Singapore and Malaysia. Specialties include Singapore kway teow—a dish of rice noodles, Chinese sausages, and clams enriched with sweet soya sauce. And the satays are some of the best in town. Snapper cooked with tamarind and spices is wonderfully fresh, superbly cooked, and deftly spiced. And the sambal ulang—prawns in homemade chile spices—can pack quite a wallop even when it is requested mild. Although service can be frantic at busy times and the kitchen may run out of a few things, in general you'll get the feeling that you're regarded with warmth and that this family business aims to please.
■ *1091 Davie St; 687-3398, $$; wine and beer; MC, V; no cheques; lunch Mon-Fri, dinner every day.*

Noor Mahal ★ Two things strike you when you enter Noor Mahal. One is the profusion of colours. The pale green walls of this tiny eatery are covered with oversize paintings of historical and mythical scenes that are bold and kitschy. But gaudy as it is, it gives you the feeling of entering a brightly decorated house, and the hospitable, helpful service completes the homey feel. The other thing you notice is the price—a definite bargain at $6 to $8 per dish. These are all full-meal deals, complete with rice, roti, chutney, pappadum, and salad. The food is hot and spicy but adjustable to order. The portions are substantial. Dosas, south Indian flatbreads made from rice, wheat, and lentil flour, are the specialty here. They come rolled, like crepes, filled with your choice of 16 fillings, including chicken, shrimp, and vegetarian specialties, among others, each accompanied by sambar—a lentil stew—and its traditional condiment, nariyal chatni—coconut chutney. ■ *4354 Fraser St; 873-9263; $; full bar; MC, V; no cheques; dinner every day.*

Nyala Restaurant ★ Many people are unaware that Ethiopia, like other African nations, has a cuisine all its own. The food is served in traditional Ethiopian style—no knives, forks, or spoons. The injera (plate-sized flatbread with a honeycomb texture) is the only utensil you need. Just tear off a little bread, fold it around bite-size portions of food, and pop the whole thing into your mouth. The food, mostly stewed or curried preparations of savoury goat, beef, lamb, chicken, fish, or vegetables, is served communally at each table on a large metal platter accompanied by an assortment of condiments (spicy sautéed cabbage, golden herbed bulghur wheat, gingered lentil purée).
■ *2930 West 4th Ave (at MacDonald St); 731-7899; $; full bar; AE, MC, V; no cheques; lunch, dinner every day.*

O-Tooz The Energie Bar ★ What started purely as a juice bar has become the darling of the health set, with its all-around-good-for-you-fast-food format. The mood is upbeat, with squeaky

Top 175
Restaurants

▲

clean yellow and grey decor and contemporary black bar stools for those with enough time to sit while they down their energy boosters. A simplified menu includes the tasteful and healthful ricepot—basmati served with a choice of spicy peanut, spinach-basil pesto, or hummus sauces, accompanied by raw vegetables. The same ingredients are served in the wrap, a whole-wheat tortilla shell. Steamed free-range chicken (the only meat you'll find here) is offered as an extra. Juices of choice are the BC trio of carrot, celery, and beet and the Hi-C, with pineapple, orange, and carrot. The healthiest bar in town—and hardly a hint of granola. Also in Royal Centre, 1055 West Georgia. ■ *1068 Davie St; 689-0208; $; no liquor; V, MV, no cheques; breakfast, lunch, dinner every day.*

Olympia Fish Market and Oyster Co. ★ The Olympia is first and foremost a fish shop, but it purveys some of the best fish 'n' chips in the Lower Mainland. Eight years ago, Robson Street fish merchant Carlo Sorace decided that what the street really needed was a good place to get fish 'n' chips. Whatever is on special in the store, which might be halibut cheeks, scallops, catfish, or calamari, is the day's special at the 12-seat counter, and is served along with the tried-and-true halibut and cod versions. Soft drinks include Chinotto (Italian herbal and fruit-flavoured sparkling water) and root beer. Eat in or take out. ■ *1094 Robson St; 685-0716; $; no alcohol; V; cheques OK; lunch, dinner every day.*

On Lock It took a friend, a gourmet at large who spends his summers in San Antonio, his winters in Singapore, and the rest of the year travelling, to point our way to one of the best bowls of wonton noodle soup in Vancouver. The rest of the food in this working-class restaurant can be ordinary and a tad greasy, but the soup is to die for. Wontons are fresh and are not made with the standard ground pork but are chunky with pork and shrimp as they should be. The noodles are chewy and firm, served in a clear stock topped with a touch of fragrant green onions. It may sound simple, but this special attention to detail is what elevated wontons from the ranks of street food to the repertoire of the gourmet. ■ *2010 E Hastings St; 253-3856; $; beer and wine; no credit cards; no cheques; lunch, dinner every day.*

The Only Seafood Cafe Vancouver's oldest restaurant, the Only opened for business in 1912 when out-of-town loggers came to East Hastings Street to spend their wages on liquor and flesh. Today, amid a neon sea of pawn shops and peep shows, a diverse sampling of humanity convenes for fresh no-frills fish. A periodic scrub and a coat of paint has brightened this greasy spoon over the years, but the time-worn design remains. There are two booths and a counter with stools, and you've got to be quick to nab one. When you do, order some fish 'n' chips.

Halibut, sole, and lingcod are snatched from the deep fryer at the instant of just-cooked perfection and served with a side of fries. One taste of halibut cheeks, oysters, Coney Island clam chowder, or pepper stew and you'll see why this diner has become a Vancouver legend. ■ *20 E Hastings St; 681-6546; $; no alcohol; no credit cards; no cheques; lunch, dinner, Mon-Sat.*

Ouzeri ★★ Traditionally, the Greek ouzeri is a place to go to drink and eat appetizers before going to dinner. In Vancouver, the Ouzeri is where you can go any time of the day and compose a meal of appetizers. The food here involves all the expected Greek specialties and then some. Chicken livers are wonderful—crisp on the outside and tender on the inside. Prawns dressed with ouzo and mushrooms are simply amazing. Friendly, casual, happy (with surely the most reasonably priced menu this side of Athens), Ouzeri proves that being Greek doesn't mean you can't be trendy. Open until 2am. ■ *3189 W Broadway; 739-9378; $$; full bar; AE, MC, V; no cheques; lunch, dinner every day.* &

Park Lock Seafood Restaurant ★ After more than a dozen years, Park Lock remains a mainstay in Chinatown. Recent renovations produced nothing more than a new coat of white paint and reupholstered chairs. No Hong Kong–style glitz here, just the simple, old-fashioned Cantonese dishes that we cut our teeth on and have learned to love. Egg foo yung comes in six varieties—including one with oysters. Black-peppered flank steak or scallops and prawns with black bean sauce come sizzling to the table on scorching cast-iron platters. The tasty, once-ubiquitous dish of steamed spareribs with yellow plum sauce that is fast becoming an anachronism can still be found here. The somewhat difficult to find second floor location is packed on Mondays with families and friends who all seem to know each other. A popular dim sum lunch is served every day. Expect a lineup. ■ *544 Main St; 688-1581; $; full bar; MC, V; no cheques; lunch every day; dinner Tues-Sun.*

Passionate Pizza ★★ The humble pizza has come a long way, and you don't have to order the Wolfgang Puck (mozzarella, smoked bacon, sweet red peppers, red onions, feta and Asiago cheeses, and eggplant) to see why. The crust is traditional (white, crisp in the thin places, chewy in the thick ones, drizzled with good olive oil, and adorned with bits of baked-on cheese), though toppings tend not to be. Vegetarians, for example, can do well here with the Granville Island Gourmet (mozzarella and Gorgonzola, caramelized onions, pine nuts, and roast garlic). The Caesar-with-a-Twist has strips of sun-dried tomatoes and giant capers hiding among the romaine and croutons. Carrot cake, peanut butter cookies, and chocolate chip cookies fill that last bit of room. ■ *1387 W 7th Ave; 733-4411; $; no alcohol; MC, V; local cheques only; dinner every day.* &

Pepitas With its staccato guitars, house margaritas, and funky Mexican decor, this friendly spot keeps the crowd happy. Good guacamole, great black beans, garlicky prawns, and paella can distract fans from what's not so good (greasy calamari and stale tortilla chips). The $13.95 platter for two, which includes chimichangas, beef burritos, and chile rellenos, can easily serve three. ▪ *1170 Robson St (and other branches); 669-4736; $$; full bar; AE, MC, V; no cheques; lunch, dinner every day.*

Peppi's ★½ On sunny days, this waterside favourite near Dundarave Beach offers unequalled Kodak moments. Misty nights, when dining is accompanied by the basso profundo of distant foghorns, are equally appealing. The restaurant is lively, casual, and roomy. The formerly pasta-centred menu has recently broadened to include BC's bounty of fresh seafood and produce. Come lunchtime, enjoy a passel of pastas, a barbecued chopped-salmon burger, scallops teamed with a raspberry vinaigrette, or a baguette heaped with crab, shrimp, asparagus, and cheese. Wisely, the restaurant still lists Peppi's Favourites at night—such as the fettuccine with mussels, salmon, and shrimp and a classic canneloni. Wild mushrooms enliven a penne dish rife with sun-dried tomatoes and pesto. Non-pasta-pickers can opt for the cioppino, the smoked Alaska black cod with a snappy cucumber caper salsa, or perhaps a steak. ▪ *150-25th St, West Vancouver; 922-1414; $$; full bar; AE, DC, MC, V; no cheques; lunch, dinner every day.*

Persia Restaurant ★ "Its namesake was the cradle of culinary civilization," says owner Neamat Meadi of his newly renovated restaurant. Greek souvlakia and Italian pastas are served, but the majority of the menu is authentically rooted in traditional Persian cookery. Start with sabzi—a plate of parsley, green onion, and radish served with feta and tafotan, a flat lacy bread, or order mast-o-mosir, yogurt with dried wild garlic. Entrées are intriguing. Sweet and sour fesenjoon, a dish of chicken in pomegranate juice and ground walnuts, is hugely flavourful. Khoreshet ghemeh teams beef and yellow beans in a cinnamony sauce, soured with dried lemon. Zereshk polo, a chicken preparation, gets its tanginess from barberries. Chelo kabob, the alleged ancestor of all kabob and brochette dishes, is meltingly tender. All dishes come with basmati rice. Leave room for dessert: a cylindrical baklava, Persian ice cream perfumed with saffron and rose water, or faloudeh—a compelling concoction of frozen noodles. Belly dancing Friday nights; live Persian music Saturdays. ▪ *710 Helmcken St; 689-1980; $; full bar; V; no cheques; lunch, dinner every day.*

Phnom Penh Restaurant ★★★ Once Vancouver's best-kept secret, this restaurant is now winning a steady stream of accolades from sources as diverse as local magazine polls and

The New York Times. The decor is still basic, but the menu has expanded from its original rice and noodle dishes to include the cuisines of China, Vietnam, and Cambodia. Hot and sour soup with sablefish is richly flavoured, redolent of lime and purple basil. An excellent appetizer of marinated beef sliced carpaccio-thin is seared rare and dressed with nuoc mam (a spicy, fishy sauce—the Vietnamese staple). Sautéed baby shrimp in prawn roe and tender slivers of salted pork cover hot, velvety steamed rice paste—a real masterpiece. Butterfly prawns with lemon-pepper dip are crisp and vibrant, chicken salad with cabbage is a refreshing twist on a pedestrian vegetable, and the oyster omelet is a dream. Service is knowledgeable and friendly. ■ *244 E Georgia St; 682-5777; $; full bar; DC, MC, V; no cheques; lunch, dinner Wed-Mon;* ■ *955 W Broadway; 734-8898.*

Pho Hoang ★ As common in Vietnam as the hamburger is here, pho is a quick meal or snack, and a great bargain besides. A large bowl of broth with rice noodles and your choice of flank, rump, brisket, tripe, or a dozen other beef cuts and combinations will cost you less than $5. You're served a side dish of bean sprouts, fresh basil, sliced green chiles, and lime to garnish as you see fit. A cup of strong Vietnamese coffee, filter-brewed at the table, is the only other thing you need. A second, equally busy location is on East Georgia Street in Chinatown. ■ *3610 Main St; 874-0810; $; no alcohol; no credit cards; cheques OK; lunch, dinner every day.*

Picasso Café Staffed by a bunch of young people eager to make a change (the menu tells you the story) and masterminded by chef Stephen Ashton, Picasso offers an inventive menu whose key word is *modern.* The decor's in tune with the food, and what might be a cliché of flowery fabrics, white wood, greenery, and ceiling fans is given a wicked spin by Ashton's changing "exhibits" of antique toasters or bizarre photos. Breakfast includes low-fat muffins or whole-grain toast with organic house-made preserves. Other times, fajitas, crêpes, focaccia, and hummus present a global village of favourites. Pizzalike pissaladieres are topped with smoked salmon and dill or chicken, apricots, and almonds in a gentle curry sauce. Salads, in every shade of green, are spiked with exceptional dressings. The handful of meat entrées link simply cooked chicken, pork, or beef with unusually inventive sauces. Desserts run to the nostalgic: Campbell's tomato soup cake, the quintessentially Canadian butter tart, and—a BC classic—Nanaimo Bars. The superb crème caramel and the service give many a four-star resturant a run for its money. ■ *1626 W Broadway; 732-3290; $; beer and wine; MC, V; no cheques; breakfast, lunch, dinner Mon-Fri.*

The Pink Pearl ★★ Tanks of fresh fish are your first clue that the Cantonese menu is especially strong on seafood. If you order the crab sautéed with five spices, you'll be further convinced. It's a spectacular dish—sometimes translated as crab with peppery salt—crisp, chile-hot, and salty on the outside, moist on the inside. A good dim sum is served every day (be sure to arrive early on weekends to avoid the lineups), and cart jockeys always seem to have time to smile as you choose among sticky rice wrapped in lotus leaf, stuffed dumplings, and fried white turnip cakes. Table clearing is an event in itself: the tablecloth is actually a stack of thick white plastic sheets; when you finish eating, a waiter will grab the corners of the top sheet and with a quick flip scoop everything up, dishes and all, and haul the lot away. A great place for kids. ▪ *1132 E Hastings St; 253-4316; $$; full bar; AE, MC, V; no cheques; lunch, dinner every day.* ⑁

The Prow ★★ Hidden away atop the bow of the ship-shaped Vancouver Convention Centre is a hideaway with a sweeping view of the North Shore mountains and the harbour. Book the Imax Theatre next door (there's a Prow discount coupon on your ticket) and take out-of-town family or friends to lunch or dinner. The location offers one of the most arresting outlooks in this view-rich city, but the creations of chef Denis Blais—accompanied by selections from an award-winning wine list—easily rival the scenery. The menu has evolved into a tidy sort of West Coast cuisine, with small touches from Italy and Southeast Asia. A recent menu featured agnolotti filled with smoked salmon; baby coho salmon and scallops in a blackberry-tarragon butter; and a tenderloin of beef flavoured with Thai chiles and coconut milk. By all means reserve a window seat for an endless view of Burrard Inlet, but bring along a sweater; window tables can be drafty. Service could use polish. ▪ *999 Canada Place, northern tip of Canada Place on Burrard St; 684-1339; $$$; full bar; AE, DC, MC, V; no cheques; lunch every day (Mon-Fri in winter), dinner every day, brunch Sun.*

Quilicum Restaurant ★★ A meal here is certainly an unusual culinary foray. You'll sample dishes you've never dreamed of—oolichan grease, for example, prepared from the oil of a native fish and spread on baked bannock bread (or as a unique side dish). Another taste thrill is caribou, barbecued or stewed, and herring roe served on a bed of healthy kelp. Not all the dishes are as spectacular as the impressive Quilicum Special—succulent parts of salmon (head, tail, and belly) barbecued and presented in a carved ceremonial bowl—but other, tamer variations on the salmon (wind-dried and steamed-smoked) are also good. The potlatch platter for two ($43.95) is heaped with barbecued salmon, smoked cod, oysters, prawns, and caribou, and will easily serve three. There are some flubs, such as overcooked fried oolichans, less-than-fresh hazelnuts, and a poor showing on the wine list. The totem poles, native masks, and artifacts among which you dine are for sale. ■ *1724 Davie St; 681-7044; $$; full bar; AE, MC, V; no cheques; lunch Wed-Fri, dinner every day.*

Raincity Grill ★★ This newcomer has proved to be the dark horse in Vancouver's culinary sweepstakes, garnering plenty of attention and awards early on. The view of English Bay from the patio is stunning; inside, a clean, contemporary look—with white linen, maroon and grey contrasts, natural wood, and plenty of greenery—is most inviting. Owner Harry Kambolis and chef Gregory Walsh have created an imaginative, regional menu based on fresh produce from Granville Island. Smoky seafood chowder (with plenty of fish and flavour) is worth a taste, as are the littleneck clams. A healthy, al dente portion of lemon-pepper linguine comes with pistachio nut pesto and grilled vegetables; juicy halibut swims in a gentle lime and chile cream, with black Thai rice on the side. Daytime offerings include one of the city's best burgers (with fresh basil mayo and excellent fries). Desserts are paired with wines (optional), such as a blockbuster Belgian chocolate and cocoa lasagne served with a glass of Quady Elysium. ■ *1193 Denman St; 685-7337; $$; full bar; AE, DC, E, MC, V; no cheques; lunch, dinner every day, brunch Sat-Sun.* 占

Raintree ★★★ The Raintree of old never quite lived up to its self-promotion, but there's an exciting renaissance afoot—a new chef in the kitchen, a cooking school, and a winemaking series. The concrete-walled space is prettied with huge flower arrangements, decorated with a simple sophistication, and, provided you are seated facing the right way, offers a spectacular view of the North Shore skyline. Chef Karen Barnaby manoeuvers the Northwest harvest of game and seafood and grape with skill, working flavour magic with pork and Alaskan black cod and delivering an on-target grilled spring salmon with bold beet and apple purée. It's a struggle to choose between the salmon bounty: kippered, smoked wild sockeye and spring salmon, Indian candy, or the seafood bowl. Dessert provokes a similar conflict, so we order the sampler and taste everything, including Raintree's signature apple pie, which contains 3 kilograms (7 pounds) of Okanagan fruit. The wine list echoes the Northwest Coast theme. At press time, Raintree is opening a similar restaurant in Victoria. ■ *1630 Alberni St; 688-5570; $$$; full bar; AE, DC, E, MC, V; no cheques; dinner every day.* 占

Raku Kushiyaki ★★ This almost-too-stark restaurant sports an innovative fusion menu that sometimes outreaches itself. It offers skewered tidbits and tiny preparations from the Far East, the Middle East, India, Thailand, France, and the Caribbean.

There are some delicious surprises here, and some pitfalls as well. Those looking for the unusual will find perfectly prepared asparagus spears with orange and pistachio butter that we have not seen elsewhere, and an excellent barbecued squid yaki. But skip the cloying grilled tofu with peanut sauce and the untrimmed fiddleheads with mustard sauce. Raku stocks four brands of sake; if you're not familiar with them, try a taster glass cold (the flavours are more distinct when sake is unheated). You can nibble, nosh, and share at Raku, but watch out—it adds up. ■ *4422 W 10th Ave; 222-8188; $; full bar; DC, MC, V; cheques OK; dinner Tues-Sat.*

The Red Onion ★★ Forget drive-ins and head to Kerrisdale for the best double dogs, cheeseburgers, and fries in town. You simply have to order the sour cream and dill french fries dip. The menu is designed to please everyone (we like the hot chicken salad; others pick the veggie soup). The wieners are the Onion's own, and so are the buns. At breakfast, the muffins (blueberry, chocolate chip, or banana) and aromatic cinnamon buns are baked on the premises (as are fantastic desserts) and served all morning. There's also takeout. The best of its kind in the city. ■ *2028 W 41st Ave; 263-0833; $; beer and wine; E, MC, V; no cheques; breakfast, lunch, dinner every day.* &

Rubina Tandoori ★★ Son Shaffeen Jamal is the congenial host; mother Krishna cooks the authentic East Indian fare. Rubina's menu is built around tandoori dishes, South Indian seafood, and Punjabi and Moghul dishes. Not surprisingly, tandoori breads are outstanding, and you can watch them being made in the new tandoori oven at the entrance of the restaurant. Fish masala is worth trying, as is a dry curry with potatoes—or any of the dishes that include Rubina's homemade paneer cheese. If you're a beginner at Indian food, try a duet (for two or more)—for example, Moglai Magic, a great, not-too-hot introduction to the cuisine. Don't pass up dessert, since the Gulab Jamun, deep-fried milk dough smothered in syrup and scented with rose water, is a soothing finale. Rubina has separate smoking and nonsmoking rooms. ■ *1962 Kingsway; 874-3621; $$; full bar; AE, MC, V; no cheques; lunch Mon-Fri, dinner Mon-Sat.*

The Salmon House on the Hill ★★ The Salmon House boasts a view that stretches from Lions Gate to Vancouver Island. West Coast native artifacts reflect the origins of much of the Salmon House menu. Recent renovations have added a striking entrance area with a new mask wall and etched window depicting the restaurant's yin-and-yang salmon motif. Other changes reflected in the menu, as well as in a more extensive wine list, suggest that the Salmon House is working toward a more regional "serious kitchen" identity. The hallmark dish is BC salmon cooked over green alderwood, which delivers the distinctive, delicate, and smoky flavour—certainly worth the drive halfway to Horseshoe Bay. Crab cakes come with crab that you can actually taste. For the indecisive, there's the Salmon House sampler, with generous tastes of smoked and alderwood-barbecued salmon, an intriguing roulade, and gravlax, all served with homemade relish and chutneys. Service is friendly and correct. ■ *2229 Folkestone Way, West Vancouver; 926-3212; $$$; full bar; AE, E, MC, V; no cheques; lunch, dinner every day, brunch Sun.*

Saltimbocca ★★½ Maverick chef Ken Bogas's perch has plenty of atmosphere and is something of a see-and-be-seen scene—a lively buzz, contemporary and casual surroundings, and a distinctive Mediterranean flair make tables here eagerly sought. The Italian-inspired menu (with some Asian influences) is prepared almost entirely on the compact open grill by three or four dexterous chefs, who add considerably to the theatre. There's no question that Bogas can work marvels, as shown by the much-celebrated tuna fillet with lime wasabe, which is indeed superb and beautifully balanced. However, for meals preceded by such fuss and for a place with such a following, the fare can be surprisingly inconsistent and presentation haphazard. Starters such as fresh scallops with black beans are worth sampling, and a solitary crab cake (with plenty of crabmeat) is tasty and deeply spiced with coriander. The wine selection is well thought out, though it contains few bargains. A reservation, while advised, doesn't necessarily guarantee dining on schedule, and service at times can be just short of nonchalant. ■ *2201 W 1st Ave; 738-0101; $$$; full bar; AE, MC, V; no cheques; dinner every day.* ⅊

Salute ★★ This cozy, relaxed spot joins the growing number of excellent eateries sprouting alongside West Vancouver's Marine Drive. The elaborate bar puts out some great martinis. Owner/chef Gamal Hanna spent several years at one of Vancouver's respected trattorias honing his skills, as reflected in his version of carpaccio: lean and moist, attractively arranged, drizzled with piquant, grainy mustard, and garnished with capers and fresh parsley, it's among the best around. Salads can sometimes be too oily, though the carciofi—a colourful mix of greens with a tasty combination of shrimp, chopped marinated artichoke hearts, and sun-dried tomatoes—is commendable. A good list of pastas is punctuated by some more rustic dishes, such as ciocicara—a gutsy, earthy combination of fusili pasta with potatoes and spicy sausage, or the Spaghetti Salute—a mix of chicken, pink and green peppercorns, garlic, chiles, black beans, and al dente pasta. A predominantly Italian wine list leans toward the high end, though there are some less expensive options. ■ *1747 Marine Dr, West Vancouver; 922-6282; $$; full bar; no cheques; lunch Mon-Fri, dinner Mon-Sat.*

Santa Fe Cafe ★ ½ Anyone who has chowed down at the Santa Fe Cafe knows it is about as close to New Mexico as Vancouver can get. And the Santa Fe team seems to have what Vancouverites want these days: food that is earthy and vibrant and a setting that is casual. No one goes to Santa Fe for privacy; at this 46-seat, storefront-size restaurant, the people sitting at the next table are really sitting at your table and are practically sharing your conversation. But nobody seems to mind—the place sizzles on Friday nights. Tiger prawns on a bed of spinach, an appetizer, is a winner, giving the perfect zap of spices. Santa Fe's chile con queso, with perfectly prepared seafood and a healthy lacing of ancho and Anaheim chiles, may be a new classic. A new location has opened in the Barclay Hotel, but it's not up to the standards of the original location. ■ *1688 W 4th Ave; 738-8777; $$; beer and wine; AE, DC, MC, V; no cheques; lunch Mon-Fri, dinner every day;* ■ *1348 Robson St; 687-3003; $$; full bar; AE, DC, MC, V; no cheques; lunch, dinner every day.* ⅃

Sawasdee Thai Restaurant The oldest Thai restaurant in Vancouver, Sawasdee doesn't offer the most sophisticated Thai food around, but it offers a fun environment in which to eat it. The mee krob appetizer—crisp noodles with shrimp, bean sprouts, dried tofu, and shredded red cabbage—will be either too sweet or addictive, depending on your taste. Order the chicken wings, deboned, stuffed with minced chicken and vegetables, and paired with a spicy-hot dipping sauce. A new item, the choo-chee talay, combines a spicy curry with prawns, squid, clams, and fish. Relaxed service. Save room for the deep-fried banana fritters with a choice of homemade coconut or mango ice cream (have both). The Granville Street Sawasdee (2145 Granville Street, 737-8222) is not as good as the original location. ■ *4250 Main St; 876-4030; $$; full bar; MC, V; no cheques; dinner every day.*

Seasons in the Park ★★ A facelift and considerable attention in the kitchen have contributed to Seasons in the Park's rapidly rising reputation. Although the park setting and the stunning view of downtown and the North Shore mountains still guarantee a line of tour buses outside, today's visitors to Seasons (including visiting presidents Clinton and Yeltsin) come as much for the food as the view. Diners are treated to a menu of just-picked produce, succulent seafood, and local wines, with such highlights as ravioli stuffed with fresh crab and spinach, veal medallions with sage butter sauce, and constantly changing salmon entrées. For dessert, a lemon espresso mousse cake with a dark-and-white-chocolate sauce is a knockout. ■ *33rd Ave at Cambie in Queen Elizabeth Park; 874-8008; $$; full bar; AE, MC, V; no cheques; lunch Mon-Fri, dinner every day, brunch Sat-Sun.*

Settebello ★ You'll find splendid pizzas and pastas at Umberto Menghi's most casual restaurant. *Settebello* means "beautiful seven" (from an Italian card game), and in contrast to Menghi's other establishments, this restaurant attempts to draw a younger crowd. Settebello is best on sunny days, as a respite from shopping, perhaps, when you can sit out on the rooftop patio nibbling at pasta or a collection of Italian tapas-style dishes. Begin with the fresh buffalo mozzarella with tomatoes, basil, and a touch of balsamico and extra virgin olive oil. Then order the first-rate trio of pastas featuring creamy tortellini, fettuccine sauced with spicy tomatoes, and the linguine with pesto. Try the salsiccia pizza, with hot Italian sausage, spinach, sun-dried tomatoes, and chile peppers. Excellent, moderately priced wine list. ■ *1131 Robson St; 681-7377; $$; full bar; AE, DC, MC, V; no cheques; lunch, dinner every day.*

Shabusen Yakiniku House ★¹/₂ *Yakiniku* is Japanese for "barbecue." The menu here highlights Korean food, and both of these big, glittery, action-packed, second-floor restaurants are more like what you'd expect to find in Hong Kong than in Tokyo. Everyone comes here sooner or later: families, couples (eating yakiniku can be a very sharing experience), and Japanese tourists marvelling at our cheap sushi. Ordering yakiniku gives you a choice of the familiar (chicken, beef, or salmon), or exotic (cuttlefish, beef tongue, or eel) to cook to your taste on the tabletop barbecue. Side dishes of pickled spinach and fiery kimchi, as well as a huge pot of rice, are included. Listings for shabu shabu—Japanese hot pots—offer a similar selection bolstered by live prawns, lobster, and geoduck. The Shabusen Special lets you eat your fill of yakiniku and shabu shabu. Sushi and sashimi round out the menu. ■ *2993 Granville St; 737-6888;* ■ *755 Burrard St; 669-3883; $$; full bar; AE, MC, V; no cheques; lunch, Mon-Sat, dinner every day.*

Shanghai Garden Restaurant ★★ For more than 15 years three restaurants have been located side by side on the east side of Fraser Street at 23rd Avenue. Like the three doors on the famous television game show, they don't always open to winners. In fact, doors one and three have changed hands more times than we can remember. But door number two, the one in the middle, has always been a sure bet. Consistency and occasional brilliance are what one gets from Shanghai Garden's years of experience. Enter and you'll be rewarded with crispy fried duck—so tender that you'll be tempted to eat the bones. Tofu steamed over sautéed spinach, wonderful five-spice beef, fat juicy Shanghai noodles, and silky drunken chicken are some of the other prizes. Recently we hit pay dirt—a live crab fished out of the tank, deep-fried in peppered salt, and tossed in garlic and chiles. In a word: outstanding. ■ *3932*

Fraser St; 873-6123; $; full bar; MC, V; no cheques; lunch, dinner every day except Wed.

Shijo Japanese Restaurant ★★ Shijo is a pleasant, uncluttered sushi bar serving excellent sushi, sashimi, and robata. Oysters, grilled on the half shell and painted with a light miso sauce, are a good bet, as are butterflied tiger prawns or shiitake foilyaki—mushrooms sprinkled with lemony ponzu sauce and cooked in foil. Meals end in a refreshing manner, with orange sherbet served in a hollowed-out orange. ■ *1926 W 4th Ave (between Cypress St and Maple St, on the 2nd floor); 732-4676; $$$; full bar; AE, MC, V; no cheques; lunch Mon-Fri, dinner every day.* &

Shinla Korean Restaurant ★ Shinla is a Korean restaurant for Koreans. The second-storey location on East Broadway has minimal signage, giving it the feeling of a private club. Private rooms surround a centre area with booth seating—all functionally decorated—with bulgogi grills on every table. The special combination for two (a hearty undertaking) is a bargain at $22.95: rib-eye steak slices, short ribs, chicken, prawns, and pork come neatly arranged on a large platter ready to be seared to taste, complemented by interesting side dishes of kimchi, pickled garlic, grilled dry minnows, sesamed spinach, and other vegetables. Sushi, tempura, and noodle dishes are also available, with sometimes inconsistent execution. But when they're good, they're very good. ■ *206-333 E Broadway; 875-6649; $$; full bar; MC, V; cheques OK; lunch, dinner every day.*

▼

Top 175
Restaurants

▲

Shiro ★★ You may have to wait, but you'll always be welcome. Hidden away in a mini-mall is one of Vancouver's best-kept secrets: a charming little restaurant run by Shiro Okano. Owner and sushi chef, he directs and stars in the show—and a highly entertaining show it is—from a stage-centre, banner-hung bar. It's a neighbourhood sushi place, and the neighbourhood loves it. Start with the cool noodle salad called wakame sunomono. Next, try Shiro's house-made gyoza, among the best in town, with their sharp and salty dipping sauce. Then order up some addictively good deep-fried squid. Or just sit at the bar, play it by ear, and eat the sushi as Shiro nimbly orchestrates. Donburi sushi, okonomi sushi, and the cone variety—temaki sushi—are all particularly good. This being the city for cuisine fusing, there's even a Tex-Mex variety made with chili sauce and mayonnaise. A happy place where you can't help but have a good time. Feel free to practise your Japanese. There's an entry-level phrase book at the back of the menu. ■ *3096 Cambie St; 874-0027; $; full bar; AE, MC, V; no cheques; lunch, dinner every day.*

Singapore Restaurant ★ The city at the crossroads of the world has bred a multicultural cuisine that's part Chinese and part Malaysian, yet has its own clear identity—as you'll discover at the Singapore. This small West Side eatery provides a cozy ambience, but it's the bargain-priced dishes, not the atmosphere, that keeps customers coming in droves. Dishes are spice-rated with one to five stars; you decide how high to turn up the thermostat. At the top of the scale, sambal bunchies, a mix of green beans and pink prawns, can scorch your palate. Peanuty fried hokkien mee—noodles studded with squid and morsels of pork and omelet, offers a milder choice. Try the pungent Singapore eggplant, the satays, or the gado gado singapura salad. Other options? Smooth-as-a-kiss, coconut-milk-based curries, a complex yellow ginger rice, a pageful of clam, shrimp, and fish dishes, interesting noodles, and more. ■ *546 W Broadway; 874-6161; $; full bar; MC, V; no cheques; lunch, dinner every day.*

The Sleighs ★ It's a good half-hour drive from Vancouver to the little fishing village of Steveston, so make an evening of it and schedule enough time for a preprandial saunter along the docks. The Sleighs is an intriguing mix. Thank British-born Stephen Sleigh for the dark green, pink, and floral English country house decor. Credit his wife, Aurora, with the Spanish menu. Chockablock with seafood and lusty with Iberian flavours, the paella is arguably BC's best. Smoked trout escabeche, uncomplicated prawn preparations, a fisherman's pot, a few meat dishes, and a vegetarian gypsy pot round out the menu. Many make a meal of the tapas: just-crisp patatas aioli is blanketed in a toothsome garlic mayonnaise. House special croquettes are crisp fingers filled with ham, chorizo, or shrimp in a creamy béchamel. Catalan pan con tomate is a triumph of simple flavours: toasted French bread spread with olive oil, garlic, and fresh tomato. You can always walk it off with another stroll after dinner. ■ *3211 Bayview St, Richmond (Steveston); 275-5188; $$; full bar; AE, MC, V; no cheques; lunch, dinner every day.*

▼

Top 175 Restaurants

▲

Sophie's Cosmic Cafe ★★ Where *Leave It to Beaver* meets Pee Wee Herman—this funky diner-cum-garage sale is a fun place to be: Don't worry about the wait—there's plenty to look at, including Sophie's collection of colourful lunch boxes and hats that were once stashed in her attic. People rave about the huge spicy burgers and chocolate shakes, but the best thing here is the stick-to-the-ribs-style breakfast. Try the great mash of Mexican eggs (with sausage, peppers, and onions and spiced with hot pepper sauce poured from a wine bottle), which is served right through lunch. Dinners run along a similar line, with the addition of chicken enchiladas, ribs, cosmic pastas, and lamb chops. ■ *2095 W 4th Ave; 732-6810; $; beer and wine; MC, V; no cheques; breakfast, lunch, dinner every day, brunch Sat-Sun.* &

Spumante's Cafe Ristorante ★★ A standout in a street of good solid Italian neighbourhood restaurants, Spumante's is a haven for the indecisive. Dark green walls and gilt-framed paintings make for attractive surroundings, and the service is contagiously enthusiastic (they love their food, and they want you to love it too). But what sets Spumante's apart is one simple, brilliant idea: instead of having to choose between linguine in a marinated lamb sauce and chicken breast with a mint and cream sauce, you can enjoy both. Spaghetti alla carbonara gets paired with pork chops sautéed in milk with peppers, tomatoes, and a touch of curry. Egg fettuccine with vegetables is teamed with stuffed baked vegetables. All in all, there are 38 different "pasta and..." combinations to pick from, all priced the same: $9.95 at lunch and $14.95 at dinner (or $9.95 for pasta alone). Meals kick off with a little plate of stuzzichini—starters—on the house. There's a handful of appetizers and, as well as the combination dishes, a half dozen additional entrées. Daytime regulars go for the inexpensive quick lunch menu. ▪ *1736 Commercial Dr; 253-8899; $$; full bar; DC, MC, V; no cheques; lunch Tues-Fri, dinner Tues-Sat.*

▼
Top 175
Restaurants
▲

Star Anise ★★★ When maitre d' Sam Laliji and chef Adam Busby hung out their shingle in early 1993, success was virtually a given: both had earned a loyal following at other venerable dining spots. Here in the heart of the trendy South Granville quartier, their chic but comfortable Star Anise has nothing to do with Chinese seasoning and everything to do with exemplary service and endlessly inventive cooking. Whether you dine here twice a week or are visiting for the first time, Laliji's welcome is invariably warm. Elegant surroundings attract anyone who is passionate about food. Dictated by the season and Chef Busby's whim, the menu is honest and unpretentious, leaning to lightness or deep, earthy comfort, with a constant theme of fresh ingredients. Lunchtime listings (a steal) may include a salad of mussels, roasted beets, and potatoes napped with a subtle curry dressing, bitter greens played against a satiny tarte of ricotta and leeks, or a sandwich of brioche-crumbed chicken with roasted red peppers. Dinner starters can range from a velvety duck confit with purple plum relish to an inspired trio of mozzarella toast, white beans, and arugula. Main courses—including pairings such as seared salmon with napa cabbage or sea scallops with a mustard seed dressing—are often inspired. The pan-roasted chicken has its own devout following. ▪ *1485 W 12th Ave; 737-1485; $$$; full bar; AE, DC, MC, V; no cheques; lunch Mon-Fri, dinner every day, brunch Sat-Sun.*

Stepho's Souvlakia ★ This is one of those little restaurants that just keeps on going, regardless of the economy or whether it's a Monday or Saturday night. This is basic, good Greek fare:

lots of pungent tzatziki; mega-salads; decent-sized hunks of pita—in a nutshell, great value, along with plenty of regulars and a staff that really seems to care. The interior is no-nonsense comfortable, with enough posters of the Parthenon to start a travel agency, bunches of fresh carnations on every table, and plenty of tiles and greenery. Despite the heavy traffic, it's also clean and the service is prompt and polite. Portions are generous: even a single, sizeable brochette fights for space on a plate loaded with rice pilaf, giant buttery roast potatoes, Greek salad with plenty of black olives, parsley, tomato, feta and peppers, a healthy serving of good tzatziki, and hot pita bread on the side for dipping. Good Greek food, cheap. No wonder people wait for it in the rain. ■ *1124 Davie St; 683-2555; $; full bar; AE, MC, V; no cheques; lunch, dinner every day.*

Steveston Seafood House ★ Appropriately located near the Fraser River and the fishing docks, the Steveston Seafood House continues to earn its reputation as "that great little seafood place in Richmond." The decor is funky, with a nautical motif featuring overhead nets, glass floats, and corny seashell knickknacks. Seafood, simply prepared and generously served on large fish-shaped plates, delivers all it promises. We recommend any of the house specialties—even ones with names like Jonathan Livingston Seafood (a mixed seafood platter)—but you shouldn't overlook simple dishes such as the juicy pan-fried halibut with lemon butter. ■ *3951 Moncton St (at No. 1 Rd), Richmond; 271-5252; $$; full bar; AE, MC, V; no cheques; dinner every day.*

▼

**Top 175
Restaurants**

▲

Sun Sui Wah Seafood Restaurant ★★★ These two restaurants are actually an extension of a Hong Kong chain, with food that has a proven track record and dining rooms that are full most nights of the week. The reason: specialties and preparations that are tried and true (and much ordered): crisp, tender roasted squab; deftly steamed scallops on silky bean curd topped with creamy-crunchy tobikko (flying-fish roe) sauce; and Kirin Fish—steamed rock cod slices interwoven with paper-thin slices of ham and fleshy mushrooms and presented on a fresh lotus leaf. The Richmond location is renowned for its platter of deep-fried "milk"—fragrant, sweet coconut in a fluffy crust. With only a few minor lapses in service, this restaurant's success is richly deserved. ■ *4940 No. 3 Rd (Alderbridge Plaza), Richmond; 273-8208; $$; full bar; MC, V; no cheques; lunch, dinner every day;* ⌖■ *4818 Main St; 872-8822; $$; full bar; MC, V; no cheques; dinner every day.*

Sun Wong Kee ★ The word is out: this little Chinese restaurant hidden away on Main Street offers some of the best, least expensive food in town. You'll find minimal decor and maximum attention to what's cooking, especially with the live crabs, rock cod, and lobsters priced just a tad above what they sell for at the market. The seafood is prepared steamed plain, served with butter and cream; baked with green pepper and black bean sauce; or baked with green onion and ginger—but the spicy, deep-fried version gets our vote. The 224-item menu runs the gamut of noodles, hot pots, congee, and pork, beef, and rice dishes; veers toward seafood (abalone to oysters); and includes such esoterica as fried milk with house special sauce. Five-course seafood dinners for four can be had for under $30. ■ *4136 Main St; 879-7231; $; beer and wine; MC, V; no cheques; lunch, dinner Wed-Mon.*

Surat Sweet ★ Vancouver's East Indian neighbourhood is home to numerous purveyors of curry, but Surat Sweet is surely among the best. Serving freshly made Gujarati food (and therefore by definition vegetarian), this pocket-size, 16-seat restaurant draws a steady stream of regulars. Samosas are fresh and commendably nongreasy. Bhajia—chick-pea-floured potato slices—are deep-fried and served with tamarind sauce and fresh grated coconut. Thalis, depending on their size (the special feeds two), include one or two curries, spiced with the subtlety of a maestro. The mind-blowingly sweet desserts are all good, but don't miss the shrikhand—thickened yogurt tinted with saffron and speckled with cardamom seeds and finely chopped pistachios. ■ *6665 Fraser St; 322-9544; $; no alcohol; MC, V; no cheques; lunch, dinner Tues-Sun.*

▼

Top 175 Restaurants

▲

Szechuan Chongqing ★ For a long time, Chongqing was the only Chinese restaurant offering authentic Sichuan specialties. The robust flavours, the piquant sauces, and the searing heat of fresh and dry chiles quickly became familiar signposts of Chinese food in Vancouver, and when the restaurant closed many were left wondering where they would find that addictively haunting plate of fried green beans. Luckily, there's a new Chongqing. Live seafood tanks line one wall, and a couple of VIP salons bring up the rear. Waiters in sleek vests briskly whisk away silk arrangements from the tables as you're being seated. The old haunt has gone upscale, and not surprisingly, the reception has been ambivalent. Whereas some pine for the lost cozy, friendly feeling, others complain that the service is confused. All this is trivial indeed, because the food remains eminently true to form. The fried prawns with chile sauce are quite simply magnificent: sweet and masterfully seasoned. The rich, smooth-crunchy Tan Tan noodles, the lingering orange-peel beef, the melt-in-your-mouth sliced pork with garlic sauce, and, of course, those worth-their-weight-in-gold beans—they're all there to attest that the Chongqing dynasty is going to be long-lived. A new West Broadway location opened at press time. ■ *2808 Commercial Dr; 254-7434 or 879-8454;* ■ *1668 W Broadway; 734-1668; $$; full bar; AE, E, MC, V; no cheques; lunch, dinner every day.* &

Tai Chi Hin ★★ Tai Chi Hin was one of the first Chinese restaurants in Vancouver to set high standards, and many other places followed suit. The decor is postmodern (glass block and pastel), the waiters are tuxedoed and give the same polished service as Swiss hotel school graduates, and the overall look is so glamorous that it makes the food appear to be more expensive than it actually is. We recommend the fried smoked duck (served in crisp chunks with coriander and dumplings,) the crab and white asparagus soup, and the garlic eel in a smooth brown sauce. The rock cod comes to your table live in a plastic case for your premeal inspection (though you're welcome to skip the preview). For something special, the Peking duck does not need to be ordered in advance, but the Beggar's Chicken does. This dramatically different dish is a whole stuffed chicken wrapped in lotus leaves and baked inside a 5-centimetre (2-inch) coating of dough. Ask the waiter to remove the rock-hard crust at the table—it's fun to watch. ■ *888 Burrard St; 682-1888; $$; full bar; AE, E, JCV, V; no cheques; lunch, dinner every day.* &

Tak Sangka Indonesian Restaurant ★★ Tak Sangka was the first Indonesian restaurant in Vancouver, and it has had many years to develop the simple elegance that it now possesses. It's not opulent and overbearing; it's immaculate, comfortable, and decorated with carefully collected Indonesian treasures. The service can be leisurely, but it is very friendly and warm—like the room and the food. A great way to graze through the 50-item menu is to order the Rijsttafels—the deluxe offers 12 dishes and a choice of 4 desserts in a symphony of tastes at $16.95 per person. Dishes include a superb spicy coconut curried chicken, an intense braised beef spiced with chiles, savoury prawns with garlic and tomatoes, and a vegetable chowder of corn, broad beans, red peppers, and cabbage subtly sweetened with coconut milk. Lively sweet pickles of cucumber and carrots cleanse the palate for the nutty, deep-fried, hard-boiled eggs marinated in sambal and the rich, crunchy gado gado salad. And that's just half of it. So bring a friend or two, relax, feast, and plan your next trip to Bali. ■ *3916 Main St; 876-0121; $$; full bar; AE, MC, V; no cheques; lunch Tues-Fri, dinner Tues-Sun.*

Tandoori Taj ★★ Chef Chander Mani Bhatt has put this East Indian restaurant on the map with his fiery sauces, prawns from the clay oven, rich buttery chicken makhani, and lamb vindaloo. Nice tandoori breads—especially the Taj special naan stuffed with chopped chicken, and the onion kulcha—are spectacular, as is the eggplant Bharta, roasted over charcoal in the Tandoor before being mashed and seasoned. Cool off with mango ice cream and special Masala tea. ■ *2189 Kingsway; 439-0157; $$; full bar; AE, MC, V; no cheques; lunch, dinner Tues-Sun.*

Tang's Noodle House ★ As Vancouver's Asian population swells, noodle houses pop up overnight like mushrooms. Tang's is still one of the best, thanks largely to owner Eddie Tang's rigorous quality control and insistence on giving good value (and there's a sign on the window saying that GST and MSG are verboten). Here, in bubblegum pink and grey surroundings, you'll find locals rubbing elbows with those who have trekked in from the distant 'burbs for a serving of fried spicy black cod or shredded pork in garlic and sour sauce. The 100-plus dishes on the menu include rice with barbecued duck, chicken, pork, or brisket, warming hot pots, and vegetarian dishes. Aficionados of incendiary dishes (thoughtfully marked with an *H*) shouldn't miss the wonton in spicy garlic and chile. Gentler flavours are found in the Singapore noodles—a golden curry-flavoured dish crunchy with bean sprouts, green pepper, and onion and generously sprinkled with shrimp and slivers of barbecued pork. Terrific hot and sour soup and bargain-priced lunch specials. ■ *2805-2807 W Broadway; 737-1278; $; beer and wine; MC, V; no cheques; lunch, dinner Mon-Sat.*

The Teahouse at Ferguson Point ★★ This stunning location is a magnet for tourists, with its park setting and spectacular view of English Bay, but a faithful following of locals attests to the consistency of fare. Appetizers run the gamut from shrimp and crab avocado cocktail to carpaccio with wild mushroom salad, from Pernod-spiked fresh seafood soup to excellent crab-stuffed mushroom caps. Salmon is always a good bet, sometimes served with a rich topping of crab and shrimp in a dill hollandaise. Rack of lamb in fresh herb crust is also a perennial favourite and certainly one of the city's best—even without the view. Recent interior changes suggest that the Teahouse may be updating its slightly staid style. ■ *Enter Stanley Park from Georgia St, follow road to Ferguson Pt; 669-3281; $$; full bar; AE, MC, V; no cheques; lunch Mon-Fri, dinner every day, brunch Sat-Sun.* ♿

Tio Pepe ★ Tio Pepe—a shoebox of a restaurant, one long, narrow room crammed full of tables, with the kitchen at the back—has reasonable prices and food unlike any other Mexican food in town. Start with margaritas and a double order of chicken flautas—some of the best around. Charbroiled lamb is marinated in wine and spices with a haunting, bittersweet taste of Seville oranges. Pascaya con huevo—date-palm shoots fried in an egg batter and served with tomato sauce—is an unusual appetizer, with a pleasantly astringent taste. The food is flavourful without being too spicy; it has a mildness typical of Yucatán cooking. If fire is your style, however, try the habaero hot sauce, distilled from the hottest peppers known to anyone. ■ *1134 Commercial Dr (between the pier and William St); 254-8999; $; beer and wine; MC, V; no cheques; dinner Mon-Sat.* ♿

▼

Top 175 Restaurants

▲

Tojo's ★★★★ Tojo Hidekazu *is* Tojo's. This beaming Japanese chef has a loyal clientele that regularly fills his spacious up-stairs restaurant, though most people want to sit at the 10-seat sushi bar—not big enough for all his devoted patrons, but the most Tojo likes to tend at one time. He's endlessly innovative, surgically precise, and committed to fresh ingredients. Show an interest in the food, and if the restaurant isn't frantically busy, he'll offer you a bit of this and that from the kitchen: Tojo tuna or perhaps special beef (very thin beef wrapped around asparagus and shrimp). Getting to be a regular is not difficult, and it's highly recommended. Sushi and sushi bar aside, the restaurant is excellent. The dining room has a view of the stun-ning North Shore mountains and plenty of table seating; Japan-ese menu standards like tempura and teriyaki are always reliable, and daily specials are usually superb. We've enjoyed pine mushroom soup in the fall, shrimp dumplings with hot mus-tard sauce from October to May, cherry blossoms with scallops and deep-fried sole with tiger prawns in the spring, and stuffed salmon and homemade egg tofu in the summer. Plum wine and fresh orange pieces or a green tea and some mango ice cream complete the meal. ■ *202-777 W Broadway; 872-8050; $$$; full bar; AE, DC, MC, V; no cheques; dinner Mon-Sat.* ㊑

▼

Top 175
Restaurants

▲

The Tomahawk ★ The Tomahawk must be the original inspi-ration for all those hokey, totem-pole theme restaurants on highways across North America. In Vancouver, it's a 72-year in-stitution, famous for its hungry-man-sized meals. The eye-open-ing Yukon Breakfast, served all day, includes five rashers of bacon, two eggs, hash browns, and toast for $7.50. For lunch, there are several hamburger platters (named after native chiefs), sandwiches, fried chicken, fish 'n' chips, and even oys-ters. Pies (lemon meringue, Dutch apple, banana cream) are baked on the premises, and the staff will gladly wrap one to go. ■ *1550 Philip Ave (at Marine Dr), North Vancouver; 988-2612; $; no alcohol; AE, MC, V; no cheques; breakfast, lunch, dinner every day.*

Tomato Fresh Food Cafe ★ Tomato is two experiences, both noisy. One is a row of tables and chairs down the centre of the restaurant, placed so close that your elbows touch your neigh-bour's. The other (our choice) is a set of roomy booths around the edge, with plenty of space to lounge. For years, this was an undistinguished diner; now it has an overlay of young, retro en-ergy, most lucidly expressed in the big, chunky, wildly coloured bowls used for serving specialties such as "teapuccino"—cap-puccino made with tea. Modern young wait-staff serve a varia-tion of Mom food: vegetarian chile with really good corn bread, a whacking slab of turkey in the turkey sandwich, a tomato and pesto sandwich, real milkshakes, brownie sundaes, and a wide selection of fresh juices. ■ *3305 Cambie St; 874-6020; $; beer* *and wine; MC, V; no cheques; breakfast, lunch, dinner Tues-Sat, brunch Sat-Sun.*

Top Gun Chinese Seafood Restaurant ★★ A visit to Top Gun is somehow a bit larger than life (by the end of 1994 the area in which it's located, known as "little Asia," will be going full force, with its Japanese mall, an education centre, and a Buddhist temple). The menu is generic Cantonese, but specials can be quite interesting, as in sautéed spiced frog's legs with fagara, chicken marinated in bean paste and then nicely fried, or sea scallops and fresh pears in a potato nest. For dessert, amble across the mall to the Rhino Cafe (next to the bowling alley) and try some of the unusual Eurasian cakes and pastries that are featured there. ▪ *2110-4151 Hazelbridge Way (between No. 3 Rd and Cambie St), Richmond; 273-2883; $$; full bar; V; no cheques; lunch, dinner every day.* &

Towkay Singapore Seafood ★★ Singapore, buoyed by its remarkable economic growth in recent years, is receiving growing recognition as a culinary destination. Its cuisine, influenced by Malaysian, Chinese, and other diverse Southeast Asian cultures, is unique and sophisticated. Fortunately for us, we don't need to travel across the Pacific to sample some of Singapore's best seafood treatments: they can be found here at Towkay on Broadway. *Towkay* means "tycoon," and the restaurant is smartly appointed to make everyone feel like one. Rich hardwood floors, comfortable rattan furnishings, and the sound of pretty waitresses draped in traditional silk cheong sums swishing among the well-spaced tables somehow harks back to gayer and more elegant times. Service is gracious and helpful. The food can be addictive, especially dishes like the spicy sambal clams or the aromatic black-pepper crab. The Singapore-style donut stuffed with squid and garnished with honeydew melon and mayonnaise is an interesting mix of textures and flavours. For those who spurn the fruits of the sea, there is always the trademark Hainan steamed chicken, rich curries, and spareribs with Singapore-style sweet and sour sauce. ▪ *02B-525 W Broadway; 872-0328; $$; beer and wine; AE, MC, V; no cheques; lunch, dinner every day.*

Tropika Malaysian Cuisine ★ The only Malaysian restaurant in town was a truck stop on Kingsway until Tropika came along offering authentic Malaysian fare. A second location recently opened in Kitsilano at 3105 W Broadway. Try the spicy spinach, pungently flavoured with dried shrimp and fish sauce. Less fiery is the tender Hainan chicken served with ginger, scallions, and a sambal dip. Rendang lembu, a beef curry, retains an element of heat, though it's smoothed with soothing coconut milk. Two rice dishes also stand out on the menu: a luxurious coconut rice and a warm, porridgey, sweet black-rice pudding. The latter is served in Bali as breakfast and makes a

▼

Top 175 Restaurants

▲

comforting late-morning meal here too. ■ *1096 Denman St; 682-1887; $$; full bar; AE, DC, MC, V; no cheques; lunch, dinner every day.*

Umberto Al Porto Umberto's Menghi's least expensive restaurant, Al Porto has a lively, colour-splashed decor. We recommend the antipasto plate or the excellent carpaccio as a starter. Pastas range from good to excellent; only the cannelloni falls short of expectations, and it would have been redeemed if it had been cooked longer. The chicken piccata is tender and plentiful, the sauce appropriately lemony and light. Serious grape nuts are drawn to the basement of this Gastown warehouse not only to choose from an estimable wine list, cleverly divided by region, but also to attend Umberto Wine Club events. ■ *321 Water St (Gastown); 683-8376; $$; full bar; AE, DC, JCV, MC, V; no cheques; lunch Mon-Fri; dinner Mon-Sat.*

Uncle Herbert's Fish & Chip Shop ★★ At Uncle Herbert's, owner Ken Mertens has crafted an old English village street atmosphere, with individually styled rooms lining either side of a main "street." The walls in one room are covered with tea towels from every English town big enough to print one, and the Windsor Room is stocked with royal memorabilia dating back to George V. Stop by from 2 to 4 for afternoon tea. For $6.95, you get a pot of tea, finger sandwiches, and scones with clotted cream and sweets. But it's the top-quality fish (lingcod or halibut) and chips that draw the crowds. The roster of pub food includes Cornish pasties, English pork pies, Scotch eggs, sausage rolls, New England clam chowder, and Yorkshire fish cakes (two large slices of potato with fish between them, like a sandwich, battered and deep-fried). Ken imports as many English beers as he can get. ■ *4866 Delta St (at Bridge St, next to the Delta Museum), Ladner; 946-8222; $; beer and wine; MC, V; no cheques; lunch Tues-Sat, dinner Tues-Sun.*

▼

Top 175 Restaurants

▲

Vanier Café The multimillion-dollar, panoramic, "don't you wish you lived in Vancouver?" view of the water and coastal mountains is what makes the Vanier Café a worthy stop. Located in the Vancouver Museum, the restaurant allows you to mix a lot of culture and a little shopping—the museum's gift store is loaded with native art and local memorabilia—with a cup of coffee. After wandering the museum's galleries, you can rest your feet while you nosh on a house-baked bran and pineapple muffin or a slice of chef Heather Vogt's popular pound cake. Lunchtime, there are meat pies, sausage rolls, pita pockets, and croissant-wiches served cafeteria style. It's a quiet place to sit, the vast grassy park outside is popular with kite fliers, the beach is a stone's throw away, and there's loads of free parking. ■ *1110 Chestnut St; 738-1533; $; no alcohol; no credit cards; no cheques; summer: lunch every day; winter, closed Mon.*

Vassilis Taverna ★★ You'll feel transported to the Mediterranean: the paper placemats are even adorned with maps of the Greek Islands. Vassilis, one of Vancouver's original Greek restaurants, is located on Broadway near MacDonald in what is loosely referred to as Little Greece. The menu is more traditional than original, but the quality is consistent. Worthy starters include lightly battered calamari (among the city's best) and rich, salty, scalding-hot saganaki (Greek kefalotiri cheese fried in oil and sprinkled with lemon juice). Spiced roast lamb is superb, and the house specialty, perfectly juicy kotopoulo—chicken pounded flat, simply seasoned with lemon juice, garlic, and oregano, and then barbecued—is special indeed. The Greek salad makes a meal in itself, or enjoy it with a succulent pile of quick-fried baby smelts on the side. For dessert, there's honey-sweet baklava or truly luscious navarino. Service is friendly, if at times sporadic. In summer the restaurant opens onto the sidewalk. ■ *2884 W Broadway; 733-3231; $$; full bar; AE, DC, MC, V; no cheques; lunch Tues-Fri, dinner Tues-Sun.* ⑃

▼

Top 175 Restaurants

▲

Villa del Lupo ★★★ Owners Julio Gonzales and Vince Piccolo boast impressive culinary pedigrees, having presided over several other fine Italian restaurants in Vancouver, and it shows. The "House of the Wolf" is a simple, elegant space with white walls and forest-green trim that balances the traditional with the contemporary. Prices tend to be high, but portions are generous (some are enough for two). Almost everything is wonderful: crab cakes bursting with crabmeat and served with a surprisingly subtle aioli, pumpkin gnocchi dressed in a lovely combination of roughly chopped hazelnuts and basil oil, and veal medallions served with a garnish of Italian mushrooms, filament-thin shoestring potatoes, and julienned vegetables in an Armagnac sauce. The osso bucco is for serious appetites only: two shanks bearing fork-tender meat in a richly seasoned sauce, with a side of orzo (rice-shaped pasta). Italy isn't the only region on the wine list (though it is represented in some depth), and grappa and eaux-de-vie are available as well. Service is always correct, if a little slow. ■ *869 Hamilton St; 688-7436; $$$; full bar; AE, DC, E, MC, V; no cheques; dinner every day.*

Vong's Kitchen ★★ With new upscale Chinese restaurants cropping up all over the city, one could get positively nostalgic about Vong's. It seems to have been around forever and is still a tiny place on unfashionable Fraser Street with steamy windows and almost stark decor inside. If you are serious about food and don't care that much about atmosphere, then Vong's will fill the bill. The place is owned and run by the Vong family, who prepare each dish with loving attention. Order the chile-sauced prawns and atomic rice (rich broth is poured on top of the crisp-cooked rice and vegetables, producing a loud sizzling noise). Although the execution of some dishes can be inconsistent, you are getting as close to a home-cooked meal as you are going to get in a restaurant. The service also gives you a sense of having just come home. Your bill is accompanied by deep-fried banana fritters. If you don't plan to arrive before 6pm, reservations are essential—even then, be prepared to wait. Perhaps this will be remedied by the new location opening after we go to press. ■ *4298 Fraser St; 327-4627; $; no alcohol; no credit cards; no cheques; dinner Wed-Sun.*

Water Street Cafe ★ ½ Across the street from the steam-powered clock, this small corner cafe is the restaurant of choice for homemade focaccia, buttery carpaccio, and Southern Italian pastas. A delightful find, especially when you can sit outside at the sidewalk tables (best to call ahead and reserve one at lunch). The menu's not long, but, lunch or dinner, there's always something that's exactly right: calamari, deep-fried with a cucumber and dill yogurt; salmon marinated in soy and balsamic vinegar, sauteed and served on a bed of greens; spaghetti tossed with chicken, sun-dried tomatoes and fresh basil; and for dessert, a rich, smooth tiramisú. The staff is warm and welcoming, providing a great place to dine alla famìglia. Two rooms upstairs (one seats 12 and has a fireplace; the other seats 45) are used for private parties. ■ *300 Water St; 689-2832; $$; full bar; MC, V; no cheques; lunch, dinner every day.*

White Spot It's as much a part of the city as Stanley Park, and Vancouverites driving into town after months or years away have been known to stop off at the nearest "Spot" for a Legendary Platter, which includes a Triple O Burger lavishly garnished with a "secret sauce." The first Spot opened as a hamburger joint in 1928, went on to become the first drive-in restaurant in Canada, and now has over 40 locations. It continues to be a fave among even the most fussy foodies. The butterhorns served at breakfast, the fish and chips, the clubhouse sandwich, and the Pirate Pak for kids are the stuff of legend. You'll also find the ultimate in comfort foods: liver and onions, a hot turkey sandwich, meat loaf, and macaroni and cheese. In keeping with the culinary correctness of the '90s, White Spot has broadened its listings to include pastas and teriyaki chicken as well as garden salads and "heart smart" items. ■ *1616 W Georgia St, 681-8034 (and branches); $; full bar; MC, V; no cheques; breakfast, lunch, dinner every day.*

The William Tell (The Georgian Court Hotel) ★★★ The elegance and charm of this Old World restaurant are a reflection of Erwin Doebeli, its dedicated owner. Doebeli, the consummate restaurateur, seems to be here, there, and everywhere, enthusiastically greeting arrivals at the door or flamboyantly whipping up a cafe diablo. Outstanding appetizers include

Swiss-style air-dried beef and BC salmon tartare with fennel and wild mushrooms on toasted homemade brioche; if you crave soup, order the double consommé or the hearty chowder. We recommend the Fraser Valley duck flavoured with an apple cucumber wine sauce, the scalloppine of veal in a sherry sauce, or the chateaubriand. The desserts, all homemade, just get better: an unequalled meringue glacé au chocolat, perfect hot fruit soufflés (try the passion fruit), and opulently rich crêpes Suzette or cherries jubilee prepared at your table. The sommelier reigns over one of the best wine cellars in the city (aficionados should ask to see the "reserved wine menu"). Sunday night is family dining with a Swiss farmer's buffet. ■ *765 Beatty St (across from BC Place Stadium); 688-3504; $$$; full bar; AE, DC, MC, V; no cheques; breakfast every day, lunch Mon-Fri, dinner Mon-Sun.* &

Won More ★ Whether you eat in or take out, Sichuan is the fieriest of Chinese cuisines. Go for the diced chicken with hot garlic sauce or dried tangerine peel, or the three-alarm spicy pork with peanuts and hot chile. Milder appetites can be appeased, but will never be bored, with a zingy lemon chicken or fresh squid with mixed vegetables. Not everything is spicy: mushu pork is subtly flavoured and good. With its intensely flavoured broth and savoury stuffed noodles, the Won More's wonton soup elevates a cliché to a classic. Particularly commendable are the Singapore noodles, lightly curry flavoured and tangled with shrimp, barbecued pork, shredded omelet, and crispy bean sprouts, every bite different. Vegetarians will have a field day here. Either location, consider takeout, then stroll down to the beach, take in the sunset, and consider coming back for just won more. ■ *201-1184 Denman St; 688-8856;* ■ *1944 W 4th Ave; 737-2889; $; beer and wine; AE, MC, V; no cheques; lunch Mon-Sat, dinner every day.*

Wonton Noodles ★½ Don't be put off by the out-of-the-way location on an otherwise charmless strip of Hastings Street. Or by the fact that apart from the couple of tables that offer a peek-aboo mountain view, decor is basic. Or that the service, though pleasant, is brisk. The food makes up for all of these shortcomings. The menu lists 176 items. Wonton soup, Peking duck, sweet and sour, hot and sour—chances are good you'll find any Cantonese dish you've ever heard of—and then some. Servings are generous. The medium-size bowl of Seaweed Bean Cake Seafood Soup, a bewitching complexity of textures and flavours, feeds three. The listing of chicken's feet, duck's tongues, and various tripe dishes is written in Chinese only, but the staff is happy to make a stab at translation. Worth a separate trip, and fast gaining a cult following, are the rock-bottom-priced snack-size specials: a single crisp-skinned, butterflied quail or pai dan, the preserved duck egg whose yolk is the colour of green marble. Worth trying too are the half-moon-shaped dumplings, the eggplant and deep-fried bean curd in hot garlic sauce, and superlative pan-fried squid with salt and hot pepper. ■ *1991 E Hastings St; 253-8418; $; beer only; MC; no cheques; lunch, dinner every day.*

Woodlands Natural Food Restaurant This is where Vancouverites enlighten out-of-towners who still believe strict vegetarian (no meat, fish, fowl, or eggs are used here) means bland. Set in the heart of counterculture country, with new age music and crystal shops all around, Woodlands customers run the gamut from business-suited professionals to erstwhile hippies. Outside there's a diminutive deck. Inside, a large, pleasant, split-level room is flanked by an L-shaped buffet where food is sold by the 100 grams. Dishes vary daily. Spicy Szechuan tofu, fukameni rice noodles, Mexican chile, and eggplant moussaka are often among the 10 or so hot entrées, each with a sign spelling out the presence—or absence—of wheat or dairy products. Samosas and soups are available and are priced separately. Customer overflow spills into the carpeted, wicker-furnished atrium, where you can order à la carte. Breakfasts are nourishing. All-day hikers fuel up on the formidably filling sesame waffles, whole-grain pancakes, or an Indian breakfast of potato- or cauliflower-stuffed chapati and yogurt. Lunch or dinner includes vegetarian pizzas (with tofu salami) and burgers, a macrobiotic plate, spinach lasagne, and a savoury Eight Jewels clay pot replete with vegetable "jewels." ■ *2582 W Broadway (above the Kitsilano Natural Food Store); 733-5411; $; beer and wine; MC, V; no cheques; breakfast, lunch, dinner every day.*

Yaohan Supermarket and Shopping Centre Where can you find over 20 varieties of Japanese soya sauce, fresh wasabe root, matsutake mushrooms, or squid with smelt roe? Try the Yaohan Supermarket at the new Yaohan Centre—the first Canadian branch of one of the largest department store chains in Asia. Here you can also find ready-for-the-pot precut sukiyaki beef; sushi-grade salmon, tuna, and geoduck; and ready-for-the-pot precut black cod, snapper, pomfret, mackerel, mushrooms, and Napa cabbage. This may be the largest supermarket fish department in the Lower Mainland. Across the concourse, in the food court, 15 outlets provide a smorgasbord of Asian fast foods, such as Buddhist vegetarian dishes, Singapore/Malaysian specialties, Vietnamese pho, Northern Chinese dim sum, ChiuChow stir-fries, Hong-Kong-coffee-shop-style food, and a Japanese yakitori bar. The centre also features retail shops on the second level with a games arcade, a medical centre, and the largest Japanese book store in the area. ■ *3700 No. 3 Rd, Richmond; 231-0601; Yaohan Supermarket; 276-8808; $; no credit cards; no cheques; bank cards in supermarket; every day.*

Zefferelli's ★½ Architectural prints, interesting paintings, and mega-sized exotic fruits are just part of the terrific decor dreamed up by doyen among local restaurant designers David Vance. These eclectic surroundings are a suitable (and comfortable) backdrop to lusty Italian (read Tuscan) cooking on Vancouver's lively Robson Street strip. The antipasto offers exceptionally good grilled veggies and lyrical chicken livers scented with sage and sherry and served up on toast. Salads go beyond the usual, pairing warm spinach leaves with smoked lamb and mushrooms, or adding onions to the Caprese salad of tomato and bocconcini. Although classic preparations are there in abundance—spaghetti bolognese, penne with hot sausage, etc.—there are some notable surprises in the pasta listings. Fettuccine comes with chicken and leeks or pancetta and chiles. Fusili can be had with pesto or, in an almost Grecian take, with lamb and artichokes. Grilled chops, scalloppine with lemon butter, chicken, and fish are nonpasta options. Terrific lunchtime sandwiches include the PLT (prosciutto, lettuce, tomato and a rustic mix of Italian sausage, garlic, and olive oil). ■ *1136 Robson St; 687-0655; $$; full bar; AE, MC, V; no cheques; lunch, dinner every day.*

Zeppo's Trattoria ★★½ Lively, upbeat atmosphere in a setting as warm as a Tuscan family reunion. A ho-hum location, but the hip and hungry crowd willingly drives kilometres for the food as, with élan and bravado, chef Tim Johnstone finesses lusty peasant flavours into memorable and often elegant dishes. There's complementary foccaccia and silken pâté to start. Antipasto is a must, hot or cold, the hot big enough to share and including shrimp, oysters, sausage, some spicy pepperonata, and a solitary escargot. What about that insanely rich polenta next? It's topped with more pepperonata and reclining on a bed of decadently rich sauce—an amalgam of Romano, Parmesan, and Edam—wicked as original sin. Fettuccine with scallops; fork-tender lamb shanks; angel hair pasta with two sauces neatly divided by a row of grill-marked tiger prawns; gnocchi with Gorgonzola cream; shell pasta stuffed with chicken, fennel, and chorizo—they're all good. The menu's rejigged every couple of weeks to accommodate seasonal tastes. Pray that the triple cream of mushroom soup is still on the menu. ■ *1967 W Broadway; 737-7444; $$; full bar; AE, DC, MC, V; no cheques; lunch Mon-Fri, dinner every day.*

Zuni Cafe ★★ Igniting Asian ingredients with Cactus Belt spice, chef Eddie Cheung was among Vancouver's first proponents of fusion cooking. Committed foodies hang out downstairs, a long skinny space furnished with brightly cushioned banquettes. The stuccoed walls showcase the work of local brush-wielders. Upstairs, more tables—and a diminutive outdoor patio. Addictive wherever you eat is Cheung's pan-fried linguine with black bean sauce, a signature dish that comes mingled with prawns or smoked chicken, in entrée and appetizer sizes. Equally toothsome, his oriental spicy lamb. Best of all, a "sampling" dinner that may include small servings of a Puck-ish pizza of crabmeat, sun-dried tomatoes, onions, pancetta, a smokily smooth grilled corn and seafood chowder, quail, Cajun barbecued scampi, and lobster stew. The bad news: as of spring '94 Eddie left to open a Zuni in Hong Kong. The good: in his place is brother Christopher Cheung of Christopher's Cafe in Berkeley. ■ *1221 Thurlow St; 681-3521; $$; full bar; AE, MC, V; no cheques; dinner every day.*

NIGHTLIFE

Nightlife Index

The Garden Lounge
Gerard Lounge
Graceland
Hogan's Alley
Hot Jazz
Hungry Eye
Joe Fortes
Kits Pub
Luv Affair
Madison's
The Marble Arch
MaRS Restaurant and
  Nightclub
Mescalero
Numbers Cabaret
O'Ryans
The Odyssey
Pelican Bay Pub
Punchlines
Railway Club
Richard's on Richards

Rio Rio
The Roxy
The Royal Hotel
Seymour Billiards
Shark Club
Soho Cafe
The Town Pump
Uncle Charlie's Lounge
Wedgewood Hotel Lounge
The World
The Yale
Yuk Yuk's

East Vancouver
Jake O'Grady's
Santos Tapas

New Westminster
California Dreamin'
Kits Pub New West

North Vancouver
The Avalon
Jack Lonsdale's

Richmond
Frank's Place
Matches

South Vancouver
The Wild Coyote

Surrey
Pancho & Lefty's

West Vancouver
Lifestyles Non-Alcoholic
  Bar and Cafe

Nightlife

NIGHTCLUBS

Big Bam Boo Several club owners pooled their methods and their moola with the goal of taking on the popular Richard's on Richards for the title of #1 nightspot. The result is this funky playroom where 19-to-49-year-olds can frolic while dressed to the nines and looking for 10s. Live duos and a fine sushi bar are offered upstairs. Downstairs, the singles cruise the aisles and live bands churn out funk, R&B, and Top 40. Wednesday offers the hottest Ladies' Night in the city. ■ *1236 W Broadway; 733-2220; full bar; Tues-Sat.*

Blarney Stone The Blarney Stone proves that there's more to Irish music than U2. This rollicking Gastown club turns every weekend into a St. Patty's Day celebration and every patron into an honorary native of the Emerald Isles. The decor is Olde Irish pub. Don't be surprised to see entire families partying together. ■ *216 Carrall St; 687-4322; full bar; Tues-Sat.*

Boone County Why do cowboy hats bend up at the side? So you can fit four people into a pickup and 300 into Boone County on weekends. This place is raucous, with a cramped layout that makes it seem busier than it really is. A large square bar fills much of the back half of the place, and raised tables and a decent-sized dance floor fill the rest. Weekends are so busy you'll have to grease your chaps to slide into a standing-room spot, so mosey in early to grab a seat. ■ *801 Brunette Ave, Coquitlam; 525-3144; full bar; Mon-Sat.*

California Dreamin' This subterranean rock pit is one of the few remaining live hard-rock bars in the Lower Mainland. Big hair is the rule for both sexes. The gents shuffle in wearing full

rock star regalia, and the women strut around in spikes, mini-skirts, and makeup that is just this side of Tammy Faye Bakker.
■ *57 Blackie St, New Westminster; 522-0011; full bar; closed Sun.*

Celebrities Nightclub Since its auspicious beginning as the Retinal Circus where the Grateful Dead came to play and the '60s hippies came to trip out, this room has been best known for its revolving marquee. Step through the doors into a massive, square, two-storey room encircled by an upper balcony and centered by a giant dance floor, Vancouver's hottest place to dance. An amplifier the size of an Oldsmobile pushes out modern dance and rock. Pedestals ring the floor and a pair of cages suspend from the ceiling, allowing the closet Fred or Ginger to step out and shine. Strippers take it off Tuesdays at 10:30pm, and a drag show takes the floor Wednesday night at 11pm.
■ *1022 Davie St; 689-3180; full bar; open every day.*

The Commodore The unsinkable flagship of Vancouver nightspots, the fabulous Commodore has been building its legend since 1929. Grand in size (1100 capacity) and grand in style, it houses the Lower Mainland's largest dance floor. Everyone from Count Basie and Duke Ellington to the world's hottest rock acts have graced the stage. Elevated side tables make viewing easy. Voted Canada's Best Live Venue in 1992. Eat your heart out, Toronto. ■ *870 Granville St; 681-7838; full bar.*

The Edge As other clubs close, the Edge fills with club-weary revellers looking for a jolt of caffeine or a last chance at romance. A pair of polished heat ducts and a lively mural run the length of this narrow room. If the recorded dance music doesn't energize the gay crowd, the full list of espresso drinks and desserts should do the trick. Open until 4am (2am on Sundays). ■ *1148 Davie St; 689-4742; no alcohol; open every day.*

Frank's Place Many a flatlander has turned 19 in this long-running Richmond institution. In a casual suburban setting, the music ranges from hard rock to funk, depending on which band is booked in that week. Monday and Tuesday are Jam Nights, and the featured attraction takes the stage Wednesday through Saturday. ■ *7100 Elmbridge Way, Richmond; 270-1800; full bar; every day.*

Frisco's If Jed Clampett were running Richard's on Richards, the result would be something like this. Both the facilities and the young patrons are a little on the grotty side, but that doesn't keep the crowds away. On Thursday and Friday, which are the big nights, you'll be forced to line up later in the evening, but don't worry, there's usually a fight or two in the parking lot to keep you entertained. ■ *2089 Lougheed Hwy, Port Coquitlam; 942-6020; full bar; Mon-Sat.*

Graceland You won't find Elvis in this humongous warehouse-size club where the 4000-watt sound system works almost too well. The music is cutting edge, alternative, obscure, and programmed with the feeling that anything a month old is a golden oldie; needless to say, the crowd is young, hip, and dressed in black. A line forms by 10pm on weekends, and Reggae Night on Wednesdays draws a full house. ■ *1250 Richards St; 688-2648; full bar; Wed-Sat.*

Hot Jazz Those hard-to-find big band and swing sounds are served up here at Vancouver's jazz institution, a real favourite among the city's jazz fans who pack the dance floor for a blast from the past. ■ *2120 Main St; 873-4131.*

Hungry Eye As grungy as the live music it presents, the Hungry Eye is Vancouver's alternative music headquarters. You can squeeze into the two small upper levels and try to withstand the sonic assault of local and imported talent, or you can retreat to the lower level for a relatively quiet game of pool. On Tuesday, guest DJs spin psychedelic-funk and disco; live bands take over Wednesday through Saturday. ■ *23 W Cordova St; 688-5351; Tues-Sat.*

Jake O'Grady's Make a run for the border, where Burnaby meets Vancouver and thirsty locals meet the blues. The decor is nothing special, just a square, windowed, 140-seat room that could just as easily be a family restaurant—were it not for a minute stage flanked by framed pictures of musical greats and loaded with musical gear. When the band starts, the small dance floor fills and the unrhythmical hit the dart boards. A tasty menu is offered from noon till closing, with food and drink specials every day and 10 kinds of beer on tap. Monday is Jam Night. ■ *3684 E Hastings St; 298-1434; full bar; every day.*

▼

Nightclubs

▲

Luv Affair Originally a haunt for the gay crowd, the Luv Affair now plays host to a very young crowd of straight suburbanites in trendy threads who bop nonstop to equally trendy tunes (industrial, acid house, etc.) played at ear-splitting volume. This is one of the most successful places in town, and there's usually a line out the door. ■ *1275 Seymour St; 685-3288; full bar; every day.*

Madison's A night at Madison's is like spending eight hours locked in the trunk of one of those boom cars that cruise Robson street. The decor is glitzy, the nonstop canned dance music is loud, and the fashion-conscious patrons range in age from 19 to 19½. Valet parking. ■ *398 Richards St; 687-5007; full bar; Wed-Sat.*

MaRS Restaurant and Nightclub The next time you're all dressed up, there *is* somewhere to go. The MaRS Restaurant and Club is 1994's resurrection of Saturno, an ambitious project that sat idle for a few years. This time around it's working, and deservedly so. MaRS is world-class—from the hardwood floors with recessed illuminated stars to the DMX fibreoptic technology that recreates the Milky Way on the ceiling three stories above. The back wall is a large glass window that showcases a computer-controlled hydroponics garden complete with a running brook, banana trees and a live volcano. A pair of galactic bars feature good wine and champagne selections, a perfect complement to the five-star offerings of the culinary team. Spinning above the ample dance floor is the Vortex, a 38-foot titanium, robotic lighting structure with cybernetic technology that issues an array of dazzling effects. Meanwhile, the sound system (designed for Michael Jackson's tour) pumps out distortion-free dance music that centers on the dancers and keeps the level tolerable elsewhere in the room. Throw in the world's most powerful video system, a 22-foot fibreoptics screen, a world exclusive nitrogen fog screen, and Hollywood special effects, and you have a truly lunar experience. Memberships offer privileges at future MaRS locations in L.A. and New York. Non-members pay a cover charge after 9pm unless you're dining in. ■ *1320 Richards St; 230-MARS (6277); full bar; open every day.*

Numbers Cabaret Regulars of all ages squeeze into Levi's and leather and cram into a room that's as interesting as the gay clientele. Corridors connect four split-levels and a pair of bars. Grab a stool down below in the Kok-Pit or head up top and practise your stroke on a trio of pool tables. The dance tunes crank up at 10pm nightly and the mid-level dance floor fills until closing with gyrating patrons. Never a cover charge (except New Year's Eve). ■ *1098 Davie St; 685-4077; full bar; open every day.*

O'Ryan's In this big, barnlike room, a pair of elevated grand pianos perch nose to nose, while a twosome of piano-pounders cranks out high-energy duets for an appreciative and raucous throng of merry-makers. You won't get the chance to warble one on your own as you would in a conventional piano bar, but you will have a boisterous good time. ■ *6 Powell St; 685-1333; full bar; Thurs-Sat.*

The Odyssey ★★ It all started as a family home—and what a family! At the Odyssey a large contingent of bisexuals mingle with gays and a growing number of straight patrons, which has motivated management to pluck gay people from the ever-present lineup. Work up a sweat on the dance floor and then cool off by stepping outside to the rear garden or strip naked and lather yourself in an elevated shower on Thursdays. Rubba dubba hubba hubba. ■ *1251 Howe St; 689-5256; full bar every day.*

Pancho & Lefty's There's no better place to kick back and listen to music about blue-collar people than the blue-collar suburb from which they came. Pancho & Lefty's is stationed in the deepest, darkest heart of Surrey, a flat, rectangular, one-storey addition to the Flamingo Hotel. Rub elbows with an eclectic mix of cowpokes, greaseballs, and plain old Surrey folks. Oddly enough, the atmosphere is peaceful and friendly, and although it's comfortably full on weekends, there never seems to be a lineup. The bands are usually topnotch and can be seen from anywhere in the room. ■ *10768 King George Hwy, Surrey; 583-3536; full bar; closed Sun.*

Punchlines From a humble beginning in the basement of the Queen Elizabeth Theatre, Vancouver's first comedy spot has grown up and moved to a 250-seat room perched on the cobblestones of Water Street in Gastown. The decor is nonexistent—just a plain blue room that allows you to focus on a small stage featuring the in-house group of Improv Players on Tuesday and Wednesday and stand-up comedy Thursday through Saturday. ■ *15 Water St; 684-3015; full bar; Tues-Sat.*

The Railway Club The setting is intimate and the entertainment is innovative, with acts running the gamut from folk to country to blues to rock, or featuring a combination thereof. This casual, second-storey spot on Pender Street is narrow, with a large square bar cutting the room in two. Try to arrive early enough to grab a seat in the front section; you'll be glad you did. Although the Railway is a club, nonmembers are welcome at a slightly higher cover charge. ■ *579 Dunsmuir St; 681-1625; every day.*

Richard's on Richards Better known as Dick's on Dicks, this is Vancouver's most venerable "meet market"—a place where hair is piled high, hemlines show lots of thigh, and silk shirts are open to the navel. The second level offers a shooter bar and a bird's-eye view of the dance floor, so if you're balding and like to comb it over, you won't be fooling anyone. Expect long lines Thursday through Saturday. ■ *1036 Richards St; 687-6794; full bar; Mon-Sat.*

The Roxy After the young suburbanites hit the mall and the college crowd hits the books, they all hit the Roxy for classic rock. Behind two bars the gin slingers do their Tom Cruise imitations, juggling joy juice, catching bottles behind their backs, and clanging a hanging bell whenever a generous donation makes its way into their tip jar. A pair of house bands splits the week. Don't miss the Surreal McCoys, Sunday through Tuesday. Casual dress, with retro '60s attire in abundance. ■ *932 Granville St; 684-7699; full bar; every day.*

Rumours Spiffy decor and a horde of decidedly unspiffy young locals jam the joint, especially on Thursdays, shaking their booty to hot dance and Top 40 tuneage spun by a DJ. ■ *2616 Shaughnessy Ave, Port Coquitlam; 944-8118; full bar; Tues-Sat.*

Shark Club Vancouver's newest and hottest arrival is an upscale, tiered sports bar offering a soothing decor of oak and brass punctuated with an assortment of sports memorabilia. In addition to the usual assortment of interpersonal games being played among the crowd, you'll find 25 screens showing games of other kinds, along with the requisite pool tables and dart boards. At 8pm sharp, a DJ fires up Top-40 and classic rock ditties and the dance floor fills fast. There's a long oak bar (offering 15 beers on tap) and a kitchen that pumps out Italian cuisine for lunch, dinner, and weekend brunch. All 180 seats are full and a line-up's in place by 9pm on Thursdays and 5pm on weekends. Reservations are accepted until 5:30pm. A valet docks your vessel Thursday through Saturday evenings, or you can do-it-yourself in the underground parking lot. ■ *180 W Georgia St; 687-4275; full bar; open every day.*

Steel Monkey This place has the feel of an out-of-control house party on Cheap Drink Night, Tuesdays, when highballs sell for an unbelievable 99 cents. Probably the hottest Tuesday night in the city, with lines forming at 7pm (the doors don't open until 7:30). Popular dance and rock tunes keep the dance floor jumping, while a pair of large go-go cages lets the exhibitionists strut their stuff. Things simmer down the rest of the week, until Ladies' Night on Friday, which is usually standing room only. ■ *2745 Barnet Hwy, Coquitlam; 941-3128; full bar; Tues-Sat.*

The Town Pump Touring acts of all kinds and all stature have played on this stage, and the club remains one of the city's most popular concert spots—in spite of some of the poorest sight lines in town. The room is long and narrow with a middle-mounted stage that faces sideways, leaving those in the seating area with a side view. If you want a front view, you'll have to stand on the dance floor. The feeling is casual and rustic, with a front lounge area for those intent on conversation. ■ *66 Water St; 683-6695; full bar; every day.*

The Wild Coyote This recent addition to the club scene proves there are more than trolls lurking under the Granville Street Bridge. The Wild Coyote is the latest offering from the owners of the Big Bam Boo, and they're packing 'em in, despite an unlikely location on the south end of Granville. The lively young crowd hails mainly from Richmond and Kits. Local bands play original material Monday through Wednesday; topnotch cover bands perform Thursday through Saturday. The Coyote features a main-level dance floor with a second level overlooking the action. Get there early. ■ *1312 SW Marine Dr, 264-ROCK (7625); full bar; closed Sun.*

The Wild Pony For many clubs, the commitment to country music extends only as far as the band of the week and a couple of wagon wheels tacked to the wall. At the Wild Pony, however, they've gone all out, and the result is the best-looking country corral in the city. Wood planking covers the floor, a desert-scape mural covers three walls, and the fourth features a weathered, western facade containing the bar, a kitchen that serves up down-home vittles, and a side area with a pair of pool tables. Friendly, sociable, and unpretentious, the Wild Pony will make you feel welcome whether you're 19 or 59. Cover charge on weekends only. ■ *6200 Kingsway, Burnaby; 434-3100; full bar; every day.*

The World Insomniacs share this space with those who can't get enough and those who've already had too much, proving there's never a dull moment at Vancouver's premier after-hours joint. The tunes are loud and alternative, the refreshments are nonalcoholic, and the doors are open from midnight until 5am. ■ *1369 Richards St; 688-7806; no alcohol; Fri-Sat.*

Yuk Yuk's This venue originated as the Flying Club during Expo 86 and is still going strong as a member of the world's largest comedy club chain. This is the perfect place for comedy, just the right size (218 seats), with a theatre-style setting that ensures a perfect vantage point from any seat in the house. Three hilarious touring acts are featured each night, Wednesdays through Saturdays. ■ *750 Pacific Blvd; 687-LAFF (5233); full bar; Wed-Sat.*

PUBS

The Avalon On weekends, this hotel lounge resembles a future Volvo owners' convention as the young middle-class North Vancouverites come out to play. An up-tempo, upscale energy fills the air as a DJ spins popular, rock, and dance music, and the revellers bop till they drop, or 2am, whichever comes first. ■ *1025 Marine Dr; North Vancouver; 985-4181; full bar; every day.*

Bar-None This newcomer to the club scene is one of the trendiest and most popular places in town. The well-dressed, well-coiffed, and well-heeled under-40 set queues up for a chance to stand crammed together like sardines, to hunch over a long row of built-in backgammon boards or checkerboards, and to play pool to the sounds of live blues, rock, and soul. The bands play Wednesdays through Saturdays, so come early, stay late, and keep your stomach sucked in. ■ *1222 Hamilton St; 689-7000; full bar; every day.*

Cat and Fiddle Cradled among the warehouses and auto-supply wholesalers of Port Coquitlam's industrial district sits one of the Lower Mainland's most successful pubs. Abundant oak and a low ceiling make for a fairly dark atmosphere, which does nothing to diminish the festive feel of the place. By 9pm Thursday through Saturday, revellers are lined up out the door, but the real wingding is Wednesday, when the place is jammed by 5pm for Cheap Wing Night. ■ *1979 Brown St, Port Coquitlam; 941-8822; full bar; every day.*

Darby D. Dawes Many Kitsilano residents start their evening in Darby's warm, convivial confines and then head over to the Fairview at closing time. Thursday through Saturday you'll find live blues, and good food is served up seven days a week. ■ *2001 Macdonald St; 731-0617; full bar; every day.*

Delaney's Customers range from suits to bikers, from 19 to fossilized, and they seem to be a sociable lot. The pub's entire front wall consists of garage doors that slide up (weather permitting) and open on to a fresh-air patio, providing relief to non-smokers. Bonuses are the occasional live blues act, a pair of pool tables, and a cozy corner offering comfortable couches and a fireplace. The budget-conscious will appreciate the daily food and drink specials. ■ *170-5665 Kingsway, Burnaby; 433-8942; full bar; every day.*

Denman Station Denman Station, a neighborhood pub, is a popular launch pad where people pop in for a cool one on their way to the clubs. Recorded music at a well-modulated volume means you can converse without shouting. The decibel and energy level comes up a bit later in the evening on Friday and Saturday as the primarily gay clientele takes to the dance floor. Pop in Monday nights at 7:30pm to play euchre (like bridge) or take the stage Sunday or Wednesday nights at 11pm and warble your best karaoke. Denman Station is popular with the lesbian crowd and offers a pool table, dart board, and a big-screen TV. ■ *860 Denman St; 669-3448; full bar; open every day.*

The Drake Show Lounge When they say that their staff bends over backwards to satisfy the customer, they're not kidding. The servers are known as "the Drakettes," and when they're not whizzing to your table with refreshments, they're doffing their uniforms (clingy red micro-shorts and low-cut bodysuits) on stage. Ironically, the stage is shaped like a cross and is flanked by a pair of 1-metre (3-foot) hexagonal ministages, where the Drakettes occasionally put on a minishow in response to your special request. Sports screens, pool tables, and decent pub-grub. ■ *606 Powell St; 254-2826; full bar; every day.*

The Fairview The Ramada Inn may seem like an unusual location for a blues club, but this is one bar that showcases some of the city's best players. Although not comfy enough to be considered intimate, the room is just the right size and there isn't a bad seat in the house. A small dance floor sits in front of the tiny stage, and when the band gets cooking, so do the dancers. The atmosphere is casual, so come as you are. ■ *898 W Broadway; 872-1262; full bar; every day.*

Fiesta's On Fridays you'll be hard pressed to find an open chair in this happening little pub in a very nonhappening location on Kingsway. The multileveled setting is fairly intimate, and the clientele likes to party hearty. Bang some balls on the pool tables or take roost on the outdoor patio and savour the hospitable atmosphere and wholesome food. ■ *6879 Kingsway, Burnaby; 525-7414; full bar; every day.*

Jack Lonsdale's A fave among the mountain-grown grown-ups of North Vancouver, this haunt delivers everything you'd expect from a pub—clean, comfortable surroundings, decent food, and a good selection of beer. Pop in during ski season after a day on the slopes. ■ *1433 Lonsdale Ave, North Vancouver; 986-7333; full bar; every day.*

The John B Neighbourhood Pub The John B is 14 years old and fighting the aging process as fervently as the neatly attired 25-to-40-year-olds who fill its seats. Live classic rock and a boisterous but well-mannered contingent of regulars keep the energy level high. A freestanding gas fireplace dominates an upper section, and 16 stools await those who like to belly up to the gorgeous oak bar with its ceiling-high backdrop of liquor bottles. The food's great, with Wing Night every Monday and Pull and Eat Prawn Night on Tuesdays. ■ *1000 Austin Ave, Coquitlam; 931-5115; full bar; every day.*

▼

Pubs

▲

Kits Pub ■ Kits Pub New West Check your attitude and your leathers at the door. This place is strictly casual: come as you are and leave as you wannabe. Both pubs are noisy and energetic, with a good-sized dance floor where the crowd gyrates to canned classic rock and Top 40. You'll find pool tables in back and a line out front, so cruise in early. The New Westminster location has a slightly younger clientele. ■ *1424 W Broadway; 736-5811; full bar; every day;* ■ *535 Front St, New Westminster; 525-2353; full bar; Thurs-Sat.*

Lifestyles Non-Alcoholic Bar and Cafe Lifestyles, a wholesale nonalcoholic beverage company, is spawning retail franchises at a breakneck pace—six stores/restaurants have opened in the past year. Tony dark wood interiors and upscale publike settings are completed with TVs and smartly dressed bartenders. The beverage menu features sparkling waters, special coffees, and over two dozen nonalcoholic cocktails made from the same flavourings that are used to flavour regular liqueurs. But the focus is on the company's two lines of nonalcoholic wines and five brands of nonalcoholic beers. At the slightest provocation, the bartenders will whip out the tasting glasses. This could become a regular haunt if the food menu ever offers more than somewhat mundane and generic pub fare. As it is, it's still a choice beginning to a new lifestyle. ■ *The Market at Park Royal, West Vancouver; 925-0506; every day; no alcohol; other branches.*

The Marble Arch Canadian laws allow exotic dancers to take it all off, whereas the United States allows them to strip to the G-string only. So it's no wonder businessmen love the downtown location, and lunchtime finds them seated suit to suit, shoulder to shoulder. All 280 seats are well served by not one but three stages, which are often found in simultaneous operation around dinnertime—a process known as "triple stage mania." Sports screens, video games, pool tables, food, and a courtesy phone for calling your wife. ■ *518 Richards St; 681-5435; full bar; every day.*

The Mountain Shadow Clad in weathered wood and stained glass, this Tudor-style inn is as good-looking as the 20-to-35-year-olds who fill it to the rafters. There's an upper level overlooking an open centre section, allowing you to hide away upstairs for a bird's-eye view of the frivolities, or mix it up in the main floor action, with a pool table, dart boards, and live music Thursday through Saturday. Weekends are jam-packed. ■ *7174 Barnet Hwy, North Burnaby; 291-9322; full bar; every day.*

Pelican Bay Pub Much like a tractor-pull with champagne, an ocean view with draft beer is hard to come by, but that's exactly what's on tap at this snazzy 70-seat hangout. Play pool, have a snack, or mingle with the jovial regulars. Sliding glass doors lead to a patio with a waterfront view. ■ *1253 Johnston St (Granville Island); 683-7373; full bar; every day.*

The Royal Hotel It's a Friday afternoon tradition—the whistle blows and downtown working stiffs trudge down to the Royal Hotel to rinse away their cares and woes. The Royal Hotel is a 238-seat, mostly gay pub with a pool table, dart board, pinball machines, and a stage that hosts live country, jazz, and blues Wednesday through Sunday. Friday is the hottest night, with a lineup from 5:30 to 9pm. ■ *1025 Granville St; 685-5335; full bar; open every day.*

The Yale To fully appreciate the blues, they should be enjoyed in the same atmosphere in which they were created—a tattered old room in the tough part of town. Welcome to the Yale. The building has been around for over 100 years, and so have many of the imported bluesmen who play there. The room is long and narrow, with a teeny stage that's hard to see from the back, but you can always squeeze yourself onto the stage-front dance floor for a closer peek. Suburban blues lovers and seedy-looking characters share the shabby surroundings. ■ *1300 Granville St; 681-YALE (9253); full bar; every day.*

The Bayside Room If you're looking for a cozy spot where you and your sweetie can look out over the ocean, don't overlook the Bayside Room. The decor is soft and loungelike, but things get rollicking on the weekend. Popular with the 25-to-40-year-olds. ■ *1755 Davie St; 682-1831; full bar; every day.*

Carnegie's Sax and sex combine with a delightful result in this very happening spot. The jazz is warm and mellow—so mellow it's ignored by most of the well-dressed singles who mingle in the stand-up lounge area. A pianist holds court with a special guest each night—perhaps a vocalist, a sax player, or a guitarist. Things heat up on Fridays, when many of the local Kits crowd stop by after work to commence the weekend festivities with a couple of cool ones in the warm, antique-oak environment. ■ *1619 W Broadway; 733-4141; full bar; open Mon-Sat.*

Delilah's Sandwiched between apartment buildings on a West End side street is one of the area's most popular hangouts. This snazzy little restaurant is credited with elevating the martini from its former status as something you might hear about in a Noel Coward play to its current status as the drink of choice, ordered in abundance by the regular patrons. You'll have to stand in the tiny lounge area up front, but with 16 varieties of martinis to choose from, it's worth the inconvenience. ■ *1906 Haro St; 687-3424; full bar; every day.*

Fiasco Fiasco has proven to be anything but for the owners of this trendy Evian watering hole, where meeting takes precedence over eating. In the Cal-Ital restaurant, the scent of a wood-burning oven mingles with the fragrance of expensive perfume, and designer clothing is de rigueur. Live R&B is the entertainment; expect long lines on Thursdays. ■ *2486 Bayswater St; 734-1325; full bar; every day.*

The Garden Lounge Sure to impress those out-of-town guests, the Garden Lounge is a stunning destination. A towering, atrium-style roof covers 130 seats set in a jungle of exotic foliage—an award-winning garden full of rare flora from Africa. The result is a soothing lounge where the soft clinking of cocktail glasses mingles with the soft tinkling of a grand piano. A drink will cost you what a case used to, but the decor is impressive. ■ *791 W Georgia St; 689-9333; full bar; closed Sun.*

Gerard Lounge (Le Meridien Hotel) How does the other half live? Very well, thank you, if this lounge in the Le Meridien Hotel is any indication. The decor is posh, with an understated elegance—about what you'd expect from Western Canada's best place for celebrity-watching. After a hard day on the set, the movie crews and stars repair to Gerard's to let their famous butts sink into the comfy couches around the fireplace. Kirstie

Alley, Richard Gere, Sharon Stone—if they're in town, they'll be at Gerard's eventually. There are only 50 seats, but a promenade with 25 more awaits, and you'll still hear the piano from there. ■ *845 Burrard St; 682-5511; full bar; every day.*

Hogan's Alley With its oak and brick livery and heritage building location, this intimate room is a superb spot to experience a musical menu that serves up smoking portions of Texas, Delta, and Southern blues. Plenty of major rock players hang out here and grace the stage. Members of Bryan Adams's and Colin James's bands, Loverboy, Long John Baldry, and even the Neville Brothers have dropped in recently. Enjoy a selection of local all-stars Tuesday to Thursday, local and import blues Friday and Saturday, and an open stage on Monday. ■ *730 Main St; 689-8645; full bar; every day.*

Joe Fortes Lawyers, stockbrokers—even decent people start their weekend festivities with a visit to the lounge area of this gorgeous restaurant named after a turn-of-the-century lifeguard. Friday afternoon finds it packed with well-heeled movers and shakers clad in suits and well-cut business attire. The mood is jubilant, and the decor resembles that of a U.S. chophouse. ■ *777 Thurlow; 669-1940; full bar; every day.*

Matches Who knows? You just may meet your match at Matches. This may look like your typical hotel lounge, but what the room lacks in personality is made up for by the personalities you'll meet there. In this crowd, over 35 is *not* over the hill. ■ *7551 Westminster Hwy, Richmond; 273-7878; full bar; every day.*

Mescalero Pretentious trendoids belly their flat stomachs up to the long oak bar and pack the front lounge area Gucci shoe to Gucci shoe on weekends. Leave your tractor-pull T-shirt in the closet and let everyone know you drive a "Vette" (no need to mention it's a Chevette). ■ *1215 Bidwell; 669-2399; full bar; every day.*

Rio Rio Food is served tapas-style, and plenty of expatriate Latins and hip west-siders come to party and have their libidos elevated by the sinewy sounds of the in-house Latin dance band known as Latin Connection. Clench a rose in your teeth, but if you're a rookie, remember to watch out for thorns. ■ *102 Water St; 685-1144; full bar; every day.*

Santos Tapas Down on the "Drive," the Sunday ritual is an afternoon visit to Santos Tapas Restaurant, where a live band churns out blues and rock with a Latin flavour. An interesting array of the colourful locals makes for great people-watching. ■ *1191 Commercial Dr; 253-0444; full bar; closed Mon.*

Uncle Charlie's Lounge ■ **Lotus Club** Perched where Chinatown, Skid Row, and Downtown converge, the antiquated Heritage House Hotel is a cultured oasis in a sea of decay. On the main floor is Uncle Charlie's Lounge, a toasty hide-away that caters to a gay crowd. A pair of opulent chandeliers, gorgeous antique furnishings, and warm colours complete the room. Snuggle into a cushy corner and swoon as the croon of Nat King Cole oozes from the speakers. Prices are reasonable, with a Sunday mug beer special that can't be beat. Down a flight of marble stairs is the Lotus Club, a small, pillared room where the ceiling is low and the attitude high. Line-dancers and two-steppers sashay on the smallish dance floor weeknights and Saturday. Friday night is "women-only." A bright spot in a blighted part of town. ■ *455 Abbott St; 685-7777; full bar; every day.*

Wedgewood Hotel Lounge Nestled in one of the city's best hotels, this elegant retreat is a 120-seat sensation. A piano player rules the roost midweek, and a combo sets up on weekends to serenade the imbibers with everything from soft rock to old standards. Attire is dressy, with wall-to-wall suits in attendance Friday and Saturday nights. Call ahead for a reservation. ■ *845 Hornby St; 689-7777; full bar; every day.*

POOL HALLS

Automotive The pool hall used to be strictly a male domain—a place where monosyllabic greasers, smelling of Brylcreem and leather, would congregate to smoke, squint, and swear. Automotive is an example of how much things have changed in Vancouver. This hip Yaletown billiard room is ensconced in a former auto dealership. White walls, a high ceiling, and abundant windows keep it bright and cheery, and the original garage door swings open (weather permitting) to keep the air as fresh as the juices and snacks that are offered up front. You'll wait anywhere from 15 minutes to an hour in the '60s-furnished holding lounge if you arrive between 8pm and 1am. ■ *1095 Homer St; 682-0040; alcohol Mon nights only; every day.*

Barracuda Like its namesake, Barracuda is aggressive—at least in its quest to put the pool hall in the forefront of Vancouver's entertainment scene. The atmosphere is darker than you'll find in Automotive but no less inviting. The floor is made of dark, weathered planks, and the walls combine rustic brick and soothing sponged blues. This former art gallery remains true to its history, with a revolving display of modern artistic works and hanging table lights fashioned from plumbing fixtures. Saturday night features a live band and dancing, and at lunchtime area workers pop in to take advantage of the exquisite food service. ■ *562 Beatty St; 687-6588; no alcohol; every day.*

Brownstone This new spot has already caught on as a lunch stop for the downtown business crowd, who seem to appreciate the streamlined, tasteful decor and tasty food. A sound system pumps out mellow jazz during the day and switches to rock when the sun goes down. All 10 pool tables are busy until 2am most nights. ■ *830 W Pender St; 684-7665; no alcohol; every day.*

Seymour Billiards This is the grand old man of Vancouver pool halls, an immense structure that's filled with 22 full-size snooker tables, six pool tables, and enough cigarette smoke to grow a tumour the size of a Buick. It's a grimy people-watcher's paradise, a grungy version of Noah's Ark, where you'll find at least two examples of virtually every form of humanity that can walk, crawl, or slither through the door. ■ *999 Seymour St; no phone; no alcohol; every day.*

Soho Cafe You can credit this establishment with instigating the wave of upscale pool haunts that are washing over the city. Since day one, the seats and pool tables have been full of Kitsilano yupsters and Yaletown hipsters. The walls are clad in the original rustic brick, and the place looks and feels super. The food alone is worth a visit. ■ *1144 Homer St; 688-1180; no alcohol; Mon-Sat.*

COFFEE AND TEA

See also Nightlife Index: Nonalcoholic

Bean Around The World Together with its sister store Bean #1 over in West Van, this retail roasting shop helps supply Vancouver's blossoming addiction to fresh-roasted beans. It's an inviting, cozy-sweater kind of place, serving a mix of sippers from early-bird exercisers and retired folk to students and parents with their kids. This coffeehouse (which serves lattes in a bowl) gives its beans a slightly lighter roast than many other beaneries. Not only does this preserve varietal distinctions, it provides more caffeine kick in the cup. There's a 45-cent discount if you provide the mug. ■ *4456 West 10th Ave; 222-1400; every day.*

The Bon Ton Sometime in the '30s, Italian-born Mr. Notte and French-born Mrs. Notte opened this tea shop. Second-generation Nottes still labour away behind the scenes, creating some of the most wickedly delicious pastries in the city: mocha filbert meringues, chocolate éclairs, Florentines, triple threats a-whirl with butter cream and chestnut paste. A selection under a plastic dome gets left on your table in the unassuming tearoom. Around teatime, you can have your tea leaves or tarot cards read by itinerant fortune-tellers. ■ *874 Granville St; 681-3058; Tues-Sat.*

British Home This experience, so authentic it causes tears to well in the eyes of expatriates, calls for a 40-minute drive from downtown to the fishing village of Steveston. Here, Ray and Mary Carter have duplicated the corner store you find on every street corner in Britain. If you've ever watched Corona-tion Street, you've seen its kind—shelves stocked with Mar-mite and steamed ginger pudding and other delicacies dear to the hearts of the British. From a counter backed by a wall crammed with pictures of royalty, the Carters dispense haggis, black pudding, boiled sweets, and tea. Jolly nice. ■ *3986 Moncton at #1 Rd, Steveston; 274-2261; every day.*

Cafe Fleuri (Le Meridien Hotel) Blissfully tranquil surroundings and a very civilized tea await those who venture through the ho-tel's chandeliered lobby. But what genre of tea? A simple pot of Chinese tea? Or the traditional Japanese tea ceremony with hand-whisked macha tea and bean jelly? Or a classic English tea? Most of the hotel guests, the corporate types, and the movie stars (celeb-spotting is a popular sport) go for the last. Fifteen bucks gets you finger sandwiches, pastries, scones, and cream. Half the price buys a duo of warm, currant-studded scones, a generous bowl of thick cream, and a trio of little pots of English preserves. ■ *845 Burrard St; 682-5511; Mon-Sat.*

Ciao Espresso Bar Smoking is practically mandatory at this smouldering '70s cafe. Here, black brew and tobacco provide the stimulus, for both the people who come to talk and the writers residing in worn booths. Try the Americano—an exquisitely thick and caramelly concoction with beautiful crema. Ciao also serves up a modest selection of Italian sandwiches, fresh juices, and desserts, including the popular low-fat muffins. ■ *1074 Denman St; 682-0112; beer and wine; every day.*

The Expressohead Coffee House Honey-coloured afternoon light slants through the generous south-facing windows while patrons work their way through provocative pleasures like Ex-presso Bolt, Steamed Moo, or Mario's Glory. The nonsmoking Expressohead has chosen its caterer well, offering outstanding desserts and yeast-free goodies from around the city. Renowned among Kitsilano regulars are the mile-high lemon meringue and hazelnut dacquoise. Why not add to your plea-sures with a unique take-home Berkley bean blend such as Sig-mund's Waltz or Zappatta Hot Wire? ■ *1945 Cornwall Ave; 739-1069; every day.*

The Gastown Garden Tea Room A rainy day tearoom that is as unpretentious as the sippers who take refuge here. The Gar-den offers 21 varieties of tea, as well as a fine cup of coffee, soups, sandwiches, and light entrées. High tea is served at any time and includes finger sandwiches, crumpets, scones, De-vonshire cream, and preserves. The occasional weathered dock worker ruminates over a pot of tea and scones with a friend who looks like Bruce Lee, making one feel more hip about sipping tea and munching dainties. ■ *342 Water St; 681-4666; every day.*

Hotel Vancouver The city's venerable grande dame among hostelries offers two locations for a cuppa: wing-back chairs and comfy sofas in the Lobby Lounge or the high-voltage urban appeal of Griffin's, with chrome-yellow walls, where tango-era tea dances were once held. A mere $1.95 gets you a silver pot of any one of 16 types of tea. But the biggest draw of all is the meal-size Garden Tea, which kicks off with sandwiches and pastries, segues into the scones, and caps it all off with strawberries and cream. ■ *900 West Georgia St; 684-3131; every day.*

Joe's Cafe Despite the seedy decor and laundromat lighting, Joe's has the feeling of a well-worn neighbourhood living room where intellectuals, bohemian philosophers, poets, feminists, and political agitators mix with pool-hustling locals. Joe's doesn't glamorize espresso or otherwise try to be popular; it just happens. Knowing hands prepare espresso standards, along with hybrids. But be prepared, after the last mouthful, cup and saucer are whisked out from under you and removed to the bar. This encourages you to get up and become part of the activity, play pool—or leave. ■ *1150 Commercial Dr; number unlisted; every day.*

▼
Coffee and Tea
▲

La Luna Lured inside by the smoky crackle of roasting beans, unsuspecting customers will find themselves in an angular cafe where halogen bulbs strung from exposed ductwork flare like stars. If it's on tap, ask for a sample of master roaster Peter Kleta's bean child, the Gastown blend. Or if you want to experience the java jitters (not a new band) quaff a Luna Cup, the equivalent of a double espresso run through twice. Caffeine collides with the shop's many pleasures, creating that marvellous, heady disturbance that the cafe's emblem suggests. ■ *117 Water St; 687-5862; other branches; every day.*

The Remarkable Dog What do you name a gift shop full of serendipitous finds with a tea shop attached whose fin de siècle decor includes a bar that once belonged to Maurice Chevalier's papa? You call it the Remarkable Dog, of course. The brain-pup of restaurant designers David Vance and Bronwen Wilson, this eclectic, delightfully oddball store became a must-see from the moment it opened. Cabbage-shaped tea cosies, teapot-shaped napkin rings, chinaware, hats, medieval jester slippers, and gourmet dog biscuits are all for sale. Tea can be supped as you sit on a bentwood chair at a tiny round table (you could be in Paris). It comes in a nice brown pot, and most people find room for a scone too. ■ *1735 Marine Dr, West Vancouver; 922-0334; every day.*

Starbucks Vancouver coffee bars can thank their lucky Starbucks for making coffee fashionable here in 1991. After a successful market probe of its first Vancouver location nearby, the Seattle-based company brought its ebony roast to Robson

Street and hit the jackpot. Service is rapid and drinks well executed by a highly trained young team of swirling baristas. Snag a cup on the run, or sit down in the sleek, Italian-style bar and put on your cheaters to eyeball and be eyeballed. Committed to freshness, Starbucks gives local charities any beans that do not sell in seven days. Like the company's other outlets, the shop stocks affordable and upscale brewing paraphernalia, including the ever-popular Bodum brewer. ■ *1099 Robson St; 685-1099; every day.*

The Tearoom at Plaza Escada Hidden away in this savagely pricey designer store is a coolly sophisticated, granite-and-black-leather spot for tea, the flagship Canadian venue for Banana Republic founder Mel Ziegler's "Republic of Tea." To showcase his exquisitely packaged offerings, this tearoom offers tea for free, provided you're content to sip Cinnamon Plum or Earl Greyer or whatever else they're sampling that day. Otherwise, it's three bucks a pop, a charge that they waive should you do any shopping, which is easy enough: surrounding you are the teas, the accoutrements of tea making such as handsomely designed teapots, and various gourmet nibbles, all highly tempting and all for sale. ■ *757 West Hastings St; 688-8558; Mon-Sat.*

Urban Expresso Hewed into the concrete base of a downtown building, this dimly lit grotto offers fast Coloiera coffee, sandwiches, salads, and baked edibles to the BC Tel bunch by day. By night, Urban's black brew fortifies the younger crowd while noise from the street blends with the pulse of the music and the hiss of the cappuccino maker. Bring your own mug to avoid paper cups. ■ *605 Robson St; 681-3987; every day.*

▼

Coffee and Tea

▲

THE ARTS

The Arts

The arts community is alive and thriving in Vancouver. Reflecting the diversity of the city, art events include multicultural festivals, traditional and innovative art forms, and impromptu events. In any given week, you may catch Shakespeare on the beach, opera by the lake, or music in the mountains.

The daily and weekly newspapers and event publications do a good job of providing current listings of a broad spectrum of events, but the **Arts Hotline** is probably the best source of up-to-date information. Staffed by the Vancouver Cultural Alliance (VCA), an umbrella service organization for some 200 members, the hotline is accessible 24 hours a day. Call 684-ARTS (2787), or visit the VCA's office at 938 Howe Street.

ART IN PUBLIC PLACES

Vancouverites make the most of their city's moderate climate, spending a lot of time outdoors. And the outdoors is almost as well decorated as the indoors. The brilliant banners that blossom on lamp standards in many of the city's main areas and on bridges are a 35-year-old institution, heralding the beginning of summer. BC artists who have designed banners include Jack Shadbolt, Bill Reid, Sam Black, Robert Davidson, Toni Onley, Barbara Shelly, and Joe Average. First sponsored by the city, local merchants' associations display their own banners in some areas. In the fall, some of these large works of art are sold at the Vancouver Museum Gift Shop (731-4158).

Vancouver is a festive city, and art is everywhere—in the air, on street corners, in parks, in gardens, and in public buildings. You can also find it in a few unexpected places. *The Search*, Seward Johnson's bronze of a woman rummaging in her purse while sitting on a park bench near the entrance to Stanley Park, has caused more than one motorist to do a double take. At Robson Square, Inuit artist Etungat's bronze *Bird of Spring* is solidly elegant. Outside 700 W Pender you can enjoy Robert Dow Reid's fibreglass *Canada Geese in Flight*. A memorial to the courage of a young man, Franklin Allen's *Terry Fox Memorial*, stands outside BC Place Stadium. Outside the Pacific Press building on Granville Street just south of the bridge is Jack Harman's *Family Group*, which caused a furor when it was unveiled in 1966, since the boy in the group is nude. Close by, on the grass near the bridge, is the stone carving *100*, which was erected in 1986 for Vancouver's centennial. In *Continuity*, the work of Letha Keate, two nude cherubic children balance on a log outside Brock House, 3975 Point Grey Road, near Jericho Beach. Farther west along the beach, at Spanish Bank West, is Christel Fuoss-Moore's fittingly nautical concrete *Anchor*.

The lobby of the Waterfront Hotel displays a map of Captain George Vancouver's third and final voyage, in 1790, to the Pacific Northwest. Beautifully hung on a mirrored wall, the antiqued map, titled *Voyage of Discovery*, includes hand-lettered quotes from his journal, some proclaiming that the Strait of Juan de Fuca does not exist. The map was created by Emily Standley and Peggy Vanbianchi of Seattle, Washington. The main wall of the Garden Lounge of the Four Seasons Hotel is dominated by a large, striking Inuit felt hanging appliquéd with caribou-skin figures depicting objects from everyday Inuit life. These seals, bears, sleds, huskies, and fishermen are the work of Susan Sinnisiaks Seelo of Eskimo Point, Northwest Territories.

First-time visitors to the airy atrium of the Hongkong Bank of Canada Building on Georgia Street invariably duck when they see the 27.5-metre-long (90-foot-long) shining pendulum of buffed aluminum gliding silently toward them. Suspended 30.5 metres (100 feet) above the floor, the pendulum, by BC sculptor Alan Storey, has a hypnotic rhythm.

Art that reacts to people adorns the lobby of Cathedral Place on West Georgia. A vast fragment of fractured glass and brass circles called *Navigational Device*, by local artist Robert Studer, has lights and brass pipes that respond to the movement and number of people in the lobby. The device, which was found on Lyell Island in the Queen Charlotte Islands, is a mythical icon. The etched hieroglyphics on the glass are indecipherable. Around the corner in the lobby of Park Place, a glowing pink glass high rise, hangs a brilliant weaving by fibre artist Joanna Staniszkis. Woven in wonderfully tactile strips, the hanging echoes scenes from the busy harbour nearby—mountains, ocean, buildings, and boats. Although it is impossible to outdo nature in Vancouver, the vast ceramic mural *The Fathomless Richness of the Seabed* comes close. Myriad textures of the ocean floor—ripple marks, fronds of coral, tubes and vents, the movement of currents, and the supple shapes of sea creatures—are captured in gentle shades of blue, green, cream, and tan. This work by Québec artist Jordi Bonet is in the lobby of the Guinness Tower on West Hastings.

Vancouver's parks and gardens contain many sculptures and fountains. **Stanley Park** alone has about 24, many of which are mentioned elsewhere in this book. The UBC campus is also home to at least 20 excellent works, but any mention of public art is incomplete if it doesn't include Charles Marega's pair of concrete lions guarding the south end of the Lions Gate Bridge.

GALLERIES

Inside, outside, upstairs, and downstairs, Vancouver has a wealth of public and private galleries. Many are on South Granville Street, throughout downtown, in Gastown, or on Granville Island. Small galleries and artists' spaces are popping up, or relocating, to the area around Victory Square (Hastings and Cambie). It's worth exploring the area for new developments.

Artist-run spaces include the refreshingly irreverent **Western Front** (876-9343), now a quarter of a century old, **Video In/Video Out** (872-8337), and **Basic Inquiry** (681-2855).

Many of Vancouver's galleries and the Vancouver Museum participate in **First Thursday**, a monthly art night sponsored by the Vancouver Cultural Alliance. On the first Thursday of each month, the galleries stay open in the evening for people unable to visit during usual hours. The Vancouver Art Gallery has a pay-what-you-can evening every Thursday. For details call the **Arts Hotline** (684-ARTS/2787) or the **Vancouver Cultural Alliance** (681-3535).

ART

Bau-Xi Gallery One of Vancouver's oldest private galleries, the Bau-Xi specializes in the works of Canadian artists such as the venerable Jack Shadbolt, Tony Urquhart, and Joe Plaskett. Uncrowded paintings are displayed against a minimalist background. Open storage allows visitors access to a lot more than what's on display. ■ *3045 Granville St at 14th; 733-7011; Mon–Sat 9:30am–5:30pm.*

Burnaby Art Gallery Housed in an elegant heritage building, with sweeping staircases, curved wooden railings, and leaded glass windows, this gallery specializes in 20th-century art, which is shown to advantage in this gracious setting. ■ *6344 Deer Lake Ave; 291-9441; Tues–Fri 9am–5pm, Sat–Sun 12pm–5pm.*

Buschlen–Mowatt Gallery This modern gallery on the edge of Stanley Park, overlooking Coal Harbour, specializes in international contemporary art, from the truly challenging, avant-garde to huge, splashy romantic works. Artists include Bill Reid, Andre Brasilier, Yehouda Chaki, Ted Harrison, and Bernard Cathelin, to name a few. ■ *111-1445 W Georgia St; 682-1234; Mon–Sat 10am–6pm, Sun 12pm–5pm.*

Diane Farris Gallery The almost-industrial feeling of this gallery is not an accident. Farris specializes in artists who work on enormous canvasses, and the moveable walls and high ceilings are essential. Farris nurtures many young artists, including enfant terrible Attila Richard Lukacs, who has the international art world lining up at his Berlin studio door. The cutting edge of contemporary local and national art. ■ *1565 W 7th Ave; 737-2629; Tues–Fri 10am–5:30pm, Sat 10am–5pm.*

Equinox Gallery Another long-established, serious Vancouver gallery, the Equinox Gallery handles only the very best North American painters and graphic artists. Works are beautifully displayed in serene surroundings. ■ *2321 Granville St; 736-2405; Tues–Sat 10am–5pm.*

Federation Gallery The Federation of Canadian Artists runs this delightfully elegant gallery and workshop, which presents the works of many of British Columbia's best artists. Group of Seven artist Lawren Harris was its first president in 1941. Less formal than many other art spaces, the gallery displays excellent exhibits that change frequently. ■ *1241 Cartwright St, Granville Island; 681-8534; Tues–Sun 10am–4pm.*

Foto Base Gallery This new Gastown gallery specializes in photography and photo-related art. The exhibitions of eclectic works from the camera may help answer the age-old conundrum, "It's photography, but is it art?" ■ *231 Carrall St; 687-7465; Tues–Sat 12pm–6pm.*

Heffel Gallery Elegantly housed in a historic stone building, the Heffel Gallery specializes in works by the august **Group of Seven** and many respected Canadian landscape artists. Exhibits can be spread over three floors, with lots of little spaces for quiet contemplation of a special work. ■ *2247 Granville St at 6th; 732-6505; Mon–Sat 10am–6pm.*

John Ramsay Contemporary Art This gallery has an exciting roster of contemporary artists whose work may be bold and beautiful or small and exquisite but is always respected across the continent. Shows range from cool still lifes to the starkly contemporary. ■ *1065 Cambie St; 685-5570; Tues–Sat 10:30am–5:30pm, Sun 12pm–5pm.*

Presentation House One of the oldest galleries in the city that is still faithful to photographic art. From elegant black and white to contemporary full colour, exhibitions are exciting and beautifully showcased in this attractive older building. ■ *333*

Chesterfield Ave, North Vancouver; 986-1351; Wed, Fri–Sun 12pm–5pm, Thurs 12pm–9pm.

Richmond Art Gallery Local and international artists are exhibited at this gallery, which is also very involved in the community. Each show has programming for children and adults, including such events as artist-run workshops, talks, and tours. Every spring a show is specifically mounted for children. ▪ *180 Minoru Park Plaza, 7700 Minoru Gate, Richmond; 231-6440; Mon–Fri 9am–9pm, Sat–Sun 10am–5pm.*

Surrey Art Gallery This cool, spacious gallery is part of the Surrey Arts Centre and benefits from strong community involvement. Exhibitions range from soothing to cutting-edge contemporary and from local to international. The gallery and the arts centre hold imaginative art-appreciation programs for adults and children. ▪ *13750-88th Ave, Surrey; 596-7461; Mon–Thurs 9am–8:30pm, Fri 9am–5pm, Sat–Sun 1pm–5pm.*

UBC Fine Arts Gallery Ever-changing exhibitions of contemporary art are featured at this gallery. It also hosts lecture series and special events. ▪ *1956 Main Mall, Main Library, UBC; 822-2759; Tues–Fri 10am–5pm, Sat 12pm–5pm.*

Vancouver Art Gallery See Major Attractions in the Exploring chapter.

NORTHWEST COAST INDIAN AND INUIT ART

Galleries

Art

Gallery of Tribal Art The main focus of this gallery is Northwest Coast Indian art, but exhibits also include art from aboriginal Australia and Papua New Guinea. ▪ *2329 Granville St; 732-4555; Tues–Sat 10am–6pm.*

Images for a Canadian Heritage This large Gastown gallery specializes in Northwest Coast native wood carvings, which account for the gallery's pleasantly aromatic smell, and Eskimo carvings in stone and bone, as well as graphics and some crafts. It also carries stone carvings by BC artists and houses a wide variety of limited-edition prints and art works. ▪ *164 Water St; 685-7046; Mon–Sat 10am–6pm, Sun 12pm–5pm.*

Inuit Gallery This longtime Gastown gallery has a well-deserved reputation as North America's leading Inuit art gallery. Collectors from across the globe buy here, and some of the beautifully produced show catalogues are collector's items. Northwest Coast work includes masks, wood carvings, and jewellery. Gallery employees know their subject and are usually delighted to share their knowledge. ▪ *345 Water St; 688-7323; Mon–Sat 10am–6pm, Sun 12pm–5pm.*

Leona Lattimer Gallery Housed in a traditional cedar longhouse on the edge of Granville Island, this gallery has an impressive collection of Northwest Coast Indian art. Works vary from limited-edition prints to carvings and from bent boxes and masks to button blankets. In addition, the gallery displays traditionally engraved gold and silver jewellery and some argillite carvings. ■ *1590 W 2nd Ave; 732-4556; Mon–Fri 10am–6pm, Sat–Sun 10am–5pm.*

Marion Scott Gallery One of the oldest galleries around specializing in traditional Inuit and Northwest Coast Indian art. Some contemporary work, including the ubiquitous cat in many delightful works, are often displayed in this comfortable downtown gallery. ■ *801 W Georgia St; 685-1934; Mon–Sat 9:30am–5:30pm, Sun 10am–5pm.*

The Three Vets Vancouver's best-kept native art secret. Behind all the outdoor equipment, clothing, and great little gadgets is a gallery/storage room filled with Northwest native art from more than 300 of BC's native people. Paintings, prints, masks, carvings, jewellery, rattles, talking sticks, bowls, and plaques are all represented, collected over 10 years by curator Jerry Wolfman. ■ *2200 Yukon St; 872-5475; Mon–Thurs 9am–6pm, Fri 9am–8:30pm, Sat 9am–6pm.*

CRAFT

The Canadian Craft Museum See Museums in this chapter.

Circle Craft Unique pottery, creative weaving, innovative jewellery, and challenging toys are just some of the items displayed in this cooperative gallery. The work is all jury selected and is the best of the best. ■ *1-1666 Johnston St, Granville Island; 669-8201; every day, 10am–6pm.*

Crafthouse Gallery This popular nonprofit gallery/shop on Granville Island is run by the Crafts Association of BC. An amazing array of clay, glass, fibre, metal, wood, and papier-mâché pieces illustrate the many talents of BC's finest craftspeople. A small side gallery showcases something special each month. ■ *1386 Cartwright St, Granville Island; 687-7270; Tues–Sun 10am–5:30pm.*

Gallery of BC Ceramics The teapot as a functional work of art is quite the norm in this gallery, which showcases the sometimes-amazing pottery of more than 60 BC artists. From funky to beautiful, useful to decorative, there isn't a clunky piece in sight. ■ *1359 Cartwright St, Granville Island; 669-5645; Tues–Sun 10:30am–5:30pm.*

Robert Held Art Glass Watch how glass is blown in this cavernous workshop/studio where the red-hot furnaces lend an unreal background to the exquisite works of art created by local artisans. Elegant vases, goblets, glasses, candlesticks, and decorative pieces are swirled through with colour, emphasizing their unique, fragile shapes. ■ *2130 Pine St; 737-0020; Mon–Sat 9am–5pm.*

CHORAL

Choral music is always popular and enjoys a healthy following locally. Both amateur and professional groups, such as the Vancouver Cantata Singers, the Vancouver Chamber Choir, and the Vancouver Bach Choir, perform in the various theatres, hotels, and churches throughout Vancouver. The **Vancouver Bach Choir** (921-8012) is known for its adventurous repertoire, and the **Elektra Women's Chorus** always dazzles audiences with its exquisite renditions of works that span the generations. The **Vancouver Men's Chorus** is also highly popular and well supported and has its own season. For choral phone listings and all other arts information, call the Arts Hotline at 684-ARTS.

DANCE

British Columbia is developing a reputation as a hotbed of contemporary dance, attracting dancers and independent choreographers from all over Canada, the United States, and abroad who offer lively and original performances to appreciative audiences. Look for regular programs by Vancouver-based choreographers Jennifer Mascall and Judith Marcuse.

Dance

Ballet British Columbia Since its inception in the mid-'80s, BC's premier contemporary ballet company has earned a glowing reputation for its bold, exciting performances. Under the artistic directorship of noted choreographer John Alleyne, the energetic company offers dance enthusiasts a potpourri of modern and classical dance each September through June as part of its popular Dance Alive series. Five programs and three special events each season range from the exquisite grace of Canada's National Ballet to the invigorating passion of Alvin Ailey's Dance Theatre of America. Ballet BC performs two programs each season, including Canadian or world premieres of innovative works by master choreographers. ■ *Queen Elizabeth Theatre, Hamilton St at W Georgia St; 669-5954.*

Dancing on the Edge Festival Dubbed North America's largest festival of independent choreographers, this two-week celebration of new dance, held each September, attracts international leaders in choreography from around the globe. Always fresh and daring, some 60 to 70 shows are offered throughout the day from early afternoon to the wee hours of the morning. Venues are as adventurous as the dance itself—from Vancouver's incomparable beaches to traditional stages. ■ *689-0926.*

Firehall Arts Centre The Firehall Arts Centre Dance Series presents contemporary dance productions October through June. A cousin of the avant-garde Dancing on the Edge Festival, the Firehall series continues the tradition of presenting the best of independent choreographers as well as local and national modern dance companies, including Karen Jamieson Dance Company, Jumpstart performances, and Kokoro Dance. The Firehall also presents several theatre productions each season, with an emphasis on Canadian theatre that reflects the cultural diversity of the nation. Resident companies are Touchstone and Axis Mime, which, in addition to performing at the Firehall, also tour. Axis Mime puts on plays for children in schools throughout the province. ■ *280 E Cordova St; 689-0926.*

Vancouver East Cultural Centre See Theatre in this chapter.

FILM

Vancouver is often called Hollywood North and stargazing is no longer the novelty it was a decade ago. Hollywood discovered Vancouver in 1969, when Director Robert Altman encountered the adaptable charms of the city while filming *That Cold Day in the Park*. Since then, the film industry has burgeoned, becoming one of the leading money makers for the province and attracting international filmmakers. The list of stars who have worked in the area during recent years grows steadily: Warren Beatty, Julie Christie, Mel Gibson, Goldie Hawn, Tom Selleck, Kirstie Alley, John Travolta, Richard Gere, Sharon Stone, Mickey Rourke, Steve Martin, Daryl Hannah, Glenn Close, Robert De Niro, John Candy, Chuck Norris, Jodie Foster, Sylvester Stallone, Richard Dreyfuss, Johnny Depp.

▼

Dance

▲

American producers flock to Vancouver to shoot movies and television features. They say we have some of the best alleys for shooting films in North America. The most-used locations in Vancouver are the **Vancouver Art Gallery** on Hornby Street (Jodie Foster and Kelly McGillis shot their courtroom scenes for *The Accused* here), **Blood Alley** just off Carrall Street in Gastown, and the alley south of Hastings Street between Cambie and Abbott streets (both of these alleys are featured in *Another Stakeout* with Emilio Estevez and Richard Dreyfuss). Both the interior and exterior of **500 Seymour Street** are well used; Hume Cronyn shot scenes here for the TV movie *Christmas on Division Street*.

Mansions in the Shaughnessy area of the city are also used constantly as locations. Many were built around the turn of the century by resource barons. Most of the residents seem to enjoy having film companies in their neighbourhood, and many are only too happy to move out of their houses for a few weeks, have their homes redecorated by professional movie designers, and at the end of the shoot, receive a fat cheque.

For up-to-the-minute local movie news read Friday columns in the *Vancouver Sun* (City Lights) and the *Province* (the Insider). Entertainment reporter **Lynne McNamara** interviews the stars in locally shot movies on BCTV's *Star Tracks* (cable 11) every Monday at 5:20pm. *Playback*, a tabloid-format industry newspaper, publishes every two weeks; *Reel West* is a bimonthly industry magazine. *Reel West Digest*, published annually, lists production personnel, studios, performers, writers, and agents. It can be picked up at most major newsstands or ordered by calling 294-4122. *The Hip List* (925-1149) is a tiny, annually updated collection of cool and groovy places to hang out that was first published for visiting producers and stars who wanted to find the best eateries, boutiques, and the like. The BC Film Commission's *Film List* of projects currently in production may be picked up at the BC Business Info Centre, main floor, 601 West Cordova, weekdays between 8:30am and 4:30pm. Or call **The B.C. Film Commission Hot Line** (660-3569) for film-listing updates.

If you'd like to see yourself on the big screen just once, or if you'd like to be an extra, there are lots of opportunities here. You'll like the work if you're already financially secure, your ego is intact, and you don't take the whole thing too seriously. The hours are long, the food's mediocre (you don't get to eat with the stars), the money isn't great (about $11 an hour), the work is sporadic, and you'll be herded around like a heifer on a cattle drive. But hey, you might get to meet your favourite star. Extras casting is done by several local agencies. Try **Universal** at 689-9056 or **Local Color** at 685-0315. You'll need a few head shots for their files, and you may be required to pay a one-time fee (between $20 and $40) to register. Other talent agencies include **The Characters**, 733-9800; **Lucas Talent**, 685-0345; **Twentyfirst Century Artists Inc**, 669-7486; and **Carrier Talent Management, Inc.**, 669-6199.

The **Vancouver International Film Festival**, in its 12th year, is the third-largest in North America and typically presents more than 350 screenings of some 200 first-run feature films from over 40 countries. Every October, viewers can catch the traditional to the avant-garde, the obscure to the mainstream from a selection of documentaries, dramatic features, animated shorts, and comedies new to the Vancouver scene.

Film festival fans frequent the **Dunbar** (228-9912), **Vancouver Centre Cinemas** (669-4442), **Starlight** (689-0096), and **Varsity** (222-2235) cinemas, where they can find an eclectic selection of independent movies and where they can often catch screenings missed during the festival. The **Ridge** (Arbutus and 16th Avenue; 738-6311) and the **Hollywood** (3123 W Broadway; 738-3211) are home to the popular, inexpensive, second-run double bills. The **Denman Place Discount Cinema** (683-2201) has triple bills. **Pacific Cinématique** (688-FILM) is touted as a year-round film festival offering retrospectives of important directors, lectures series, classic foreign films, and a variety of independent and experimental Canadian films.

Film

Screenings are evenings only, six days a week, excluding Tuesdays, when the mega-theatres drop their prices.

Two blocks along Granville Street, and many of the city's malls, boast multiplex theatres run by the corporate giants Cineplex Odeon and Famous Players, screening Hollywood's latest multimillion-dollar extravaganzas. The **Omnimax Theatre** at Vancouver's Science World (268-6363) and **CN IMAX Theatre** at Canada Place (682-IMAX) offer film lovers a new dimension with omnipresent screens. Both are legacies of Expo 86.

THEATRE

Vancouver's theatre scene is flourishing, offering a mosaic of live performances from glorious extravaganzas to impromptu events and practically everything in between. Two large-scale companies and many small, innovative groups keep theatregoers entertained year-round with a wealth of diverse performances. The University of British Columbia, Simon Fraser University, and Langara Community College mount excellent productions while classes are in session. Other companies, performing in Vancouver and on tour, include Pink Ink; the Headlines Theatre Company, which does powerplay theatre, concentrating on plays about social issues; and the Tamahnous Theatre, which gave much of the city's senior talent its start.

Arena Theatre Company The eccentric charm of suburban White Rock includes a quietly successful summer theatre company. Founded in 1976, the company offers three plays—one thriller, one comedy, one classic work—in repertory from late June through the end of August. Some programs are based on a theme, whereas others are simply a blend of popular plays. ■ *N Bluff Rd at Anderson, White Rock; 536-1343.*

The Arts Club Theatre Situated in the heart of lively Granville Island, the Arts Club Theatre and the neighbouring Arts Club Revue Theatre, run by Bill Millerd, have become local institutions. This is the largest regional theatre in Western Canada, and the year-long offerings on the main stage include a smorgasbord of drama, comedy, and musical classics, with a focus on 20th-century works. For those who enjoy a drink with their theatre, the cabaret-style Revue Theatre is the perfect spot for light theatre and musical comedy. Intermission on the False Creek dock or at the bustling Arts Club bar is an added attraction. The bar, which supports the theatre, has its own programs and is also a popular spot to hang out with musicians and artists and enjoy some music. ■ *The Arts Club Revue Theatre, 1585 Johnston St, Granville Island; 687-1644.*

Bard on the Beach Imagine—Shakespeare all summer long, set against a magnificent backdrop of city, sea, and mountains. Colourful red and white tents provide the stage for the two

Shakespearean masterpieces that are offered in repertory during the summer months. Come as you are in comfortable and layered clothing—the sunsets are breathtaking, but it can be cool. Ticket prices are not quite as low as 17th-century levels, but they are a pleasant surprise nonetheless. Cushions recommended. ▪ *Vanier Park; 733-1910 (summer tickets); 325-5955 (year-round).*

The Burnaby Arts Centre So successful is this performance and teaching centre that it has outgrown its current space and is raising money to expand. Although it holds some performances, the centre focuses on teaching visual and performing arts. Classes include dance, film, acting, photography, stage managing, pottery, painting, and piano. The Centre's best-known graduates are Michael J. Fox and the Kimura-Parker brothers. ▪ *6450 Deer Lake Ave, Burnaby; 291-6864.*

Firehall Arts Centre See Dance in this chapter.

The Fringe Festival The good, the bad, and the ugly are on show every September at the second-largest fringe theatre festival in North America. Billed as "an uncensored opportunity for performers to express ideas, challenge conventions, and stage innovative works with minimum financial risk," this 10-day theatre extravaganza features performers spanning all ages and levels of experience. The 100 performers are accepted on a first-come, first-served basis—there is no juried process—and content includes everything from outrageous comedy to challenging drama to performance art. Performances are held in various venues; admission is reasonable, since performers set their own ticket prices. ▪ *Various locations; 873-3646.*

Theatre

Queen Elizabeth Theatre and Playhouse On the Queen E's spacious stage, gorgeous glitz and glitter are commonplace. This elegant, comfortable 2,800-plus-seat theatre is Vancouver's main venue for the lavish large-scale touring musicals, dance companies, and special musical events that frequently add an international flavour to Vancouver's already-multi-faceted entertainment scene. ▪ *649 Cambie St; 665-3050.*

Theatre Under the Stars [KIDS] The sweetly familiar strains of "Some Enchanted Evening" take on new meaning at a performance of Theatre Under the Stars (TUTS). Two Broadway musicals are offered in repertory from mid-July through mid-August each summer in Canada's only truly open-air theatre. Casts feature a combination of professional and amateur performers, lending the event a wonderful enthusiasm that makes for perfect family entertainment. Festival seating accommodates some 1,200 people amid a spectacular backdrop of forests, stars, and the moon—who could ask for anything more? Bring a cushion and warm clothing. ▪ *Malkin Bowl, Stanley Park; 687-0174.*

Vancouver East Cultural Centre [KIDS] This beautifully restored 1914 church is one of Vancouver's most intriguing performance venues, where the tried and true shares the stage with the brand new. Known to locals simply as the Cultch, the centre makes diversity the key ingredient in its programming. Music to keep your toes tapping or your heart swelling, daring dance, alternative theatre, and performance art all come alive in this intimate 350-seat theatre space. Home to Masterpiece Music, a delightful six-Sunday chamber music series, where the city's top musicians gather to pool their creative talents. The popular Kids' Series offers theatre, music, and madness for children, including a performance by the highly acclaimed resident company Green Thumb Theatre for Young People, which specializes in developing lighthearted and intelligent scripts based on complex social issues. ▪ *1895 E Venables St; 254-9578.*

Vancouver International Children's Festival See Parks and Beaches in the Exploring chapter.

Vancouver International Comedy Festival [KIDS] They call it the funniest festival of all. For 10 days at the beginning of every August, Granville Island is transformed into a veritable comedy lover's paradise. With more than 100 free performances and some 30 ticketed events, mime artists, jugglers, and comedians seem to be everywhere. From noon to five each afternoon, roaming performers entertain onlookers, and each evening paying audiences savour the humour in clubs around the city. Performers hail from around the globe, but as the saying goes, the language of a smile is universal. ▪ *683-0883.*

▼
Theatre
▲

The Vancouver Playhouse Theatre Company The Vancouver Playhouse is the biggest show in town, producing six shows during its October through May season. One of western Canada's largest regional theatre companies, the Playhouse blends the classic and the modern in its repertoire, including Canadian premieres and Broadway plays. The Playhouse recently celebrated its 30th anniversary and welcomed a new artistic director, Susan Cox, who came West from the Shaw Festival. Cox plans to continue the company's successful formula, but she also wants to "celebrate the imagination of the artist, the playfulness and whimsy, romance, fantasy, passion, and truth of the theatre." The Playhouse is home to many of Canada's finest actors, and productions are invariably top quality, with spectacular sets, luscious costumes, and terrific soundscapes. ▪ *Vancouver Playhouse, Hamilton St at Dunsmuir St; 873-3311.*

Vancouver Theatresports League Murder, talk shows, politics— nothing is sacred when in the hands of the Vancouver Theatresports League. A five-time world improvisational champion, Theatresports offers hilarious, affordable late-night entertainment seven nights a week at the cozy Back Alley Theatre. The content of this Canadian creation varies—on any given night, the 30-member ensemble might improvise on a specific theme, satirize the hottest TV shows, or stage competitions in which three-member teams vie for audience approval as they create vignettes based on audience suggestions. Expect the riotously unexpected. ■ *Back Alley Theatre, 751 Thurlow St; 688-7013.*

MUSEUMS

From large, world-renowned museums to tiny specialized collections tucked into remote corners, Vancouver has museums for everyone, from aviation buffs to those who are interested in ancient cultures and even those who are considering cloning a dinosaur.

BC Museum of Mining [KIDS] [FREE] Take an hour-long drive along the scenic Upper Levels Highway toward Squamish to this mine site and museum, which have recently been declared a National Historic Site. The old Britannia Copper Mine, which in the 1920s was one of the largest copper mines in the world, once processed more than 6.4 million kilograms (14.1 million pounds) of ore daily. Guided underground tours on electric trains give a glimpse of what working life was like for the miners, and there are demonstrations of diamond drilling and copper mining. The museum contains exhibits of hundreds of old photographs, artifacts, and a slideshow. You can also pan for gold. "Colours" guaranteed means visitors are sure to find traces of gold dust in their pans. ■ *Take Highway 99 to Britannia Beach on Howe Sound; 688-8735 or 896-2233; open May 15 to Oct 11. Prearranged tours all year.*

Burnaby Village Museum [KIDS] A delightful re-creation of a turn-of-the-century town, built to honour BC's centennial in 1958. Step backwards through time and visit a blacksmith's shop, a sawmill, a printer, and much more. There are more than 30 buildings and outdoor displays depicting daily life from 1890 to 1925, including an 1890 dentist's office. Authentically costumed "residents" welcome you into their homes—which might be a pioneer log cabin—and workplaces. A church and schoolhouse are also shown, and the ice-cream parlour is operational. A miniature train, the Burnaby Central Railway, takes children for a ride around the village. A lovingly restored 1912 carousel, called "Carry-us-All," was once an attraction at the Pacific National Exhibition. Kids and adults alike will delight in a ride on this beautiful antique. ■ *6501 Deer Lake Ave, Burnaby; 293-6501. Open seasonally, call for information.*

Canadian Craft Museum [KIDS] [FREE] Located off the elegant courtyard behind the impressive facade of Cathedral Place, the

Canadian Craft Museum is Canada's first national museum devoted to crafts. Local, national, and international pieces all emphasize the beauty of handmade items and reflect the patience and care that go into these mostly one-of-a-kind pieces. A permanent collection and changing exhibits include everything from fragile glass perfume bottles to large pieces of furniture. Exhibits include tapestries, pottery, glass, jewellery, baskets, and sculptures. There is an excellent gallery gift shop. ■ *639 Hornby St (in the courtyard of Cathedral Place); 687-8266; Mon–Sat 9:30am–5:30pm, Sun 12pm–5pm.*

Canadian Museum of Flight and Transportation [KIDS] The fascination of vintage aircraft is evident in this Surrey outdoor museum, which has a great collection of early aircraft that seem too fragile to fly. The transparent skin of a lumbering World War II supply plane, the Lysander, reveals just how they do fly. Early flying machines on display include a Tiger Moth and a Flying Banana helicopter. There is also a short runway, as well as old trucks and fire engines and some military machines. Those interested in the technical side of things can browse in the library and the gift shop. The museum is an hour's drive from downtown Vancouver. Admission: $3 adult, $2 youth, $10 family (two adults and up to four youths), under 6 free; every day. ■ *13527 Crescent Rd, Surrey; 535-1115. Open seasonally, call for information.*

▼

Museums

▲

Geology Museum—UBC [KIDS] [FREE] Pieces of glowing amber and 80-million-year-old *Lambeosaurus* dinosaur bones are just some of the treasures to be found in this fascinating place. Displays of glittering crystals and minerals, as well as fossils that are so beautiful they outshine gemstones, encompass about 4.5 billion years of mineral and fossil history. More than 9,000 specimens are displayed. Collector Shop, open Wednesday afternoons. ■ *Geological Science Centre, UBC; 822-5586; Mon-Fri.*

Hastings Mill Store Museum [FREE] The handmade glass is wavy and distorts the beach scene visible through the windows, but it only adds to the charm of this cluttered museum inside Vancouver's oldest building, one of only a handful to survive the fire of 1886. Set in a little park beside the Royal Vancouver Yacht Club, this building started life as a company store for a lumber operation and, before Vancouver became a city, was the fledgling town of Granville's first post office. Old muskets, Indian baskets, satin clothing, chiming clocks, and a coach are only some of the items sheltered in the cool, dim interior. ■ *1575 Alma St; 228-1213; open weekends June through mid-September.*

Museum of Anthropology [KIDS] "Stunning" seems an inadequate word to describe this incredible soaring glass and concrete building overlooking the Strait of Georgia. From the moment you walk through the carved wooden doors it is difficult to know which is more awe-inspiring—the building or its contents. In the Great Hall, monumental totem poles with carvings of ravens, bears, eagles, frogs, and beavers gaze into the distance, seemingly imbued with the spirit of their Northwest Coast Indian artisans. Spotlit on the podium of the Great Hall is Haida artist Bill Reid's *The Raven and the First Men*, depicting how raven opened a clamshell and the first people emerged. The museum uses visible storage—visitors are encouraged to open any of the hundreds of drawers that contain one of the most comprehensive collections of Northwest Coast native culture in the world. A ceramic wing, displays of intricately engraved gold and silver jewellery, argillite (black slate) sculptures, baskets, and ceremonial masks are also displayed. Besides this amazing permanent collection, there are ever-changing temporary exhibits and many special events. The gift shop is excellent. [FREE] Tuesdays, admission is free.

[KIDS] [FREE] Outside, between the museum and the Point Grey cliffs, is another display. Totem poles tower over grassy knolls and two beautifully carved Haida buildings—a family dwelling and a mortuary chamber, which blend perfectly into the cliff-side setting. Signs give information about the animals that are represented on the poles, as well as the history of the buildings. You can enjoy the totem poles and the breathtaking views from this little park whether the museum is open or not. ■ *UBC, 6393 NW Marine Dr; 822-3825; Tues 11am–9pm, Wed–Sun 11am–5pm.*

Museums

Vancouver Maritime Museum and *St. Roch* [KIDS] Vancouver's seagoing tradition is spectacularly documented in this museum, suitably perched on the southern shore of English Bay. A Kwakiutl totem pole stands in front of the entrance, a replica of the 30.5-metre (100-foot) pole presented to Queen Elizabeth to mark BC's 1958 centennial. The museum is the home of the 1928 ketch the *St. Roch*, now a National Historic Site. This Royal Canadian Mounted Police patrol boat was the first sailing vessel to navigate the Northwest Passage from west to east, a dangerous voyage that took 28 months. The museum's permanent displays honour the city's growth as a port, the modern fishing industry, and 18th-century explorers. Subjects of temporary exhibits have included the ill-fated *Titanic* and whale watching. The museum also holds workshops, talks, and demonstrations, all with a nautical flavour. ■ *1905 Ogden Ave, Vanier Park; 257-8300; every day from July to mid-September, Tues–Sun remainder of the year.*

Vancouver Museum [KIDS] Part of the planetarium complex, this museum has a white, cone-shaped roof based on the woven hats worn by Coast Salish people. Thousands of artifacts

include archaeological and ethnological items, ceremonial objects, carvings, and intricate masks, both ancient and contemporary. Displays feature the early settlement of the BC coast, the pioneers, and the growth of Vancouver from a rough-and-ready mill town to a major city in less than 100 years. Memorabilia range from railroad passenger cars and a replica of a sawmill to elaborate 19th-century evening dresses, Victorian bedrooms, and beautifully carved native cradles. Regularly changing exhibits run the gamut from wildlife art to royal commemoratives. Admission: $5 adult, $2.50 seniors and students, seniors free on Tuesdays. ▪ *Vanier Park, 1100 Chestnut St; 736-7736; every day May through Sept; Tues–Sun Oct through April.*

Vancouver Police Centennial Museum [FREE] From clues to ancient unsolved murders to gambling displays to counterfeit money, this little museum has it all. Old photographs from the days when the police wore British bobby helmets contrast with gleaming modern guns and the grim faces of some of Vancouver's most notorious crooks. Uniforms, badges, and other artifacts are also on display. A recent addition is a forensic pathology display in the old city morgue, which isn't for everybody. Exhibits include graphic photographs and bullet-riddled skulls. ▪ *240 East Cordova St; 665-3346; Mon–Fri Sept through April, Mon–Sat May through Aug.*

▲

MUSIC SERIES

Vancouver has always enjoyed a vital music scene, but over the last decade the city has witnessed a renaissance in the proliferation of classical, jazz, and world music. Musical institutions such as the Vancouver Symphony and the Vancouver Opera have spread their wings, and smaller chamber music series are flourishing.

Coastal Jazz and Blues Society and the du Maurier Jazz Festival It's the rebirth of cool. Jazz has witnessed an incredible renaissance in Vancouver during the last decade, thanks to the indefatigable efforts of the Coastal Jazz and Blues Society. Although the society presents an eclectic mix of alternative, avant-garde, and straight-ahead performances throughout the year, its mainstay is the superb **du Maurier International Jazz Festival**, considered by many to be the best jazz festival in North America. For approximately 10 days starting in late June, the city is transformed into a jazz mecca that spans the entire jazz spectrum, with hundreds of ticketed performances and free music everywhere. ▪ *Venue: various locations; 682-0706.*

Early Music Vancouver and Vancouver Early Music Summer Festival In times past, early music seemed to be the domain of a select following, but more and more converts are discov-

ering these sublime sounds. Early Music presents a series of
performances, including various recitals, chamber orchestras,
and choirs, held in churches and concert halls throughout the
city from fall through spring. Music from the Middle Ages to
the 18th century is performed on original instruments by some
of the finest early music specialists. As an extension of the organization's main season, each summer the sounds of harpsi-
chords, lutes, and violas da gamba sweeten the UBC campus.
From mid-July through mid-August, local and international
proponents of early music share the stage and classrooms, providing a feast of musical pleasures for both the novice listener
and the advanced music scholar. ■ *Venue: various locations;*
732-1610.

Enchanted Fridays In spring and summer the Dr. Sun Yat-Sen
Classical Chinese Garden presents Enchanted Fridays. The
grounds are illuminated with lanterns, providing a soft glow for
music and dancing. ■ *578 Carrall St; 662-3207.*

Friends of Chamber Music Devotees of chamber music may
feel they have discovered manna with this 10-concert series.
From October through April (on Tuesdays), Friends of Chamber Music presents the crème de la crème of chamber music
ensembles, such as the Emerson String Quartet. The group recently received accolades for its special presentation of the
complete Beethoven quartets, featuring the renowned Bartok
String Quartet. ■ *Venue: Vancouver Playhouse; 437-5716.*

Masterpiece Music See Vancouver East Cultural Centre in
Theatre section of this chapter.

Music in the Morning Concert Society Experience the grace
of the European salons of the 18th century with a visit to one
of Music in the Morning's concerts. Born in the living room of
Artistic Director June Goldsmith almost 10 years ago, the concert series has blossomed into a well-respected and innovative
event. The repertoire includes the old and the new, performed
by local or imported artists. The society also presents the Musical Conversation series for those who want to learn more
about music in a relaxed setting. ■ *Venue: 1270 Chestnut (by*
Vanier Park); 736-5650.

Vancouver New Music Society Eclectic, alternative, on the
cutting edge—whichever expression you choose, the Vancouver New Music Society has earned a reputation for presenting
the hottest composers of contemporary music on an international scale. Unlikely as it may seem, you may well be hearing
music history in the making. The majority of concerts are
staged at the Vancouver East Cultural Centre, where the
intimacy of the hall provides a wonderful ambience. Concerts
are also held at other venues scattered throughout the city.
■ *Various locations; 874-6200.*

Vancouver Recital Society For a preview of who's going to be who in the classical music world in the years to come, catch one of the seven concerts in this recital series. Artistic Director and General Manager Leila Getz seems to have a canny sixth sense about young, up-and-coming artists, and that, matched with her impeccable taste, has enabled Vancouver audiences to hear some of today's foremost performers when they were aspiring musicians. In addition, the society presents a handful of superstars each season—for example, the enchanting singer Cecilia Bartoli, opera diva Jessye Norman, and violin master Itzhak Perlman. ■ *Venue: Vancouver Playhouse, Hamilton St at Dunsmuir St; 736-6034.*

Vancouver Symphony Orchestra [KIDS] This granddaddy of the classical music scene makes its home in the magnificent 1927 Orpheum Theatre, where thick red carpets, ornate rococo gilding, and sweeping staircases transport you back to an earlier, more gracious era. Under the leadership of Maestro Sergiu Comissiona, the 79-member orchestra has reached new heights of artistic splendour. Eight subscription series offer music lovers a wide variety of aural delicacies, from traditional symphonic fare to a more adventurous repertoire to pops concerts. An ever-increasing focus on Canadian artists and repertoire has added a new dimension, although a number of illustrious soloists, such as Yo-Yo Ma, Alicia de Larrocha, and Pinchas Zukerman, continue to grace the Orpheum stage. More recently, the Vancouver Symphony Orchestra (VSO) has brought forth the sounds of silents, presenting screenings of original silent film classics accompanied by the orchestra, as well as by guest artists on the vintage Wurlitzer organ. The popular Kids' Koncerts provides an opportunity for children to experience the joys of symphonic music in a fun, relaxed atmosphere. ■ *Venue: Orpheum Theatre, Granville St and Smithe St; 876-3434.*

[FREE] In addition to its main-stage concerts and special events, the VSO also performs free concerts in the parks and on the beaches of the Lower Mainland during the summer. The high point of a symphonic summer is the annual Whistler mountaintop concert, where glorious music resounds amid the mountain peaks.

OPERA

Chinese Cultural Centre Opera is just one of the many events presented at the centre by local organizations in the Chinese community and from around the world. The centre also has fascinating exhibitions of paintings and photography, as well as book launchings and dance and musical programs. ■ *Chinese Cultural Centre, 50 E Pender St; 687-0729.*

Vancouver Opera Association Opera is once again firmly entrenched in the Vancouver arts scene. Once the domain of the ladies who lunch, it is now one of the hippest tickets in town. And thanks to clever marketing, a re-evaluation of the organization's artistic vision in recent years, and the influence of the mega-musicals such as *Phantom of the Opera*, audiences have flocked to the opera in droves. Under the astute leadership of General Director Robert J. Hallam and Music Director David Agler, the Opera Association presents five productions each season, primarily tradition-based repertoire, with a minimum of one 20th-century work each season. Although the repertoire is tried and true, the sets are spectacular and the artists are of international calibre. In addition, some of Canada's brightest singing lights frequently grace the stage of the Queen Elizabeth Theatre. ■ *Venue: Queen Elizabeth Theatre, Hamilton St at W Georgia St; 682-2871.*

Exploring

MAJOR ATTRACTIONS

DOWNTOWN VANCOUVER
Between Beach Ave and Hastings St, Chilco St and Pacific Blvd

Vancouver's sprawling downtown stretches over numerous city blocks with no real main core. Glance north down any street, and catching glimpses of the mountains between buildings, you will see that the city ends at the water. All around, glass-sheathed high rises glitter in the sunlight, offering stunning reflections of the neighbouring buildings. Many buildings are set back from the street, with flower-filled courtyards built around fountains or pools.

These glass and steel office towers are in striking contrast to the mellow stone of lovely old **Christ Church Cathedral** (Burrard and Georgia streets), the oldest-surviving church in Vancouver. Across from the cathedral is the venerable **Hotel Vancouver,** with its famous griffins and gargoyles, green copper roof, and hushed, spacious lobby. Behind the hotel is the main branch of the **Vancouver Public Library** (Burrard Street and Robson Street). The building can no longer house all the books, so a new library complex is under construction half a dozen blocks east, and it promises to be a city showpiece. The gleaming white, stylized sails of **Canada Place**, on the edge of the harbour at the bottom of Howe Street, are a city landmark. **[FREE]** Walk around the "decks," enjoy the sea breeze, and admire the views. The **Marine Building** (Hastings Street and Burrard Street) is an art deco masterpiece, and for a decade after it opened in 1930 it was the tallest building in the British Commonwealth. The intricate, richly diverse carvings and sculptures in and outside this building emphasize a marine

121

and transportation theme in terra cotta, brass, stone, and marble. **Cathedral Place** (Georgia Street near Hornby Street), with its gargoyles and elegant facade, is newly "old."

Three of the city's major department and specialty stores are clustered at the corners of Granville and Georgia streets—the ornate facade of **The Bay** contrasting with the modern **Eaton's** building and the **Holt Renfrew** store, called Holt's by locals.

Robson Street is the city's most fashionable shopping street. Once called Robsonstrasse because of its many German delis and hearty restaurants, it has now been taken over by designer boutiques and cafes. It is the liveliest place in Vancouver in late evening, as people stroll along window-shopping, linger in sidewalk cafes, meet friends, or people-watch. The **Vancouver Art Gallery** and **Robson Square** (Hornby and Robson streets) are across from the **Provincial Courthouse**, a soaring glass structure designed by West Coast architect Arthur Erickson. Embellished with trailing greenery, the courthouse resembles a dignified greenhouse.

CHINATOWN
Between Abbott St and Heatley St, Prior St and Powell St

[KIDS][FREE] Vancouver has North America's second-largest Chinese community; only San Francisco's is larger. Chinese immigrants began arriving in Vancouver in the late 1850s. In the 1880s, thousands of Chinese arrived to work on building the railway across the West. By 1890, Vancouver's Chinatown had a population of more than 1,000, many of whom ran their own businesses.

Today's Chinatown, which lies mostly between Carrall Street and Gore Avenue, is a crowded, bustling area where shop owners loudly advertise their wares. Stores sell fruit and vegetables, jade, ivory, rattan, brass, china, silk, and brocade. It's easy to spend hours browsing through the cramped, incense-perfumed stores, unearthing delicately embroidered tablecloths or blouses. Enticing aromas waft from bakeries and restaurants. Wander along the busy streets, dodging women laden with bulging shopping bags, and admire streetlights decorated with golden dragons, phone booths topped with pagoda-style roofs, and ornamental street signs in both Chinese and English. Parking is difficult.

On the corner of Pender and Carrall streets is the famous **world's thinnest office building**. The **Sam Kee Building**, built in 1913, is only 1.8 metres (6 feet) wide and two storeys tall. Once a store selling beautiful silks, it is now an insurance office.

GASTOWN
Between Hastings St and Waters St, Homer St and Columbia St

[KIDS][FREE] Vancouver's first community was where Gastown now stands. In the 1860s, it grew up around the Globe Saloon, owned by **Gassy Jack Deighton**, a former river pilot renowned for his volubility—hence the nickname Gassy. After the fire that levelled the infant city of Granville in 1886, the city moved westward and changed its name to Vancouver. The old Gastown gradually disintegrated into the city's skid-row area.

In the late 1960s, the renovation and restoration of the area began. The streets were paved with cobblestones or red brick, decorative streetlamps were installed, and trees were planted in front of glittering boutiques and restaurants. In 1971, Gastown was designated a heritage site.

In Gastown, all roads—Carrall, Powell, Water, and Alexander streets—lead to **Maple Tree Square**. Nightclubs, art galleries, antique stores, and jazz clubs all add to the attractions of this pleasant place. Tucked into corners are flower-filled courtyards with names like Gaoler's Mews, and except for the presence of some elegant boutiques, they seem unchanged from the turn of the century. Gassy Jack himself has not been forgotten—his statue stands proudly in the centre of Maple Tree Square.

[KIDS][FREE] The 2-tonne (almost 2 tons) **Gastown Steam Clock**, on the corner of Cambie and Water streets, operates on steam tapped from the underground pipes of nearby buildings. The 5-metre-tall (16.4-foot-tall) clock whistles every 15 minutes and sends forth clouds of steam every hour. With a big glass face on all four sides, a 20-kilogram (44-pound) gold-plated pendulum, and a gothic roof, the clock is a popular stop for photographers. Around the corner and beside the train tracks, Ray Saunders, who designed the clock, has a store filled with antique clocks and watches.

GRANVILLE ISLAND
Underneath south end of Granville St Bridge

[KIDS][FREE] Granville Island is a success story that has confounded critics who argued that derelict warehouses and crumbling boathouses were pretty shaky foundations on which to build a vision. In 1917, the island, which is really a peninsula, was a filled-in mudflat that held the city's main industrial area. As the city expanded, businesses gradually moved away and the island became a grimy embarrassment. In the early 1970s, two Vancouver businessmen decided the area had potential and began developing one small part of it, arousing enough interest to get the federal government involved. Now this bustling people place with imaginative buildings that are faithful to its industrial beginnings is as popular with locals as it is with visitors.

The way to enjoy the island is at a leisurely pace. Allow lots of time to wander and wonder—at the endless marine traffic, from skimming canoes to stately yachts to picturesque paddlewheelers, and at the airy art galleries, the fearless seagulls looking for lunch, the downtown skyline, the uptown skyline, the pottery, jewellery, books, and blossoms—and the people. You'll want to stop at many of the colourful stalls, heaped high with fruits and vegetables, candy, bread, fish, and meat. For nightlife, the island boasts two theatres and an eclectic mix of restaurants, and you can still watch the boats—and the people.

In common with all success stories, the hardest thing about visiting Granville Island is the parking, especially on weekend mornings, despite the recent addition of covered pay parking places to supplement the free outside spaces. Try parking around Fourth Avenue and Fir Street and take the Granville Island bus. There's also a tiny shuttle **aquabus** from the downtown side of serene False Creek to the island.

[KIDS] The **Kids Only Market** near the entrance to the island, on Cartwright Street, is filled with everything a child, or an adult, could wish for. Games, gifts, hobbies, art and craft supplies, toys, video games, and live entertainers all contribute to the fun.

At the west end of the island is the waterside wharf edging Broker's Bay. Millions of dollars' worth of yachts are berthed here, and it is a good place to rent or charter a boat.

The sprawling public market housed in a huge renovated warehouse on the north corner of the island on Johnston Street (which bisects the island east to west) has more than 50 shops and stalls offering fresh produce, pasta, fudge, fish, crafts, and much more. The market is open daily except Mondays in the winter months. On Thursdays, from late May to October, there's the **Truck Farmers' Market** in the Arts Club Theatre parking lot, where you can buy local fruit, vegetables, and flowers from the backs of trucks from BC farmers. Nearby, the **NetLoft** houses small shops and big craft displays, with everything from beads to Northwest Coast native carvings. All around are wonderful aromatic bakeries, bookshops for browsing, and art and craft galleries. Boat shops, boat rentals, and boat repairs are on Duranleau Street; floating homes and marinas are on False Creek; and the Emily Carr College of Art and Design is on Johnston Street.

[FREE][KIDS] Visit the **Water Park** and adventure playground off Cartwright Street beside grassy Sutcliffe Park. Most restaurants on Granville Island have capitalized on their waterfront setting, and there's no shortage of sights to watch while you relax over coffee or a meal.

There's a pleasant walk along the seawall, a wide waterfront walkway paved in a mixture of surfaces—flagstones, wood, or concrete—where you will find sheltered courtyards, inviting plazas, and grassy, landscaped areas, as well as benches where you can sit and watch all the activity. Canada geese perch on boulders rising from the large duck pond. Three marinas cluster along the shore of False Creek, where sailboats, kayaks, and canoes abound. Cormorants wait patiently for dinner to swim by.

The seawall divides into a cycle path and walkway to form a loop around the north and south shores of False Creek. Start at Granville Island and wander east to the Cambie Street Bridge, then head north over the bridge and turn west to pick up the path that parallels the north shore. Follow the path west under the Granville Street Bridge and continue for a few minutes more to the west side of the Burrard Street Bridge, where you can take the tiny aquabus across False Creek back to the island. The loop takes about two hours to walk.

[KIDS] Each June, as part of the **Dragon Boat Festival** (669-4555), dragon boat races are held on False Creek. Slender, brilliantly coloured, exotically decorated boats come from around the world to take part in the races. The festival also includes a fireworks display and an international food fair.

GROUSE MOUNTAIN
Top of Capilano Rd, North Vancouver, 984-0661

[KIDS] Sailing 1128 metres (3,700 feet) through the sky in an aerial tramway could be considered one of the more pleasurable ways to scale a mountain. The scenery is amazing, from the feathery firs just beneath you to the city spread out at your feet and Washington State's San Juan Islands more than 160 kilometres (100 miles) to the south. Well known as a ski resort, Grouse is a different mountain in summer. From energetic hikers to those who prefer relaxing strolls, Grouse Mountain, just a 15-minute drive from downtown Vancouver, has something to please everyone. The **Skyride**, an enclosed gondola, glides up the mountain and drops you into the centre of the alpine activities. The peak chairlift will take you right to the top of the mountain for breathtaking views and enchanting sunsets.

Major Attractions

Harbour Centre Tower

A notice board outside the Skyride station has a map of the trails and general information. The nearby **Blue Grouse Trail** winds gently through the trees to a tiny jewel of a lake, which supplies the resort with its water. For this reason, swimming is not allowed. But it's a perfect place for a picnic. Although this 15-minute hike is ideal for small children, only experienced hikers should tackle the challenging **Goat Ridge Trail**, which takes about six hours, round trip. In between are hikes for every level of fitness. Kids also flock to the adventure playground, and in summer there are pony rides, horse-drawn wagons, and helicopter tours. Round out the perfect day with a visit to the multimedia **Theatre in the Sky**, or attend one of a series of summer concerts.

HARBOUR CENTRE TOWER
555 W Hastings St, 689-7304

[KIDS] Get a bird's-eye view of Vancouver and never leave the ground—take a trip to the top of the Harbour Centre Tower.

Glass elevators whisk you up 167 metres (548 feet) in less than a minute to a 360-degree vista of the city. Burrard Inlet, the North Shore mountains, Burnaby Mountain with Simon Fraser University perched on top, the Port of Vancouver, Stanley Park, downtown, West Vancouver, Bowen Island—all are on display. There are also photo-fact plaques, historical displays, and a video on Vancouver. Enjoy a meal or a snack in the revolving restaurant while you take in the view.

QUEEN ELIZABETH PARK AND ARBORETUM
Cambie St and 33rd Ave

[KIDS][FREE] This jewel of a park is set on the highest point of the city, 150 metres (500 feet) above sea level, offering a stunning 360-degree view of the surrounding area. Beautifully landscaped, the park has visual treats at every turn—fountains, rock gardens, waterfalls, flower beds bursting with brilliant blossoms, and a placid pond where ducks preen beneath graceful willow trees.

This park was created from two old quarries—crushed volcanic rock was used to pave the city's first roads—and the paths swoop up and down or twist around the steep sides. Landscaping of the largest quarry was finished in 1954, and the second quarry was finished in 1961, in time for Vancouver's 75th anniversary.

In spring the park's grassy slopes glow with colour from rhododendrons, azaleas, and other indigenous BC shrubs. When Vancouver revels in a rare snowfall, these slopes are quickly claimed by young tobogganers. The rose garden is a perfumed delight, as is the tiny Japanese garden with a stone lantern surrounded by dwarf trees and a small fountain.

At the top of Little Mountain, as the park was called before the name was changed to commemorate a visit from King George VI and Queen Elizabeth, an open reservoir has been filled and transformed into a spacious plaza with water gardens and fountains. A beautiful bronze sculpture by Henry Moore, *Knife Edge—Two Pieces*, graces the plaza and is a favourite with children, who squeeze between the sculpture's two sections. The park's popularity as a setting for wedding party photographs is reflected in another bronze sculpture—a life-sized family group by Seward Johnson called *Photo Session*. Tennis courts, pitch and putt, and lawn bowling add to the attractions of this family park.

[KIDS] The silver triodetic dome of the **Bloedel Conservatory** is the crowning point of the park—1,490 little Plexiglas bubbles that are illuminated at night. From the walkway around the conservatory, you get a panoramic view of Vancouver, the harbour, the North Shore mountains, the Fraser River delta, and the Strait of Georgia. Plaques along the way tell you which mountains you are looking at and how high they are.

Inside the dome is a warm, moist rain forest and a miniature desert. Tropical plants and shrubs from Mexico, Africa, Australia, and South America spread their leafy branches overhead. Brightly hued birds flit through the trees or peck at cunningly disguised feeders. A curving path winds through the shrubbery, leading to a little desert where cacti flourish. The floral displays change with the seasons—at Christmastime, the conservatory is a blaze of crimson poinsettias (872-5513).

SCIENCE WORLD
1455 Quebec St, 268-6363

[KIDS] Fondly known as the city's "golf ball," Science World is housed in what was the World Expo Centre at Expo 86. Now this futuristic building on the False Creek waterfront features permanent and travelling exhibits that dazzle the senses, offering hands-on experiences that range from buzzing around a beehive to mastering the essentials of light and sound. Three main galleries explore the realms of biology, physics, and music; the fourth gallery is reserved for travelling exhibits. Uncover the secrets of the universe and still be home in time for dinner. There is a great gift shop with a science-oriented theme.

At the **Omnimax Theatre** in **Science World**, the largest wraparound screen in the world puts you right in the picture. Separate admittance.

SEABUS AND LONSDALE QUAY
North Vancouver, bottom of Lonsdale Ave,
SeaBus information: 264-5000

[KIDS] Take a boat ride on a "bus"—the SeaBus that hustles back and forth across the harbour from downtown Vancouver to the North Shore. The Vancouver terminal is in the beautifully renovated **Canadian Pacific Railway Station** at Cordova and Granville streets, where, above the small shops and coffee bars, a series of wonderful paintings depicts views of the Rocky Mountains. On the North Shore, the SeaBus terminal is in Lonsdale Quay, a lively area of boutiques, coffee shops, restaurants, and a public market. Beside the terminal is Waterfront Park, a delightful place to stroll along the oceanside and view the city from a different angle.

The SS *Beaver* and the SS *Otter* take 12 minutes to sail across the sheltered waters of Vancouver's inner harbour. This is history repeating itself. In 1900, years before any major bridges were built, a ferry linked Vancouver and the then-small North Shore population.

Activity is all around as the SeaBus sails serenely across Burrard Inlet. Freighters steam by to load and unload, while sailboats skim over the waves. To the north are the majestic peaks of the Coast Mountains, and to the west lies the green bulk of Stanley Park, framed by the elegant span of the Lions

Gate Bridge. During the four-month summer season, gleaming white cruise ships glide by. Southward, office towers and high rises cluster behind the shining sails of Canada Place. The SeaBus is also a wonderful mini-cruise to take at night, when the city's myriad lights are reflected on the water.

Lonsdale Quay is a soaring glass and steel structure sheltering three levels of shops, boutiques, and restaurants. At ground level the public market offers a vast array of fruits and vegetables, fish, breads, flowers, and meats. Have coffee outside in the sunshine and admire the stunning view. On the second level are gift shops and boutiques, and on the third level is the entrance to the Lonsdale Quay Hotel.

[KIDS] Take a left turn at the SeaBus Terminal for Waterfront Park. There's plenty to see on a stroll around the paved walkway that circumnavigates the small park. Along the seawall, plaques identify several outstanding downtown buildings, and a huge modernistic sculpture, *Cathedral*, by Douglas Senft, sits on the lawn. At **Sailor's Point Plaza**, which is dedicated to those who have lost their lives at sea, is an elegant sundial by Tim Osborne titled *Timelines*. A plaque also commemorates Captain George Vancouver, the European who discovered and named Burrard Inlet. At the far end of the park is the **Pacific Marine Training Institute**, which is full of boats, ropes, and outboard engines for students working toward a marine career.

During the summer this park is busy. Concerts are held on many Sunday afternoons, and numerous clubs hold festivals, exhibits, dances, and competitions here.

STANLEY PARK
Vancouver Park Department; 2099 Beach Ave; 681-1141

[KIDS][FREE] Thanks to the farsightedness of Vancouver's pioneering city founders, the 400 glorious hectares (1,000 acres) that became Stanley Park were set aside in 1886. The park was officially opened by Mayor David Oppenheimer in September 1888. Long before the Spanish explorers and Captain Vancouver arrived in the late 18th century, Chief Khahtsahlano lived at Chaythoos, now **Prospect Point**, the highest area of the park.

Natural woodlands, manicured gardens, sports facilities, leafy glades, winding trails, golden beaches, calm lagoons, an aquarium, a summer theatre, a haven for wildlife, and a wonderful park to spend a day, or several days, exploring—Stanley Park is all this and more. Much of Vancouver's reputation as a beautiful city is linked with the wonders of Stanley Park, one of the largest urban parks in North America.

Attractions are spread throughout the park, but the best way to get acquainted with its many charms is to walk, run, or cycle the **Stanley Park seawall**. (A bike rental outlet is at the foot of Georgia Street near the park entrance.) The seawall, the longest in Canada, is 10.5 kilometres (6 miles) long and was constructed over 60 years; it was finally completed in 1980. It can be circumnavigated in two hours of brisk walking, or you can take a day to stroll around it, veering off to check out the surrounding attractions, stopping for coffee or lunch, or sitting in the sun marvelling at the views, which are always incredible.

Start at **Lost Lagoon**, a haven for Canada geese, trumpeter swans, imported mandarin ducks, and more. The fountain in the centre, built in 1936 to mark the park's Golden Jubilee, is illuminated at night. (A path around the lagoon is separate from the seawall.) Single sculls and eights from the **Vancouver Rowing Club** can often be seen skimming over the harbour waters. A statue of Robbie Burns is opposite the Rowing Club. The **Rose Gardens** are a few minutes' walk from the seawall, and nearby, in a country-garden-like setting, is the **Stanley Park Pavilion Cafeteria**, built in 1932 and now a heritage building.

Intriguing totem poles of the Squamish people, the first inhabitants of this coast, stand near **Brockton Point**—a prime spot for photographs. The Nine O'clock Gun, which used to call fishermen home at night, is still used by residents to check their watches. Be warned, it is loud. On summer weekends watch an unhurried cricket match at **Brockton Oval**. At low tide you can see a bronze statue titled *Girl in a Wet Suit* created by Elek Imredy. A wooden fire-breathing dragon on the seawall here is a replica of the figurehead from the old *Empress of Japan*, a passenger ship that regularly called at Vancouver.

[KIDS][FREE] Popular **Lumberman's Arch** is a rolling meadow for picnics or playing, with a delightful children's water park bordering the ocean and a busy concession stand nearby. Watch for brave bunnies who hop in and out of the bushes. This lively, cheerful area was once a native village, and literally tonnes of shells from the village midden were used to surface the first road into the park in 1888.

The most developed area of the park is the **Vancouver Aquarium**. (See Vancouver Aquarium in this chapter.) Kids of all ages love the miniature train that puffs over 1.2 kilometres (0.75 mile) through forest and lake (weather permitting).

Beaver Lake, where water lilies speckle the smooth surface, is a quiet place for contemplation or a gentle walk. Behind the lake are numerous forest trails weaving through hemlock, cedar, Douglas fir, maple, and spruce. Popular with walkers and joggers, these isolated trails should not be tackled solo.

Besides offering breathtaking views of the North Shore, Prospect Point (north of Beaver Lake on the seawall) also displays a cairn in memory of the Pacific Coast's pioneer steamship, the SS *Beaver*, which sank near here in 1888. Nearby is a popular restaurant with an outdoor deck beside the Lions Gate Bridge, as well as the large, grassy Prospect Point

Major Attractions

Stanley Park

picnic area, suitable for groups.

Siwash Rock, a rocky pinnacle, has defied the elements for centuries. Various native legends have grown up around this rock, which has one tiny tree clinging to its top. Past Siwash Rock off Stanley Park Drive stands a tree of a different sort, the remains of the once-mighty **Hollow Tree**, which was large enough for automobiles to drive through. **Third Beach**, a wide, sandy beach with excellent swimming, is also near here. At **Ferguson Point**, locals bring visitors to the **Teahouse Restaurant** to admire the scenery.

[KIDS] **Second Beach** is one of the best places in town to watch the sunset, and children love the playground and picnic area. [FREE] Several nights a week in summer, the paved area is a mass of dancers—Scottish dancers, ballroom dancers, and square dancers all kick up their heels here. This is also a sports area, with pitch and putt golf, shuffleboard, lawn bowling, and busy tennis courts. **The Fish House** restaurant is also located at Second Beach.

Numerous annual events are held in Stanley Park; call the Parks and Recreation Board office for information and maps (681-1141).

UNIVERSITY OF BRITISH COLUMBIA
2075 Wesbrook Mall, 822-2211

With a student population of more than 40,000, it is hardly surprising that the University of British Columbia is a city within a city. Founded in 1908, the university is in a spectacular setting, on a wooded peninsula stretching into the Strait of Georgia, and is less than half an hour from downtown. Beaches and cliffs, dense woods, grassy meadows, expansive lawns, and spectacular views of the surrounding mountains make this one of the most beautiful campuses in the country. Buildings range from old and imposing to modern and spare.

There are four main entrance roads into the campus: West 16th, which becomes Southwest Marine Drive; West 10th, which becomes University Boulevard; West 4th, which divides into Chancellor Boulevard and Northwest Marine Drive; and SW Marine Drive. West Fourth and West 10th have frequent bus service.

Part of **Pacific Spirit Park** and the **University Endowment Lands** is on the south side of West 16th, which leads to the **Thunderbird Stadium** (home of the UBC football team, the Thunderbirds), and the **Botanical Gardens**. Nearby is the **Thunderbird Winter Sports Centre**, with ice rinks and curling, racquetball, and squash courts all open to the public at specific times. Student residences and many of the largest student parking lots—some are a 15-minute walk or more from lecture and laboratory facilities—are found in this area. University Boulevard ends at the [KIDS] **Aquatic Centre and Empire**

Pool, which includes excellent indoor and outdoor (seasonal) swimming pools, and the **War Memorial Gym**. [KIDS][FREE] Children are entranced by the **Geology Museum**. The spacious **U.B.C. Bookstore** stocks more than 70,000 titles for study, with special sections devoted to children and general interest, computers, and accessories and souvenirs. The **Main Library,** the second-largest library in Canada, is nearby. It is open to everyone, and library cards can be purchased by nonstudents and nonstaff. The library's elegant old facade and sweeping steps are popular with the many film and television people working in Vancouver and have appeared in numerous productions, as has the **Ladner Clock Tower** opposite. The **Astronomical Observatory** and the **Geophysical Observatory** both offer fascinating tours (822-2802). From Chancellor Boulevard and Northwest Marine Drive the superior **Museum of Anthropology**, and the **Beach Trails**, **SUB**—the Student Union Building—**Nitobe Gardens**, and **Faculty Club** are all easily accessible, as is the **Frederic Wood Theatre**, where students put on several excellent productions each year (822-3880). There is also the **Music Building**, which holds concerts, an opera, and summer events (822-3113).

To get an idea of the university's size, scope, and facilities, a map is essential (822-2211). In summer, some student residences are available as visitor accommodations, one of the best bargains in the city (822-5442). Reservations are required.

VANCOUVER AQUARIUM
Stanley Park, 682-1118 or 685-3364

[KIDS] Guarding the entrance to the Vancouver Aquarium in Stanley Park is Haida artist Bill Reid's magnificent 5.5-metre (18-foot) bronze killer whale sculpture. Inside, everything from the Arctic to the Amazon awaits you. The aquarium is Canada's largest and is rated as one of the best in North America. With more than 8,000 species of aquatic life, representing almost 600 separate species from the world's seas and oceans, the aquarium is also an important educational and research facility and provides tours, talks, films, and field trips (685-3364).

A highlight of the aquarium is the **beluga and killer whale presentations**, held in the new $14 million marine mammal area. Small bays, beaches, and rubbing rocks around the pools closely replicate the beluga and orca whales' natural environment. The whales carry out amazing acrobatics each day, for which they are rewarded with herring treats—they eat up to 60 kilograms (132 pounds) each day. They also soak the unwary—the splash area by the pool is well named.

The **Pacific Northwest Habitat** offers a close look at the inhabitants of local waters, from playful sea otters to gliding octopus. Scuba divers feed the fish and harvest the waving fronds of kelp. **The Amazon Gallery**, 10 years in planning, is the only exhibition in Canada that re-creates part of the Amazon Basin. Fish, reptiles, birds, insects, and plants thrive in the tropical humidity, created partly by computer-generated tropical rainstorms. The creatures in the gallery are amazing—four-eyed fish, scarlet ibis, anacondas, and fluorescent fish.

The **Arctic Canada** exhibition allows visitors to hear the language of the whales, walruses, and seals that live in the cold blue world beneath the ice. Fascinating displays illustrate just how fragile this hostile northern environment is—and you can go nose to nose with a smiling, curious beluga whale.

VANCOUVER ART GALLERY
750 Hornby St, 682-5621

Designed in 1907 by Victoria architect Francis Rattenbury—who also designed Victoria's Empress Hotel and Legislative Buildings—the imposing structure of the former provincial courthouse, with its impressive stone lions and Greek columns, now houses the Vancouver Art Gallery. Another famous architect, Arthur Erickson, transformed the cramped interior into four spacious floors flooded with light from the new glass-topped dome above the elegant rotunda.

▼

Major Attractions

Vancouver Aquarium

▲

The **Emily Carr Gallery** is filled with the glowing works of British Columbia's most revered artist. A native of Vancouver Island, Emily Carr captured the majesty of the coastal rain forests, the towering totem poles, and the natives who created them. Many of these works are from the turn of the century. The gallery has a permanent collection of contemporary local and Canadian artists, and a collection of European and North American masters, including the Group of Seven and such luminaries as Pablo Picasso. Frequently changing travelling exhibits offer everything from photography to videos to sculpture. [KIDS] The **Children's Gallery** also has changing exhibits. Short talks are held several times a week. There are children's and adult workshops, as well as concerts (682-5621).

The Gift Shop, off the main lobby, is an excellent place for souvenirs; including postcards, posters, jewellery, books, and prints. Visit the **Gallery Cafe** for coffee or lunch. Sit outside if weather permits and watch the crowds on Robson Street.

On the Georgia Street side of the Vancouver Art Gallery are attractive well-kept gardens and the **Centennial Fountain**. Surrounded by a blue, green, and white mosaic, the rough-hewn rock in the centre has carvings of Celtic legends. Designed in 1966 by R. H. Savery, the fountain commemorates the union of the crown colonies of B.C. and Vancouver Island in 1866.

PARKS AND BEACHES

Whether you are looking for a seaside stroll or a strenuous workout, dazzling views or deep, aromatic forests, tennis courts or a shady picnic spot, one of Vancouver's 160 parks will provide it. And, most likely, there's a glorious, sandy beach nearby for good measure.

Ambleside Park [KIDS] This aptly named West Vancouver park is an ideal place to amble along the seawall, enjoying the superb scenery that forms a backdrop for the bustling marine traffic. For the energetic, there are playing fields, pitch and putt golf, a fitness circuit, and jogging trails, as well as picnic areas and a playground. The beach is popular with families on summer days. Impromptu volleyball games take place most evenings. Bird-watchers appreciate the bird sanctuary on an artificial island in the tidal slough. The nearby **SPCA** building sells birdseed. ■ *Along Marine Dr, turning South at 13th St, West Vancouver.*

Barnet Beach Park [KIDS] Once the site of a busy mill town, this heritage park in north Burnaby is the perfect place to spend a day by the water. Traces of the old mill workings that resemble a medieval castle are a joy to youngsters. Safe, guarded swimming areas, a wharf for fishing and crabbing, picnic areas, barbecue pits, and a nonpowered boat launch area make this park a local favourite. On summer weekends the parking lot is often full, but there's plenty of parking on nearby side streets. ■ *East along Inlet Dr to Barnet Rd, Burnaby.*

Belcarra Regional Park [KIDS] It's well worth the hour's drive from downtown Vancouver to this park, which is really two parks in one—Belcarra and White Pine Beach. The huge, grassy sweep of the Belcarra picnic area slopes gently down to Indian Arm on Burrard Inlet and is ideal for individual and group picnics. Sasamat Lake has one of the warmest beaches on the Lower Mainland. There are also well-marked trails that edge the ocean at White Pine Beach, and the sheltered coves make perfect picnic and sunning spots. Tidal pools with their varied marine life are an endless source of entertainment. Crabbers and fishers bask in the sunshine on the dock, waiting for a bite (permit required). Kids love the imaginative adventure playground. Mud flats on the southern tip of Bedwell Bay provide interesting beachcombing. Busy on weekends. Signs along Ioca Road tell you if the park is full. ■ *Along Hastings/Barnet Hwy to Ioca Rd N and N to 1st Ave (follow signs); group picnic reservations, 432-6352; group camping reservations, 879-4018.*

Burnaby Lake Regional Park The focal point of this huge, 300-hectare (740-acre) park is 12,000-year-old Burnaby Lake, which has the best rowing facilities in the province. There's a public canoe launch area at the Rowing Pavilion. Other sports facilities include tennis courts, grass hockey, rugby, and soccer fields; a skating rink; a swimming pool; and an archery range. In addition, there's a fitness circuit and an equestrian centre with riding rings and a large network of trails. [KIDS] The **Nature House** has children's programs in summer. Throughout the park, pleasant walking trails are liberally scattered with birdhouses, providing accommodation for everything from tiny chickadees to wood ducks. A bird-watching tower offers a sweeping view of the lake, which is usually busy with rowers and canoes. ▪ *Between Kensington Ave and Caribou Rd, Hwy 1 and Winston St, Burnaby.*

Capilano River Park [KIDS] This park spans North and West Vancouver with everything from the urban to the wild. The immense **Cleveland Dam**, named after Vancouver's first water commissioner, Ernest Cleveland, harnesses the Capilano River and supplies Vancouver's water. There are great viewpoints of the spillway from clearings beside the dam. Pleasant picnic areas abound near the colourful flower gardens. [FREE] Follow signs through the woods to the fish hatchery, where a glass-fronted observation area shows the fishways that assist salmon battling their way upriver to return to their birthplace. Displays chronicle the life cycle of Pacific salmon, and breeding tanks hold minute salmon and trout fry. Below the hatchery is wilderness, with long and short hikes beside the rushing river and inland. Fishing in Capilano River can be rewarding. ▪ *Along Capilano Rd N at the Fish Hatchery, North Vancouver; 987-1411.*

Central Park [KIDS] [FREE] One of the oldest parks in the city, straddling the boundary between Vancouver and Burnaby, this lovely park was named after its New York counterpart. Once a military reserve for the defence of New Westminster, the park has an award-winning playground that was specially designed with disabled children in mind. On the trails around the lake, which is rimmed with elegant weeping willows, you are likely to be waylaid by ducks looking for handouts. The ducks, however, are smart enough to keep clear of the remote-controlled boats on the nearby artificial lake. Longer trails for joggers and cyclists meander through the park. In spring, rhododendron blossoms make a brilliant display. Horseshoe pitches, pitch and putt golf, tennis courts, a swimming pool, and lawn bowling greens ensure this park has something for everyone. ▪ *Between Boundary Rd and Patterson Ave, Kingsway and Imperial St, Burnaby.*

Cypress Falls Park This West Vancouver park is perfect for those who like their wilderness manageable. Trails are steep and can be muddy and rough, but they are well marked. Trees are huge and old, with thick, textured bark. Swirling mist in the topmost branches adds to the feeling that you are a long way from civilization, when, in fact, the parking lot is a short walk away. Cypress Creek has carved a deep, narrow canyon, and the roar of the water foaming through the steep walls echoes around the park. From the canyon, the creek plunges in a spectacular cascade to the wide creek bed and its smooth, water-worn boulders. The main trail, which can be muddy and slippery, climbs steadily upward through heavy forest and underbrush, occasionally opening into natural viewpoints. ▪ *Along Hwy 1 W to Woodgreen Dr and Woodgreen Pl, West Vancouver.*

English Bay Beach [KIDS] In the 1920s and 1930s, Vancouverites thronged to the wide, sandy beach and the pier. Plays were performed on the roof of the 1931 English Bay bathhouse, where a windsurfing school operates now. A Jamaican seaman, Joe Fortes, lived in a little cottage on the beach and for 25 years was the self-appointed lifeguard, teaching many youngsters to swim. A bronze drinking fountain in tiny Alexandra Park, across Beach Avenue, stands in tribute to Fortes. [FREE] There is also a delightful gingerbread-embellished bandstand here, where the band plays on warm Sunday afternoons. The pier is gone, but crowds still come to swim and sunbathe. [KIDS] In July, English Bay is the setting for the **Vancouver Sea Festival** (684-3378), which celebrates the city's nautical heritage. Fireworks, parades, concerts, and the **Nanaimo-to-Vancouver Bathtub Race** draw an enormous audience. ▪ *Along Pacific St and Beach Ave between Denman St and Burrard St.*

Fraser River Park [KIDS] The wooden boardwalk paralleling the Fraser River in this Marpole area park bridges ponds and marshy areas where thick grasses attract birds and insects. Signs set at intervals along this walk relate the history of the river and its delta and the river's importance as a marine highway, highlighting local wildlife, geology, and native history. The Interpretive Court at the south end of the park offers additional information. Have a seat on one of the benches to watch the endless river traffic, or sit on one of the huge logs strewn along the riverbank. An open grassy area is popular with picnickers and frisbee throwers, and a long wooden pier jutting into the river puts you almost within touching distance of log booms. Wading children delight in waiting until the last possible moment before running from the waves thrown up by passing tugboats. This park is a wonderful place to watch the sunset and to view planes landing and taking off from Vancouver International Airport, across the river on Sea Island. ▪ *Along 75th Ave between Barnard St and Bentley St.*

Garry Point Park [KIDS] This park is on the extreme southwestern tip of **Lulu Island** and is rich with the history of boat building and the lore of fish canneries. At the turn of the century there were more than 2,000 fishing boats waiting at the mouth of the Fraser to set out into the Strait of Georgia. Nearby, the town of Steveston is preserved much as it was a century ago when the first cannery went into operation. It is still an important fishing area. You can buy fish fresh off the boat from Steveston quay, or enjoy a meal in one of the many excellent fish 'n' chip restaurants nearby. This is also the perfect place to watch freighter traffic heading up the main arm of the Fraser. Equally popular is picnicking in one of the many sandy bays that edge this park (beach fires permitted). A small Japanese garden pays tribute to the strong Japanese presence in Steveston. Kite fliers flock to the open grassy field where steady breezes from the strait provide a challenge. North from the park are scenic riverside trails along Richmond's dikes, which are well used by walkers and cyclists. ■ *7th Ave at Chatham St, Richmond.*

Iona Beach Park [KIDS] Based on the premise that if you can't hide it, flaunt it, one of Vancouver's major sewage outfall pipes has been transformed into a unique walking and cycling path that extends 4 kilometres (2.5 miles) into the Strait of Georgia. The pathway, which is on top of the pipe, evokes the sensation of being at sea on an ocean liner. At the end of the walkway a viewing tower gives a bird's-eye vista of the strait and, on clear days, distant glimpses of Vancouver Island and the mountains of the Olympic Peninsula. [KIDS] Beaches are sandy and flat, ideal for kite flying, swimming, and sunning. The waters are sheltered for canoeing and kayaking. Driftwood trims the shore, and the river marsh on the island's south shore is a haven for migrating birds that stop over on their way to and from Arctic breeding grounds. Ducks, songbirds, and sandpipers congregate here in vast numbers. ■ *Along Ferguson Rd near airport to Iona Island Causeway, Richmond.*

Kitsilano Beach [KIDS] This great sandy sweep of beach was once part of an Indian reservation and is named after Chief Khahtsahlano of the Squamish band. In summer families flock to its warm, safe swimming area, while sun worshippers pack the grassy area towel to towel. Tennis courts, a children's play area, and basketball courts are equally busy. [KIDS] **Kitsilano Pool**, open seasonally, is the largest outdoor pool in Vancouver, with areas for serious swimmers and for small children, as well as a generous anything-goes section. This heated pool is always crowded. [KIDS] [FREE] On the south side of the pool is the **Kitsilano Showboat**, a local institution of beachside entertainment that has been running every summer since 1935. Local amateur groups sing and dance three evenings a week, weather permitting. The shoreline path is the perfect place for a summer evening stroll, and benches allow comfortable people-watching. Cyclists use this path too. The route curves along the beach, past the Maritime Museum, the Vancouver Museum, and the planetarium, all the way to Granville Island, a pleasant 30-minute walk. ∎ *Along Cornwall Ave and Point Grey Rd, between Arbutus St and Trafalgar, Kitsilano Pool; 731-0011.*

Lighthouse Park Driving along West Vancouver's Marine Drive, where houses are perched on top of cliffs, you might anticipate a beach park. Instead, you find a dense forest edged with rock. No logging has been allowed here since the area was set aside as a reserve in 1881. Allow at least half a day for exploring. Numerous trails meander through the park and to the tidal pools. There are maps and information boards in the large parking lot, which can fill early on summer Sundays. The main trail to the ocean and the Point Atkinson lighthouse (built in 1914) is well marked and is a mere 10-minute downhill walk through gigantic Douglas fir, some 61 metres (200 feet) tall and 2 metres (6.5 feet) in diameter. [KIDS] [FREE] Tours of the lighthouse are given daily in summer—just show up. Bring a sweater, since it can be cool in the woods. Unspoiled wilderness only 30 minutes from downtown Vancouver, spectacular sunsets. ∎ *Along Marine Dr to Beacon Lane, West Vancouver.*

Locarno Beach [KIDS] Locarno is the oldest settlement in Point Grey. Bones and shells that were once part of a native midden date back 3,000 years. This is also one of the most spectacular beaches in the city. At low tide it seems you can walk to West Vancouver across miles of tide-rippled sand, speckled with shallow tidal pools. Warmed by the sun, these pools are perfect for children. Seagulls stalk around the water's edge, herons hunch in the shallows, and eagles sometimes circle overhead. A wide dirt path, which is well used by walkers and cyclists, runs along the top of the beach. Between the path and the road is a broad, grassy area with picnic tables and benches. A few trees add shade. All along this shoreline beach you can see the green of Stanley Park, the wilderness of Lighthouse Park, and the gleaming fingers of the high rises in the West End. Locarno and Jericho beaches blend into each other, creating a beach lover's, windsurfer's, and sailor's paradise. ∎ *Along NW Marine Dr between Trimble St and Blanca St.*

Pacific Spirit Park Pacific Spirit Park is one of the Greater Vancouver Regional District's newest parks, offering over 800 hectares (2,000 acres) of wilderness adjacent to the University of British Columbia. More than 55 kilometres (34 miles) of trails (designated for walkers, cyclists, and horseback riders) plunge through thick, second-growth forest, edge deep ravines, and wind along cliff tops overlooking beaches with spectacular views of English Bay, Howe Sound, and the north arm of the Fraser River. There's plenty of small wildlife here, and early in the morning you may even catch a glimpse of a coyote. Just above the Locarno Beach cliffs on the Spanish Trail is an open area covered with wild roses, fireweed, and salmonberry bushes. It's called the Plains of Abraham, and a dairy farm operated here at the turn of the century (traces of the brick foundation remain on the south edge). A serene forest on the edge of the city, Pacific Spirit Park is well named. ■ *Between NW Marine Dr and SW Marine Dr, Camosun St and UBC.*

Stanley Park See Major Attractions in this chapter.

Vanier Park [KIDS] Ocean breezes blowing over the wide, grassy space on English Bay have made this one of the best places in town to fly a kite. At the end of May, families flock to the red-and-white-striped tents of the **Vancouver International Children's Festival** (687-7697), where performers from around the world entertain multitudes of children with their unique brand of Belgian theatre, African rhythms, or native storytelling. There's also the **H. R. MacMillan Planetarium** (736-3656), considered one of the best planetariums in North America. The planetarium and the **Vancouver Museum** (736-7736), which has displays chronicling the history of Vancouver and the Lower Mainland, offer frequently changing shows. Both are in the building with the conical roof that is shape of a traditional native woven cedar-bark hat, a fitting tribute to the coastal native tribes that once lived on this tip of land jutting into English Bay. Outside the building is the wishing pool guarded by George Norris's stainless steel fountain, *The Crab.* Just south of the museum parking lot is the **Southern Observatory** (736-7736) with free tours for stargazers on clear nights. East of the museum are the City of Vancouver Archives and a music school, the Vancouver Academy of Music. On the west side of the museum parking lot is the [KIDS] **Maritime Museum** (737-2212), which shelters the historic RCMP vessel the *St. Roch,* as well as offering fascinating information about Vancouver's seagoing heritage. [FREE] Nearby is Heritage Harbour, where a unique collection of ordinary and unusual vessels, including a Chinese junk and a Haida canoe, are moored. ■ *Just west of the Burrard St Bridge, north of Cornwall Ave at Chestnut St.*

▼

Parks and Beaches

▲

Wreck Beach Take it off or keep it on—the choice is yours. Vancouver's famous, and only, nude beach lies beneath the cliffs toward the northern tip of the University of British Columbia. Over the years it has generated strong criticism, but more recently a live-and-let-live attitude seems to prevail. Vendors weave between the sun worshippers, offering cold drinks and a variety of food. Fun in the sun with no tan lines. ■ *Below NW Marine Dr at the University of British Columbia.*

GARDENS

Gardens, parks, and green spaces are tucked into the corner of a city lot, squeezed between houses, stretched across a campus, or set in front of public buildings. High on the mountainside or beside the ocean are tiny private domains as well as sprawling hectares for public pleasure. The temperate climate and soft, plentiful rains encourage exuberant growth in limitless combinations of species. The dogwood is British Columbia's provincial flower, and in spring the spreading tree is jam-packed with fragile, creamy blossoms. Following are descriptions of some of Vancouver's wonderful gardens.

Dr. Sun Yat-Sen Classical Chinese Garden This authentic Ming Dynasty (1368–1644) garden is the first of its kind to be built inside or outside China since 1492. Rocks, wood, plants, and water are used with deceptive simplicity, but gradually contrasts are revealed—large and small, dark and light, hard and soft, straight and curved, artificial and natural. Windows frame courtyards, intricate carvings, or a rock whose heavily textured surface changes with the play of light. Pavilions connected by covered walkways edge the milky jade waters of the pond, whose surface is speckled with water lilies. Most of the materials used were imported from Suzhou, China's foremost garden city. Adjoining this serene, starkly elegant garden is Dr. Sun Yat-Sen Park, a simplified version of the main garden. ■ *578 Carrall St; 662-3207.*

Nitobe Garden This tranquil garden should be explored at leisure. As you stroll along gently curving paths, note the care that went into the placement of every rock, tree, and shrub to harmonize with nature. Wander counterclockwise, accompanied by the soothing sounds of the lake, waterfalls, and tiny streams, for the gardens move from a beginning through growth and change to an ending. Native and imported plants and trees, azaleas, flowering cherry, irises, and maples provide colour the year round. ■ *UBC; 822-6038.*

Park and Tilford Gardens [FREE] Created in 1968, these glorious gardens are a popular place for summer weddings, and it's easy to understand why. A choice of eight theme gardens provides the perfect setting—from a stunning display of roses to the cool formality of the **White Garden**. The **Display Garden** features colourful spring bulbs and spreading annuals. The **Oriental Garden** features traditional bonsai trees and a tranquil pond, and in the **Native Garden**, a footpath winds through a small, aromatic Pacific Coast forest. There's also the **Herb Garden** and the shady **Colonade Garden**, with its soothing rock pool and numerous other botanical delights. ■ *440-333 Brooksbank Ave, North Vancouver; 984-8200.*

University of British Columbia Botanical Gardens The oldest, and one of the finest, botanical gardens in Canada, the UBC Botanical Gardens is really five gardens in one. Each has a different theme and character. Spread over 28 hectares (70 acres), the gardens provide a trip around the botanical world.

The **Asian Garden**, nestled in a second-growth coastal forest of firs, cedars, and hemlocks, has fragile magnolias and more than 400 varieties of brilliant rhododendrons. Climbing roses and flowering vines twine around the trees, and the rare blue Himalayan poppy and giant Himalayan lilies bloom here. The **BC Native Garden**, displaying more than 3,500 plants found in the province, offers over 3 hectares (8 acres) of diversity, encompassing water meadows, dunes, bogs, and a desert. The **Alpine Garden** provides the challenge of growing high-elevation plants at sea level. Specially imported soil, boulders, and rocks give protection for vibrant, rare, low-growing mountain plants from Australia, South America, Europe, Asia, and Africa. The **Physick Garden** re-creates a 16th-century monastic herb garden. The traditional plants, which grow in raised brick beds, are all used for medicinal purposes. The **Food Garden** is an amazing example of efficient gardening. Espaliered trees serve as fences, and grapevines, berries, 136 fruit trees, and even kiwi fruit all grow on 0.10 hectare (a quarter of an acre) of land in the coldest garden on the Lower Mainland. Fruit and vegetables are harvested regularly and donated to the Salvation Army. Regular lectures, on everything from pruning to growing trees in tubs, are given for gardeners. ■ *UBC, SW Marine Dr; 822-4208.*

VanDusen Botanical Gardens [KIDS] Once a golf course, the gardens are named for W. J. Van Dusen, who was president of the Vancouver Foundation when it joined forces with the city and the provincial government to buy the rolling 22.25-hectare (55-acre) site and transform it into a botanical garden. Set against the distant backdrop of the North Shore mountains, the garden is a series of small, specialized gardens within the framework of the main garden. The gardens boast Canada's largest collection of rhododendrons, which in springtime line the Rhododendron Walk with blazing colour. The hexagonal Korean Pavilion is a focal point for the garden's Asian plant collection. Sculptures abound on the lawns, under trees, and between shrubs, and several are in the Children's Garden, where a chubby cherub presides over a wishing fountain. A latticework of paths wanders through 40 theme gardens—skirting lakes and ponds, crossing bridges, and winding through stands of bamboo and under giant redwoods. ■ *5251 Oak St, 266-7194.*

ORGANIZED TOURS

Sometimes the best way to get to know what's going on (and where) is to take a tour. Tours by bus, boat, train, plane, and motorized trolley are all available. In addition to organized tours, there are plenty of individual ones, including walking tours, horse-drawn buggy tours, luxury limo tours, tours of the university, museum tours, and art tours.

Don't overlook the obvious. Investigate **BC Transit's** (261-5100) flexible *Discover Vancouver on Transit Guidebook*, and ride the bus, SkyTrain, and SeaBus to places far and near. Available at Travel InfoCentres.

TRAINS AND BOATS

Paddle Wheelers [KIDS] Take to the water in another way— Harbour Ferries offers a 90-minute tour of the city in a delightful paddle wheeler that churns through Burrard Inlet. ▪ *Harbour Ferries (north foot of Denman St); 687-9558.*

Rocky Mountaineer Railtours The Canadian Rockies offer some of the most breathtaking scenery in all of North America, but most trains travelling from Vancouver to Jasper or Banff cross much of the mountains in the dark. Rocky Mountaineer stops for the night in Kamloops to let you make the most of the view outside your window. Breakfast, lunch, and snacks served to you in your seat. Extended trips to Edmonton or Alaska also available. Larger groups can customize their own itineraries and themes. ▪ *340 Brooksbank Ave, Suite 104, North Vancouver; 984-3131.*

Royal Hudson, North Vancouver [KIDS] It's a steamy experience—riding the rails on the Royal Hudson Steam Train. Engine 2860, the sole survivor of the 65 steam trains that crisscrossed Canada 50 years ago, takes you on a majestic trip along spectacular Howe Sound to Squamish, 65 kilometres (40 miles) north of Vancouver. There's a 90-minute stop in Squamish for sightseeing and lunch. Reservations are essential. ▪ *Royal Hudson Steam Train, BC Railways, McKeen Ave between Pemberton Ave and Philip Ave, North Vancouver; 984-5246; June to Sept.*

Royal Hudson and MV *Britannia* [KIDS] Take the Royal Hudson one way and the MV *Britannia* the other way. It's almost the same scenic trip, but cruising on the water offers a different perspective of the same views. ▪ *MV Britannia, Harbour Ferries (north foot of Denman St); 688-7246 or 687-9558.*

SS *Beaver* [KIDS] Explore the matchless scenery around Vancouver and take a cruise on a modern replica of a 19th-century paddle wheeler. Enjoy a salmon barbecue along the way. For romance, there's an evening cruise in the harbour, or a longer one to the lovely sheltered waters of Indian Arm. ▪ *SS Beaver, north foot of Bute St; 682-7284.*

RIVER TOURS

Fraser River Tours [KIDS] British Columbia's history is closely tied to that of the mighty Fraser River, where native people fished for salmon, explorers paddled canoes, and prospectors discovered gold. A Fraser River tour allows a close-up of tugs,

▼
Organized
Tours

River Tours

some hauling log booms, freighters, and other assorted vessels that work on this busy waterway. ■ *Fraser River Tours; 250-3458.*

TROLLEY

The Vancouver Trolley Company [KIDS] Take a jolly ride upon a trolley. It's an ideal way to familiarize yourself with the myriad charms of Vancouver. At any one of 17 stops you can jump off and explore, catching the next trolley 30 minutes or even three hours later—and you only pay once. Reproductions of the trolleys common on Vancouver's streets around 1890, these bright red and gold vehicles trundle you unhurriedly through the city. A relaxing, fun way to explore. ■ *255-2444.*

BUS TOURS

City and Nature Sightseeing City and Nature Sightseeing Tours whisks you through the city in a comfortable minibus that stops at museums and allows time for shopping and exploring at other attractions. ■ *683-2112.*

Gray Line [KIDS] Most city tours take about 3½ hours. Evening excursions may include a stop for dinner at an ethnic restaurant or an evening boat tour—or a drive along the North Shore. The choice is up to you. ■ *681-8687.*

Organized Tours

River Tours

Pacific Coach Lines The long and the short and the tall. Pacific Coach Lines has half a dozen tours, from a short tour of major attractions to an all-day tour that includes an aquabus to Granville Island and the Grouse Mountain Skyride. ■ *662-7575.*

PLANES AND HELICOPTERS

Harbour Air or Vancouver Helicopters You can cover a lot of ground in an airplane and avoid traffic problems. Several different tours are available, depending on the amount of time you want to spend and what you want to include. There's a special thrill to walking on ancient glacier ice, and on one of the chopper trips you can do just that. Various flights from downtown or Grouse Mountain. ■ *Contact: Harbour Air, 688-1277; or Vancouver Helicopters, 683-4354.*

SHOPPING

Shopping

SHOPPING DISTRICTS

Chinatown Although the Chinese-Canadian population of Vancouver is spread throughout the Lower Mainland, the old Chinatown is still a vital and interesting area to visit and shop in. It consists of a few blocks east and west of Main Street on Pender and Keefer streets. The little stores look as though they've been there for generations, and of course many of them have, so you'll get a good idea of the architecture of Vancouver in the first few decades of the 20th century. The Dr. Sun Yat-Sen Garden at 578 Carrall Street is definitely worth a visit. Many of the buildings there were built by artisans from China in a style that cannot be found anywhere else outside China. Other stores to check out include the original Ming Wo cookware shop at 23 East Pender Street and Chinese Linen & Silk at 27 East Pender. Just take a leisurely walk up one side of the street and down the other. Be sure to stop at the Oriental Dragon at 154 East Pender, the Man Sing Meat Centre for a little barbecued pork or duck, and the Ten Ren Tea & Jinseng Co. at 550 Main Street.

Commercial Drive Once known as Little Italy, the section of Commercial Drive between 1st and 12th avenues is now an amalgamation of many different cultures. The Italian Cultural Centre is the hub of the still-thriving Italian community, but many other Latin groups and Asian people live in the area, and the stores along the drive reflect this diversity.

Downtown The area bounded by Stanley Park to the west, Main Street to the east, False Creek to the south, and the harbour to the north has experienced a lot of growth recently. Notable buildings to see include the Marine Building at Pender and Hastings streets (a tribute to art deco inside and out), the

Hotel Vancouver at Burrard and Georgia streets, the fabulous old Orpheum Theatre on Granville Street, and the Hudson's Bay Building at the corner of Georgia and Granville streets. There's also the magnificent Canada Place at the foot of Burrard Street, with its sails perpetually raised. But also like many centres, the shopping action has moved underground to malls such as Pacific Centre, Vancouver Centre, Royal Centre, Bentall Centre, and Harbour Centre.

Granville Island Under the Granville Street Bridge, across False Creek from the Expo 86 site, warehouses and factories have been transformed into a public market and craft-y shops. There's still a cement plant down there, so watch out for large trucks, but the rest of the place is a tourist mecca. Locals flock to the public market for a tremendous selection of fresh food and gourmet items. It's a walk along the seawall from the many False Creek condos, co-ops, and townhouses; or a ferry ride from the apartments of the West End. Most of the shops are closed Mondays in winter.

Kerrisdale This area is arguably the best shopping neighbourhood in town for variety and quality of selection. You can find it spread along 41st Avenue for about four blocks east and west of West Boulevard and along West Boulevard from around 39th to 49th avenues. There is a decidedly English flavour to the neighbourhood. The stores are all well maintained, and there is a strong residential community to support them, as well as a community centre with a pool and a library. You'll find lots of fashion shops, like Margareta, Torri's, Martinique's Fashions, and Rose Marie's of Kerrisdale. There are shops for the home decorator, such as Hobbs, Linen Collection, Affordables, Salar Persian Carpets, Courtyards, and Ragfinders. And there are specialty shops for everything from cheese to chocolates. No wonder Kerrisdale shoppers are so loyal—they have no reason to wander.

Point Grey This university district runs along West 10th Avenue for about five or six blocks before you get to the gates of the University of British Columbia. Specialty shops run from decorator stores like Peasantries, the Cloth Shop, and Splish Splash Bath Boutique to stores selling imported fashions like Bali Bali and La Papillon to the very practical Hewer Home Hardware and Françoise knitting shop. There is also a Safeway (with lots of parking). This is a great area for browsing, crowds are sparse, and the quality of the merchandise is very high. It has a true neighbourhood feel to it, and it is set in an old and prestigious part of town.

Robson Street This street is the meeting place of cultures and couture, as *tout le monde* can be found strolling among its many shops every day. Weekends can be very crowded, but there's lots to see, since the street runs from the Granville Mall right down to Denman Street in the West End. You'll find the Vancouver Art Gallery, the Provincial Courthouse and its below-street-level Robson Square, the current central branch of Vancouver Public Library (the new one is under construction a few blocks east), and a number of designer boutiques, coffee shops, and neat little international-flavour restaurants.

West Vancouver Apart from the massive Park Royal Shopping Centre, the shops along Marine Drive in West Vancouver reflect the British heritage of the original European settlers of West Vancouver. The stores are quaint but carry a good stock of quality merchandise, whatever they may be selling. There are some nice little restaurants and galleries too. West Vancouver is one of the more prestigious neighbourhoods in the Lower Mainland, so expect the prices to reflect that.

ANTIQUES

Canada West Antiques Authentic pine antiques from Eastern Canada mix with country furniture and decorator pieces. Be sure to see the selection of grandmotherly folk crafts—quilts, hooked rugs, and more. ▪ *3607 W Broadway; 733-3213; every day.*

Folkart Antiques Besides antiques, this charming and fanciful place features unique pieces of folk art that are simply irresistible. There's a good selection of pine furniture as well. ▪ *3715 W 10th Ave; 228-1011; every day.*

▼

Auctions

▲

Old Country Antiques A homey atmosphere and a wide selection of pine furniture. Be sure to pick up a jar of the shop's own antique-pine wax for the care of your purchase. The delightful garden and patio statuary and benches are perfect for your own "secret garden." ▪ *3720 W 10th Ave; 224-8664; every day.*

Stewart's Antiques Take about 372 square metres (4,000 square feet) of space and fill it with antiques and reproductions, and you have not just a store but an experience. Be sure to leave enough time for extensive browsing. And brass lovers, beware—the store's selection is tantalizingly varied. ▪ *4391 Main St; 872-1155; every day.*

AUCTIONS

Love's Since 1912, Love's has been helping bargain hunters get the best prices on all kinds of items. Auctions are held every Wednesday at noon and at 7pm. Watch the papers for items to be auctioned. Merchandise varies: one day you could pick up a priceless antique; the next, some repossessed restaurant equipment. Love's also does appraisals. ▪ *1635 W Broadway; 733-1157; Mon-Fri.*

Maynard's Another long-time Vancouver fixture, Maynard's has been around since 1902. Auctions are held every Wednesday at 7pm, and you're invited to view your potential treasures on Tuesdays between 10am and 6pm. The store also has a large retail area with liquidated inventories going for a song. There's quite a range of quality and price, but some genuine bargains can be found. Constant vigilance is the key. ■ *415 W 2nd Ave; 876-6787; every day (Sunday retail only).*

BOOKS, MAPS, MAGAZINES

Banyen Books & Banyen Sound Known for its extensive stock of new age and self-help books, Banyen Books also has a great selection of vegetarian cookbooks and religious texts—and tarot cards too. The store provides hours of contented browsing in a quiet, friendly atmosphere. Banyen Sound, next door, has new age music recordings and spoken text cassette tapes. Many unique-to-the-area offerings. ■ *2671 W Broadway; 732-7912;* ■ *2669 W Broadway; 737-8858; every day.*

Blackberry Books Bright and attractive locations provide the perfect backdrop for extensive selections of popular fiction and nonfiction books. There are satisfying classic and craft sections as well. Appealing book reviews can be found at the Broadway location, where staff read books and post their comments for customers. ■ *1663 Duranleau St (Granville Island);* ■ *2206 W 4th Ave; 733-1673;* ■ *2855 W Broadway; 739-8116; every day.*

Auctions

Bomber Joe's Aviation Books Appropriately located at the Vancouver Airport's South Terminal, this store could really take off. Strictly for those with no fear of flying. Handbooks, regulation books, maintenance manuals—even video-format pilot training programs. ■ *South Terminal Bldg, 29-4440 Cowley Crescent, Richmond; 278-8021; Mon-Sat.*

The Comicshop It's true that the books here are comic books, but the shop has such a comprehensive collection that it deserves mention. New issues and collector's items. ■ *2089 W 4th Ave; 738-8122; every day.*

Duthie Books The true bibliophile must make a pilgrimage to one of Duthie's six locations. Since 1957, Duthie Books has been serving the literati and the hoi polloi alike with its comprehensive selection of the popular and the obscure. Helpful, knowledgeable staff. A new outlet just opened at 2239 West 4th. ■ *919 Robson St; 684-4496;* ■ *4444 W 10th Ave; 224-7012;* ■ *4255 Arbutus St; 738-1833.* ■ *Foreign language books and magazines at Duthie's Manhattan Books and Magazines, 1089 Robson St; 681-9074.* ■ *Duthie's Technical & Professional Books, 1701 W 3rd Ave; 732-1448; every day.*

Granville Book Company This store provides a browse-fest for bibliophiles, with a good selection of the latest best-sellers, and a very good Sci-Fi/Fantasy section. ■ *850 Granville St; 687-2213; every day.*

Mayfair News Can't find your hometown newspaper? Need a copy of an obscure magazine? Next time, try the Mayfair News collection of over 3,000 periodicals. ■ *1535 W Broadway; 738-8951; every day;* ■ *Royal Centre; 687-8951; Mon-Sat.*

Peregrine Books A fine and well-respected bookstore featuring a large variety of titles on women's studies. Used section in the back, bargain table in the front, and an interesting selection in between. ■ *2932 W Broadway; 738-6523; every day.*

Pink Peppercorn Before you head down to the Granville Island Public Market, drop by and pick up a new cookbook from the Pink Peppercorn's selection of more than 5,000. Every taste is catered to, from the connoisseur to the fast-food fanatic. Knowledgeable staff. Their storewide end-of-summer sale offers some real bargains. ■ *2686 W Broadway; 736-4213; every day.*

Siliconnections Books Callow beginners and hardened hackers alike shop at Siliconnections, where there is an impressive stock of manuals to guide you through the software jungle. ■ *3785 W 10th Ave; 222-2221; every day.*

Sport Book Plus There are fewer than a dozen bookstores in the world that are dedicated solely to sports, and Vancouver boasts one of the best. If a book has been written about a sport, chances are owner Mike Harling will have it in his stock of more than 5,000. The fitness section is particularly strong, and there are some excellent selections on sports nutrition. ■ *2100 W 4th Ave; 733-7323; every day.*

Travel Bug Off to the Serengeti? The Outback? The Bronx? Owner Dwight Elliot can find you just the right travel guide and foreign language phrase book from his stock of over 6,000 titles. Then he'll equip you with the essential travel accessories, from money belts to electrical converters to head rests. He can even provide the carry-on luggage to stow it all in. ■ *2667 W Broadway; 733-1122; every day.*

Vancouver Kidsbooks To say this store is dedicated to children's literature is a terrible understatement. There are books and book talks and book readings and book launchings. And did we mention the books? The staff are especially helpful in choosing gifts for out-of-town children. ■ *3083 W Broadway; 738-5335; every day.*

Wanderlust When it's time for those boot heels to go wanderin', Tony McCurdy and his helpful staff can make sure you're ready to go anywhere. They carry thousands of books about foreign lands, with entire bookcases devoted to some countries. Travel accessories include water purifiers, mosquito nets, maps, convertible packs, and language tapes. ▪ *1929 W 4th Ave; 739-2182; every day.*

White Dwarf Books For a vacation in another dimension, get one of the science fiction or fantasy tomes in White Dwarf's incredible selection. For an "unreal" getaway, try a role-playing game. ▪ *4368 W 10th Ave; 228-8223; every day.*

Women in Print Books by women, for women, on women's issues. Also books by men on topics of interest to women. ▪ *3566 W 4th Ave; 732-4128; every day.*

World Wide Books and Maps Wherever you're going, this store can help you find your way. It has one of the largest map and travel guide selections in Canada. ▪ *736A Granville St (downstairs); 687-3320; every day.*

CAMERAS

Future Shop This chain operates on the "more selection for less money" philosophy of retailing. It also carries a massive selection of all kinds of electronic gadgetry—from phones and answering machines to big-screen TVs and computers—and has stereo equipment for all budgets, with brand names like Sony, Hitachi, and Panasonic. ▪ *1322 W Broadway; 738-6565; every day; other branches.*

▼

Books, Maps, Magazines

▲

Lens & Shutter Cameras Serious, dedicated shutterbugs will tell you that it's not the camera that costs so much, it's all the accessories. That's why they shop here. This chain of stores has an incredible assortment of its own line of accessories as well as every single thing you ever wanted in the photography line. The knowlegable staff of photographic professionals will not intimidate. ▪ *2912 W Broadway; 736-3461; Mon-Sat.; other branches.*

Leo's Camera Supply Outside you'll find an unprepossessing exterior in one of the seedier sections of the Granville Mall, but inside is a shutterbug's dream. The store boasts of being one of the country's largest dealers of professional supplies and carries a huge selection of used photo equipment. If you're looking for a hard-to-find antique camera, chances are you'll find it here. Franchised for all the major manufacturers. Shipping available. ▪ *1055 Granville St; 685-5331; every day.*

London Drugs This store has an exceptional selection of moderately priced cameras at competitive prices. The staff is helpful and can usually answer any questions that beginners might have. ▪ *665 W Broadway; 872-8114; every day; other branches.*

CLOTHING: CHILDREN'S

Bratz Stroll down South Granville until you come to a window full of colourful, adorable, definitely wearable children's clothing. Haircuts and hair styling specifically for tots is also available. ▪ *2828 Granville St; 734-4344; Mon-Sat.*

Danica Designer fashions and accessories for the young, well-dressed set (newborn to 16), with a large selection of imported styles. ▪ *2069 W 41st Ave; 266-1711; Mon-Sat.*

Isola Bella Exclusive designer togs for tots—much of the stock is imported from France and Italy—with European quality. You'll also find footwear for fashionable feet and beautiful gift items for children. From newborn to size 16. ▪ *5692 Yew St (Kerrisdale); 266-8808; Mon-Sat.*

Please Mum Fun and functional clothing and shoes for the younger jet set. ▪ *2951 W Broadway; 732-4574;* ▪ *319-650 W 41st Ave (Oakridge Centre); 263-3534;* ▪ *2002-100 Park Royal S; 925-0338;* ▪ *123 Carrie Cates Centre (Lonsdale Quay), North Vancouver; 988-2038; and five other locations; every day.*

Spoilt Designed and made locally, these classic children's fashions are constructed to last through several hand-me-downs. The helpful staff are very tolerant of tired and temperamental tots. ▪ *Oakridge Centre; 261-2377; other branches; every day.*

▼
Clothing: Men's

CLOTHING: MEN'S

▲

Boboli The stone archway is fabled to have come from a ruined Mexican cathedral. Inside, designer fashions and footwear await discriminating shoppers. The store stocks many imports, including Claude Montana, Pal Zaleri, and Gianni Versace. ▪ *2776 Granville St; 736-3458; Mon-Sat.*

Bretton's A classically designed store that sets the tone for the upscale fashions you'll find. Top lines of international and Canadian designers. ▪ *Eaton Centre Metrotown, Burnaby; 433-6264; every day.*

Chevalier Creations Definitely for the man on the way up. Custom suits from tailor Gabriel Kalfon in linen or mohair blends and 100 percent wool. Custom-made shirts in silk, linen, or cotton. Make an appointment. ▪ *2756 Granville St; 731-8746; Mon-Sat.*

E. A. Lee for Men Classic designs: Hardy Amies, Hugo Boss, and Versace. ▪ *464 Howe St; 683-2457; Mon-Sat.*

Edward Chapman Men's Wear Traditional in every sense of the word, Edward Chapman has been synonymous with classic British clothing for four generations. The store carries

I

Liberty of London, Burberrys, and other British designers. ▪ *833 W Pender St; 685-6207; Mon-Sat.*

Harry Rosen Another long-time supplier of natty men's attire, the two stores offer a complete selection of sportswear, shirts, and accessories, as well as designer suits from world-famous makers. ▪ *Pacific Centre; 683-6861;* ▪ *Oakridge Centre; 266-1172; every day.*

Hill's of Kerrisdale Top-quality clothing with labels such as Polo, Tommy Hilfiger, and Anne Klein for everyone in the family. Timberland and Dr. Martens footwear, as well as Martha Sturdy jewellery, are carried here. It's also the location of an Aritzia in-store boutique stocking the Aritzia line of youth-oriented fashion. ▪ *2125 West 41st Ave; 266-9177; every day.*

Leone Worth a visit—if only for the sheer architectural splendour of it all. Many designers are exclusive to Leone, and it carries a very fine house label as well. Complete lines of accessories and fragrances for men and women. ▪ *Sinclair Centre, 757 W Hastings St; 683-1133; every day.*

Mark James Everything for the fashionable man, from classic jeans to suits from Armani and Versace. Designer shirts and accessories. Savvy shoppers on the store's large mailing list get in on tremendous savings during its big biannual sales. ▪ *2941 W Broadway; 734-2381; every day.*

Clothing: Men's

Michael McBride Casual clothes, including a lovely selection of sweaters and shirts. A great place to stock up on suspenders and bow ties. ▪ *4426 W 10th Ave; 222-4433; Mon-Sat.*

Quorum Fashion Emporium Designer names in a sleek setting for the man with more taste than money. Quorum offers prices up to 33 percent lower than you'll find elsewhere. A little hard to find but worth the search. ▪ *206-1008 Homer St; 684-1223; every day.*

S. Lampman Set in a building with charming trompe l'oeil second-storey windows, this shop stocks sporty separates from designers like Calvin Klein, Christian Dior, Lyle & Scott, and Alan Paine. Suits available by order. ▪ *2126 West 41st Ave; 261-2750; every day.*

Tilley Endurables Adventure Clothing For the truly adventurous—or those who want to look as though they are. Functional yet somehow funky, these incredibly practical clothes have been worn all around the world. Their fame is built on hidden vents, secret pockets, and durable fabrics. Top it all off with one of those fabulous Tilley hats. ▪ *1537 W Broadway; 732-4287;* ▪ *1194 Marine Dr, North Vancouver; 987-6424; Mon-Sat.*

CLOTHING: WOMEN'S

Alfred Sung This chain contains the Alfred Sung Boutique, which is couture for the modern woman, and Alfred by Alfred Sung, moderately priced fashions for the young of heart from this popular designer. The latter contains mostly sportswear and coordinated casuals, but some items are suitable for the office. ■ *1143 Robson St; 687-2153; every day; other branches.*

Aritzia Six locations in the area feature high-end, high-tech fashions for the woman on the go. Hot, in, definite fashion statements for the very brave or the very young. Designers like Esprit, Betsey Johnson, Comrags, and Kookai grace the racks. Dr. Martens footwear is available at Robson Street and Metrotown. ■ *2125 W 41st Ave (in Hill's of Kerrisdale); 266-6446;* ■ *Metrotown Centre, Burnaby; 435-7975;* ■ *Oakridge Shopping Centre; 261-2202;* ■ *Park Royal Centre South, West Vancouver; 926-7666;* ■ *Richmond Centre, Richmond; 244-1614;* ■ *1068 Robson St; 684-3251;* ■ *Aritzia Dr. Martens, 1208 Robson St; 689-4998; every day.*

Bacci's For the bold and the beautiful. Are you ready for Madonna's favourite designer, Jean-Paul Gaultier? Other high-fashion designers for the *autre-couture* are also sold here. ■ *2788 Granville St; 733-4933; Mon-Sat.*

Bali Bali An eclectic combination of imported and domestic fashions. Owner Mooh Hood shops the exotic East for fashions, accessories, and jewellery. ■ *4462 W 10th Ave; 224-2347; every day.*

Bellevue Landing Seven solid shops have joined together in a new concept—an open arrangement under one roof. They state that they are "always striving to surpass your expectations," and frankly, they do! Ladies' fashions can be found in Bellevue Landing Boutique (926-1475) and Ruby's (922-8715). Men's fashions are in The Mensroom (925-1812). Children are catered to in Welcome to the World (925-2810), for clothing, and 2 Cute 4 U, for hair care. The Shoe Tree (926-6640) offers European footwear for men and women, and Leumas (926-1450) has gifts for all occasions. More than exclusive and enticing fashions and accessories, Bellevue Landing offers exceptional service. They have refreshments, coat and parcel check, home delivery, and even a limousine service with free pick-up for seniors (on 24-hour notice). The stores also combine for "Make-over Mondays," and for a fashion show every month. ■ *1403 Bellevue Ave, West Vancouver; 926-1404; every day.*

Byblos No, this is not a bookstore. Byblos offers a selection of very stylish clothes and shoes that are not quite in the book, either. ■ *2790 Granville St; 737-0368; Mon-Sat.*

▼
Clothing: Women's
▲

Cabbages & Kinx Fashions for those who like to make it up as they go along. Leggings, tops, boots, leather, and lace in very interesting combinations. For the very, very chic. ■ *306 W Cordova St; 669-4238; every day.*

Celine Sophisticated fashion imported from France. ■ *755 Burrard St; 685-2353; Mon-Sat.*

C'est Ça This classically hip shop is located in the same trendy Yaletown building as Quorum Fashion Emporium Menswear. The owners have exquisite taste and a strong sense of their market. Norma Kamali and Magaschoni, Lilicube, and others are available. You can also get jewellery, accessories, and handbags. ■ *204-1008 Homer St; 682-3552; every day.*

Chanel The little store that Coco built can include Vancouver as part of its far-flung empire. This shop carries Chanel fashions, accessories, and perfume, and its ebullient Francophone staff is a pleasure to visit. ■ *755 Burrard St; 682-0522; every day.*

E. A. Lee For Women Right next to the men's shop, this is full of imported designers, Karl Lagerfeld being the most easily recognized. Expensive and worth it. ■ *466 Howe St; 683-2457; Mon-Sat.*

▼
**Clothing:
Women's**
▲

Edward Chapman Ladies Shop For over 40 years, this name has been synonymous with quality imported women's wear. Somewhat conservative in its selection, the store carries top names from England and Europe (notably Germany) in well-cut, well-made fashions. Mother may have got her tweeds here, but they are very popular with the career women downtown too. ■ *2596 Granville St; 732-3394; every day; other branches.*

Enda B A warning to casual browsers: Enda B has a large selection of designer natural-fibre fashions and the savviest wardrobe consultants in town. Don't enter unless you're fully prepared to walk out with something you love. Liz Claiborne, Guess, Alfred Sung, Steilmann, Adrienne Vittadini, and Jones New York, among others, fill the store. You'll also find lingerie, a good shoe section, a children's play area, and a cappuccino bar. ■ *4346 W 10th Ave; 228-1214; every day.*

Esmode Boutique High-quality, authoritative clothing by Canadian designers. Renowned local designer and owner Rose-Marie Cuevas has fashioned her Jacqueline Conoir line to be classic and confident. ■ *3035 Granville St; 732-4209; every day.*

Exquisite Boutique The loyal clientele is addicted to select designers such as Laborn Modell, Louis Feraud, and Jobis. Fashions for work, play, and evening—many are one of a kind. ■ *Park Royal North, West Vancouver; 922-5211; every day.*

Ferragamo Extraordinary fashions in an exclusive international boutique. This is the only Canadian operation of this company that can be found in major cities around the world. Separates, shoes, handbags, and accessories are offered, along with a handsome selection of men's footwear and accessories. ▪ *918 Robson St; 669-4495; every day.*

Holliday's Funwear Famous throughout the area for its selection of swimsuits and cruise wear. The winter selection is great. Travel accessories are also sold. ▪ *5507 West Blvd; 263-6821; Mon-Sat.*

Laura Ashley The English country style popularized throughout the world by these stores is still going strong. This shop carries women's fashions from the Laura Ashley Collection and will special-order wallpaper and fabrics for your home. ▪ *1171 Robson St; 688-8729; every day.*

Leone Set like a jewel in the exquisite Sinclair Centre, this store showcases international designers in separate galleries— Versace, Armani, Donna Karan, DKNY, and many more. There is a large selection of classic accessories, as well as fragrances. ▪ *757 W Hastings St; 683-1133; every day.*

Lesley's Think globally, dress locally. This is the first stop for chic Canadian designs—more than three-quarters of the merchandise is Canadian designed. Very helpful staff. ▪ *4440 W 10th Ave; 222-4900; every day.*

Lesliejane This store has been a mainstay in West Vancouver for many years, and shoppers depend on it for a good selection of wearable, versatile designer clothing. Several exclusive lines, and a good range of accessories. ▪ *1480 Marine Dr, West Vancouver; 922-8612; every day.*

Margareta Design Classics, designed and manufactured for the store's own label. Styles range from the elegant to the casual. Custom-made and custom-fitted fashions are a specialty. ▪ *948 Robson St; 681-6612;* ▪ *1441 Bellevue Ave, West Vancouver; 926-2113;* ▪ *5591 West Blvd; 266-6211;* ▪ *1959 152nd St, Surrey; 538-6688; every day.*

Nancy Lord Soft, supple leather fashions in classic and eclectic styling. Clothes are manufactured by the shop, and made-to-measure styles are available. The colours are beautiful and the quality is high. ▪ *1666 Johnston St (Granville Island); 689-3972; every day.*

Rodier Paris Boutique Members of the fashionable chain you see all over the world, these shops feature European-style knitwear and matching accessories. Also Rodier Hommes. ▪ *100-1025 Robson St; 682-1155;* ▪ *Oakridge Shopping Centre; 261-5121; every day.*

Roots The area boasts three of this popular North American chain's shops, carrying casual, ruggedly styled clothes and shoes for men, women, and children. They also sport a good selection of accessories perfect for weekends in the great outdoors. ▪ *Pacific Centre; 683-5465; every day; other branches.*

Simply Grand Clothing Co. Comfortably chic fashions in sizes 14 to 56, including evening and business wear and casual separates. Ask about the store's customer files for out-of-town orders. ▪ *4695 Central Blvd, Burnaby; 439-1313; every day.*

Sonia Rykiel This Parisian designer of haute knitwear is represented by fashion, jewellery, and accessories from her collection. ▪ *199 Water St; 685-5678; Mon-Sat.*

Suttles and Seawinds Truly Canadian—made in Nova Scotia—fashions and gifts. Separates and coordinates come in distinctive fabrics. Quilts and accessories are also sold. ▪ *Waterfront Centre, 200 Burrard St; 688-1612; every day.*

Suzanne Bell's Fashions A generous collection of the latest fashions and fabrics in size 16 and up, both imported and created by Canadian designers, both casual wear and dresswear. Customer sizes and preferences are kept on file for future orders. ▪ *5794 Victoria Dr; 324-7394; Mon-Sat.*

Tayari Tayari has a terrific array of forward-fashion women's clothing and accessories for hip women of all ages. The young staff couldn't be more helpful—they'll even accompany you down the street to choose shoes for your new ensemble. ▪ *4412 W 10th Ave; 224-5589; every day.*

Wear Else? The dependable fashion consultants can outfit you with an entire wardrobe—or the classic pieces that will be its foundation. Both international and Canadian designers are represented, and there is a large selection of accessories. Wear Else Weekend is available at the West 4th Avenue location and offers more casual clothing and accessories for leisure wear. ▪ *2360 W 4th Ave; 732-3521;* ▪ *789 W Pender; 662-7890; Oakridge Shopping Centre; 266-3613;* ▪ *Park Royal South, West Vancouver; 925-0058; every day.*

Zig Zag Boutique Great mix of singularly attractive accessories, shoes, handbags, and separates. ▪ *4424 W 10th Ave; 224-2421; every day.*

Zonda Nellis Unique loomed fabrics are used to create simple yet distinctive fashions. Nellis is a local designer with an international clientele. ▪ *2203 Granville St; 736-5668; Mon-Sat.*

CONSIGNMENT

Bobbitt's This children's consignment store sells quality clothes, toys, furniture, and equipment. You can also find Kindersling baby carriers here. ▪ *2951A W 4th Ave; 738-0333; Mon-Sat.*

The Comeback A consignment shop with designer labels. There's a fast turnover, so shop often. ▪ *3050 Edgemont Blvd, North Vancouver; 984-2551; Mon-Sat.*

Fine Finds Here you'll find discounts of 50 percent or more on new clothing. There is a large selection of sportswear, dresses, and evening wear, as well as an impressive accessories selection and many imported items. ▪ *6272 East Blvd; 261-8813; every day.*

MacGillycuddy's For Little People A consignment store for children, selling clothing, footwear, furniture, some hand-knits. ▪ *4881 MacKenzie St; 263-5313; Mon-Sat.*

Oz B'Coz New and consignment shop for children. Some designer labels; cute kids' hats. ▪ *7966 Granville St; 264-6161; Mon-Sat.*

Turnabout Collections Ltd. High-quality consignment, carrying some designers. In any case, you'll get top fashion for your dollar. ▪ *3121 Granville St; 732-8115;* ▪ *3636 W 4th Ave; 731-7762; every day.*

COOKWARE

Basic Stock Cookware Enter this store and instantly feel like a chef. There is rack after rack of shining pots and pans of every size and description, and gadgets, gadgets, gadgets. A selection of coffees and teas, and everything you need to make them in, is also offered. ▪ *2294 W 4th Ave; 736-1412;* ▪ *2150 W 41st Ave; 261-3599;* ▪ *986 Denman St; 685-2414; every day.*

The Cookshop When we say that the Cookshop in City Square has a comprehensive selection of kitchenware basics, name brands, and gadgets, it's no exaggeration. In its 372-square-metre (4,000-square-foot) space, the friendly and knowledgeable staff has assembled anything you'd need or want to furnish your kitchen the right way—from Finnish El-Rod stainless steel cookware to butcher blocks and prep tables, and from John Boos to German Bosch kitchen machines. Cooking classes, offered in a separate kitchen, feature local chefs. ▪ *11-555 W 12th Ave; 873-5683; every day.*

Ming Wo Since 1919, Ming Wo has maintained the highest standards of quality in the cookware and kitchenware it carries. A large stock of hard-to-find items and a reputation for value have kept Vancouverites loyal to the store. ▪ *2707 Granville St; 737-7885;* ▪ *23 E Pender St (the original store); 683-7268;* ▪ *2170 W 4th Ave; 737-7885; and suburban shopping centres; every day.*

Cookware

CRYSTAL AND CHINA

Atkinson's Just visiting Atkinson's is a luxurious experience, and the lure of the European crystal, silver, and china can charm the credit card right out of your pocket. Splurge on Lalique, Baccarat, Lladro, and Limoges, or treat yourself to bed, table, and bath linen imported from Pratesi's of Italy. ■ *2415 Granville St; 736-3378; Tues-Sat.*

Presents of Mind Fine china, decorative items, and gifts. ■ *3153 Granville St; 736-6463; Mon-Sat.*

FABRICS

Chintz & Company Floor-to-ceiling racks of fabrics and all the notions you'll need to whip up terrific-looking home decoration projects. Custom work is available. The store also carries furniture and collectable accessories. ■ *901 Homer St; 689-2022; every day.*

The Cloth Shop Just strolling into The Cloth Shop makes your fingers itch to create. You'll discover great quilting fabrics and supplies and lots of ideas for homey crafts. The shop runs its own classes on a variety of fabric crafts. ■ *4415 W 10th Ave; 224-1325; every day.*

Dressew Supply Ltd. The weeks before Halloween this store is jammed with home-sewers looking for the perfect fabric and notions to create a costume. There are miles of aisles of supplies, thread, buttons, trims, and patterns, as well as fabric by the kilometre. ■ *337 W Hastings St; 682-6196 (phone lines are open 9-10am); Mon-Sat.*

Mode Fabrics This tiny shop contains a surprisingly large selection of natural fibres, fashion fabrics, laces, silks, and satins. It also carries Simplicity and Style patterns. ■ *2259 W 41st Ave; 266-7232; Mon-Sat.*

Mr. Jax Fashion Fabrics Even if you can't sew a stitch, it's worth picking up some of this great-quality fabric to take along to your favourite dressmaker. You'll also find notions and (im)perfectly lovely "seconds" from the Mr. Jax line. ■ *316 W Cordova St; 684-7004;* ■ *7771 Alderbridge Way, Richmond; 276-8222;* ■ *218-4567 Lougheed Hwy, Burnaby; 291-6369;* ■ *104-2748 Lougheed Hwy, Port Coquitlam; 464-3100; every day.*

Ragfinders Decorators can often be found in this Kerrisdale store, chatting with the knowledgeable sales staff and comparing swatches. Good-quality manufacturers and the latest decorator fabrics are represented here. ■ *2045 W 41st Ave; 266-3611; every day.*

▼

Crystal and China

▲

FASHION ACCESSORIES

Edie Hats Owner Edie Orenstein has been a mainstay of the local fashion scene for years. The store carries her own delicious creations, as well as those of other local milliners. Imports too. ▪ *1666 Johnston St (Granville Island); 683-4280; every day.*

Eleanor Mack A visit to this shop makes you nostalgic for the days when every well-dressed woman wore a hat. A great selection of chic imports as well as custom pieces. ▪ *971 Park Royal South; 922-4630; every day.*

Satchel Shop A local favourite for purses, handbags, good-looking back packs, and luggage. Lots of convenient locations. ▪ *Pacific Centre; 669-2923;* ▪ *1060 Robson St; 662-3424;* ▪ *2186 W 41st Ave; 261-8713;* ▪ *Metrotown Centre, Burnaby; 437-6151;* ▪ *Lansdowne Park, Richmond; 278-5665;* ▪ *Park Royal South, West Vancouver; 588-2144;* ▪ *Coquitlam Centre, Coquitlam; 464-8621;* ▪ *Surrey Place Shopping Centre, Surrey; 583-3229; every day.*

FLORISTS AND GARDEN SHOPS

▼

▲

The Avant Gardener This is a great store for the serious gardener or the confirmed browser (and what gardener isn't both?). Gardening stock and patio furniture sit alongside decorator accents and designer T-shirts. ▪ *1460 Marine Drive, West Vancouver; 926-8784; every day.*

Bomar's Flowers, Gifts & Crafts Craft-y types already know about this place, with its huge selection of everything you need to create your own floral arrangements. A well-stocked array of prepared baskets and arrangements is also available. ▪ *2825 Grandview Hwy; 430-5027; every day.*

Dig This This is a faux-ivy-covered cottage on South Granville with supplies for indoor and outdoor gardening, as well as decorator accents. A larger stock of garden and outdoor furniture can be found at the Granville Island location. ▪ *3084 Granville St; 739-1725;* ▪ *1551 Johnston St (Granville Island); 688-2929; every day.*

The Flower Show A great place to pick up a bouquet. Lots of lush stock and reasonable prices. ▪ *4430 W 10th Ave; 224-3711; Mon-Sat.*

Garden Rooms If your idea of backyard furniture is restricted to beach chairs and tire swings, here's your chance to redecorate the out-of-doors. Garden Rooms' furniture, accents, and handy gadgets make outdoor living gracious living. ▪ *2083 Alma St; 224-8900; every day.*

Thomas Hobbs Florist One of the finest florists—and certainly the best-known one—in the Vancouver area. Tasteful and creative arrangements are presented in handsome containers. ■ *2127 W 41st Ave; 263-2601; Mon-Sat.*

FURNITURE AND ACCESSORIES

Bali Bali Galleria A favourite importer of the exotic and the exciting; a delightful source of handicrafts and objets d'art from the fabled East, including Bali, Java, India, and Tibet. ■ *3598 W 4th Ave; 736-2172; every day.*

Byron & Company How can you look like a world traveller and avoid those pesky immunization shots? Sprinkle a few pillows, bowls, and artistic items from this shop around your home. Imports from Asia and South America. ■ *5635 West Blvd; 266-1043; Mon-Sat.*

Chintz & Company Exotic and intriguing-looking wooden tables and accessories are offered here, along with racks of tassels, piles of carved wooden fruit, and shelves and shelves of lovely decorator fabric. Custom work is a specialty. ■ *901 Homer St; 689-2022; every day.*

Country Furniture If anything is going to convince you of the beauty and simplicity of pioneer life, it's a visit to this store. Okay, so the pioneers may not have had these brilliant designs and whimsical decorative accents, but they should have. ■ *3097 Granville St; 738-6411; Mon-Sat.*

Form & Function Furniture, simply designed, simply beautiful. Much of the stock is made by the store's crafts people. Custom furniture is also available. ■ *4357 W 10th Ave; 222-1317; Mon-Sat.*

Industrial Revolution This store manages to make high-tech look romantic, and it has lots of those handy little accessories you didn't know you needed—till you fell in love with them here. ■ *2306 Granville St; 734-4395; Mon-Sat.*

Kaya Kaya Is it a furniture store? Is it a gift shop? Is it a clothing boutique? Who cares? Beautiful Japanese imports with something for everyone. ■ *2039 W 4th Ave; 732-1816; Mon-Sat.*

Motiv There is a lot of cleverly wrought wrought iron here—and ceramic plates and bowls and primitive-looking baskets and throws. This is a sister store to Ming Wo (see Cookware section). ■ *2064 W 4th Ave; 737-8116; every day.*

GIFTS AND JEWELLERY

Birks When Henry Birk opened his doors in the beginning of the last century, he could hardly have known that one day his empire would stretch from sea to sea. Birks stores are to be found in every major Canadian city. For generations, brides have received their engagement rings from Birks, have registered with Birks, and have received their subsequent anniversary presents from Birks, all in that distinctive blue box. It carries a cachet as exciting as the gift it holds. ▪ *Vancouver Centre; 669-3333; every day; other branches.*

Cavelti Tony Cavelti is an award-winning goldsmith and jeweller and a Vancouver tradition, and his store on Georgia Street is a magnet for the rich, the powerful, and the beautiful. But we all can afford to gaze into his shop windows. ▪ *565 W Georgia St; 681-3481; Mon-Sat.*

Chachkas ▪ Chachkees Whether you're looking for the perfect little gift for a friend or a selfish little treat for yourself, you'll find plenty to choose from at these sister stores, which carry a large selection of jewellery, decorative items, prints, and imports. ▪ *1070 Robson St; 688-6417; ▪ 1075 Robson St; 687-6639; every day.*

Georg Jensen Jensen's classic turn-of-the-century designs—all executed in silver—vie for attention with modern styles. This store is part of the international chain founded by the Danish designer and features high-quality jewellery, crystal, and decor items. ▪ *Pacific Centre; 688-3116; every day.*

▼

Gifts and Jewellery

▲

Lightheart & Co. Whoever said that it is better to give than to receive probably had this store in mind. It has the most divine ready-made gift baskets, containing jars of fruits in liqueur and other tasty treats—much of which is locally made. Staff members will do custom baskets if you give them enough notice. Brides flock here for the terrific registry service, which includes a discount for the bride, free gift wrapping and delivery, and a fabulous selection of crystal, china, decorative items, and linen. ▪ *535 Howe St; 684-4711; other branches; every day.*

Martha Sturdy A local star with international impact, Martha Sturdy creates simple, charming jewellery designs. Although her artistic renderings change to reflect current fashions, her jewellery remains a classic collectible. ▪ *3065 Granville St; 737-0037; Mon-Sat; ▪ 775 Burrard St; 685-7751; every day.*

Panache Handcrafted silverware exclusive to the shop and a good selection of jewellery, crystal, and china. ▪ *4475 W 10th Ave; 224-2514; Mon-Sat.*

Tiffany The first name in jewellery can be found in Holt Renfrew in Pacific Centre. Conscious of Vancouver's loyalty to Birks jewellers, sales staff members point out that they are "the other blue box." You can expect to find classic Tiffany items, watches, and Paloma Picasso–designed jewellery. ▪ *Holt Renfrew in Pacific Centre; 681-3121; every day.*

Treemendous Many, many lovely items you have absolutely no use for are to be found here. The store stands by its motto, "Don't need it, we got it." Unique gifts for that person who has everything. ▪ *2384 W 4th Ave; 731-5368; every day.*

Yerushalem Imports You can expect to find Hebrew greeting cards and seasonal items for Jewish holidays, but this shop also contains a treasure trove of gift ideas for recipients of every age and religious persuasion—all imported from the Holy Land. ▪ *2375 W 41st Ave; 266-0662; every day.*

HARDWARE

Hewer Home Hardware One of those neighbourhood hardware stores where you're just as likely to pick up a toaster as a power tool or a can of paint. Serves the Point Grey area. ▪ *4459 W 10th Ave; 224-4934; Mon-Sat.*

Lumberland At first, this chain of stores looks just like any other building supply outlet. The differences are subtle but telling. This local, privately owned chain buys almost all its stock from local suppliers, ensuring that stock on hand is current and complete. And because they're not paying for transport and storage, prices are usually lower than the competition's. Hey, even contractors buy here. ▪ *2889 E 12th Ave; 254-1614; every day; other branches.*

▼

Gifts and Jewellery

▲

Paine Hardware Limited This hardware-cum-general store has been around since 1908—and it looks it. You can get a fishing licence or outfit your RV, and you'll find everything from penny nails to lawn mowers to explosives. ▪ *90 Lonsdale Ave, North Vancouver; 987-2241; every day.*

Steveston Marine & Hardware This is the place to find those great-looking brass fittings to add that nautical look to your home. The shop's fabulous antique brass stock varies, giving you an excuse to drop by to see what's on hand or to stock up on power tools, hoses, or marine paint. ▪ *3560 Moncton, Richmond; 277-7031; every day.*

HEALTH FOOD AND PRODUCTS

Alive Health Centre This chain of stores, found in many of the city's major shopping centres, exudes health and goodwill. There are shelves upon shelves of herbs and vitamins, a good selection of cosmetics, and every yogurt maker and juicer imaginable. A great selection of books to teach you how to get healthy and stay that way. Seniors' discount. ▪ *Oakridge Centre; 263-3235; every day; other branches.*

Capers Long the private haunt of the health-conscious in West Vancouver, Capers has at last come to Kitsilano. These are the largest "whole foods" markets (and restaurants) in the Lower Mainland, with some 557 square metres (6,000 square feet) in West Vancouver and even larger premises in Kits, devoted to bringing healthier foodstuffs our way. Milk is sold in glass bottles, the eggs are free range, and the fresh meat is organic. ■ *249 Marine Dr, West Vancouver; 925-3316;* ■ *2285 W 4th Ave; 739-6685; every day.*

Finlandia Pharmacy When the subject of healthy lifestyle comes up (as it inevitably does in Vancouver), the name Finlandia Pharmacy is often quoted as the "only" place for vitamins, herbal products, and herbal teas; yet inside this spacious and scrupulously clean store there is much, much more. You'll find energy boosters, wellness books, natural sponges and bath brushes, homeopathic allergy remedies, and the full line of BWC (Beauty Without Cruelty) cosmetics. ■ *1964 W Broadway; 733-5323; every day.*

Gaia Garden Herbal Apothecary The walls here are lined with oak apothecary cabinets filled with large jars of familiar and exotic herbs. Herbalist Chanchal Cabrera takes appointments for private consultation and also leads "wildcrafting" workshops for the uninitiated. If you're seeking a healthy diet plan or cleansing regimen, this is the place. ■ *2672 W Broadway; 734-4372; Mon-Sat.*

Hearts Natural Foods Jim Mathias and his crew have done a remarkable job of bringing fresh, organic, and reasonably priced produce and health food products to South Granville, an area given to extremes of high prices and off-price clothing shops. This full-service supermarket stopped selling cigarettes long ago, sells ecologically correct canvas bags, and generally follows the philosophy its owners embrace. ■ *3002 Granville St; 732-4405; every day.*

▼

Linens

▲

The Vitamin Experts Bulk up with bulk vitamins. This chain has some discounts on larger sizes. It also offers personalized service and advice, and carries lots of new and used books if you want to look it up yourself. Mail order service. ■ *Pacific Centre; 685-8487; every day.*

LINENS

Covers Luxurious bed, bath, and table linen in a brilliant selection of colours and patterns. You'll also find decorator accents, accessories, and great gift ideas. ■ *4454 W 10th Ave; 224-5116; Mon-Sat.*

Ed's Linens The largest and best-known discount linen merchant, with a huge selection at all five stores. There are lots of designer names and famous manufacturers, and the price is right. ▪ *7800 Alderbridge Way, Richmond; 270-3318;* ▪ *530-329 North Rd, Coquitlam; 936-2722;* ▪ *4801 Marine Dr, North Vancouver; 986-5203;* ▪ *101-15355 Fraser Hwy, Surrey; 583-5220;* ▪ *3301 W Broadway; 731-2700; every day.*

Pacific Linen You'll find an enormous selection of manufacturers, including many designer names. And the colour selection will knock your eyes out. Many small accessory items. ▪ *Metrotown, Burnaby; 451-8824;* ▪ *Capilano Mall, North Vancouver; 980-8922;* ▪ *Lansdowne Shopping Centre, Richmond; 244-3119; every day.*

LINGERIE

Diane's Lingerie and Loungewear You'll receive kid-glove treatment from the helpful staff when choosing a gift. The store offers a large selection of underpinnings in all sizes from well-known manufacturers, as well as sleepwear ranging from prosaic jammies to sexy negligees. ▪ *2950 Granville St; 738-5121; Mon-Sat.*

Flutterby's Lingerie & Hosiery A good stock of lingerie, including cotton and stretch cotton nightgowns. ▪ *2278 W Broadway; 731-8194; every day.*

La Jolie Madame Ultra-feminine lingerie in a wide range of sizes. Much of the stock is imported. Friendly, knowledgeable staff. ▪ *Pacific Centre; 669-1831; every day.*

Vanity Hosiery A huge selection of everything, from bras to hostess gowns, and a staff that is fanatic about fit. A great assortment of hosiery—including hard-to-find petite sizes. ▪ *2189 W 41st Ave; 261-0041; Mon-Sat.*

NATIVE ART AND CRAFTS

Hill's Indian Crafts Located in Gastown, Hill's carries a wide selection of aboriginal art and handiwork, spread over three floors. Art ranges from original paintings and limited editions to carved gold and silver jewellery (the design is carved into the metal, not cast). Each is signed. Hill's is also the best-known source for beautiful, durable Cowichan sweaters. ▪ *165 Water St; 685-4249; every day.*

Leona Lattimer This small gallery features aboriginal art of extremely high calibre. Many items are purchased for collection. You'll find carvings, jewellery, prints, ceremonial masks, and drums and totems—all created by native artists in the traditional motifs of the Northwest Coast aboriginal people. ▪ *1590 W 2nd Ave; 732-4556; every day.*

The Museum of Anthropology In addition to a fine selection of Northwest Coast Indian art and books, the museum shop features Inuit prints and soapstone sculpture and other hand-made craftwork. ■ *UBC, 6393 NW Marine Dr; 822-5087; Tues-Sun.*

ONE-OF-A-KIND SHOPS

The Flag Shop Fly your colours. This is the place to find flags for the country, the province, and the city—as well as a surprising number of nonflag items like pins, crests, decals, and even wind socks. The shop will take orders by phone. ■ *1755 W 4th Ave; 736-8161; Mon-Sat.*

Golden Age Collectables It's hard to say which age these folks consider golden, but they do have a fine selection of movie posters, baseball and other sport cards—some bearing autographs—and other flotsam of youth. There are also video rentals of classic films, lots of comic books and posters, and T-shirts with comic and comical designs. ■ *830 Granville St; 683-2819; every day.*

The Umbrella Shop Given Vancouver weather, it's easy to believe that this shop has been in business for over 50 years. You'll find a veritable deluge of bumbershoots in all sizes, shapes, and fabrics. Many of the umbrellas are constructed on the premises, will last for years, and can be repaired at the shop. ■ *534 W Pender; 669-9444; Mon-Sat.*

▼

ORIENTAL CARPETS

▲

Ararat Oriental Rug Company Amid a proliferation of "here today, gone tomorrow" carpet stores, Ararat remains a constant, having offered high-quality carpets at the same location since 1930. The large stock includes Boukara, Tabriz, and Hamadan carpets. Repairs and cleaning are also handled here. ■ *2221 Granville St; 733-5616; Mon-Sat.*

Salar Persian & Oriental Carpets Although the shop owners "guarantee the best selection and lowest price in BC," a good many of their beautiful antique or modern imported rugs and kilims will set you back a bundle. Check sale merchandise for significant savings. Large stock; repairs; free parking. ■ *2134 W 41st Ave; 261-3555; every day.*

Vancouver Rug Import Thousands of handmade rugs from all over the world, ranging in size, quality, and price. You can find some remarkable pieces, including a good selection of handmade silk rugs. ■ *101 Water St; 688-6787; every day.*

RECORDINGS

A & B Sound You can't always get what you want, but chances are you'll leave satisfied. Immediately identifiable by their orange buildings, these stores boast a large stock of records, tapes, and CDs, as well as a good selection of electronics. Their biannual sales draw lineups around several blocks. ■ *556 Seymour St; 687-5837;* ■ *3433 E Hastings St; 298-0464;* ■ *732 SW Marine Dr; 321-5112;* ■ *2219 Cambie St; 879-2966;* ■ *3434 Cornett Rd; 430-8585;* ■ *10280 135th St, Surrey; 589-7500;* ■ *4568 Kingsway St, Burnaby; 439-0223; Mon-Fri.*

Black Swan If you're tired of browsing your local chain store hoping for some international jazz or Latin rhythms, check out Black Swan, which specializes in these plus folk and blues. The store carries some rare recordings, many hard-to-find numbers. Mail order is available. ■ *2936 W 4th Ave; 734-2828; every day.*

Bogart Discs A small store, but full of tapes (new and used), records, and CDs. ■ *2579 Granville St; 739-1124; every day.*

Broadway Records and Tapes This store has a very good selection of modern popular rock, middle of the road, country, and so on. If it's not in stock, the very helpful staff will gladly special-order it for you. ■ *3207 W Broadway; 736-1281; every day.*

Collectors RPM This Gastown shop features the good old sounds of the '50s and '60s with everything from country and western to rock 'n' roll. There is also a Beatles museum, where much of the memorabilia is for sale. (There's an admission charge for the museum.) ■ *19 Water St; 685-8841; every day.*

D & G Collectors Records Ltd. You'll find original discs from the "golden age" including '50s and '60s classics, and CD reissues of discs from those eras. Mail-order service and special orders, too. ■ *3580 E Hastings St; 294-5737; every day.*

Highlife Records and Music This shop carries music from around the world, specializing in Latin, African, and Caribbean, as well as a selection of instruments. ■ *1317 Commercial Dr; 251-6964; every day.*

The Magic Flute Predictably, this store carries an extensive selection of classical music. It's a great gathering place for true classics fanatics, and it contains a good selection of printed material and some laserdiscs. ■ *2203 W 4th Ave; 736-2727; every day.*

Neptoon Records An eclectic mix of just about everything. You'll find lots of music-related memorabilia, including some hard-to-find concert posters from as far back as the '60s. ■ *5750 Fraser St; 324-1229; every day.*

Odyssey Imports Don't look for folk songs here. This is alternative and punk, dance, and "house" music territory, with imports from the UK, France, Belgium, and Germany. T-shirts, posters, and magazines are also sold. ■ *534 Seymour St; 669-6644; every day.*

Sikora's Classical Records In this huge store you can expect to find the usual stock of classics and some unusual recordings too. The staff is helpful. ▪ *432 W Hastings St; 685-0625; every day.*

West Indies Records and Tapes If your taste runs to reggae and calypso, this is the place for you. A good selection of Caribbean music. ▪ *1855 Commercial Dr; 254-4232; every day.*

Zulu Records New wave, punk, folk, grunge, hip-hop, reggae, rap, and other modern sounds. The store also carries its own label of independent recordings. ▪ *1869 W 4th Ave; 738-3232; every day.*

SEAFOOD

Jet Set Sam Jet Set Sam's operation specializes in packaging fine BC salmon for travel, and it has five separate retail locations at the Vancouver International Airport—which explains why they suggest you "Catch your salmon at the airport." They'll mail corporate gifts—in special cedar presentation boxes with personalized engraving—anywhere in the world. Among the varieties of seafood are several species of salmon (smoked, of course), Indian candy (salmon cured in brown sugar, then cooked and smoked), salmon jerky, canned smoked salmon, many varieties of crab, fresh whole salmon, salmon steaks and roasts, salmon pâtés and salmon butter, pickled smoked salmon, shrimp, prawns, and scallops. ▪ *Vancouver International Airport; 279-9521; every day.*

Seafood

The Lobster Man Buy your lobsters while they're still kicking and recreate the famous scene in *Annie Hall.* In addition to live lobsters, the Lobster Man sells a wide variety of seafood-related gift items (utensils, accessories, and spices, among other things) for those hard-to-please friends. They'll cook your crustaceans at no extra charge and pack them for travel or shipping. ▪ *Maritime Market, 1807 Mast Tower Rd (Granville Island); 687-4531; every day.*

Longliner Sea Foods The Longliner is one of the best fish markets on Granville Island. Expect to find Vancouver's professional cooks eyeing the goods along with you. Pristine scallops, giant prawns, squid, and whole fish shine alongside less common fishy fare. The staff is generous with cooking advice. There's also a location at Lonsdale Quay in North Vancouver. ▪ *1689 Johnston St (Granville Island); 681-9016; every day in summer, closed Mon in winter.*

The Salmon Shop Once upon a time, the Salmon Shop ran its own fishing boats, but alas, no more, and the prices reflect that change. Still, if you want premium quality, it's here for the taking. Stock includes mahimahi and swordfish as well as the best of the local catch, such as octopus, lingcod, and salmon. The smoked salmon is wonderful. ■ *Robson Public Market, 1610 Robson St; 688-FISH(3474); other branches; every day.*

SHOES AND BOOTS

Dr. Martens Store Once the Model T of footwear—available only in black—these shoes and boots are now available in several styles and colours. This is the largest selection of these comfortable English-made shoes and boots in Vancouver. ■ *1208 Robson St; 689-4998;* ■ *Metrotown Centre, Burnaby; 431-7993; every day.*

John Fluevog Yes, Virginia, there really is a John Fluevog, and he is alive and creating great footwear right here in Vancouver. Indescribably funky shoes. Doc Martens too. ■ *837 Granville St; 688-2828; every day.*

Rainbow Shoes Kids' shoes, cute and comfortable. There's a healthy stock of Keds, Nike, Reebok, and so on. Look for Neat Feet, the hand-painted canvas runners made in Vancouver. ■ *Kids Only Market, 1496 Cartwright St (Granville Island); 688-7463; every day.*

Salvatore Ferragamo High-quality Italian shoes for men and women from this world-famous maker. Choose a classic style and, with care, you'll still be wearing these shoes years from now. ■ *918 Robson St; 669-4495; Mon-Sat.*

Simard & Voyer Shoes Fashion-and-quality-conscious men and women enjoy these stylish shoes. Well-made imports are a specialty. ■ *1049 Robson St; 689-2536; every day.*

Stephane de Raucourt Locals are fanatic about footwear from this retailer. Fashionable, high-quality women's shoes from Italy, fitted by an especially helpful staff. ■ *1067 Robson St; 681-8814; Oakridge Shopping Centre; 261-7419; every day.*

Valucci Shoes, boots, handbags, and accessories. ■ *4331 W 10th Ave; 222-3122;* ■ *2154 W 41st Ave; 266-3131; every day.*

Western Town Boots Serious wranglers—and wrangler wannabes—come here for boots from Tony Lama, Lucchese, and Larry Mahan and other real Western duds. ■ *2490 Main St; 879-1914; every day.*

SKIN AND HAIR CARE PRODUCTS

Bianchés Health & Beauty Clinic Ltd. The 90-minute facial is a mini-vacation. Manicures, pedicures, eyelash tints, and aromatherapy massage are also available. ■ *2741 Granville St; 732-7265; Mon-Sat.*

The Body Shop Anita Roddick's concern for health and the environment is reflected in her shops' large selection of beauty and body products that do the body (and the soul) good. ▪ *Oakridge Centre; 261-3381;* ▪ *Guildford Town Centre, Surrey; 588-5440;* ▪ *Lonsdale Quay Market, North Vancouver; 984-7273;* ▪ *Pacific Centre; 681-7622;* ▪ *Lougheed Mall, Burnaby; 420-1316;* ▪ *Park Royal South, West Vancouver; 925-2157;* ▪ *Lynn Valley Centre, North Vancouver; 980-5033;* ▪ *Lansdowne Shopping Centre, Richmond; 278-0454;* ▪ *Eaton Centre, Burnaby; 439-9833;* ▪ *2-1141 Robson St; 688-9777;* ▪ *Coquitlam Centre, Coquitlam; 944-1611;* ▪ *Richmond Centre, Richmond; 278-7649; every day.*

Crabtree & Evelyn Choose a gift for a friend and one for yourself at this English shop, which is world famous for its most delightful old-fashioned scented soaps and bath accessories. The shop also sells some of the best teas, jams, and biscuits this side of the Thames. ▪ *Pacific Centre; 662-7211;* ▪ *Oakridge Centre; 263-4323; every day.*

La Raffinage Pampering the body and the mind is the specialty of this full-service spa. Become a member and receive a 10 percent reduction in service fees and specials twice a month. ▪ *501 W Georgia St; 681-9933; every day.*

London Drugs This local phenomenon is not a drugstore in the true sense of the word. Yes, you can get your prescription filled and your film developed and find your favourite hair and skin care products. But locals go to London Drugs for the scope of the selection and the competitive pricing. Small electrical appliances are the store's specialty, and it sells sound equipment and video equipment and maintains an excellent camera department. Brand names are everywhere, from Braun and Melitta to Canon and Sony. Computers too. ▪ *655 W Broadway; 520-9004; every day; other branches.*

Optaderm This skin care shop, and the skin care products and cosmetics of the same name, have garnered a fanatical following over the past decade. Drop by for one of the shop's luxurious European facials and pick up some fabulous lotions and potions. All products are made locally, and you'll likely get a wonderful gift with your purchase. ▪ *250-2184 W Broadway; 737-2026; Tues-Sat.*

SPECIALTY FOODS

A. Bosa & Co. Ltd. From patrone Lui Bruschetta on down, everyone working at Bosa's is some kind of member of the family. They sell fine European foods; restaurant and delicatessen supplies; California grapes for winemaking; and everything you need for Italian cooking—including the finest extra virgin olive oil. ▪ *562 Victoria Dr; 253-5578; Mon-Fri.*

All India Foods Here in the heart of bustling "Little India," around Main Street and 53rd Avenue, you'll find unlimited choices of specialty foods and seasonings at this supermarket-size Indian food emporium. The narrow aisles are crowded with more stock than you can imagine. Choose from a vast array of chutneys, curry powders, cardamom seed, saffron, chilies, and other items in more varieties, sizes, and forms than anywhere else in town. There are also bulk foods, fresh produce, and some of the cheapest milk prices around. Next door, All India Sweets offers confections and a warm and hospitable sit-down cafe. ■ *6517 Main St; 324-1686; every day.*

Famous Foods The key to Famous Foods' bargain prices is that they repackage bulk quantities into small packages themselves, reducing the time spent measuring and weighing. The savings are passed along to their customers. Unlike bulk food outlets, there's no worry about bin contamination, and constant turnover ensures that grains, pasta, and spices are fresh. Added to their superior stock of spices are special deals on bulk peanut butter, honey, and grains, as well as an impressive assortment of cheeses. ■ *1595 Kingsway; 872-3019; every day.*

Forster's Fine Cheeses Steve Forster stocks more than 200 types of cheese, cheese spreads, and biscuits. He'll be happy to tell you anything and everything he knows about cheese, while convincing you to try his richly flavoured St. Florentin—an unripened French triple cream cheese. Noncheese items, such as meat and fish pâtés and Italian pickled onions in balsamic vinegar, are available as well. ■ *2104 W 41st Ave; 261-5813; Mon-Sat.*

▼

Specialty Foods

▲

Fujiya These stores are the best sources for Japanese foods and pearl rice in town. They also have weekly specials and carry a wide variety of inexpensive kitchenware, including steamers, woks, and kitchen tools. You'll find some of the best buys in sushi supplies here, such as those hard-to-find bamboo mats for rolling rice in nori. Takeout sashimi available. ■ *453 Powell St; 251-3711; other branches; every day.*

Galloway's The combination of herbs, spices, Indian chutneys, curry pastes, and dried fruit makes Galloway's an aromatic spot for leisurely shopping. This is also the place to find that elusive Mexican vanilla and crunchy Indian snacks such as roast green peas, pumpkin seeds, and nuts. ■ *1084 Robson St; 685-7927;* ■ *Pacific Centre Mall; 669-3036;* ■ *702B 6th Ave, New Westminster; 526-3036; Mon-Sat.*

La Grotta Del Formaggio Here is where you find the city's largest variety of Italian cheeses. The store also stocks tarragon-flavoured balsamic vinegar, imported tinned fish, olive oils, Italian cookies, pannetone, and fresh yeast for the bread baker. ■ *1791 Commercial Dr; 255-3911; every day.*

Olivieri Foods Vancouver's oldest and most popular Italian supermarket makes an impressive array of fresh pasta and sauces. People crowd the aisles on weekends in pursuit of unusual canned items, olive oils, imported pasta, marinated vegetables, and deli meats. ■ *1900 Commercial Dr; 255-8844; every day.*

Parthenon Wholesale & Retail Food It's not a Greek island, but on a rainy day it's great to make believe while nibbling such delicacies as taramosalata, baklava, dolmades, Greek olives, and feta. Signs in Hellenic-style lettering add to the ethnic shopping experience. ■ *2968 W Broadway; 733-4191; every day.*

Que Pasa Mexican Foods Que Pasa is Vancouver's best source for the elusive spices and ingredients needed for Central American cooking. This small shop (there's one at Lonsdale Quay too) carries a variety of Mexican deli items and fresh vegetables for Mexican cooking: tomatillos, chiles, cactus, and jicama. There are many brands of salsa, including the store's own chunky style (in hot, medium, and mild) as well its superlative tortilla chips. We also discovered piñatas, Mexican plates, candles, margarita glasses, and candle holders featuring green glass cactus-shaped bases. Que Pasa also sells a practical *molcajete*—a kind of mortar and pestle for grinding rice into flour—and has a good stock of Mexican cookbooks. ■ *3315 Cambie St; 874-0064; every day.*

South China Seas Trading Co. It's easy to see why people flock to Kay Leong's South China Seas Trading Co. on Granville Island—Leong is familar with every item and is always ready with advice. The shop stocks an incredible variety of spices, fresh herbs, condiments, sauces, noodles, and prepared ethnic items from Asia, Southeast Asia, Africa, and the Caribbean. Fresh herbs are flown in direct from the country of origin. ■ *1689 Johnston St (Granville Island); 681-5402; summer, open every day; winter, closed Mon.*

SPORTING EQUIPMENT

Coast Mountain Sports Affordable camping, hiking, climbing, and travel gear. Boots, sleeping bags, water purifiers, and high-tech items such as freeze-dried food and satellite tracking systems. Knowledgeable staff. ■ *2201 W 4th Ave; 731-6181; every day.*

The Diving Locker Equipment sales, rentals, and instructions. In business over 20 years. ■ *2745 W 4th Ave; 736-2681; every day.*

Doug Hepburn's Gym Equipment Setting up a home gym? Get your serious weight-training equipment here. ■ *38 E 4th Ave; 873-3684; every day.*

Hanson's Fishing Outfitters Everything you need to outwit the wiliest fish. Clothing, books, and equipment. Knowledgeable staff. Charters can be booked at the store. ■ *580 Hornby St; 684-8988; Mon-Sat.*

Mountain Equipment Co-op Join for a few dollars, then shop to your heart's content amid racks of all the gear you'll need to enjoy the great outdoors. There's a good cycling section, helpful staff, and a large selection of clothing. ■ *428 W 8th Ave; 872-7858; Mon-Sat.*

Ruddick's Fly Shop The first—and many say the best—fly-fishing shop in Western Canada. It's the exclusive licensed retail outlet for Orvis rods, clothing, and accessories. The shop also sells custom-tied flies and offers classes in fly tying and fly casting, as well as group expeditions to famous fishing locations. ■ *3726 Canada Way, Burnaby; 434-2420; Mon-Sat.*

Taiga This local manufacturer with an international reputation sells high-quality tents, sleeping bags, and sportswear. There's also a great range of fashions in Goretex and Polartec. ■ *390 W 8th Ave; 875-6644; Mon-Sat.*

▼

Sporting Equipment

▲

Three Vets One of the oldest and most respected outfitters in the area, Three Vets is famous for its low prices. You'll find good-quality basic equipment for entry-level campers and hikers. Check out the store's small collection of native art. ■ *2200 Yukon St; 872-5475; Mon-Sat.*

STATIONERY AND ART SUPPLIES

Behnsen Graphic Supplies Ltd. This is a store for serious graphic artists and designers, but rank amateurs will find a wealth of inspiring colours and supplies. Behnsen sponsors free educational seminars on how to get the most out of its merchandise. Computer graphic artists will appreciate the store's hardware and software offerings. ■ *1016 Richards St; 681-7351; Mon-Sat.*

Paper-Ya Try your hand at creating your own art paper. You'll find a terrific selection of paper from around the world, as well as papermaking kits for fledgling artists. ■ *1666 Johnston St (Granville Island); 684-2531; every day.*

The Vancouver Pen Shop The giant pen in the window is your first clue to the giant selection of pens offered here: Sheaffer, Montblanc, Cross, Waterman, and Dupont pens, as well as inks and cartridges. The shop also stocks sketching tools and lower-priced pens. ■ *512 W Hastings St; 681-1612; Mon-Sat.*

The Write Place Custom stationery, cards, and writing implements. ■ *2843 Granville St; 732-7777; every day.*

Einstein's Besides an enormous selection of science books, this store offers lots of hands-on experiments, perfect for ever-curious young scientists. Science is just learning about the world around us—and Einstein's makes it so simple, you don't have to be a genius to understand. ▪ *4424 Dunbar St; 738-3622; Mon-Sat.*

Kaboodles This is the perfect place for stocking goody bags for kids' parties, but there's much, much more than a great selection of low-cost crowd pleasers. Check out the umbrellas, the back packs, and the colourful stuffed toys. Cards and wrap too. ▪ *4449 W 10th Ave; 224-5311; every day.*

Kids Only Market Not *just* toys, of course. The market features over 20 specialty shops and services, including clothing, art supplies, and more. It's where you'll find the best kite shop in the city, and kids just love to visit. ▪ *1496 Cartwright St (Granville Island); 689-8447; every day.*

The Toybox High-quality toys and lots of them. Some of the merchandise is "up-market" (read: expensive), but there are lots of lower-priced items that will please and games galore. ▪ *3002 W Broadway; 738-4322; every day.*

▼

Toys

▲

Windmill Toys Canadian-made Little Tikes Toys are exclusive to Windmill Toys in Vancouver. There are also imported lines from Germany, including Steiff and Lehmann model trains and a terrific selection of other kiddy favourites. ▪ *2387 W 41st Ave; 261-2120; every day.*

LODGINGS

Lodgings

HOTELS

DOWNTOWN

Buchan Hotel ★★ Above Vancouver's popular, boisterous Delilah's restaurant is this three-storey 1930s apartment-hotel located adjacent to Stanley Park on a lovely tree-lined cul-de-sac in the residential heart of the West End. The 66 small rooms are clean, comfortable, and pleasant enough, especially for the price. The brightest rooms overlook a small city park to the east. There are few amenities (no individual telephones), but the staff is friendly and helpful. The biggest hassle is finding a parking spot. Bring your walking shoes; Stanley Park is only steps away, and the centre of downtown is a 15-minute stroll along fashionable Robson Street. Weekly rates are available; there is a laundry room. ■ *1906 Haro St, Vancouver, BC V6G 1H7; 685-5354; $; AE, DC, MC, V; no cheques.*

Coast Plaza Inn ★★ Situated just off the main artery through the vibrant West End, this former apartment tower offers 267 large rooms, including a dozen two-bedroom suites. All have balconies, and more than two-thirds of the rooms have complete kitchens, making this a great place for vacationing families and Hollywood film crews working in Vancouver (the stars stay elsewhere). Amenities include 24-hour room service, a minibar, and a small fridge. But the hotel's strongest point is its proximity to Stanley Park. Request a room with a park view. Guests are welcome at the adjoining health club (popular with local singles). ■ *1733 Comox St, Vancouver, BC V6G 1P6; 688-7711 or toll free (800) 663-1144; $$$; AE, DC, MC, V; cheques OK.*

Delta Place ★★★ Mandarin International built this richly appointed, 197-room hotel in time for Vancouver's world exposition in 1986 but sold it shortly thereafter to Delta Hotels. Nonetheless, the hotel remains worthy of the Mandarin name. From the Italian marble in the bathrooms to the silk draperies, the solid oak cabinetry, and the exquisite art throughout, the Delta Place is a jewel in every respect—some people consider it one of Vancouver's best-kept secrets. Located in the heart of downtown Vancouver's business and financial districts, it offers oversize, soundproofed deluxe rooms with balconies and peek-aboo views of the city. There are 18 palatial suites, outstanding concierge service, nightly turn-down service on request, 24-hour room service, a full-scale business centre, and one of the finest hotel health clubs. (There are even television sets in the saunas.) Delta Place also offers a club floor and several programs for families with children (kids six years and under eat free). Le Café serves breakfast, lunch, and dinner. The Clipper Lounge's weekday Asian luncheon buffet is a holdover from the Mandarin days that has proved too popular to change. Rates start at $220, but special weekend rates plunge to $99. ■ *645 Howe St, Vancouver, BC V6C 2Y9; 687-1122 or toll free (800) 268-1133; $$$; AE, DC, MC, V; no cheques.*

Hotels

Downtown

▲

The Four Seasons ★★★★ The upscale chain of Four Seasons hotels is well known for pampering guests, and the Vancouver hotel only enhances that reputation. Arrival is awkward, however, since guests must enter from a small driveway wedged between concrete pillars and then ride an elevator to the lobby, which is also connected to the Pacific Centre shopping mall. Once the hurdle of check-in has been overcome, guests wallow in luxury. Although the hotel is located smack-dab in the centre of high-rise downtown, many of the guest rooms offer surprising views of the city. Amenities include bathrobes, hair dryers, VCRs, a complimentary shoeshine, 24-hour valet service, a year-round indoor-outdoor pool, and a rooftop garden. Kids are welcomed with complimentary milk and cookie on arrival. Chartwell (see Restaurants chapter) is one of the best dining rooms in the city. The Garden Lounge, just off the lobby, is a place to see and be seen. ■ *791 W Georgia St, Vancouver, BC V6E 2T4; 689-9333; $$$; AE, DC, MC, V; no cheques.*

Georgian Court Hotel ★★★ Compared with the other pricey hotels in the city, there's good value to be enjoyed at this intimate and luxurious 180-room European-style hotel situated across from BC Place Stadium and the Queen Elizabeth Theatre. All rooms feature desks, minibars, three telephones, nightly turn-down service, and (at last) good reading lamps. Among Vancouverites, the Georgian Court Hotel is best known as the home of the William Tell Restaurant (see Restaurants chapter), where for years flamboyant owner Erwin Doebeli has set the standard for fine dining in Vancouver. The hotel's strong point is value for dollars in a luxury hotel, but a guest, or any visitor to the city, would be remiss not to dine in the William Tell. ■ *773 Beatty St, Vancouver, BC V6B 2M4; 682-5555 or toll free (800) 663-1155; $$$; AE, DC, DIS, E, JCV, MC, V; cheques OK.*

Hotel Georgia ★ This attractive stone 12-storey hotel, built in 1927, offers old-fashioned charm, with its small oak-panelled lobby, elaborate brass elevators, and comfortable rooms furnished with contemporary oak furniture, but it has the feel of a hotel for travelling salespeople and bus tours. The rooms with the best views face south to the Vancouver Art Gallery, but they are on a busy, noisy street. Executive rooms have a seating area that is useful for conducting business. The hotel's location couldn't be more central. The Georgia has two bars that are popular with locals (especially for their pub-style lunches). ■ *801 W Georgia St, Vancouver, BC V6C 2W6; 682-5566; $$$; AE, DC, MC, V; no cheques.*

Hotel Vancouver ★★★ This is one of the grand French chateau-style hotels built in 1939 by the Canadian Pacific Railway barons to entice visitors to ride the train across Canada. The green, steeply pitched copper roof that dominated the city's skyline for decades remains a less-obvious landmark today. The 508-room hotel is popular with conventions; nonetheless, service remains quite good and includes complimentary coffee and newspapers in the morning. Dinner dances take place in the Roof Restaurant and Lounge—it's that kind of hotel. An executive floor called Entrée Gold includes premium rooms with a dedicated reception desk and concierge, continental breakfast and canapés, and secretarial services. The hotel has a health club with a sky-lit lap pool. Try for a room high above the street noise. ■ *900 W Georgia St, Vancouver, BC V6C 2W6; 684-3131 or toll free (800) 441-1414; $$$; AE, DC, DIS, E, JCV, MC, V; cheques OK.*

Hotels

Downtown

Hyatt Regency ★★ No surprises here. This is a good Hyatt Regency, like all the others around the world. It's popular with conventions and tour groups yet continues to offer personalized service. Good views of the harbour and mountains are available from north-facing upper floors. Try for a corner room with a balcony. Two Regency Club floors, with special keyed access, have their own concierge, complimentary breakfast, late afternoon hors d'oeuvres, and evening pastries. A health club and pool are available. Standard rooms (which are among the largest standards in the city) start at $175. ■ *655 Burrard St, Vancouver, BC V6C 2R7; 687-6543 or toll free (800) 233-1234; $$$; AE, DC, DIS, E, JCV, MC, V; cheques OK.*

Le Meridien ★★★★ Vancouver's most elegant hotel is another outstanding legacy of the city's world exposition held in 1986. Le Meridien would rank as a top hotel in any European capital. All 397 soundproofed rooms in this sumptuous residential-style hotel look and feel like a beautiful home, which they do. The king-size beds are extra large: the furnishings are reproductions of European antiques. (There are plenty of spectacular original pieces throughout the hotel's public spaces.) The maids faithfully appear twice a day with all the amenities one could wish for—including fresh flowers, umbrella, and complimentary shoeshine. There are nine nonsmoking floors and the fastest elevators in town. The lobby recalls a European manor and posts a 24-hour concierge service. Le Meridien's restaurants and lounges have been popular with locals since the day they opened, with the richly panelled Gerard Lounge ranking as one of the best watering holes in the Northwest (see Nightlife chapter). Le Spa offers a swimming pool, fitness room, and beauty salons. Room rates in season range from $180 for a standard double to $1250 for the Presidential Suite; however, special getaway weekend packages are available. Ask for a deal, then spoil the one you love. ■ *845 Burrard St, Vancouver, BC V6Z 2K6; 682-5511 or toll free (800) 543-4300; $$$; AE, DC, DIS, E, JCV, MC, V; no cheques.*

Pacific Palisades ★★★ The internationally celebrated Shangri-La chain purchased the Pacific Palisades in 1991 and promptly began a complete renovation of what was already a good hotel. The 233 rooms, most of which are one-bedroom suites, have long been popular with the many movie production crews that visit Vancouver. Part of the appeal comes from the hotel's personal attention to guests' needs, but the major draw is spacious rooms, all with a mini-kitchen that includes a fridge, microwave, and coffee-maker. There's a health club and a swimming pool. The location on Robson Street is tough to beat if you want to be where the action is. ■ *1277 Robson St, Vancouver, BC V6E 1C4; 688-0461 or toll free (800) 663-1815; $$$; AE, DC, E, JCV, MC, V; no cheques.*

Pan Pacific Hotel ★★★ No hotel in Vancouver has a more stunning location, a better health club, or a more remarkable architectural presence. As part of Canada Place, the Pan Pacific juts out into Vancouver's inner harbour with its five giant white signature sails. The building, which is also the embarkation point for the thriving summertime Alaska cruise ship market, hasn't achieved the fame of Sydney's Opera House, but it was meant to. The first four floors of the building comprise the World Trade Centre Vancouver, but up on the eighth, where the guest rooms begin, things become more diminutive. Standard guest rooms (high season rates start at $265) are among the smallest of Vancouver's luxury hotels, and the decor is all a bit disappointing after such a grand facade. Nonetheless, perhaps the spectacular views make up for any shortcomings. The best views face west, but you can't beat a corner room (with views from your tub). A complete range of guest services is offered. The fine-dining restaurant, the Five Sails, has achieved a fair bit of attention for its exquisite Pacific Rim cuisine (see Restaurants chapter). The Cascades Lounge, just off the lobby, is a must-stop if you want to watch ships sail into the sunset while seaplanes land beneath you against the backdrop of the North Shore mountains. ■ *300-999 Canada Pl Way, Vancouver, BC V6C 3B5; 662-8111 or toll free (800) 937-1515; $$$; AE, DC, E, JCV, MC, V; no cheques.*

Sylvia Hotel ★★ A favourite for price and location. This ivy-covered eight-storey historic brick hotel is a landmark adjacent to English Bay, Vancouver's most popular beach and strutting grounds. Try for a south-facing room. A low-rise addition was built to compensate for the busy summer season when you might just need to settle for *any* room. Doubles begin at $55, and reservations are required well in advance. All 116 rooms (quite standard) have baths. Families or small groups should request the large two- and three-bedroom suites with kitchens ($80 to $120). The hotel also offers covered parking, a restaurant, and a lounge—reportedly the first cocktail bar in Vancouver (opened in 1954), and on some winter afternoons it looks like the original clientele is still there. Pets permitted. ■ *1154 Gilford St, Vancouver, BC V6G 2P6; 681-9321; $; AE, DC, MC, V; cheques OK.*

Hotels

Downtown

Waterfront Centre Hotel ★★★ The tasteful rooms in the newish 23-storey Waterfront Centre are among the best in the city. Their size and rich appointments clearly outclass the Pan Pacific Hotel, just across the street on Vancouver's inner harbour. Underground passageways connect the Waterfront Centre to Canada Place and the convention and trade centre. Expect wonderful surprises, such as third-floor guest rooms with private terraces and gardens concealed from the street level. A club floor called Entrée Gold caters to every whim, offering a private concierge, continental breakfast, nightly hors d'oeuvres, and private conference room. Of the 489 guest rooms, there are 29 suites and one that's fit for royalty. Operated by Canadian Pacific, the Waterfront Centre ranks among the top hotels in Vancouver (along with Four Seasons, Le Meridien, Wedgewood, and Delta Place), and as new as it is, it has the most Canadian feel to it. There is an excellent health club, complete with outdoor pool (a view-and-a-half), nightly turn-down service, nonsmoking floors, and rooms designed for people with disabilities. The works of Canadian artists are prominently displayed throughout the hotel's public spaces and guest rooms. Don't miss the upbeat gospel music at

Sunday brunch. ■ *900 Canada Pl Way, Vancouver, BC V6C 3L5; 691-1991 or toll free (800) 441-1414; $$$; AE, DC, DIS, E, JCV, MC, V; no cheques.*

The Wedgewood Hotel ★★★ Owner and manager Eleni Skalbania takes great pride in the Wedgewood Hotel. And Ms. Skalbania has much to be proud of. This is a hotel you will want to return to time and time again. Ideally located in the heart of Vancouver's finest shopping district, and across the street from the art gallery, the gardens of Robson Square, and the court-house built of glass, the Wedgewood offers Old World charm and scrupulous attention to every detail of hospitality. From the complimentary Belgian chocolates (fruit baskets during the summer months) on arrival to the potted flowers flourishing on the balcony of every room to the renowned Bacchus Ris-torante, this 93-room hotel is all that a small urban luxury ho-tel should be. This is the only luxury hotel in the city where you won't find tour buses unloading swarms of visitors. The finely appointed rooms, which are surprisingly large and are deco-rated with new, vibrant colours and genuine English antiques, feel like a home. Nightly turn-down service, a bare-essentials fitness room, and 24-hour room service are offered. This is the place to spend your honeymoon (and many do), but any week-end at the Wedgewood is a weekend to savour. ■ *845 Hornby St, Vancouver, BC V6Z 1V1; 689-7777 or toll free (800) 663-0666; $$$; AE, DC, DIS, E, JCV, MC, V; no cheques.*

Westin Bayshore Hotel ★★ The Bayshore sits on the south-ern shore of Coal Harbour next to the main entrance to Stan-ley Park. Set back from busy Georgia Street, this is the only downtown hotel that resembles a resort (children love it here). Rooms look out over a large outdoor pool, with Coal Harbour's colourful marina as a backdrop and the North Shore mountains beyond. The Hertz counter in the hotel rents bicycles, and if you're up for a one-hour ride, you can't beat the scenery along the connecting Stanley Park seawall. Amenities include all that you'd expect from a Westin. Guest rooms in the tower all have balconies. There's also a health club with an indoor pool. The major business and shopping areas of downtown are a pleasant 15-minute walk away. The staff could use a week or two at the Wedgewood or Le Meridien for some ad-vanced training. ■ *1601 W Georgia St, Vancouver, BC V6G 2V4; 682-3377 or toll free (800) 228-3000; $$$; AE, DC, MC, V; cheques OK.*

AIRPORT

Delta Pacific Resort ★★ Formerly called the Delta Airport Inn, this is one of two Delta hotels in the vicinity of Vancouver International Airport. Both are well run and offer a wealth of recreational facilities. This 4-hectare (10-acre) resort includes three swimming pools (one indoor), year-round tennis courts under a bubble, a play centre and summer camp for kids (ages 5 to 12), exercise classes, volleyball nets, and a golf practice net. There are meeting rooms and a restaurant, cafe, and bar. There's also free shuttle service to and from the airport, and major nearby shopping centres. ■ *10251 St Edward's Dr, Richmond, BC V6X 2M9; 278-9611; $$$; AE, DC, DIS, E, JCV, MC, V; no cheques.*

Delta Vancouver Airport Hotel ★★ The closest hotel to Vancouver International Airport (formerly called the Delta River Inn) spreads along the banks of the Fraser River. There is an outdoor pool, bar, and barbecue, as well as bicycle and running trails. All in all, not a bad place to lay over if you are passing through Vancouver. East-side rooms face the river and marina. Downtown is 30 minutes away. The 400-plus guest rooms and over a dozen meeting rooms are popular for conventions and corporate travellers. Kids under six eat free in the hotel's dining facilities. There are other hotels in the vicinity of the airport, but the Delta Vancouver Airport Hotel is the best of the lot. ■ *3500 Cessna Dr, Richmond, BC V7B 1C7; 278-1241; $$$; AE, DC, DIS, E, JCV, MC, V; no cheques.*

GREATER VANCOUVER: NORTH SHORE

Lonsdale Quay Hotel ★ Few visitors take the time to explore the North Shore, which has the best wilderness areas of perhaps any other major North American city. The pleasant Lonsdale Quay Hotel, located inside the enjoyable Lonsdale Quay market and across the harbour from downtown Vancouver (yet only 15 minutes away via the SeaBus), gives you a comfortable place to stay (as long as you don't need to be pampered). French doors on south-facing rooms open up to the Vancouver skyline, a dazzling sight at night, with the lights reflecting off the water. ■ *123 Carrie Cates Court, North Vancouver, BC V7M 3K7; 986-6111 or toll free (800) 836-6111; $$$; AE, DC, DIS, E, MC, V; no cheques.*

Park Royal Hotel ★★ A perfect setting for an ivy-covered 30-room Tudor-style hotel. Too bad the rooms aren't a little nicer, or the staff a little friendlier. Located just off the north end of Lions Gate Bridge along the quiet backwaters of Capilano River, the Park Royal Hotel offers a bit of old England just minutes from downtown and with quick access to the road to Whistler. During summer reservations can be hard to get, especially for a riverfront room. The dining room is extremely pleasant, opening onto a lovely garden fronting the river. ■ *540 Clyde Ave, West Vancouver, BC V7T 2J7; 926-5511; $$; AE, DC, E, MC, V; no cheques.*

INNS AND BED AND BREAKFASTS

English Bay Inn ★★★ Owner Bob Chapin devotes meticulous attention to his romantic five-room English Bay Inn. Down comforters rest atop Louis Philippe sleigh beds beneath alabaster lighting fixtures. The pièce de résistance is a two-level suite on the top floor with a fireplace in the bedroom. Extras include terrycloth robes, evening sherry, and phones in each guest room. All rooms have a private bath, and two back rooms open onto a small garden. A fabulous breakfast is served in a formal dining room with gothic dining suite in front of a crackling (albeit gas) fire and the ticking of a grandfather clock. Stanley Park and English Bay are just minutes away by foot. ■ *1968 Comox St, Vancouver, BC V6G 1R4; 683-8002; $$$; AE, V; cheques OK.*

Laburnam Cottage Bed and Breakfast ★★ This elegant country home is set off by an award-winning English garden, tended with care over the past four decades by Innkeeper Delphine Masterton, who raised five children here before opening the home to lodgers. The main house, furnished with antiques and collectibles, features three guest rooms, each light and airy, with private bath and garden view. The Summerhouse Cottage—situated in the midst of the garden and accessed by a footbridge that traverses a small creek—is a Rosamond Pilcher novel come to life, perfect for honeymooning couples. Another, larger cottage, with private entrance, kitchen, fireplace, and children's loft, sleeps six. Delphine's warm gift for welcome, and ability to weave strangers into friends over the cheerful breakfast table, make a stay here all it should be. ■ *1388 Terrace Ave, North Vancouver, BC V7R 1B4; 988-4877; $$$; MC, V; cheques OK.*

Penny Farthing Inn ★★ This Edwardian 1912 home is an historic treasure in Vancouver's trendy west side Kitsilano district. Try for the attic room overlooking the overgrown English garden backdropped by the North Shore mountains. Owner Lyn Hainstock is a professional innkeeper with a wealth of information about Vancouver. Breakfast is a gourmet's feast. ■ *2855 W 6th Ave, Vancouver, BC V6K 1X2; 739-9002; $$; no credit cards; cheques OK.*

River Run Floating Cottage ★★ River Run Floating Cottage is a jewel on the Fraser River. Located in historic Ladner, 30 minutes south of downtown Vancouver and close to the ferries to Victoria, this floating cottage docked among a community of houseboats offers a closeness to nature—ducks, swans, leaping salmon, and bald eagles all put on a show. Views from the rear deck include the North Shore mountains and Vancouver Island. Open only during the summer, the cottage is nicely appointed, including a claw-foot tub, a wood-burning potbelly stove, and cooking facilities. A hot breakfast is delivered on board. Another one-bedroom cottage on shore is set to open in mid-1994. ■ *4551 River Rd W, Ladner, BC V4K 1R9; 946-7778; $$; MC, V; cheques OK.*

West End Guest House ★★ Don't be put off by the blazing pink exterior of this early-1900s Victorian home, located on a residential street close to Stanley Park and just a block off Robson Street. Owner Evan Penner runs a fine nine-room inn (seven with private bath), and during summer a vacancy is rare. Rooms are generally small but nicely furnished, and there are antiques throughout the house. The staff members have all worked in major hotels and know what hospitality is. Sherry is served in the afternoons. Nightly turn-down service, feather and lambskin mattress covers, terrycloth robes, and telephones are provided in every room. Breakfast is a bountiful cooked meal served family style or delivered to your room. There is guest parking (a rarity in the West End). Families with children are accepted, but just be careful with the antiques. ■ *1362 Haro St, Vancouver, BC V6E 1G2; 681-2889; $$; AE, DIS, MC, V; cheques OK.*

CONDOMINIUMS

Barclay Mansions ★ This is a typical bland 1960s-style West End apartment building with furnished rooms available weekly or monthly. The furnishings are modern-motel, but the rooms are clean and the building is well run. The location is just off Burrard Street (next to the YMCA), two blocks south of Robson Street in downtown Vancouver. Most of the 40 rooms are one-bedrooms ($440 per week; $1,320 monthly), but there are also a few suites. The mostly corporate clientele receives twice-a-week maid service and free parking. ■ *1040 Barclay St, Vancouver, BC V6E 1G6; 683-8939; $$; AE, DC, MC, V; no cheques.*

La Grande Résidence ★★★★ The best rental condominiums in the city are located in a separate building connected to Le Meridien in the heart of downtown. La Grande Résidence provides all the amenities of a luxury hotel in 162 spiffy one- and two-bedroom suites with kitchens and balconies. Maid service, valet parking, concierge, and secretarial, laundry, and room services are all available. A state-of-the-art security system ensures privacy. Telephone calls and visiting guests are received by the hotel's front desk. The minimum stay is a month (starting at $3,500 for 30 days). ■ *845 Burrard St, Vancouver, BC V6Z 2K6; 682-5511 or toll free (800) 543-4300; AE, DC, DIS, E, JCV, MC, V; no cheques.*

Outings

BOWEN ISLAND

Vancouver senior citizens fondly remember the Moonlight Cruises to the Happy Isle back in the 1930s and 1940s. For $1 on a Wednesday or Saturday night, you could dance across Howe Sound on board luxury steamships like the *Lady Alexandra*, follow the orchestra up the fragrant rose-arboured path to the Dance Pavilion (the largest in BC), and then sail back again.

More than 100 cottages, built by Union Steamship Company and the Hotel Monaco (later Bowen Inn), catered to summer pleasure seekers, but these are largely gone. So is the company. But the 52-square-kilometre (20-square-mile) island of 2,700 people is undergoing a resurgence as a new generation discovers the year-round pleasures of living on an island only 20 minutes away.

There's a festive feeling when the ferry pulls into **Snug Cove**, where pleasure boats are docked at the new **Union Steamship Co. Marina** and welcoming flags fly from the cheery green wooden **Doc Morgan's Inn**. Commuting baby boomers who have moved their families from the mainland to Bowen (which has the highest ratio of schoolchildren under 10 in BC) have created a market for more upscale stores on the main drag (the only drag) in Snug Cove.

From Horseshoe Bay, it's a pleasant ferry ride aboard the *Queen of Capilano*, one of BC's newer ferries, which departs almost hourly until 9:35pm (685-1021), carrying 85 cars. Once on Bowen, how you spend your day on the 6-kilometre-wide (3.7-mile-wide) by 14-kilometre-long (8.7-mile-long) island depends on whether you're travelling by car, bike, or foot (you can park in Horseshoe Bay or ride the blue Horseshoe Bay bus right from downtown Vancouver, on Georgia at Granville). When you disembark onto Government Road, you'll confront virtually every service on Bowen from the **Oven Door Bakery** and **Whirling "Dervish" Coffee House** to the Chevron gas station, so this is your chance to pick up information, directions, fuel, food, and a copy of *Undercurrent*, Bowen's weekly paper.

Caroline's Deli (Government Road, 947-2907) has an impressive range of meals and makings, as well as French pastries. Check out the adjoining **Dunfield & Daughter Whole Food** mini-grocery and the **Lady Rose Bookstore** upstairs while you're there. **Crafty People** (Bowen Berries, Snug Cove, 947-0892) do picnics or backpacks to go and will meet you at the ferry.

The big red building closest to the ferry landing is the renovated **Union Steamship Company General Store**, now a tourist information centre. [KIDS][FREE] Pick up the excellent free brochure entitled *Happy Isle Historic Walking Tour*, which has old photos keyed to the numbered stops along the 2.5-kilometre (1.5-mile) easy route along roads and trails

through **Crippen Regional Park**, which today encompasses much of the Union Steamship Company's former resort. Two other options: walk to the old United Church near the Collins Farm (ask for trail directions) or past the fish ladders (check with Federal Fisheries, 921-7811, to see if coho or cutthroat are running in October and November) to **Killarney Lake**, which is warm enough for summer swimming.

You can drive or bike to Killarney Lake to swim, canoe, or kayak, but the 75-minute trail *around* the lake is strictly for hikers. There are plenty of benches and a boardwalk that crosses a marsh at one end of the lake. At 760 metres (250 feet), **Mount Gardiner** is Bowen's highest point, and the views of surrounding islands and the Lions peaks are well worth the all-day hike. [KIDS][FREE] Swimmers should head for **Bowen Bay's public beach** (Grafton Road to Bowen Bay Road). A happy thought: registered massage therapist Judith Mallett, who once coordinated the Pan Pacific Hotel's massage service, now takes day trippers' bodies in hand at her Bowen home (947-0422).

Drivers and cyclists can't circumnavigate Bowen, because there are only three main roads, all branching out from Snug Cove. Nonetheless, there are a number of artists, such as Sam Black, whose studios can make a pleasant tour. Among other creative island residents not on the tour: Nick Bantock, author of *Griffin & Sabine*, and photographer Barbara Woodley, whose bare-shouldered photograph of former Canadian prime minister Kim Campbell inspired Japanese media to dub the first female prime minister "Canada's Madonna."

The flagship of Bowen's new marina resort (including

docks, renovated cottages, a chandlery/gift shop, and board-walks) is Doc Morgan's marine pub/restaurant. The owners are enthusiastic and the patios are tempting, despite the over-powering canned music, but high points so far are the fries and microbrews.

If you can't get enough of the Happy Isle in one day, there are bed and breakfasts and rental cottages that are a slice of renovated Union Steamship history, each with cheery wood stove and kitchen. Summer weekends are booked up as much as a year in advance (Snug Cove, 947-0707). Jeannet and Bruce Murdoch's pretty New England–style **Bowen Island Bed and Breakfast** (981 Grafton Road, 947-2013) is inland, overlooking Mount Gardiner. The historic **Evergreen Hall** is unbeatable for the sheer size and charm of its newly added guest suite (with separate entrance, kitchen facilities) overlooking the old dance pavilion and hotel site (464 Melmore Road, 947-0312).

FRASER VALLEY THROUGH HARRISON HOT SPRINGS
To drive through rural Fraser Valley farmland east of Vancouver is to slip into a slower time when neighbours didn't lock their doors and you knew where your eggs came from. It's a leisurely day's drive through wonderfully peaceful countryside to Harrison Hot Springs, since there are lots of interesting stops along the slower back roads (2½ hours, without stops).

You have a choice of two highways out to Mission: the Trans-Canada (Highway 1) or the Lougheed (Highway 7), which is more scenic but can be grim getting out of Vancouver. From there, travel in a long, easterly loop, which begins on the north side of the Fraser River, crosses south of Agassiz, and returns along the south side.

To get a jump on the day, drive east on the Trans-Canada 70 kilometres (43.5 miles) to the Highway 11 turnoff and head north through Abbotsford. Keep an eye out for Clayburn Road on your right. Be sure to take this short detour down to the lit-tle-known old **Clayburn Village**. You'll think you've missed it as you head through a new suburb of massive houses, but keep going and you'll suddenly round a bend onto a street of small brick bungalows facing the village green.

[FREE] Clayburn is not a tourist village but rather a real community of people determined to save what was once the employees' town for one of Canada's largest brick mills. Few people know that it was designed by BC's noted arts and crafts architect Samuel McClure. Stop at the **Clayburn Village Store** (Clayburn Road, 853-4020) for tea, coffee, scones or pastries, imported British sweets, and local history. During Clayburn Heritage Day (usually the third weekend in July) a number of private homes and the church are open to the public, tea is served, and a visiting historian provides intriguing background.

Ask for directions back to Highway 11 without retracing your route for the 10-minute drive to Mission.

Mission, the rhododendron capital of BC, has a small-town friendliness and an artful new coffee house in **Glass Bean Espresso Gallery** (33128 First Avenue, 826-2766), where you'll find peaceful music, '50s red Naugahyde and chrome stools, and in back, the work of some 10 local artists. Cheerful owner George Jaeckel is happy to give you tips about more off-the-beaten-track spots in the valley. Ask directions (this town of railway tracks and one-way streets can be confusing) to the locally popular Mexican **Locomotive Club Cafe**, operated by an ebullient Italian/Polish Canadian (end of Glasgow Road, 826-7759; closed Mondays; dinner only Sundays).

[FREE] The splendid hilltop setting of **Westminster Abbey Seminary of Christ the King**, Canada's smallest arts university, with some 40 students training for the priesthood, was built over a period of 28 years by and for members of the Benedictine order. The founders of the site dropped to their knees in praise when they saw the vistas and rolling hills beyond. St. Benedict's Holy Rule 53: "All visitors who call are to be welcomed as if they were Christ, for he will say, 'I was a stranger and you took me in.'" You're free to wander the peaceful woodland trails—where PAX is carved into a stump—anytime, but if you want to see the inside of the impressive contemporary cathedral, with its massive sculptures and 64 stained-glass windows, you may do so from 1:30pm to 4:30pm weekdays and from 2pm to 4pm Sundays, or come for public worship; dress modestly. Bells are rung Sundays at 9:45am and 4:15pm. Couples, single men, or two or more women seeking solitude may arrange with the guestmaster (826-8975) to stay overnight.

▼

Day Trips

Fraser–Harrison

▲

[KIDS][FREE] If you're looking for a picnic spot, head back to Highway 7 and drive five minutes to Sylvester Road. Turn left, drive 20 minutes (when the road forks, stay right), park at the **Cascade Falls** sign, and walk down the trail. Back on Highway 7, continue east on the prettiest section of the winding road (between Dewdney and Deroche) to signs for **Kilby General Store Museum**.

[KIDS] This is one historic site—showing a once-bustling community that was bypassed—that shouldn't be missed. The General Store, in operation until the 1970s, was built on pilings (this area was formerly a floodplain), and the view is splendid. The Tearoom has tasty light lunches, and an intriguing selection of gifts, including colourful replicas of early canned salmon tins. Generally open May to September; weekends only October and November (call 796-9576).

From here, depending on how much time you have, you could drive the 15 minutes north on Highway 9 to **Harrison Hot Springs** for a quick look at a classic old-time lakefront resort, [KIDS] now home to the **World Championship Sand**

Sculpture Competition each September. Stop for a cold one or a snack at the **Old Settler** log pub on the way up to the springs (outside seating overlooks the water lily–laden Miami River, which is overhung with willows). Cross the Fraser River south of Agassiz.

This will put you on the more rural **Yale Road** through Chilliwack, where cars still angle-park, before reconnecting with the Trans-Canada. Boot it back to Highway 11, where you first turned north, and turn north again, passing Clayburn Road to turn left (west) at Harris Road, which will lead you along a delightful stretch past communities like Mount Lehman and **Bradner** (with fields of flowers such as daffodils, gladioli, and tulips and lots of seasonal roadside produce stalls). Eventually you'll feed back onto the Trans-Canada, which will take you to Vancouver.

GIBSONS

[KIDS][FREE] This simple seaside village known to television viewers in 40 countries as the setting for 19 seasons of *The Beachcombers* is well worth the price of a ferry ticket from West Vancouver's Horseshoe Bay terminal to **Langdale**. A 5-kilometre (3-mile) drive from Langdale lands you in front of the familiar Welcome Back sign on **Molly's Reach**, which presumes you have surely been here before, if only via television. (Stephen King movie fans will also see Gibsons in *Needful Things*.) The cafe setting is only a facade, but there's enough in the marina, shops, restaurants, and nearby hiking trails and beaches to assuage visitors' initial disappointment.

There are stairs just below Molly's Reach leading down to the marina and government wharf. You can follow **Gibsons Sea Walk** to either the left (glance up at vintage waterfront residences above) or the right past **Smitty's Marina** and marine enterprises servicing the active fishing and recreational port. The walk takes one detour up to the road, just below the **Elphinstone Pioneer Museum**, before continuing along to the **Mariners' Locker** general store, a good place to get really functional boating, fishing, and weather gear. Signs in the marina advertise fishing charters and kayak and boat rentals if you cannot resist the lure of the sea. The Elphinstone museum recreates the turn-of-the-century office, bedroom, and kitchen of early settlers and includes photos of old Gibsons' streetscapes, a native dugout canoe, a double-ender fishing boat, and equipment from early commercial ventures in logging, fishing, and the W. M. Malkin cooperative jam cannery. Open Monday and Tuesday 1pm to 5pm; Wednesday to Sunday 9am to 5pm.

At **Gibsons Fish Market** the crisp, battered fish and chips are always freshly cooked. Farther down the road, **Truffles** offers up heavenly baked goods, hearty soups and sandwiches, quiche, cappuccino, and decadent Belgian truffles.

Next door **Flurry Fast Hot Foods** ironically sells 16 flavours of ice cream. For a beer seaside, head for **Grandma's Pub** by the government wharf.

There are a number of small galleries showing the work of local artists and artisans, but at **Quay Works Gallery and Shop** (across the street from Truffles and downstairs), you have a chance to talk to artists as they work. **Molly's Lane Market**, between Gower Point Road and Molly's Reach, is worth a browse for the chance to pick up antiques, old books, and local crafts.

There's a spectacular overview of the town and surroundings, best reached by car, since the road is steep. Drive up School Road to reach **Soames Hill Park Trail**, or the Knob (via North Road west, turning right onto Chamberlin Road, then left on Bridgeman). Park here and get ready for a steep (but rewarding) half-hour climb.

[FREE] Gibsons is surrounded by a well-marked network of hiking trails called the **South Elphinstone Heritage and Recreation Trails**, entwined with the roads and camps from the early logging trade (expect to see the remains of old Japanese and Chinese labour camps and the Drew-Battle 1903 steam-powered sawmill at First Camp). [KIDS] The most popular family beach destination is **Chaster Provincial Park**, 5 kilometres (3 miles) past Gibsons.

The **Bonniebrook Lodge**, across the street from the park (886-2188), is now run by the former chef of Vancouver's Pan Pacific and La Gavroche, Philippe Lacoste, and his wife, Karen. They have transformed this seaside lodge into a first-class retreat, with four Edwardian-style bed and breakfast rooms available. Downstairs, **Chez Philippe Restaurant** has become the newest spot on the Sunshine Coast for fine dining. Remember: the last ferry leaves at 8:30pm!

It is possible to visit Gibsons without taking your car on the ferry (and so avoiding the irritating weekend lineups). Bus service starts right at the ferry dock, and funky taxicabs in town can get you out to Chaster Park. Or you can do the whole excursion easily by bicycle. Any time of the year is a delight on the Sunshine Coast.

LADNER

Slip back in time and enjoy the sensory delights of this farming community tucked against the reaches, sloughs, and marshes at the mouth of the mighty Fraser River. It's also an ideal starting point for side trips to the **Reifel Bird Sanctuary** on **Westham Island** and the less-known **Deas Island Regional Park**.

Take the River Road exit off Highway 99 (the first exit immediately south of the George Massey Tunnel, also known as the Deas Tunnel). You're soon driving down a road where fat

ponies graze next to old wooden houses with graceful veran-
dahs, and hollyhocks grow in the yards on one side and ditches
are lined with waist-high grass on the other. **[KIDS][FREE]** Cross
a wooden bridge past pretty sloops and fish boats to **Ladner
Heritage Park,** home to dozens of friendly wild rabbits and
trails through the cottonwoods to view the dock and new condos.

[KIDS][FREE] A stroll along the old village, centred on
Delta Street and 48th Avenue, should include a visit to the delightful **Delta Museum & Archives** (4858 Delta Street, 946-
9322) housed in the 1912 Tudor-style former municipal hall and
jail. You'll find some good, affordable native art in the gift shop.
Next door, at quirky **Uncle Herbert's Fish & Chip Shop,**
you have to be from Yorkshire to appreciate "true mushy peas,"
but not the fine fish and chips. Across the street, **Stillwater
Sports** (4849 Delta, 946-9933) has a cougar in the window and
enough decoys to fill a punt. Movie set decorators occasionally
check out **Ladner Estate Liquidators** (5040A-48th Avenue,
946-6330).

Head down River Road West, past the fruit stands to the
sign at the bridge directing you to turn right to Westham Island. First drive on another 15 metres (50 feet) and stop at the
Canoe Pass Village sign. Clamber up the dike bank for a jaw-
dropping gander at mega-houseboats, some complete with
kayak davits. If you have a bike, you might want to cycle down
one of the farm roads, inhaling the earthy smells as you go.

Day Trips

Ladner

[KIDS] The **Reifel Bird Sanctuary** (946-6980), 9.5 kilometres (6 miles) west is a rural remnant of the once-vast Fraser
estuary marshes, now home to thousands of migratory birds
on their ages-old path along North America's Pacific flyway.
Over 240 species can be sighted throughout the year, from the
Canada goose to the uncommon black-crowned night heron
and the extremely rare Temminck's stint. In winter, the sight
of thousands of snow geese rising up as one, on their journey
to California from their Arctic breeding grounds off Siberia, is
unforgettable. Early risers should start with Reifel, returning
to Ladner for lunch or tea. In season, look for pick-your-own
berries on Westham.

Back in town, stop in the 5000 block for a look at an old
church (now a Montessori school), the restored **Bridgeport
School,** and Heritage House Interiors.

[KIDS][FREE] Peaceful **Deas Island Regional Park** is
technically located right above the George Massey Tunnel.
Here you can enjoy the river's breeze or cast your line toward
salmon-loaded gill-netters or freighters carrying cars from
Japan. Wander to the viewing tower for a dreamy view of river
traffic and wildlife. People picnic here year round but the second Sunday in August is devoted to the annual Teddy Bears'
picnic, when stuffed bears and their owners gather.

If you plan to be near Ladner around dinnertime, make

reservations for a leisurely dinner at **La Belle Auberge** (4856 48th Ave, 946-7717).

PITT RIVER AND WIDGEON MARSH RESERVE

[KIDS][FREE] Coquitlam's Pitt Lake, about a 35-minute drive from Vancouver, is the largest freshwater tidal lake in North America, but the true attraction is **Pitt River** and the **Widgeon Marsh Reserve**, 432-6350. The Greater Vancouver Regional District Park's newest acquisition is already well known to birders. You can walk or cycle the series of dikes ringing nearby Pitt Polder (two hours around the bottom; three around the top, with bird-watching towers en route), thanks to Holland's grateful Queen Juliana, who (in appreciation for her stay in Canada during World War II) provided the funds to employ returning servicemen, who helped build the dikes.

A better way to get close to the wildlife and appreciate the calming beauty of these pristine wetlands surrounded by steep mountain slopes, is to rent a canoe at **Ayla Canoes** ((604) 941-2822) from March through October ($25 a day). Owner Gordon Williams knows the area well and can tell you about the 44,000 salmon that return to spawn and the bird species found here. At present, boats are the only way in to Widgeon Marsh Reserve, purchased in 1992 as a park reserve for the future.

Directions: Follow the Lougheed Highway (Highway 7) to Port Coquitlam. Cross the Pitt River Bridge into Pitt Meadows and turn left onto Dewdney Trunk Road. Follow it for 6.2 kilometres (3.85 miles) and turn left onto Neaves/208th Street, which becomes Rannie Road and finally ends in the parking lot by the public boat launch at the mouth of Pitt Lake. (The lake can become dangerous when a wind pipes up.) Cross Pitt River to Widgeon Creek on the west side. Instead of the direct 10-minute crossing, you can take the more leisurely route around Siwash Island. Along the way watch for herons, ospreys, and eagles atop the mooring posts that tether log booms.

Head north up the narrow channel between **Siwash Island** and the western river bank, where marsh marigolds bloom in spring. Drifting silently with the current, you may slip past red-tailed hawks, widgeons, swans, and sandhill cranes, whose nesting areas in the polder are closed to dike-walking visitors from April through June. The paddle up Widgeon Creek to a covered picnic area with campsites takes about one hour. Look for the lime green garbage cans, which are easier to spot than the white and brown sign reading "Widgeon Creek BC Forest Service Recreational Site." Pull up on the beach for a picnic and swim. You can leave your canoe here, and follow well-marked Forest Service trails upstream for a view of the impressive **Widgeon Falls**, a delightful three-hour round trip. Tip from the foresters: if you're hiking in the fall or winter, take the drier road for the first three kilometres if there's been a lot of rain.

It will merge back into the trail. A signed fork on the trail directs you to Widgeon Falls or Widgeon Lake. Only those in good shape should tackle the nine-hour round-trip, steep hike to Widgeon Lake. It is spectacular, and the trout fishing is great at this emerald in the sky.

SEYMOUR DEMONSTRATION FOREST

[KIDS][FREE] One of the best-kept secrets on Vancouver's North Shore opened to visitors in 1987. Now the 5600-hectare (13,837-acre) **Seymour Demonstration Forest** (north end of Lillooet Road, 432-6286) attracts enthusiastic regular hikers, cyclists, and inline skaters drawn by the 50 kilometres (31 miles) of paved and gravel logging roads and trails, as well as access to the Seymour River. The area has been off-limits since 1928, when it was designated a future watershed. That designation still holds, but the future won't arrive until well into the 21st century.

The idea is to help people understand that logging can work if the forest is managed well. Because of the controversy in BC about clearcut logging and the bad press that the province has received, people want to learn more—and are surprised to discover that many of the big western redcedar, western hemlock, Douglas fir, *amabilis* fir, and Sitka spruce are only 75 years old. Visitors will also learn what makes sap rise in a tree and how to spot stumps left from logging in the 1900s.

Follow Lillooet Road north past Capilano College and the cemetery, and a gravel road will take you to the parking area and information centre where friendly staff are happy to point you to the best routes for your ability. For families with children, there is the pleasant **Forest Ecology Loop Trail** around pretty **Rice Lake**. It's one of the few freshwater lakes on the North Shore, and you can fish for trout from the small docks, provided you have a provincial fishing licence (available from any tackle shop).

The big draw is the 22-kilometre (13.7-mile) round-trip trek to **Seymour Dam**, which includes a broad, spectacular vista from **Mid Valley Viewpoint**. Walking is easy, although most people seem to be on two wheels, enjoying the broad, paved road (no vehicles weekends or evenings). The prettier trail beside the river takes almost double the time of the road.

If you've packed a picnic, there are swimming holes between the main gate and Mid Valley, and the water is warm compared with the better-known but chilly Lynn Creek (but keep an eye out for bears). Or plan to eat at the base of the massive dam, whose dramatic concrete architecture would have fit right into Terry Gilliam's *Brazil*. It's worth the short climb up to overlook the lake and the short detour to the nearby fish hatchery. [KIDS] No dogs at any time; bikes are permitted on the paved road to Seymour Dam on evenings and weekends only. Public hours are not steadfast, but generally the public is welcome 7am to 9pm in summer, 8am to 5pm in winter. Access for canoeing and kayaking is by special-use permit only ((604) 987-1273).

STEVESTON

Steveston, once the biggest fishing port in the world, with over 50 canneries, has not a single operating cannery left. It is still Canada's largest port, with over 1,000 vessels, most of which are commercial fishing boats. It's a colourful place that still smells of the sea and history, a place where you can often buy fresh prawns, salmon, snapper, sole, and crab right off the boats.

Drive out from Vancouver south along Highway 99 to the Steveston Highway turnoff, or take the 406 or 407 bus from downtown Vancouver. Park or get off the bus at **Steveston Park**, which pays tribute to the Japanese-Canadians who helped build Steveston and were later evacuated to the Interior during the Second World War. The nearby **Martial Arts Centre** is the first *dojo* house ever built outside Japan. This house, built specifically for martial arts, has two halls—one with hardwood floors for kendo and karate, the other with tatami mats for karate.

Old-timers may grumble about the incursion of walkers, joggers, and cyclists on the new bike trails and the upscale **Steveston Landing** retail complex (3800 Bayview Street), but these developments have saved the wetlands (the salt marshes of Sturgeon Bank are Canada's largest wintering spot for ducks) from turning into oil tanker docks.

Plan to spend the morning wandering through the old historic fishing village centred on Bayview, Moncton, and Chatham streets. Pick up fish and chips from the take-out window at **Dave's Fish and Chips** (3460 Moncton Street, 271-7555) or **Pelican Pete's** (3866 Bayview Street, 275-7811) on the waterfront, or spoon up some chowder at **Pajo's**, a boat restaurant anchored at the dock (summer only).

Danny's Rainbow Charters, a converted deep-sea Dutch-built diesel-powered lifeboat, leaves on demand from the dock at the foot of Second Avenue for a 30-minute narrated harbour tour past boats, eagles, great blue herons, and sea lions. Or see the harbour by land via the dikes that wrap around the southwestern edge of Steveston (a leisurely walk could take up to 2½ hours).

Try the Spanish paella or the crab served on the outside patio at **Sleigh's Restaurant** (3711 Bayview Street, 275-5188). **Steveston Seafood House** (3951 Moncton Street, 271-5252) is something of an institution; the decor is no-surprises nautical, but the wine list is surprisingly good.

Moncton Street is a mix of new boutiques and authentic fishing gear stores in one-storey false-fronted buildings. The **Steveston Museum** (3811 Moncton Street, 271-6868, Mon-

Sat) was erected as a prefab bank in 1905 and now doubles as a post office. [KIDS][FREE] Most of what you'll want to see lies to the west, eventually ending with a view of river traffic from **Garry Point Park**, where the Musqueam people camped for over a thousand years when following the salmon runs. **Britannia Heritage Shipyard**, the oldest building on the waterfront, is a huge timbered dry dock that began life as a cannery. Old-timers have revived the art of wooden shipbuilding and repair. With any luck, you'll catch them working on an old wooden seiner.

The cedar plank pathway was once Steveston's Main Street, when the town was a heady Saturday night boomtown with more than 10,000 people strolling the boardwalks between hotels, saloons, and houses of prostitution. Nearby, drop in for a piece of Judy's deep-dish pie at the **Steveston Cannery Cafe** (3711 Moncton Street, 272-1222), a turn-of-the-century cook house.

[KIDS][FREE] Another landmark at the foot of Third Street is the former **Gulf of Georgia Cannery**, dubbed the "monster cannery," which Parks Canada plans to open as a National Historic Site for its centenary in the summer of 1994. In summer, you'll also have a chance to shop at the many roadside fruit and vegetable stands in this prime farming area or to join in on the July 1 (Canada Day) Salmon Festival, Canada's largest one-day community festival.

VICTORIA
See also Victoria in Excursions section of this chapter.

The Royal Sealink catamaran harbour-to-harbour service that made a car-free day trip from Vancouver to Victoria on Vancouver Island such a delight has shut down service. There are other options, however. **Pacific Coach Lines** (662-8074) offers frequent reliable service between the two downtown areas from Vancouver's new bus terminal at 1150 Station Street. The ferry through Active Pass past numerous Gulf Islands is 1 hour and 40 minutes, but allow about 3½ hours downtown to downtown. If you prefer to drive yourself, call **BC Ferries** (669-1211) for sailing times (recorded information, 685-1021).

Helijet Airways (455 Waterfront Road, 273-1414) and **Air BC's** floatplane service (foot of Bute Street, 688-5515) are pricier, but they do provide 35-minute harbour-to-harbour service. (Helijet also links downtown Victoria direct with Vancouver International Airport.) The two best times to travel to Victoria are on a crisp, clear day in early December when the sea is calm, and in the summer months, despite the many tourists. Here's why. In December, the **Empress Hotel** is decorated for Christmas. Settle back into an earlier, gentler time in the **Bengal Lounge**, where a buffet of assorted curries is served up for a warming tiffin. After lunch, check the Empress archives on the lower level for the days when a suite was $15, the William F. Tickle Orchestra played, and wartime menus urged: "All persons in ordering their food ought to consider the needs of Great Britain and her Allies and their Armies for wheat, beef, bacon and fats."

In summer, there isn't a more heavenly way to spend the afternoon than in the gardens of **Point Ellice House** (2616 Pleasant Street, (604) 387-4697). Walk a few blocks first to local eatery **C'est Bon** (Bastion Square), notable for its home-made soup, breads, and croissants and a new view to the harbour since the city removed a wall. [KIDS] From the Inner Harbour, board the mini **Victoria Harbour Ferry** for the 10-minute ride up the gorge to the Point Ellice House, where you step up onto the landing dock and back into the 19th century. Until 1977, this was the home of the gardening-besotted Ellice family, whose slip into genteel poverty allowed them to retain all the Victorian furnishings of a family who once hosted Sir John A. Macdonald (Canada's first prime minister).

Afternoon tea is still served on the croquet lawn 1pm to 4pm Thursday to Sunday (summers only; reservations suggested); in June, the dreamy garden, still being carefully renovated, is heady with the scent of old-fashioned damask roses. Sundays are best (and quietest) for, sadly, Point Ellice is the last bastion of peace on the now quite noisy Pleasant Street.

Victoria's charm lies in its comfortable human scale, which you can enjoy year round as you stroll up Government Street. Few buildings in the heart of the city are over seven storeys. Being on foot makes sense here, since 90 percent of what most visitors want to see is within two blocks of the waterfront. [KIDS] In under an hour you can walk across town or stroll most of the waterfront past the sailboats and floatplanes. Then go on to Bastion Square, where the less well known but fascinating **Maritime Museum** houses *Trekka*, a 6-metre (20-foot) ketch that sailed solo around the world in the 1950s, and *Tilikum*, a converted 11.5-metre (38-foot) native dugout canoe that made an equally impressive two-year passage to England at the turn of the century. Aviation buffs will enjoy **The Aviator**, a new shop in Bastion Square, close to **Dig This**, a great gardener's shop.

The return trip down the very English Government Street takes you past the gleaming mahogany and stained-glass interiors of heritage buildings like the century-old tobacco shop **E. A. Morris** ((604) 382-4811), which ships tobacco throughout the world but also stocks nifty shaving gear, seltzer bottles, and walking sticks. You will also pass **Munro's** ((604) 382-2464), which *Maclean's* columnist Allan Fotheringham calls the best bookstore in Canada, and **Rogers' Chocolates** ((604) 384-7021), whose near-hockey-puck-size Victoria creams wrapped in waxy, pink-gingham paper have been shipped to

Buckingham Palace. Most locals will recommend the **Royal British Columbia Museum** as one of the best in the country, with dramatic dioramas of natural BC landscapes and full-scale reconstructions of Victorian storefronts. Of particular interest: the Northwest Coast First Nations exhibit, rich with spiritual and cultural artifacts. Open every day, Belleville and Government; (604) 387-3701.

It's only a short walk from there to 74.5-hectare (184-acre) Beacon Hill Park with its splendid ocean views and the hand-holding couples who stroll the walkways and give retirement a good name. A lovely spot to get away from the shopping mania downtown.

George Straith Ltd. styles itself as the best of the British clothing stores (you can be measured for a suit here that will be tailored in England), but it is pricey and the women's clothes in particular appeal to those with traditional taste. Piccadilly Shopper British Woollens specializes in good-quality women's clothes; Sasquatch Trading Company, Ltd. and the Indian Craft Shop both have some of the best Cowichan sweaters. Two quick side excursions off Government Street worth doing: first, dip into the Eaton Centre for a gander at British Importers, whose present store, complete with Italian leather floor tiles and hand-made lighting fixtures, won them a national design award. Their exclusive products go beyond English Brollies and Bally shoes to Armani and Valentino designs. Then turn up from Government Street to 606 Trounce Alley, where the Nushin Boutique, one of Victoria's elite women's clothing stores, brings together many European designers. Some, less well known, are surprisingly good values.

Day Trips

Victoria

For a not-so-British take on shopping, head for Chinatown's **Fisgard Street** and **Fan Tan Alley**, Canada's narrowest street, or the funky shops along **Johnson Street**. There are some intriguing home design, furnishings, and surplus stores just beyond Chinatown on **Herald Street** (Surplus City) and **Store Street** (North Park Design, Capital Iron, Attica). Serious antique hunters head for Antique Row in the 800 to 1000 blocks of **Fort Street**.

Although Victorians do weary of being touted as a little bit of old Blighty, let's face it: an early Victorian man-about-town once shared a mistress with the Prince of Wales (later Edward VII), the Empress Hotel still pours 1.6 million cups of afternoon tea a year, and horse-drawn vehicles have been clopping along the Inner Harbour since the city started sightseeing tours in 1903. And where else can you visit Anne Hathaway's cottage and see Queen Victoria in wax, alongside replicas of the crown jewels, without crossing the Atlantic?

EXCURSIONS

BARKLEY SOUND

[KIDS] The stout Scottish-built 1937 packet freighter MV *Lady Rose*, and her "new" companion, the MV *Frances Barkley*, are both working freight vessels that carry mail and supplies to remote communities along the Alberni Inlet and on the distant islands of Barkley Sound leading out to the west coast of Vancouver Island. They also carry passengers, since the trip makes for a scenic diversion.

There are two routes. The year-round scheduled run to **Bamfield** operates every Tuesday, Thursday, and Saturday. Come summer, on Monday, Wednesday, and Friday the boats drop kayakers at the spectacular **Broken Islands** before heading on to **Ucluelet** (easily reached by Pacific Rim Highway other months). The best trip is to Bamfield (population 270), which holds more charm than the larger Ucluelet. From early July through Labour Day, a special Sunday sailing does just that. Call to be sure ((800) 663-7192 or 723-8313).

Along the way, the boat stops to drop supplies at tiny floating fishing and logging camps, newspapers at solitary cabins, or ice at fish farms. Or sometimes it just stops to sell a candy bar to a fisher with a sweet tooth. The *Lady Rose*'s happy band of 100 passengers ranges from loggers, fishermen, and scientists to kayakers, hikers, and tourists along for the 9-to-10-hour return trip ($32 to $36; kids under seven are free). It can be breezy even in summer. Take warm clothes, a camera, extra film, and binoculars.

Besides being a better way to reach Bamfield than over rough dirt roads filled with logging trucks, the four-hour cruise down Alberni Inlet is breathtaking. Given the 8am departure time from the Alberni Harbour Quay, you'll probably have to overnight in Port Alberni. Breakfast and lunch are served in the little galley. Or take along a loaf of cheese bread from Port Alberni's the **Flour Shop** (723-1105).

Bamfield spans the inlet, which acts as the main street of the town. A local water taxi joins west and east Bamfield. [KIDS][FREE] The tiny fishing village is heavily populated by marine biologists at the nearby Marine Research Station (half-hour visits are available summer weekends at 1:30pm to coincide with the boat arrivals, but it's a good idea to call ahead at 728-3301).

[FREE] Take a short walk to **Brady's Beach** or hike farther along to **Cape Beale Lighthouse** and the wild beaches just beyond. The stretch of coastline from here south to Port Renfrew is one of the most rugged and unforgiving shores in the world. With one shipwreck for every 1.5 kilometres (1 mile) of coastline, it became known as the Graveyard of the Pacific and spurred the building of the West Coast lifesaving trail. If time allows, hike to the northern end of the trail at **Pachena Bay**, just 5 kilometres (3 miles) from Bamfield. (This is the prettier end of the 77-kilometre (48-mile) trail: some hikers just take the short route to **Nitinat Narrows** and retrace their steps.) The comfortable **McKay Bay Lodge** (728-3323) has only seven guest rooms (those upstairs and out front are best), so call early. Full meal packages are available and suggested, since there's not a lot of choice in tiny Bamfield.

COAST MOUNTAIN LOOP

This circle route takes you past mountains, glaciers, canyons, and Chilcotin wilderness, and best of all, into the Cariboo. The **Duffey Lake Road**, which links Whistler to BC's cattle country, has long been familiar to four-wheel-drive owners. Thanks to the recent paving of the old logging road, this spectacular drive has opened to the rest of us. Any BC Tourist InfoCentre can provide a brochure and map detailing the Coast Mountain Circle Tour, which takes you north on Highway 99 from the year-round resort of Whistler (see Whistler section in this chapter) through near-desert Lillooet to the high plateau country of Cache Creek and Ashcroft, where grass was once as high as a horse's belly and smart men found real money raising cattle for hungry gold miners.

From there, you'll circle south to Vancouver on the Trans-Canada (Highway 1) through the dramatic Fraser Canyon, past the rafting capital of Lytton (which routinely records Canada's highest summer temperatures) and Hope before turning west through the farmlands and distant mountains of the Fraser Valley (see Fraser Valley in Day Trips section of this chapter) to the coast.

Driving time from **Whistler** to Cache Creek is about 3½ hours. If you're just looking for a scenic drive with a few stops along the way, you can certainly do the whole circuit in two days, but it's a pity not to spend three or four exploring this fascinating route, which follows much of the historic Gold Rush trail from the late 1850s and early 1860s. In summer, with any luck, this can be a hot, sunny drive, so load up the cooler with cold drinks and picnic goodies.

[KIDS][FREE] **Lillooet Museum and InfoCentre** (Main Street, 256-4308 in summer, 256-4556 off-season), set in a disused Anglican church that was packed in piece by piece on the backs of miners, is a reminder of Lillooet's Gold Rush days, when, with 15,000 people, it was the second-largest city north of San Francisco. Another whole section is devoted to one of BC's best-known newspaper women, feisty Ma Murray. The nearby **Hanging Tree** (the key limb has rotted off) is a reminder of "Hanging Judge" Matthew Begbie's stern days when killers were hanged.

[KIDS][FREE] **Pavilion Lake** is a great spot for a swim

after the drive across the peaceful big-sky plateau country where every breath smells of sagebrush and pine. **Historic Hat Creek Ranch** (north of Cache Creek, junction of Highways 97 and 12, 457-9722) is a must. You can take a guided wagon or trail ride around the last remaining intact Cariboo Wagon roadhouse and its buildings (well-trained, fat 'n' sassy retired ranch horses match your level as a rider, giving as good as they get). Admission by donation.

Carry on through Cache Creek (mostly gas stations and motels at this highway crossroads) past the benchlands to nearby **Ashcroft** for a fine meal or afternoon tea in the shade of leafy acacia trees at the delightful **Ashcroft Manor** (Highway 1, turnoff to Ashcroft, 453-9983), a former stopping house that now operates its own museum and arts and crafts house.

For a delightful (and reasonable) night's stay and an excellent dinner, drive south 43 kilometres (27 miles) to **Spences Bridge** and the historic (1890s) **Steelhead Inn** operated by chef Jeremy Lewis (458-2398). Curiously, there are few notable places to stay along the Coast Mountain route, but there are plenty of motels. One alternative is to take a detour west from Pemberton or Lillooet to the $3 million newly hewn log **Tyax Mountain Lake Resort** (238-2221), which is open year-round and whose broad range of activities in the Chilcotin wilderness— heli-everything, hiking, fishing, canoeing, and horseback riding in summer and skiing, snowmobiling, tobogganing, and skating in winter—draws families and guests from Europe and Japan. Some find it a bit overwhelming.

[KIDS] Good fall steelhead fishing at Spences Bridge and most whitewater rafting happens on the stretch of the Thompson River between here and **Lytton** (named for Sir Edward Bulwer-Lytton, British civil servant and novelist who penned the immortal line: "It was a dark and stormy night . . ."). It's an unforgettable experience. Rafting operators are based in both towns. [KIDS][FREE] Along the road, keep an eye out for two small provincial parks: **Goldpan** (beside the river) and, even better, the lesser-known **Skihist** (above the highway), a very special near-desert location with prickly pear cactus and the occasional Pacific rattlesnake. Here you'll also find impressive river panoramas and occasionally sight Rocky Mountain bighorn sheep. If you don't go rafting, **Hell's Gate Airtram** (south of Boston Bar) will give you a 153-metre (502-foot) trip across the turbulent river. It draws a lot of tourists daily during the mid-April to mid-October season (there's even a Christmas Shop at the bottom of the tram), but the trip across the river is worth doing once to see the fish ladders or to sample the salmon chowder at the Salmon House Restaurant. To make your travels along the old wagon trail through **Boston Bar** and **Yale** more interesting and educational, pick up material on the Gold Rush history at any of the information centres along the way.

Many people blast through **Hope** (junction for the Fraser Canyon or the Hope-Princeton route east), but do stop to see the site of the 1965 **Hope Slide** (Highway 3, 15 minutes east of Hope) where two of the four people killed in a massive avalanche remain entombed; a related mud slide filled the valley to a depth of 61 metres (200 feet). The **Othello Tunnels**, off Highway 5, are less well known to tourists and even British Columbians, although Sylvester Stallone fans will recognize the dramatic setting from *First Blood*. Ask at the **InfoCentre** (919 Water Avenue, 869-2021) for directions to the five tunnels carved out of rock to link the Kootenays and used by the Kettle Valley Railway until 1961. The tunnels drip, and they're closed in winter, but they're fascinating to walk through, with views to the Coquihalla River roaring by in the 100-metre-high (328-foot-high) gorge.

HORNBY ISLAND

This funky, laid-back, northern Gulf Island is seldom described in detail in guidebooks or even government publications. The 1,600 locals like it that way. For one, it's a five-hour, three-ferry journey from Vancouver. Take the Horseshoe Bay ferry to Nanaimo, then allow two hours for the 80-kilometre (50-mile) drive north on Vancouver Island to **Buckley Bay**. From there, catch the 10-minute ferry to the sister island of Denman, cross the pastoral and artistic island, and catch the next short ferry to Hornby. Ferries are timed so you can make it easily.

Compared with other Gulf Islands, Hornby has relatively few restaurants or places to stay, other than campgrounds or private cabins; however, for people happy to schlep around in old shorts and thongs, Hornby is heaven. The tiny bucolic island is filled with characters from the '60s, barefoot earth mothers who were not even born in the '60s, permanent artists like potter Wayne Ngan, and longtime summer families of architects, musicians, and such painters as Jack Shadbolt and Robert Bateman. You can kayak around the island in a long day or cycle the few roads in a couple of hours.

There are three social hubs to Hornby: the local **recycling depot**—a sort of communal Dogpatch, complete with **Free Store**; the local hobbit-house-like **community centre/theatre** where movies like *Bugsy* alternate with subtitled films like China's *Ju-Dou*. This woodsy complex includes the **Hornby Island Cooperative** grocery store, 335-1121 (which makes it unnecessary to pack in your own Asiago cheese, basmati rice, and the like), some artists' stores, and two tiny food stands: **VORIZO** (Hornby's postal code) for cappuccino and quesadilla addicts and **Jan's Cafe** for carnivores and vegans alike.

A bike trip around the occasionally hilly island (rent at the **Hornby Island Off-Road Bike Shop**, 335-0444) is a pleasant blur of artisans' studios and produce gardens (don't miss the small sign for dreamy **Gordon's Garden** just before Ford Cove), punctuated by stops for a cold draft at the **Thatch** by the ferry, or inland at the island's only bakery, the **Cardboard House Bakery and Cafe** (Central Road, 335-0733).

If you've never tried ocean kayaking, call **Zucchini Ocean Kayak Centre** (335-0045), which rents kayaks and runs guided trips for novices. The staff is happy to tell you about prevailing winds, tides, best beaches, and chances for seeing mink, seals, eagles, and, perhaps, an orca. Best view from a kayak: hugging the coastline stretch between Tribune Bay and Whaling Station Bay, where cormorants hang off the sandstone cliffs of Helliwell Park. Detour to Flora Island, where curious seals bob off the most easterly point. Or simply stroll along the dramatic grassy tops of the seaside cliffs. Best white sand beaches: Whaling Station Bay and Tribune Bay, aka Big Trib (around the next bay, Little Trib is a nude beach).

You can stay in one of the three pretty (but small) waterfront rooms at Joyce Cunningham's **Grassy Point Bed and Breakfast** (Grassy Point, 335-2224). Dinner choices on the island are simple: the **Thatch** by the ferry for pub-style meals and summer barbecues, and the **Sea Breeze Lodge** (335-2321) at Tralee Point, which takes reservations for nonguests (the cottages—unpretentious but comfortable—overlook the ocean; the newest cottages have fireplaces). Simplest of all, ask which nights the bakery will be cranking out great pizza. Plan to eat in the bakery's garden or phone ahead for takeout.

If you've got time to kill, plan a day of cycling or driving on neighbouring Denman, touring the studios of weavers, potters, painters, and other artisans, especially **Beardsley Pottery** (4920 Lacon Road, 335-0308), always open.

MV UCHUK III

[KIDS] More northerly, remote, and historic than the *Lady Rose* is the MV *Uchuk III* (head west from Campbell River). The 41-metre (135-foot) converted American minesweeper built in 1943 carries passengers, mail, and cargo year-round from Gold River to Tahsis and Kyoquot Sound. Come summer, the boat adds two summer "tourist cruises" (reservations: 283-2325). Departure for the day trip is at noon, so overnight in **Campbell River** and drive to Gold River in the morning. The six-hour round trip (Tuesday and Wednesday, July and August) via fjordlike inlets to historic **Nootka Sound** includes a one-hour stop at Yuquot or **Friendly Cove** (Captain James Cook's first known landing place on the west coast in 1772 triggered the sea otter fur trade). Britain and Spain also vied for power here (in the 18th century, *Nootka Incident* played in a theatre in London's West End, yet most British Columbians today couldn't place Nootka on a map).

The $7 landing fee includes a guided tour by local native

people. The stained-glass windows in the small Catholic church commemorating the early explorers are a recent gift from Spain. Walking on a spongy trail under the tall spruce trees, cast a thought back to Cook's men, who once brewed spruce beer here. The second trip is an overnight cruise to **Kyoquot**, a secluded fishing village located on a small sheltered bay. The price of $130 (free for kids under 12) includes accommodation in Old Co-op (four small bedrooms, with breakfast in the host's home). On both trips, stops are made as required at logging camps and settlements in the area to deliver supplies and passengers. Expect to see seals, clearcuts, salmon, passing trollers, south polar skuas on their flight to colder climes. Part of this trip is in open waters—not for the queasy.

OKANAGAN WINERY TOUR

Despite more than a century of history behind it, the BC wine industry has only just begun to flourish. Today oenophiles can savour a tour of the Okanagan wine country, where the hanging benchland surrounding the shores of Okanagan Lake provides an extraordinarily beautiful setting for growing and bottling the noble grape.

Getting there from Vancouver is a comfortable four-hour drive via the Trans-Canada Highway (Highway 1) to Hope, then along the scenic Coquihalla Highway (Highway 6) into Merritt, and from there along the Coquihalla Connector into the valley.

The Okanagan Valley runs north-south, wrapping itself around Okanagan Lake from Vernon to Penticton and then spreading south to the border. Over two dozen wineries operate in the region, ranging from a few large commercial concerns to many small estate wineries to a few tiny farm gate businesses operating from a house or garage.

The estate wineries are responsible for British Columbia's growing reputation, and almost all welcome visitors. You can obtain maps and information about hours at most tourist information kiosks between Vancouver and the Okanagan. If you want to meet the winemaker and tour the facility beyond the tasting room, be sure to call ahead for an appointment. The **British Columbia Wine Institute** (BCWI) can help you, and the more notice you can give them the better. Contact the BCWI in Vancouver at (604) 986-0440.

The following is a brief look at the leading properties in the region, beginning some 20 minutes north of Kelowna at Winfield.

Just west of Winfield, over the hills on Camp Road, is **Gray Monk Estate Winery** (1051 Camp Road, (604) 766-3168), etched perilously into the slopes above Okanagan Lake. Owners George and Trudy Heiss, two of the best ambassadors the region could have, recently celebrated their 20th year in the valley. There is no better way to pass a warm summer's day than by sitting on their sun-drenched balcony, overlooking the lake, sipping on a Gray Monk Rotberger, a pinot gris, or one of their fabulous late-harvest wines.

Leaving Gray Monk, head back south along Highway 97 into Kelowna and look for Lakeshore Road. Turning left (south) will point you toward **CedarCreek Estate Winery** (5445 Lakeshore Road, (604) 764-8866), tucked neatly into the hillside high above the eastern shores of Okanagan Lake. Bring along some bread and cheese and stop at one of the picnic tables nestled among the steep-sloping vineyards to sip winemaker Ann Sperling's award-winning chardonnay, pinot blanc, merlot, or chancellor.

On the way back toward Kelowna, not far from Cedar-Creek, you will find **Summerhill Estate Winery** (4870 Chute Lake Road, (604) 764-8000), the region's first commercial sparkling wine producer. Transplanted New Yorker and owner Stephen Cipes (rhymes with *pipes*) is turning out a number of good sparkling wines under the watchful eye of winemaker Eric von Krosigk. The nonvintage Cipes Brut is sure to catch your attention, as will a number of other upscale sparklers.

Upon your return to Kelowna, cross the floating bridge and follow Highway 97 south as it winds its way to Penticton. First up, just north of Peachland, is **Hainle Estate Vineyards** (5355 Trepannier Bench Road, (604) 767-2525). Proprietors Tilman and Sandra Hainle offer another beautiful vista, high above the lake, from which to sip their ultra-dry wines. The Hainles have produced the valley's first ice wine—a sweet dessert wine that is a must-taste—and are leaders in the endeavour to produce natural wines using totally organic methods.

Farther south on the northern edge of Summerland is the hilltop estate winery of **Sumac Ridge** (Highway 97, (604) 494-0451). Owner Harry McWatters is among the valley's leading wine historians and is an invaluable resource for anyone seeking information about the Okanagan wine industry. Don't miss the Sumac Ridge Reserve Gewürztraminer or the winery's *méthode champenoise* sparkler.

Penticton is the next stop, and while you're there, plan to stay overnight at the Coast Lakeside Resort at the lake's southern end. The farm gate wineries of Naramata are a quick jaunt from the hotel, and 20 to 30 minutes south you will find Blue Mountain Vineyard and Gehringer Brothers.

Blue Mountain Vineyard and Cellars (Oliver Ranch Road, (604) 497-8224) is one of BC's newer estate wineries—although owners Jan and Ian Mavety have actively grown grapes on site for many years. Nestled in a canyonlike setting at the northern end of Vaseaux Lake, Blue Mountain is making some of the valley's best pinot gris and pinot blanc, as well as chardonnay and pinot noir produced in both still and sparkling formats.

Continue south past Oliver. On your right-hand side you will see a rising bench that is home to **Gehringer Brothers Estate Winery** (Highway 97 and Road 8, (604) 498-3537). Walter Gehringer has been producing fine German-style varietals here for years, and riesling fans must make a stop. The lineup runs from ice wine to dry riesling, with some wonderful, floral, fruity pinot auxerrois and ehrenfelser thrown in for good measure.

QUADRA ISLAND

When General Norman Schwarzkopf wanted bigger fish to fry, he headed for **April Point Lodge** on **Quadra Island** (April Point Road, 285-2222), possibly the toniest fishing resort in the Pacific Northwest. BC is world famous for salmon fishing, and Vancouver Island's Campbell River, home of the mighty tyee (chinook weighing over 14 kilograms or 30 pounds), helped put it on the map. Take the 10-minute ferry ride from **Campbell River** to tiny Quadra Island, where the Peterson family, long-time lodge owners, has drawn such celebrities and serious fishermen as John Wayne, Julie Andrews, and Kevin Costner, and you'll be hooked too.

There are some 50 professional fishing guides to help you land that 60-pounder (27 kilograms). Boston whalers take two guests out for a minimum of four hours, and the price includes boat, fuel, tackle, bait, rain gear, and guide. You can fly-fish for northern coho, troll or mooch for chinook, or row for the tyee (the best time to catch one is from July to September).

The one- to six-bedroom guest houses facing west are expensive but spacious, beautifully furnished, and graced with large fireplaces. North-facing thin-walled cabins overlook the marina; you could be kept awake by late-drinking or early-rising fishermen in adjoining rooms. There are also suites and single rooms in the sunny and cheerful main lodge. The food—from fresh Dungeness crab to Gulf Island lamb—is always good, thanks to chef Dory Ford. Your catch is expertly cleaned, frozen, and packaged in coolers for travel. You can also have it smoked, canned, or made into lox. Instead of having the Big One mounted, ask April Point's guide Eiji Umenura to make a gyotaku, a Japanese "fish print" suitable for framing.

If you're not there to fish—really fish—you may sense a good-natured (more likely slightly puzzled) fish or cut bait attitude from guests who come only to do just that. Although there are no other amenities at April Point, **Quadra Island** has lots to offer. About 8 kilometres (5 miles) in either direction are exceptionally lovely beach walks. To the south, you can walk along the shore to **Cape Mudge's** lighthouse. To the east lies the **Rebecca Spit Provincial Park**, where a shallow bay offers surprisingly warm swimming.

Or if you've caught your limit, head for the **Kwagiulth Museum and Cultural Centre** (285-3733), one of BC's best small museums, which has an outstanding historical collection of Northwest Coast Indian art, thanks to the return of goods once confiscated by the government when potlatches were banned. Ask where you can see petroglyphs across the street. Summer workshops open to the public include rubbings of these ancient carved "drawings" in stone.

The same Cape Mudge Band recently opened the **Tsa-Kwa-Luten Lodge** (Lighthouse Road, 665-7745 or (800) 665-7745), the only resort owned and operated by native people in Canada that features authentic native culture. On Friday nights, the contemporary lodge, built in the architectural spirit of a longhouse, offers buffet dinners (open to anyone) featuring local foods (salmon cooked over an open fire, clams, mussels, berries, fiddleheads). A tribal dance follows.

On your way home, try a final cast from Campbell River's 180-metre-long (590-foot-long) wooden Discovery Pier (first built in Canada specifically as a saltwater fishing pier), where 16 tyee were caught in 1992. As you head for Nanaimo, keep an eye out for Fanny Bay, where you can buy direct from **Mac's Oysters** (335-2233). Farther on, **Dot's Cafe** (5921 North Island Highway, 390-3331) is famous for Lemon Meringue Mile High Pie. For a final thrill, drive 25 minutes south of Nanaimo to tie a line to yourself at Nanaimo's **Bungee Zone** (753-5867). Yes, you can jump naked. Stormin' Norman didn't bungee jump, but back at April Point, he did use a skip fly—an extremely difficult and esoteric method—to land a 25½-pound spring salmon.

SALTSPRING ISLAND

Named for the unusually cold and briny springs on the north end of the island, Saltspring is the largest and most populous of the Gulf Islands chain. Its population has been growing steadily since the first permanent settlers (black Americans) arrived in the 1800s. The last influx consisted of burned-out urbanites clutching copies of *The Electronic Cottage*. The island even has a nine-hole golf course. Like the other islands, it's generally drier and warmer than Vancouver and has the bark-shedding arbutus tree to prove it.

Saltspring is **accessible by three ferries**: from Tsawwassen (to Long Harbour, 1½ hours); from Crofton, near Duncan on Vancouver Island (to Vesuvius, 20 minutes); or from Swartz Bay (32 kilometres [20 miles] from Victoria) on the Saanich Peninsula (to Fulford Harbour, 30 minutes). Crofton is the best route from Vancouver, via Horseshoe Bay. Locals caught in a Fulford lineup, knowing that the ferry has only machine-dispensed snacks and drinks, pass the time at nearby **Rodrigo's** restaurant and ice cream window.

All roads lead to **Ganges**, as the natives are fond of saying. Ganges, the largest town in the Gulf Islands, has a colourful Saturday morning **[FREE] Farmer's Market** (early morning to

2pm) with high-quality crafts, as well as a growing number of pleasant cafes and restaurants, a condominium complex overlooking the harbour, and a flurry of new retail development. Just when your nostrils catch the whiff of yuppification, you stumble onto **Mouat's** (537-5551) department store, an island mainstay since 1907 and still owned by the same family.

For light meals and snacks (vegetarian too) try **Stella's Boardwalk Cafe** (Mouat's Mall, 537-1436), which has indoor and outdoor seating (check out Stella's daughter's adjoining mini-garden shop, **Boardwalk Greens**), the **New Deli Cafe** (waterfront in the Grace Point complex), or **Glad's Ice Cream** (across from Mouat's, 537-4211). For a relaxing dinner, the tiny blue and white Scandinavian **House Piccolo** (108 Hereford Avenue, 537-1844) is charming and the local lamb yummy; the upper deck of **Alfresco's** (3106 Grace Point Square, 537-5979) overlooks boats bobbing in the Ganges harbour. For a more casual night, head for a verandah table at the lively, rebuilt **Vesuvius Inn** (180 Vesuvius Bay Road, 537-2312) for decent burgers and cold draft; only the overly loud music detracts from the passing seals and the sunset. Backgammon board and dart boards provided. However, it is **Hastings House** (160 Upper Ganges Road, 537-2362) that put Saltspring Island on the international map. Just minutes from Ganges, nestled among trees overlooking a rolling lawn and the sea, this splendid resort is undeniably luxe, and the dining room (under chef Lars Jorgenson, formerly of Vancouver's William Tell) is quite wonderful. Prices, as suspected, are stiff.

There are also **camping facilities** at St. Mary Lake, Ruckle Park, and Mouat Provincial Park on the southeastern tip of the island, where you'll find a spectacular mixture of virgin forest, rock and clamshell beach, and rugged headlands.

If your idea of comfort begins with a breakfast of crème fraîche and strawberries, a sorrel and asparagus soufflé, and freshly baked cinnamon buns, head for the **Old Farmhouse Bed & Breakfast** (1077 Northend Road, 537-4113). Like Hastings House, it is minutes from Ganges, the Vesuvius ferry, and the community centre that doubles as a movie theatre. It is a newly restored 100-year-old heritage farmhouse (complete with benign, hatted ghost of a former eccentric owner) with a separate guest wing (all rooms with private bath and balcony or patio). Hosts Karl and Gerti Fuss (she trained in European hotel school and managed Vancouver's Il Giardino restaurant) have combined solid wood doors, gemlike stained-glass windows, and antique pedestal sinks with pine floors and cheerful, crisp contemporary chintzes in the rooms. Some rooms seem less soundproof than others. You might ask about this when booking.

Any of the island's 90-plus B&Bs and hotels can provide you with a map of Saltspring. If it's Sunday, drive around the island armed with the **Sunday artists'** studio tour map. Summer visitors can see most work represented in the summerlong **Artcraft** show in Mahon Hall—convenient, but not nearly as interesting.

[KIDS][FREE] There aren't kilometres of sandy beaches on this island, but there is a pretty little beach at the end of **Churchill Road** (near Ganges) and a beautiful shell and sand beach at the end of **Beddis Road** (eastern side of the island). Drive to Ruckle Park to stroll the paths and explore the rock pools left by the receding tide. Some members of the Ruckle family still reside in the farmhouses you see scattered throughout under a tenancy-for-life agreement made after they donated the land as a park in 1973. The park warden's home, built in 1938 for Norman Ruckle's bride-to-be, was never lived in, since the wedding failed to take place. Instead, it was used to store potatoes! Be sure to stop at the nearby **Everlasting Summer Dried Flower & Herb Farm** (194 McLennan) to wander the formal herb and rose gardens and gape at the ceilings full of drying flowers.

For an astounding view of the archipelago from Saltspring to the American mainland, pick a clear day and drive up Cranberry Road to the top of **Mount Maxwell**.

SOOKE

Forty-five minutes west of Victoria on Highway 14, you are truly on the Pacific Ocean—next stop, Japan. The small communities of **Sooke**, **Jordan River**, and **Port Renfrew** contain excellent parks and dozens of trails leading down to wild surf-flung beaches where trees have been blown almost horizontal. Some of the beaches have good waves for daring surfers. Ask at the Sooke Information Centre for the locations of **French Beach Provincial Park**, **Sandcut Beach** (it's easy to miss the sign), **China Beach Provincial Park** (which has a 15-minute trail to a secluded sandy beach with a hidden waterfall at the west end; benches ease the steep climb back), and **Mystic Beach** (a rugged 20-minute trail takes you there).

Where you stay depends on your budget, mood, and desire to cook in or eat out. The white clapboard 1931 **Sooke Harbour House** (1528 Whiffen Spit Road, 642-3421) has gained international attention for its kitchen dedicated to the freshest natural local ingredients. It's worth stopping just to see the herbal gardens. Each room is singular, with views, decks, fresh flowers, and decanters of port a given. At the more reasonably priced **Sooke Harbour Bed & Breakfast Cabins** (5259 Sooke Road, 642-7929), which straddle the Galloping Goose Trail just east of Sooke, breakfast appears in a basket at your door.

French Beach Retreats (646-2154) relies largely on word of mouth for its two private getaways in ocean-front settings. While filming on location, Sharon Stone rented the 167-square-metre (1798-square-foot) contemporary home, complete with antiques, woods and trails, and a vegetable garden for guests to use (there are a sandbox and swings for little guests). The smaller octagonal Ocean Tree House is ideal for twosomes who prefer to eat out. Within Sooke, try dining at the funky **Good Life Bookstore and Cafe** (2113 Otter Point Rd, (604) 642-6821); **Mom's Cafe** (Sooke Road at Shields, (604) 642-3314) for halibut and chips; or **Margison House** (6605 Sooke Road, (604) 642-3620), an elegant cottage in pretty grounds just off the highway serving up the best afternoon tea in these parts as well as light lunches.

[FREE] Consider a detour from Sooke into **Lester B. Pearson College of the Pacific** on Pedder Bay. Open since 1974 with a two-year program to foster international understanding, Pearson is one of only seven United World Colleges, and the setting and architecture by well-known West Coast architect Ron Thom are both worth seeing (self-guided tours anytime; for occasional guided tours, call 478-5591).

Twenty-four kilometres (15 miles) west of Sooke, **Point No Point Resort** draws a faithful following who can live without TV and telephones in 15 cabins set above 1.6 kilometres (1 mile) of beach and among 16 hectares (40 acres) of wooded trails. Some of the older cabins are rustic and quite dark, but four new cabins hang right over the water, where you sleep lulled by the crashing of rolling swells. Firewood is supplied, but pick up food en route. Afternoon tea and light lunches only are served in a convivial (and simple) dining room.

The paved but twisty road continues for about a half hour to Port Renfrew, where it ends. From there, you're on foot on the famous **West Coast Trail**, one of the greatest (and most demanding) coastal hikes in the Northwest. (Average hiking time to Bamfield is five days one way.) [KIDS][FREE] Time your drive to coincide with the low tides at **Botanical Beach** just south of Port Renfrew. Here exceptionally low tides in early summer expose kilometres of sea life and sculpted sandstone. Check with the local gas station about conditions on the deeply grooved road leading to the beach.

Make a slow loop out of the drive via the 55-kilometre (34-mile) gravel logging road from Port Renfrew through the forest and past woodland lakes to Lake Cowichan. A paved highway connects you back to Duncan and Highway 1 leading to Nanaimo or Victoria.

SUNSHINE COAST

Vancouverites have caught on. Not only is there more to see and do on the Sechelt Peninsula (aka the Sunshine Coast) than on many of the Gulf Islands, the ferry travel time is shorter and often half the price. And what rain forest denizen could resist the promise of a sunshine coast, even if Environment Canada's records suggest that the popular name is a bit misleading? Curiously, this coast is part of the mainland but, like an island, is accessible only by boat or small plane. BC Ferries (669-1211) is the link from Vancouver.

Lack of direct road access has probably saved this beautiful peninsula from rapid development. But each year lineups are longer for the pleasant 40-minute ferry ride from **Horseshoe Bay** to Langdale or for the spectacular ride through the fjordlike waters of Jervis Inlet between **Saltery Bay** and **Earls Cove** at the north end of the peninsula. If you can, travel midweek to avoid lines, or at least leave Vancouver early afternoon Friday or late Saturday morning and return early on Monday. (The gift shop on the spiffy Langdale ferry, believe it or not, has a rich selection of regional books and magazines.)

Strung along the main road running south to north between the two ferry terminals are two main pockets of population—Gibsons and Sechelt—and a series of delightful getaways: Roberts Creek, Redroofs, Smugglers Cove, Secret Cove, Pender Harbour, Garden Bay, Irvines Landing, and Egmont. Amazingly, the entire drive nonstop is only one hour and 25 minutes, but you can easily spend a week here.

[KIDS] Drive into **Gibsons** for at least a quick look at the town where *The Beachcombers* television series was once shot. Molly's Reach may just be a prop, but the marina is very real. If you were smart enough to stay in the gift shop rather than the restaurant on the ferry, this is a good place to eat (see Gibsons in Day Trips section of this chapter).

If you take the upper road (North Road) off the ferry, you will bypass Lower Gibsons and meet up later with Highway 101. Northbound, the **Roberts Creek Road**, just past the public **Sunshine Coast Golf and Country Club**, leads to "the Creek," an intimate spot to be waylaid, have an ice cream at the funky General Store on Flume Road, read the newsy bulletin board, walk the long pebble beach, or indulge in a sumptuous European-style dinner at the **Creekhouse Restaurant**, long considered the best on the Sunshine Coast (reservations: 885-9321). At the **Country Cottage Bed & Breakfast** (near Roberts Creek Road and Cedar Grove Road), owners Philip and Loragene Gaulin cook gourmet breakfasts for guests on their 1927 wood cookstove. Additional treat: afternoon tea (885-7448). The nine-hole **Sunshine Coast Golf and Country Club** near Roberts Creek is open to the public. Hikers stroll through **Cliff Gilker Park** adjacent to the course.

There are few sandy beaches on the Sunshine Coast, and of those the best is at **Davis Bay**, which explodes into view after a sharp bend in the highway just before Sechelt, 30 minutes from the ferry. As you arrive into **Sechelt**, the massive, unappealing structure on the left is the **House of Hewhiwus** (House of Chiefs), administrative centre of the Sechelt Indian

Government District, which in 1988 became Canada's first self-governing Indian band (behind the building stands a commanding circle of totem poles commemorating this event). The complex contains the South Campus of Capilano College, a small but interesting museum of local history and native artifacts, the Tsain-Ko Gift Shop (which sells native arts, crafts, clothes, and jewellery, as well as books on native culture), and the **Raven's Cry Theatre** (call 885-4673 for a schedule of live performances and movies).

Sechelt's **Blue Heron** (885-3847) gets raves for its outstanding meals and its equally outstanding view of the inlet. For lighter meals and small shops, cruise Cowrie Street: the **Family Bulk Food and Delicatessen** (885-7767) does excellent packed lunches; **Kafe Kitago** (885-7606) is the latest "in" spot for cappuccino, tasty soups, quiche, and mouth-watering desserts; and in the summer the artsy outdoor **Cappuccino and Dessert Bar** (885-7606) tucked behind the **Shadow Baux Gallery** offers entertainment Friday evenings.

Tickets sell out in spring for readings by the biggest names in Canadian literature and journalism at Sechelt's annual August **Festival of the Written Arts**, held at the woodsy Rockwood Centre. Plan ahead by calling 885-9631.

Redroofs Road, 6 kilometres (3.8 miles) north of Sechelt, leads to a unique getaway, **Halfmoon Bay Cabin** (bookings a must, 885-2589). The rustic yet luxurious 120-square-metre (1292-square-foot) waterfront cabin, with a massive stone fireplace and skylights throughout, sits on a hill surrounded by an English country garden and has a huge sundeck (with a shower and gas barbecue) overlooking its own beach.

The scenery gets wilder as you continue north, offering great **hiking options**, such as the Saturday morning excursions with Friends of Caren (883-2807) to see Canada's oldest forest, the newly discovered nesting ground of the rare marbled murrelet. The 1.6-kilometre (1-mile) round-trip hike around **Smugglers Cove Marine Park** (2 kilometres [1.2 miles] west of Halfmoon Bay) is an easy and wonderful way to experience it firsthand. At **Secret Cove**, 2 kilometres (1.2 miles) farther north, settle onto the restaurant decks of either the **Jolly Roger Inn** (885-7038) or **Lord Jim's Resort Hotel** (885-7038), both great spots for a lingering drink and a bird's-eye view of Thormanby Island beyond. **Blackberry Bed and Breakfast** (885-3567) provides a two-bedroom house with breathtaking view from the deck (breakfast fixings supplied, right down to the homemade blackberry jam and plates with blackberry pattern, but you do the cooking).

[KIDS] At **Madeira Park** locals gather at **Frances' Hamburger Takeout**, where the best hamburger, milkshake, and fries on the Sunshine Coast are miraculously produced out of a 2.4-metre-by-6-metre (8-foot-by-19.6-foot) trailer. Head for the

▼

quieter picnic area in front of the Harbour Gallery for your first beautiful view of the indented waterway known as **Pender Harbour**. Wind along Highway 101 past Madeira Park to Garden Bay Road, which gets you to the other side of the harbour.

Garden Bay and nearby **Irvines Landing** have recently added chic to faultless natural beauty and abundant recreational choices. Check out **John Henry's General Store and Post Office** (an ice cream, local gossip, and booze outlet with info on chartering almost anything that floats plus info on local dinner cruises). The **Garden Bay Hotel Restaurant** includes fine dining, a pub, and a deck (883-2674) and overlooks the Royal Vancouver Yacht Club outport, which along with the West Vancouver and Seattle yacht clubs attracts the well-heeled. The landmark **Sundowner Inn and Restaurant** (883-9676), renovated under new owners, is worth visiting if only for the fact that meals are served in what was the women's ward of this converted hospital.

At Irvines Landing reserve the **Seaside Bed & Breakfast** (883-9929). There's a 180-degree view of the sea (hot tub, TV, and fridge are included, as well as a deluxe breakfast served on your own private deck). It's a short walk from here to the area's primo fish and chips at **Irvine's Landing Pub**.

Climb **Pender Hill** for a view of the whole harbour or hike up cone-shaped **Mount Daniel**, spurred on by the knowledge that Sechelt native women once hiked up daily to bring food to girls who were isolated on the mountaintop for four months during their puberty rites. The **Pender Harbour Golf Club**, carved out of the rain forest north of the Garden Bay Road turnoff, is worth a few lost balls in exchange for the challenge and the scenery.

One of BC's greatest natural sites—**Skookumchuck Rapids** near Egmont—lies at the northern tip of the peninsula. To get there it's an easy 8-kilometre (5-mile) round-trip hike to see the largest saltwater rapids on the West Coast. Tide changes trigger iridescent turquoise cascades in this bottleneck, resulting in whirlpools that are 18 metres (59 feet) across and 2.5 metres (8 feet) high and that daredevils actually fly across in kamikaze speedboat joyrides. Lie safely on the smooth rocks on shore and feel the vibration. Timing is everything. Check local newspapers **Coast News** (885-3930) and the **Press** (885-5121) for best viewing time or call **Bathgate's Store and Marina** in Egmont (883-2222). Greatest tidal range: early June. Nonhiking option: take the cruise up the inlet from Porpoise Bay. Call **Tzoonie Outdoor Adventures** in Sechelt (885-9802) or **Cruise Tours** in Garden Bay (883-2280), which also runs tours up to beautiful Princess Louisa Inlet and organizes winter diving. Later, hit Egmont's **Back Eddy Pub** for great burgers, cold beer, and yet another postcard view.

From here take the quaint 50-minute ferry trip from **Earls**

Cove through the fjords of Jervis Inlet to **Saltery Bay**. Once there, take the road that ends 54 kilometres (33.5 miles) later in the tiny fishing village of **Lund**, literally the last of the coastal roads in BC. Check out historic **Lund Hotel** (483-3187), a small town—restaurant, post office, pub—all in one with accommodation in the hotel. Call the Sliammon Indian Band (483-4111) about its guided tours of a chum salmon enhancement facility. Eagles gather in the hundreds at salmon spawning creeks October to December (InfoCentre, 485-4701).

TOFINO AND LONG BEACH

Each year some 600,000 people visit Vancouver Island's **Pacific Rim National Park**, more commonly known as Long Beach. (In fact, the three-part Pacific Rim Park really encompasses the Broken Islands Group and the West Coast Trail as well.) This spectacular stretch of Vancouver Island's rugged mid-island west coast manages to absorb all these visitors, even in the busy summer season. Visitors in the know prefer spring or fall, and even winter, when wild winter storms have their own beauty on the 11-kilometre-long (7-mile-long) beach.

The entire trip along Highway 4 from the Parksville Bypass north of Nanaimo to Tofino (where the road abruptly ends) is only 166 kilometres (103 miles). There's a lot to see along this winding route, so allow at least two hours.

[KIDS][FREE] Within minutes of the Parksville Bypass, you'll want to consider stops along the road at **Englishman River Falls Provincial Park** (picnicking in a forest setting on a fine fishing river); **Coombs** (a lively community known for music festivals, goats on the sod-roofed Old Country Market, and Butterfly World); and 90-hectare (222-acre) **Cathedral Grove**. This park is a jaw-dropping must-see. Park and walk some of the trails on either side of the highway. Some of the giant old-growth Douglas fir, western redcedar, and western hemlock were growing here when King John signed the Magna Carta in 1215.

[KIDS][FREE] Travelling west, at the **Port Alberni** junction—the logging town that survived the 1964 tsunami from the Alaska earthquake—you'll pass by a number of Indian reserves of the 14-band West Coast Indians, now referred to as Nuu-Chah-Nulth (pronounced *ne shaw nulth*). For a unique picnic spot, turn in at **Sproat Lake Provincial Park**. Chances are good that you will see the lake's fabled mirror reflections, and you may catch the Martin Flying Tanks, the world's largest water bombers, scooping up 27 tonnes (30 tons) of water in 22 seconds, for forest-fire fighting (West Coast Rangers, 723-2952).

The small towns of Ucluelet and Tofino bracket Pacific Rim National Park, and both celebrate the **Pacific Rim Whale Festival** from mid-March to mid-April, when some 20,000 Pacific grey whales—virtually the world's population—migrating from Baja, Mexico, to the Arctic Ocean, pass by. **Ucluelet** (BC's third-largest port for landed fish catch), at the south end, is closer to Highway 4 and claims to be the whale-watching capital of the world, but you can do that from Tofino too, which has more charm.

Tofino is also the gateway to Clayoquot Sound, one of the last virgin timberlands on the West Coast, whose future is hotly disputed by environmentalists and forest companies. Stop at the **Pacific Rim Park InfoCentre** (726-4212) just five minutes after turning north to Tofino from the Highway 4 junction. The stretch of surf-swept sand that is Long Beach is best explored by hiking the beaches, headlands, and woodland trails, so pick up a free *Hiker's Guide*. Ask for tips on whale watching and where to see the permanent colonies of basking sea lions. [KIDS][FREE] There are also daily evening interpretive lectures at Green Point Theatre and occasional guided storm walks.

[KIDS][FREE] The much-loved old Wickaninnish Inn is gone, but the timbers, rafters, and stone hearth have been built into the new **Wickaninnish Interpretive Centre** (halfway to Tofino from the junction, 726-7333), operated by Parks Canada (closed winters) on the same picturesque point at the end of Long Beach Road. The centre tells the stories of the whales using exhibits, film, and telescopes on the observation decks. Plan on having lunch or dinner at the restaurant here, which overlooks Long Beach. Beach fires are allowed, but you'll need to gather firewood while it's still daylight.

Lots of campsites, motels, and cabins are available, but the delightful new ocean-front **Middle Beach Lodge**, which is five minutes from Tofino (725-2900), is the best bet. Rates for the 25 rooms vary according to whether they have a view of the ocean or the forest. Some have balconies overlooking what amounts to a private beach. All come with pretty private bathrooms, cozy duvets, and continental breakfast. Guests are invited to sign up for dinner on Tuesday, Wednesday, Friday, and Saturday only.

Walkable Tofino (population 1,103) is a relaxed town and a popular reprovisioning spot for sailors circumnavigating Vancouver Island. You'll find locals at the **Common Loaf Bake Shop** behind the bank (it has wonderful cheese buns, and come summer nights, bread dough becomes pizza dough), and at the pink and turquoise **Alley Way Cafe** (also behind the bank and probably the island's only organic restaurant outside of Victoria). Everything, right down to the mayonnaise on the clam burgers, is made by Christina Delano-Stephans.

Be sure to visit well-known native artist Roy Vicker's **Eagle Aeries Gallery**, inspired by the traditional form of a West Coast longhouse (725-3235). [KIDS][FREE] For a unique tour, drop by the **Coast Guard Rescue Station** (725-3231) during the daily informal open house, 10am to 2pm, and imagine turning turtle in the self-righting rescue vessel.

Other things to do include sailing, cruising, or flying to **Hot Springs Cove**, which has an unforgettable forest hike into the 43°C waterfalls and pools, shared by tourists, shampooing boaters, and fishermen. Bring a bathing suit and money—the floating store has a surprisingly fine selection of books and homespun wool. You can also take a whale-watching trip (some whales remain here through the summer) on a 10-passenger rubber Zodiac, if you don't have back problems. There are various operators from Tofino, Ucluelet, and Hot Springs Cove; check with **Tofino's Information Centre**, 380 Campbell Street, 725-3414. In addition, sea kayaking trips for novices are offered, from introductory half-day to week-long excursions (Vancouver-based Tofino Expeditions, 737-2030, or Tofino-based Klahanie Kayaking Adventure, 725-2538).

VICTORIA AND BEYOND
See Day Trips section in this chapter for transportation to Victoria information.

Although Victoria was recently ranked by *Conde Naste Traveler* magazine readers as one of the top 10 cities to visit in the world, its greatest charms may be the delightful places that lie just outside BC's small capital city on southern Vancouver Island. Victoria's "backyard" includes a variety of landscapes from nearby Saxe Point naval base to the wild West Coast just around the southern tip of Vancouver Island, where Pacific waves pound in from Japan (see sections on Tofino and Sooke).

Best day trip: the so-called Western Communities of **Colwood** and **Metchosin**, one of the oldest settled communities in British Columbia. Highlights en route include fascinating **Fort Rodd Hill National Historic Park** (603 Fort Rodd Hill Road, 380-4662), where men manned the guns from 1878 to 1956, and the display inside **Fisgard Lighthouse**, the oldest on the coast. Drive along Ocean Boulevard Spit, where navy wives wave tearful goodbyes alongside the bird sanctuary to manouever-bound destroyers. Nearby, golfers weep over a missed putt on **Royal Colwood Golf Course** (off Sooke Road), ranked as BC's best.

The Metchosin area is loaded with great parks, including **Witty's Lagoon** nature park and beaches, which are an afternoon in themselves (the Nature House, on the lagoon trail, is open weekends year-round). Along the way you can see **Chosin Pottery** (Canadian award-winning ceramics), roadside "honour" boxes for vegetable and egg stands, and in spring, wild orchids on the grounds of **St. Catherine's Church** in Metchosin.

For sustenance, pick up unusual picnic goodies at **Rebecca's** (1127 Wharf Street in Victoria, 380-6999) from the 7 metres (20 feet) of take-out. The chefs cook different dishes

▼

▲

every day, but look for Dungeness crab, samosas, burritos, 10 different salads, and 10 homemade desserts, including chocolate espresso torte. Eat on the grounds at Ford Rodd (summer military concerts are held on Sunday afternoons). Or stop for a draft at **Spinnakers** brew pub (308 Catherine Street, 386-2739) and for halibut fish and chips (yeast for batter is supplied by the on-site brewery).

[KIDS] Back in Victoria, find time to visit **Craigdarroch Castle** (1050 Joan Crescent, 592-5323) built by coal baron Robert Dunsmuir to induce his Scottish wife to live in distant Victoria; the award-winning **Royal British Columbia Museum** that even antsy kids love (Belleville and Government streets, 387-3701); and the **Art Gallery of Greater Victoria** (1040 Moss Street, 384-4101), complete with the only Shinto shrine outside Japan and a fine gift shop housed in a modern building and an Edwardian house.

The Old Cemeteries Society offers year-round walking tours of Victoria's many cemeteries on Sunday (and on Tuesday and Thursday evenings in summer), but the majority of tours go to **Ross Bay Cemetery**, with good cause. It's a who's who of Victoria, including coal magnate Robert Dunsmuir and artist Emily Carr (Fairfield Road at Memorial Drive, 384-0045). You can also buy a booklet at Munro's bookstore and do a self-guided tour anytime. The annual Ghost Walk takes place on October 31. Call 384-0045 for meeting locations.

You cannot fail to rest your head happily in such splendid small inns as **Abigail's** (906 McClure Street, 388-5363), where the halls smell of good coffee and beautiful women, and **Holland House Inn** (595 Michigan Street, 384-6644), all artful bliss and duvets; or B&Bs like **Joan Brown's** less central but gracious Georgian mansion, once home to a lieutenant governor (729 Pemberton Road, 592-5929), or **Mulberry Manor** (611 Foul Bay, 370-1918), designed by renowned architect Samuel McClure.

Overnight guests at the handsomely renovated **Empress Hotel** (721 Government Street, 384-8111), where Bob Hope once hit golf balls off the front lawn, are offered a free tea if they present either an Elvis stamp or the Canadian series of five 43-cent stamps depicting CP hotels, including the Empress. The hefty price and amount of tea are normally reason enough to arrive for the 12 noon "tea" sitting in the main Tea Lobby in lieu of lunch. Those without reservations or proper attire (suit jacket for men; no jeans, jogging suits, shorts, or tennis shoes) may still find tea in the Bengal Lounge or nearby Lobby Lounge. From October to May be sure to ask for reservations at the best room rate (harbour views are wonderful); there are often unadvertised specials. For the best view of the Empress or the illuminated Parliament Buildings, ride the tiny "ferry" across to the newly opened **Ocean Pointe Resort** (360-2999).

Some find the interior decor in the public areas a bit too international/modern I-could-be-in-any-major-city, but the fine-dining **Victorian Room** is charming and popular for tea and dinner.

Dinner recommendations include the excellent high-energy **Herald Street Caffe** (546 Herald Street, 381-1441); the **El Terrazzo** (555 Johnson Street, 386-4747), which was the former Grand Central Cafe, for a cozy brick-walled patio; the hip angel-ceilinged **Met Bistro** (1715 Government Street, 381-1512) for Heavenly Lunch; and sister restaurants **Villa Rosa** (1015 Fort Street, 384-5337), which is more Italian, and San Remo (2709 Quadra Street, 384-5255), which is more Greek. Farther afield and much pricier is the elegant **Chez Daniel** (2524 Estevan, 592-7424).

Best-kept secret: Victoria Harbour Ferry's bargain $8 mini–moonlight cruise of the harbour aboard a mini-ferry. Show up at the Inner Harbour or reserve at the Tourism Victoria InfoCentre on the Inner Harbour. Daytime cruises up the Gorge or over to Ocean Pointe are a pleasant diversion, too.

WHISTLER

Highway 99, running north from Vancouver to Whistler, is an adventure in itself. Allow two hours on the aptly named Sea to Sky Highway, whose curves hug fir-covered mountains that tumble sharply into Howe Sound. On a clear day, look for the spectacular **Tantalus Range** pull-off north of Squamish. As an alternative, take Maverick Coach Lines or the scenic BC Rail train trip from North Vancouver, or fly via Helijet Airways' shuttle from Vancouver International Airport. For details, call Whistler Activity and Information Centre, 932-2394.

Along the way: Just north of Lions Bay, golfers should check out the spectacular new Robert Muir Graves–designed **Furry Creek Golf & Country Club** (896-2216), which opened in mid-1993 after building where everyone said it was impossible to build. The course is partially open to public play until all memberships have been sold. [KIDS] Stop at Britannia Beach (once the largest processor of copper in the British Empire) for seasonal underground mining museum tours and sustenance: **Mountain Woman's** (no phone) for great burgers and fries; **Twin Gables Tearoom** (896-2265) for home-baked goods, breakfast, lunch, and tea; **Jane's Coffee House** (896-2245) for cappuccino, cinnamon buns, textiles, and collectibles; or the **99er** (896-2497) for quick, cheap coffee to go. South of Squamish, 61 kilometres (38 miles) from Vancouver, look for the imposing 650-metre (2,133-foot) granite mass that is **Stawamus Chief**, drawing climbers from around the world.

Rated North America's number one ski resort by *Snow Country*, **Whistler Resort** has gained a reputation as a world-class year-round resort. In ski season, you'll hear plenty of Southern US, European, and Japanese accents in the chair lift lineups along with those of the many Aussie lifties. The huge European-style resort is actually two communities: pedestrian-only Whistler Village and Upper Village (also known as Black-comb Resort). A smaller, third, less expensive "base" a few miles closer to Vancouver is the Whistler Creek area (down at Whistler's original south side). New this year: the Market Place, across from the Blackcomb Hotel in Whistler Village. It's home to shops, cafes, post office, and liquor store, and there is lots of parking. This is the first part of Village North, which will eventually be three times the size of Whistler Village.

Accommodation outside the Village and Blackcomb is cheaper, but you'll need a car, taxi, or thumb if you're not on the bus route. Reservations are recommended far in advance. Call **Central Reservations** for info on luxury hotels, lodges, condos (some of the best among North American ski resorts and a popular choice with locals), and pensions: 932-4222; from Vancouver, dial 685-3650; United States and Canada toll free (800) 944-7853. Many lodgings now require 30 days' cancellation notice with a three-day minimum stay in peak season. The $75 million **Chateau Whistler** (938-8000—ask for special packages) is a peaceful resort in itself (Robin Leach proclaimed the Mallard Bar "the premier address at Whistler"), where the staff's goal is a happy guest. Don't miss the art-filled lobby, brunch at Wildflower, or the shops below. The best Whistler has to offer in a traditional alpine country inn is the **Durlacher Hof** ((604) 943-1924) located a mile north of Whistler Village. The seven guest rooms have private baths, balconies, and views of Whistler, Blackcomb, or Wedge Mountain.

The **Whistler-Blackcomb ski area** has two mountains with the largest high-speed lift system in North America. The friendly rivalry benefits the skier as each mountain jockeys for the best runs, grooming, restaurants, and service. Knowing how to take in North America's longest vertical—given the 200-plus runs, 3 glaciers, and 6 massive, high alpine bowls—is a challenge.

The best way for first-time visitors to discover the two mountains is to sign on for the fun-filled three- and four-day **Ski Esprit** packages (932-3400) for a guided introduction and instruction by friendly local instructors. **[FREE]** It is also a good idea to attend the Sunday night welcome and orientation at the Conference Centre. If you want to ski two mountains in one day, ski Blackcomb first. At noon, ski to Whistler's gondola base, have lunch in the village, and then take the 14-minute gondola ride to the top. Summit to summit is 40 minutes. Non-skiers are welcome to go topside for the view and lunch (many resorts don't allow this).

Biggest thrill for intermediates: riding up Whistler's steep Peak Chair knowing there is an easy way down the back as well as an unforgettable view over the back of bowls, glaciers, and Black Tusk. Blackcomb's double black diamond (Canada's

▼

Excursions

Whistler

▲

first) Saudan Couloir is still a badge-of-courage gulper. Advanced and expert Vancouver skiers regularly sign up for adult camps (moguls, masters, women only), 938-7710. The best ski tuning: **First Tracks** in the Delta Hotel; best boot refitting: George McConkey at **McCoo's** (reserve ahead). In winter it pays to reserve at older favourite restaurants such as romantic **Rim Rock** (932-5565) and Umberto's **Il Caminetto** (932-4442), which some Vancouver skiers prebook for the season. An absolute must for the best French cooking in BC is **Val d'Isère** in Whistler Village. Regulars are dreamy-eyed when considering Chef Roland Pfaff's house onion pie, grilled venison steak, and interesting seafood, duck, and veal dishes. Après-ski, enjoy leisurely patio viewing from **Monk's Grill** or the Chateau, or lively beer drinking at **Merlin's** (Blackcomb base) or the **Longhorn** (Village). Later try **Buffalo Bill's**, which usually has good, sometimes great, live bands; **Savage Beagle** and **Tommy Africa's** attract younger crowds.

If you haven't tried **paragliding, snow-boarding**, or **heli-skiing**, do. Call Whistler Activity and Information Centre (932-2394) and ask about dogsledding, snowshoeing, snowmobiling, and sleigh rides as well. When the lights go down low and it snows, cross-country ski in the moonlight on the peaceful track-set trails (rentals in Village), stopping in for a bargain meal and beer at the Chateau Whistler Golf Clubhouse.

Whistler has done a lot to develop year-round recreation and is definitely worth checking out even when there's no snow on the ground. Again, the Whistler Activity and Information Centre (Conference Centre, 932-2394) is a useful clearinghouse (from Vancouver: 985-6107, extension 161). In summer, you can go glacier skiing; hikers can take chair lifts to a network of alpine trails; Ski Esprit guide John Nemy offers **stargazing** on Blackcomb (932-3467); and mountain bikers can board their cycles onto Blackcomb's express chairs or Whistler's gondola for the ultimate mountain descent.

[KIDS] In-line skating is hot, and **Blackcomb Ski & Sport** (938-7788) offers bargain instruction packages. **The Escape Route's** professional guides can introduce you to Whistler's back country (day hikes to expeditions), 932-3338. **Whistler Outdoor Experience Company** (Chateau Whistler lobby, 932-3389) is the best adventure source.

Come summer, guests for Blackcomb's **Sunset Dinner** series take the chair up to **Christine's** mile-high restaurant for a luxurious dinner while the sun sets, followed by a twilight ride down to the village (check dates). Eating out is a major activity at Whistler, with more than 45 restaurants scattered through the village. Try **La Rua** in Upper Village (in Le Chamois Hotel, 932-5011) for comfortably elegant, eclectic dining (great appetizers), or **Settebello** (932-3000), one of Umberto Menghi's three Whistler restaurants, for wood-fired pizza. **Border Cantina's** new owners have put in a softer look and a tapas-like Southwestern menu (Shoestring Lodge on highway north of Village, 932-3373).

Local hangouts: **South Side Deli** (Whistler Creek), known for rock 'n' roll breakfasts, switches management at night and turns into the **Flipside** (932-3368). It has a small menu but great, cheap food in a dinerlike atmosphere. Condo-cooking tourists shop at the **Grocery Store** in the Village; locals shop at **Nester's** on the highway. Go to **Cork and Cheddar** in the Village for primo BLTs and lunch packs to order.

Water sports are hot on all five local lakes (windsurfing began on Alta Lake in Canada); the Arnold Palmer–designed **Whistler Golf Course** (932-3280)—his first Canadian course—and newly opened rugged links-style **Chateau Whistler Golf Course** (938-8000) by Robert Trent Jones Jr. are both championship courses. The latter's clubhouse reflects the Chateau's usual high standards.

Concerts are performed almost daily on the Village stage from June to September, and the resort hosts Labour Day, Canada's Birthday (July 1), and Octoberfest celebrations as well as a country and blues festival (mid-June), a classical music fest with a mountaintop concert by the Vancouver Symphony Orchestra (mid-August), and a jazz festival (mid-September).

North of Whistler, Deanna Pilling's new **Spirit Circle Art, Craft and Tea Company** (on Highway 99, 894-6336) incorporates some 100-year-old timbers of the Mount Currie elders' lodge formerly on this site. It's a welcoming place with relaxed, home-cooked meals and cappuccino as well as bannock and intriguing local Salish herbal teas and artwork (daily, 894-6336). [KIDS][FREE] The long hike up into the glorious **ancient cedar grove** (ask directions at the Whistler Activity Centre) is well worth it; you can smell the grove before you see it. For a much flatter stroll, take the pleasant half-hour walk into dramatic **Nairn Falls**, 32 kilometres (20 miles) north of Whistler. Access is on the right-hand side of the highway as you drive from Whistler toward Pemberton. Another fun free excursion is to four-wheel-drive in to **Meager Creek Hot Springs**. Take your suit (although some don't) and soak away your cares in these natural hot waters. Be sure to ask for directions and a map at Pemberton's gas station.

RECREATION

Recreation

BICYCLING

Vancouver's superb recreational cycling trails offer expansive views of the sea and mountains as they wind through breathtaking stands of fir, cedar, and hemlock and follow the shoreline of numerous bays and inlets. Not all of the treasures are 100 percent natural: along the way there are plenty of places to stop for cappuccino, pizza by the slice, fish and chips, and frozen yogurt. Cyclists with more time can explore the Sunshine Coast and Gulf Islands with the help of the largest ferry system in the world. A helmet and filled-up water bottle are mandatory; bring a shackle-style U-lock if you plan to stop and shop or walk around. It's against the law to cycle while wearing a headset, so keep it in the daypack. The best one-stop source for bicycling information is the resource library of **Cycling British Columbia** (1367 West Broadway Avenue, 737-3034). You'll find maps, bike routes, guidebooks, and a competition calendar. Racers should note that time-trials and criteriums are held each week throughout the summer at UBC. Call the Cycling BC event hotline at 290-4455 for further information.

Here are some of the best rides around the city. For further information, refer to the Mountain Biking section in this chapter.

Gulf Islands From March to October, cyclists use the BC Ferries dock at Tsawwassen as a departure point for exploring the southern Gulf Islands. Saltspring, Galiano, Mayne, North and South Pender, and Saturna are the most popular. Accommodation ranges from Provincial Park campgrounds to a range of

B&Bs. Swimming coves, pubs, and shady arbutus trees provide welcome relief from the occasional hill. You can take ferries from Tsawwassen or Horseshoe Bay near Vancouver, and schedules change from season to season. If you're taking a vehicle, be prepared for lengthy lineups during the summer months. Call BC Ferries (386-3431) beforehand for sailing times.

River Road to Steveston [KIDS] A fun, flat 36-kilometre (22.5-mile) loop in the suburb of Richmond. Families often do just a portion of this circuit, parking their cars at the RV park on the west side of the Dunsmuir Bridge. Cycle along the gravel dyke-path to the fishing village of Steveston for ice cream or to buy the catch of the day. The finely pebbled route is level but twisting in spots. There is no finer place to watch the sun go down than Garry Point Park, just west of Steveston.

Seaside Bicycle Route A terrific 15-kilometre (9.4-mile) route linking the Seawall with other waterfront pathways around False Creek, Vanier Park, Kitsilano Beach, Jericho Beach, and ending below UBC at Spanish Banks. A less-crowded alternative to the Seawall, this route offers more rest-stop options: a cappuccino on Cornwall Avenue, swimming at Kits Pool or Jericho Beach, and kite flying in Vanier Park. Parts of this route follow city streets; look for the green and white bike-route signs. Maps can be picked up at several info kiosks along the way. **Recreation Rentals** (2560 Arbutus Street, 733-7368) rents hybrid bikes suitable for bike paths and urban riding, as well as mountain bikes (some with suspension) rugged enough to go anywhere.

▼

Outdoor Sports

Bicycling

▲

Stanley Park Seawall No cycle visit to Vancouver is complete without a spin around the 9-kilometre (5.6-mile) seawall. Watch sea planes taking off and landing in Burrard Inlet, stop and smell the rose gardens, brace yourself for the Nine O'Clock Gun from Hallelujah Point, and gulp great breaths of the cedar forest while trying not to disturb nesting Canada geese around Lost Lagoon. To escape the crowds, venture off the pavement onto other dirt-packed trails inside the park's core. There are many bike-rental shops near the entrances to Stanley Park; the best-known is **Stanley Park Rentals** (676 Chilco Street, 681-5581). They rent five-speed bikes as well as tandems. As its name suggests, **Spokes Bicycle Rental and Espresso Bar** (1798 West Georgia Street, 688-5141) combines cycling and coffee, the favorite passions of many Vancouverites.

CANOEING AND KAYAKING

British Columbia doesn't have a canoe on its coat of arms, but it could. Over 50,000 residents of the province are regular canoeists or kayakers, and paddlers can take their pick of thousands of lakes and rivers, as well as explore over 6,500 offshore islands.

On any day of the year, marine enthusiasts carry on the Northwest coast native tradition by paddling modern versions of the baidarka, or sea kayak. The sea kayak is longer and sleeker than its whitewater cousin, and some boats are specially constructed for tandem paddlers. Most of the bays and inlets around Vancouver are perfect for even novice paddlers, but taking an introductory course offered by the **Ecomarine Ocean Kayak Centre** (689-7575) on Granville Island is a good idea. Learn the basic paddle strokes and self-rescue techniques, then rent single or two-person kayaks at Jericho Beach or False Creek. The waters of English Bay toward Stanley Park and by Kits Beach and Spanish Banks offer a mix of benign and moderately challenging conditions. Watch for unpredictable winds and tides around Spanish Banks and around Lighthouse Park in West Vancouver. Sea kayakers are prohibited from using the busy harbour area between the Lions Gate and Second Narrows bridges.

Indian Arm is a finger-shaped fjord which bends northward for 30 kilometres (18.8 miles) deep into the heart of the Coast Range mountains. See impenetrable forests growing on impossibly steep hillsides, rising from the shoreline for hundreds of vertical metres. You can rent boats at the **Deep Cove Canoe and Kayak Centre** (929-2268) and paddle across 1.6-kilometre- (1-mile-) wide Indian Arm to Jug Island, Combe Park, or Belcarra Park. A paddle south leads to Cates Park, where Malcolm Lowry wrote *Under the Volcano*. It takes about four hours (one way) to reach to the head of this glorious fjord. Inexperienced paddlers should beware of wake-swells from larger yachts, speedboats, and sailboats.

Betty Pratt-Johnson is the grande dame of whitewater trips in the province. A number of her books cover kayaking and canoeing across British Columbia. John Ince and Hedi Kottner's *Sea Kayaking Canada's West Coast* is an indispensable guide to exploring the province's 27,000 kilometres (16,875 miles) of coastline. Marine charts and tide tables are available from most Vancouver marine stores and from the Canadian Hydrographic Service, Department of Fisheries and Oceans, Institute of Ocean Sciences, 9860 West Saanich Rd, Box 6000, Sidney, BC V8L 4B2; (604) 356-6358. Sea kayaking is the best way of getting a cormorant's eye view of the **Gulf Islands**. The paddling here is done in safe, scenic waters. Tiny coves harbouring soft-pebble beaches overhung with shady rust-barked arbutus trees beckon the weary paddler. **Saltspring Kayaking**, (604) 653-4222, offers guided outings. If you have your own boat, just get on the ferry and follow your maps. Although this area is one of the sunniest and most temperate in the province, the water is frigid, even in summer. Less experienced kayakers should stay close to shore, where an easy swim leads to safety in case of a spill. The **Powell River Canoe Circuit**, located on the

Outdoor
Sports

*Canoeing
and
Kayaking*

Sunshine Coast, takes in over 57 kilometres (35.6 miles) of canoeing and 8 kilometres (5 miles) of portages. There are eight lakes in the loop, but easy access to various parts of the route via logging roads makes day trips popular. The entire circuit takes a week to complete and provides good views of coastal rain forest and glimpses of inaccessible, seldom-visited mountain peaks. This route is best paddled between April and November, since the higher lakes are frozen during the winter months and roads become inaccessible. Call Sunshine Forest District at (604) 485-4033 for maps and directions.

The Canoeing Association, the Whitewater Kayaking Association, and the Sea Kayaking Association of British Columbia are useful sources of information about paddle sports in the province. They can be contacted through the Outdoor Recreation Council of British Columbia at 737-3058.

CLIMBING AND MOUNTAINEERING

The Coast Mountains stretch northward from the 49th parallel, the largest portion of a massive cordillera extending from the Mexican border to Alaska. Within its huge geographical boundaries there are still hundreds of unclimbed summits and cross-country traverses to be done. Virtually every kind of mountaineering challenge can be found within a day's drive of downtown Vancouver, from frozen-waterfall–climbing in Lillooet to rock-climbing the sun-baked granite of the Smoke Bluffs near Squamish. Spectacular glacier ascents can be done in Garibaldi Provincial Park and on the peaks surrounding the Joffre Lakes Recreation Area east of Pemberton.

Some of the best views of the city can be seen from the summit of several prominent peaks that dwarf the city skyline. Most of these peaks are accessible by well-maintained hiking trails. Fog, rain, wind, and freezing temperatures can turn even the least-technical climb into an ordeal, so always carry extra food and clothing, even for a day trip. With its gondola towers and lighted ski runs visible from many parts of the Lower Mainland, **Grouse Mountain** (1,128 metres or 3,700 feet) is one of Vancouver's best-known natural landmarks. Purists can walk up the trail under the Skyride to the Grouse Nest restaurant and follow the ski run to the top, or you can take the the tramway up. Trail maps are available at the guest services booth at the Grouse Mountain Skyride ticket office. **Mount Seymour Provincial Park** is a 30-minute drive from downtown. Hiking to the top of the three rounded summits, each slightly higher than the last one, provides a surprisingly authentic wilderness experience if you go there midweek or in the winter on snowshoes. Your reward is an unparallelled view northward into the heart of the Coast Range, southward beyond the urban sprawl to the Gulf and San Juan islands, easterly to Mount Baker and the Cascades, and west toward

Vancouver Island. The 8-kilometre (5-mile) return trip takes about four hours. [KIDS] Black Mountain in **Cypress Provincial Park** can be climbed on foot or reached by chairlift. Nearby Cabin Lake is on the Baden-Powell trail and provides a refreshing midsummer dip. The two-hour Black Mountain Loop Trail is perfect for introducing the family to the joys of hiking in the mountains. **Garibaldi Provincial Park** is accessible from several points along Highway 99 en route to Whistler. Diamond Head, the Black Tusk Meadows, Singing Pass, and Wedgemount Lake provide varying degrees of challenge and are suitable for daytrips or overnight expeditions. Perhaps the most outstanding landmark is the volcanic plug of the 2,315-metre (7,595-foot) **Black Tusk**. The trail to the base of starts at Taylor Campground. Because of crumbling rock and high exposure, climbing the tusk itself is for experienced hikers only. Contact BC Parks at 898-3678 for trail and weather reports.

Many local rock climbers learn their craft indoors at the **Edge Climbing Centre** (984-9080) in North Vancouver. This is the rock climber's version of an indoor jungle-gym, and the carved holds and textured surfaces provide a stunningly realistic simulation of routes and situational problems found on the real crags. All of the routes are rated, with varying degrees of difficulty. Even if you get vertigo standing too close to a guardrail, it's a fun place to go and watch human spiders in action. You can take courses, rent shoes and harnesses, and play until 11pm, seven days a week. For a taste of the real thing, drive 60 kilometres (37.5 miles) north to Squamish. The **Stawamus Chief** is the second-largest freestanding granite outcropping in the world, next to the Rock of Gibraltar. There are over 280 climbing routes on its various walls, faces, and slabs. The dramatic University Wall climb, ending on the Dance Platform, is rated the hardest rock climb in Canada. The vehicle pullout north of Shannon Falls provides an excellent vantage point to see climbers in action. Less dramatic (but equally challenging) climbs can be found in **Murrin Provincial Park** and on the **Smoke Bluffs**. Novice climbers will like the grippy granite and easy moves on Banana Peel, Diédre, Cat Crack, and Sugarloaf.

There are so many hiking and mountaineering organizations in the Lower Mainland that they have their own umbrella group, the **Federation of Mountain Clubs of British Columbia** (737-3053). Trail building, safety and education, wilderness preservation, and public awareness of mountain recreation issues are all part of their mandate. Their partially-subsidized courses provide the best introduction to the wilderness currently available.

Outdoor Sports

Climbing and Mountaineering

DIVING

The clean, cold, and clear waters between Vancouver Island and the Lower Mainland are home to over 450 fish species, 600 plant species, 4,000 invertebrates, and the ghosts of countless sunken vessels. The best time to dive is in the winter, since plankton growth in the summer months often obscures visibility. Betty Pratt-Johnson's *141 Dives in the Protected Waters of Washington State and British Columbia* is essential reading for divers. Wreck-divers should pick up a copy of Fred Rogers's *Shipwrecks of British Columbia*. Get air, tanks, and the latest news on what's hot from **Diver's World** (732-1344) at the corner of 4th Avenue and Burrard Street.

Whytecliff Park in West Vancouver is a fine undersea park close to the city. It contains a variety of marine life in its protected cove and nearby waters. Copper Cove, Telegraph Cove, and Cates Park in Deep Cove are also local favourites. Be sure to check local regulations before harvesting edibles like crabs. With more than 100 dives mapped by local enthusiasts, **Powell River**, at the top of the Sechelt Peninsula on the Sunshine Coast, is officially the scuba diving capital of Canada. Charters, rentals, air, and guides are all available through Beach Gardens Resort (485-6267). Wreck-diving is the attraction here. Look for the remains of the *Shamrock* off Vivian Island. Rare red coral thrives in these waters, as do octopus and wolf eels. Many divers seek out the underwater mermaid, a sunken statue that resides near the BC Ferry dock at Saltery Bay.

FISHING (FRESHWATER AND SALTWATER)

BC's scenic coastline provides a magnificent backdrop for great fishing opportunities and makes up for the rare occasion when anglers get skunked. Freshwater anglers can catch trout, char, and salmon. Saltwater fishers can try for five species of salmon (including the fabled chinook), rockfish, and halibut.

Two government agencies administer sport fishing. The **Federal Department of Fisheries and Oceans** (666-3545) regulates saltwater fishing and the provincial **Ministry of Environment, Lands, and Parks** (582-5200) regulates freshwater fishing. Licences are required for both. You can purchase these at tackle shops throughout the Lower Mainland, which are also great sources of information about where the fish are biting. Shops and tourist information centres also have copies of the Provincial Sport Fishing Regulations. The section on catch-and-release streams and lakes is particularly important for the freshwater angler.

Fishing in the creeks and rivers off the Coquihalla Highway, north of Hope, is usually rewarding, especially after spring runoff. The feeder creeks and tributaries of the Fraser and Thompson rivers number in the thousands, and yield coho salmon, rainbow trout, and the much-prized steelhead.

Horseshoe Bay/Hole in the Wall Howe Sound, the 40-kilometre- (25-mile-) long inlet that starts at Horseshoe Bay, is perfect for saltwater fishing. Whether you're out to hook the fish of your dreams or just want a relaxing few hours on the saltchuck, **Sewell's Marina** (921-3474) offers a fleet of 60 rental boats as well as a regularly scheduled group fishing tour. Rock cod and salmon can be caught at the legendary Hole in the Wall, several kilometres north of the marina.

Rice Lake This lake is in the Seymour Demonstration Forest on the North Shore. To get there, take the Mount Seymour Parkway exit from Highway 1 and follow Lillooet Road past Capilano College to the road's end. This lake is wheelchair-accessible. The Seymour River provides excellent angling opportunities as well.

Salmon Lake Resort Set high in the rolling grasslands of the Nicola Plateau on the Douglas Lake Ranch (Canada's largest cattle ranch), Salmon Lake Resort offers superior fly-fishing and the thrill of stalking trophy-size Kamloops rainbow trout. A 3½-hour drive northeast of Vancouver via the Coquihalla Highway, the resort's number is (800) 663-4838.

Spences Bridge Spanning the waters of Thompson River, Spences Bridge is the place to go for steelhead fishing. It's a four-hour drive north of Vancouver on Highway 1.

GOLFING

The popular Lotusland myth of going skiing in the morning and golfing in the afternoon is not as far-fetched as you might think. Although courses aren't exactly in prime condition in December or January, by the time April rolls around many of the Lower Mainland links are in midsummer shape. Golf has been the fastest-growing activity for some time now, and new courses are being installed as quickly as developers can acquire land. North of the city, two brand-new courses take advantage of the spectacular mountain scenery. The **Furry Creek Golf and Country Club** just past Porteau Cove is carved from a mountainside and hugs the shoreline of Horseshoe Bay in several places. The breathtaking Robert Trent-Jones–designed **Chateau Whistler Golf and Country Club** complements the decade-old Arnold Palmer–designed **Whistler Golf and Country Club**. Both Whistler tracks are true tests of a golfer's talent; thankfully, the scenery makes those bogeys more bearable. For more small-town ambience, the **Squamish Golf and Country Club** boasts a mature layout with several holes straddling the Mamquam River. Watch for bald eagles soaring overhead.

The City of Vancouver operates several municipal golf courses, and some privately owned courses are open to the public as well. Following is a sampling of the best.

▼
**Outdoor
Sports**

Golfing

▲

Fraserview Golf Course On some days it seems that every golfer in Canada has descended onto the fairways of this south Vancouver course, which overlooks the Fraser River. Featuring wide-open fairways for most of its 6,346-yard length, Fraserview is a pleasant course—and the busiest in the province. ▪ *7800 Vivian Ave at 54th St; 327-3717.*

Mayfair Lakes "Water, water, everywhere" might be the unofficial motto of this very attractive course in the suburb of Richmond. Not as tree-lined as some of the more established tracks, but definitely a must-play in terms of challenge and design. Par 72, 6,225 yards. Watch for salmon jumping in some of the water hazards. ▪ *5460 No. 7 Rd, Richmond; 276-0505.*

Peace Portal Golf Course Glance to the right on Highway 99 as you enter Canada and you'll see one of the Lower Mainland's oldest courses, Peace Portal Golf Course, named after the international boundary monument that straddles the border. Established in 1928, this mature course is open year-round and is a local favourite. ▪ *16900-4th Ave, Surrey; 538-4818.*

Queen Elizabeth Pitch and Putt Serious golfers might scoff at the inclusion of a lowly pitch-and-putt, but this course offers some of the most breathtaking views of the city from its vantage point atop Little Mountain. Non-golfers can stroll the adjacent grounds of Queen Elizabeth Park or visit the Macmillan Conservatory. ▪ *Cambie St at 33rd Ave; 874-8336.*

University Golf Club A gorgeous course, well-maintained and a treat to play in almost any condition. You do not need any connection with the university to play here, and many people attend classes under the tutelage of seven certified CPGA pros. ▪ *5185 University Blvd; 224-1818.*

HIKING

A telltale sign of the popularity of hiking in Vancouver is that David and Mary Macaree's *103 Hikes in Southwestern British Columbia* is now into its fourth edition. A companion volume, *109 Walks in the Lower Mainland*, is almost as popular. The Macarees know their terrain well, with distances and estimated hiking times not being based on the dawdler. Several of the most popular hikes are listed in the Climbing and Mountaineering section; what follows is a more diverse selection.

Garibaldi Provincial Park This park is the jewel of West Coast mountain parks, with over 60 kilometres (37.5 miles) of developed hiking trails. The trails near Singing Pass can be reached by taking the Whistler Gondola Express and following a well-defined trail over the Musical Bumps. This is particularly beautiful in August, when the meadows are filled with blooming lupines, Indian paintbrush, and saxifrage. Cheakamus Lake,

Diamond Head, and Black Tusk meadows are all worthwhile day trips. If you're going to Black Tusk, avoid the crowds and mind-numbing boredom of the infamous "Barrier switchbacks" by using the alternative Helm Creek trail (same access as the Cheakamus Lake turnoff). ▪ *(604) 898-3678.*

Golden Ears Provincial Park
Although many hikers like the rugged trails of Garibaldi Park and the North Shore, Golden Ears (east of the city) provides some spectacular views of seldom-visited glaciers and mountains. The best part about climbing Golden Ears is that although it looks incredibly steep from its precipitous west face, the route up the east side, calling for some use of hands on the way up, is little more than an exerting hike. Fit hikers can tackle the 1,706-metre (5,597-foot) North Ear, but an early start is necessary as the trailhead is almost at sea level. Once on top you can marvel at Pitt and Alouette lakes, two large bodies of water nearby. The latter is suitable for swimming after you descend. This is not a short day trip and should only be attempted after the upper meadows are free of snow. ▪ *463-3513.*

Howe Sound Crest Trail
Strong day-hikers might want to tackle the Howe Sound Crest Trail, a 30-kilometre (18.8-mile) (one way) trek across several summits, including Black Mountain, Mount Harvey, Mount Brunswick, and Deeks Peak, and ending in Porteau Cove. Portions of this trail can be reached at various points along Highway 99 north of Horseshoe Bay, but to do the whole trip you need to park one car at Cypress Bowl and another at Deeks Creek. There are stiff hills and slippery descents en route, and weather can change very quickly. Still, this trail provides awesome views of Howe Sound and the Strait of Georgia. ▪ *463-3513.*

Lighthouse Park
On the bluffs above West Vancouver's Point Atkinson, Lighthouse Park features one of the few remaining stands of old-growth Douglas fir trees. Next to the California redwood, Douglas firs are the second-tallest tree species found in North America. This park is fun to walk in regardless of the weather. Crowds are most easily avoided during the misty, moody winter months. The smooth igneous rock surrounding the lighthouse provides an ideal spot to rest and enjoy a picnic. Eagles' nests, rust-red arbutus trees, and the red and white lighthouse casting its beam across the water complete this very beautiful West Coast postcard. ▪ *463-3513.*

Manning Provincial Park
[KIDS] A three-hour drive east on the Trans-Canada Highway and Highway 3 (take the Hope-Princeton route at the Hope interchange), Manning Park is especially spectacular when in bloom. In June, stop at the Rhododendron Flats pullout near the highway; in August, see the brilliant carpet of alpine wildflowers at higher elevations.

Trained park naturalists are on duty during periods of peak bloom, and the trail to the alpine meadows is ideal for children as well. If they're restless, have them smell the fragrant sitka valerian, a white wildflower known for its mild narcotic effect. ▪ *(604) 875-7161.*

Pitt River Dykes The Pitt is a major tributary of the Fraser and a walk along its dykes can be enjoyed at any time of the year. You can drive directly to Pitt Lake and take in the breathtaking view of the Coast Range to the north, then work your way south along the river's edge, past Chatham Reach and on toward the Pitt's confluence with the Fraser. If you go on different days and wonder where all of the water has gone, your eyes will have not deceived you. The Pitt is subject to changing river levels due to tidal activity. There's great bird-watching here, too.

HORSEBACK RIDING

Cowboys roam the ranges on the Ponderosa-size ranches of the Cariboo and Chilcotin, but city slickers can don hats and boots for horseback riding in the Fraser Valley.

Outdoor Sports

Hiking

Campbell Valley Regional Park This nature park features equestrian trails, cross-country jumps, picnicking, and nature study areas. Hop off your horse and pick a handful of blackberries at summer's end. Open every day. From Highway 1 take the Langley 200 Street exit southbound. ▪ *Travel 14.5 kilometres (9 miles) and turn east on 16th Avenue for the North Valley entrance; 530-4983.*

Golden Ears Provincial Park A great place for both urban cowboys and the saddle-savvy to trail-ride. Commercial stables in Maple Ridge organize summer day rides to Alouette Lake. Hitch your horses, swim in the lake, then head 'em home. Golden Ears Riding Stable is located 48 kilometres (30 miles) east of Vancouver on Highway 7. ▪ *23103-136th Ave, Maple Ridge; (604) 463-8761.*

Manning Provincial Park This park, which is less than three hours east of Vancouver in the Cascade Mountains, is a spectacular place to ride horseback. Several hundred kilometres of horse trails crisscross the park. Bring your own horses or rent one through the Manning Park Corral. ▪ *Manning Park Resort; (604) 840-8844.*

Whitbread Stables II The fragrant, fertile farmlands of the Fraser delta near Ladner are the fields of play for Whitbread Stables, who offer a superlative range of riding possibilities. Choose from Western and English-style classes, horseback-riding picnics, and even horse-drawn carriage lessons. A favourite venue for movie actors learning to get back in the saddle. ▪ *4409 66 St, Ladner; 946-6802.*

Fraser Valley Langley airport serves as the base for **Fantasy Balloon Charters**. They specialize in dawn or dusk champagne flights, taking wing once the air is cooler and less susceptible to turbulent currents. It's the most relaxing way to get an eagle's eye view of Mount Baker, Golden Ears, the North Shore, and the patchwork quilt of rich farmland bordering the Fraser River. ▪ *2628 Granville St; 530-1974.*

Whistler Area **Sea to Sky Balloon Adventures** is one of the few ballooning companies to fly in high alpine territory. Their early morning summer champagne brunch flights soar above the Pemberton Valley. Watch for coyotes, bald eagles, and moose on the shores of the Lillooet River. ▪ *Twenty minutes north of Whistler; free shuttle service from Whistler hotels; (604) 932-7752.*

ICE SKATING

Unlike Canadian cities with below-zero temperatures, Vancouver has a mild winter climate less conducive to traditional winter recreation like tobogganing and ice skating. Nevertheless, several recreation facilities are open to skaters, and some outdoor ponds are suitable for a quick pirouette or double axel when an infrequent cold-snap hits.

▼

Outdoor
Sports

Ice Skating

▲

Karen Magnussen Recreation Centre [KIDS] Named after an ex-Olympic medallist who grew up in the neighbourhood, this North Vancouver facility is the premier skating rink on the North Shore. ▪ *937 Lynn Valley Rd, North Vancouver; 987-7529.*

Kerrisdale Cyclone Taylor Arena [KIDS] This West Side arena holds special parties to commemorate events like St. Patrick's Day. Open fall and winter; call ahead for a public skating schedule. ▪ *5670 East Blvd; 261-8144.*

Kitsilano Community Centre Year-round public skating is available at this popular West Side recreation centre. The arena is closed for six weeks in April and May. ▪ *2690 Larch St; 734-1415.*

Lost Lagoon, Stanley Park, and Other City Parks [KIDS] [FREE] When Arctic air comes pouring out of the north, many of the ponds in Vancouver parks freeze over. The Parks Board cordons off part of Lost Lagoon in Stanley Park for free public skating until rising temperatures and precipitation make ice levels unsafe. Other ponds are located in Queen Elizabeth Park, along the south shore of False Creek, and on Como Lake in Coquitlam.

Robson Square Join power-lunching businessmen whirling around the outdoor rink on the lower level of Robson Square from November until early March. Rentals are not available, so bring your own skates.

IN-LINE SKATING

A decade after the introduction of in-line skates (or roller-blades), it's apparent that they have led to an established recreational activity and will not be the hula-hoop of the 1990s. Vancouver's rather hilly geography means that you should have your braking techniques mastered, especially if you're going to be out chasing traffic on city streets.

Kerrisdale Cyclone Taylor Arena Like many other Vancouver ice-skating arenas, when the ice comes out in the spring, Kerrisdale becomes a popular in-line skating centre, and even has an energetic street hockey league for boys and girls. Flat. ■ *5670 East Blvd; 261-8144.*

Stanley Park Seawall Bladers can travel on parts of the 9-kilometre (5.6-mile) seawall, taking in the spectacular viewpoints. This is a busy pedestrian and cycling area, so etiquette prevails. Mostly flat.

University of British Columbia Skaters can share an undulating cycle path that loops along 16th Avenue through Pacific Spirit Park and back along Chancellor Boulevard into University Village. The paved shoulder of Marine Drive from 16th Avenue to 49th Avenue is also prime skating territory. The closest rental store is **Recreational Rentals** at 2560 Arbutus Street; 733-7368.

KITE FLYING

When the winds blow whitecaps on the waters of English Bay, it's time to unravel the kite strings and join other fliers at one of the seaside parks. **Vanier Park** on Kits Point is a frequent-flyer spot, where many enthusiasts fly high-performance combat kites that engage in exciting dogfights.

Garry Point Park The windswept knolls surrounding the mouth of the Fraser River in Steveston are flat and very exposed to south and westerly winds. This park isn't visited often by Vancouverites, but it's well worth the trip. Drive south across the Oak Street Bridge (Highway 99) to the Steveston Highway turnoff, then west (right) along Steveston Highway to the end and turn south (left) to the park. If the wind dies, you can always enjoy a beach bonfire.

MOUNTAIN BIKING

Although many recreation-oriented towns claim to be mountain-biking meccas, there is a good case for making Vancouver the fat-tire capital of North America. Every possible accessory and kind of bike you could ever expect to find is available in Vancouver-area specialty stores, and some of the finest frames and components are built right in Vancouver. Designers test their prototypes on some of the most technically difficult trails to be found anywhere.

Pacific Spirit Regional Park This large tract of land was one of the earliest places to be discovered by mountain bikers, and it still remains popular despite numerous trail closures and a policy of prohibiting cyclists on trails. Park wardens patrol the area to fine offenders who still ride in these restricted areas. Trails are especially muddy (and uncrowded) after a few days of rain.

The Secret Trails Society In most mountain communities in North America, hikers and mountain bikers have shared, at best, an uneasy coexistence. Ross Kirkwood is a local enthusiast who took matters (or a chainsaw) into his own hands and fashioned the the most challenging riding (and environmentally impact-resistant) trails in North America in places where hikers seldom wander. These trails are so "secret" that a comprehensive trail guide and map to the area does not exist. General areas to pick up the trails are below Cypress Bowl, behind Grouse Mountain, and in the Seymour Demonstration Forest. Local bike shops like Mountain and Beach at 100-68 East 2nd Avenue (876-2683) and the Deep Cove Bike Shop (929-1918) can provide details. The Great Bicycle Co. (988-1800) on Mountain Highway at Lynn Valley Road offers rentals and is the closest shop to the largest network of easily-accessible trails. This terrain is not suitable for novice riders, and should never be cycled alone. Frequent riders are asked to help maintain the trails and obey proper etiquette when encountering other users.

Whistler Area Once the snow melts and Whistlerites have retired their skis and snowboards for the season, the toys of summer come out. Whistler offers as much variety for mountain bikers in the summer as it does for skiers in the winter—from wide-open cross-country ski trails to old logging roads leading to magnificent stands of old-growth redcedar to some of the gnarliest and most technically difficult riding imaginable. Not all of the trails are easy to find, so pick up the newest edition of the *Whistler Off Road Cycling Guide* by Grant Lamont and Charlie Doyle. The Cheakamus Challenge, the largest mountain bike event in Canada, is held on the last weekend in September each year. The 63-kilometre- (32-mile-) long course features gear-grinding ascents, white-knuckle descents, and a great post-race party. Novices will enjoy the Lost Lake Loop (stop for a refreshing dip either at the public beach on the south side of the lake or at a clothing-optional dock on the east side). The Lost Lake trail is easily accessible from the Village and its many bike shops. For greater challenge and a bit more solitude, Brandywine Falls and Cheakamus Lake are ideal trips, often scheduled by one of the local guiding companies like Backroads Bicycle Tours (932-3111), Whistler Outdoor Experience (932-3389), and Spicy Sports (938-1821). Hardcore riders will head straight for legendary trails like the Emerald

*Mountain
Biking*

Forest, A River Runs Through It, Northwest Passage, and the Rebob Trail.

NATURE OBSERVATION

Although the intrusion of civilization has had a devastating effect on the ecosystem habitat of indigenous flora and fauna, there are many areas where one can still observe the rhythms and life cycles of the natural world. Birds, whales, fish, and mammals are constantly foraging for food in the same places that native tribes hunted them centuries ago. Other locations like the Fraser River delta are favourite stopping points for migrating flocks of snow geese, brants, and terns.

Many clubs and associations provide detailed information on nature observation in the province. Some of the local natural history societies sponsor field trips and can provide information about tour operators who specialize in wildlife viewing. The umbrella organization for the province is the **Federation of BC Naturalists** (737-3057), who can provide details of area clubs.

Bird Watching Naturalists come from all over the world to the [KIDS] **George C. Reifel Migratory Bird Sanctuary** on Westham Island at the mouth of the Fraser River, 9.6 kilometres (6 miles) west of Ladner. Over 250 species of birds can be sighted; the peak viewing season is between October and April. This wetlands environment is especially attractive to shorebirds like herons, geese, and ducks. Occasionally, migratory birds from Asian countries lose their way and end up here, drawing crowds of ornithologists seeking to cross another exotic bird off their "life-lists." Kids love to feed seeds to the squeaking hordes of ducks looking for a free handout. Take a picnic, sneak into a bird blind, or climb up a viewing tower, particularly in November during the Snow Goose Festival (946-6980). Eighty kilometres (50 miles) north of Vancouver on Highway 99, the small community of **Brackendale** calls itself the Bald Eagle Capital of Canada. During January hundreds of these majestic birds flock to the banks of the Squamish River to feed on the spawned-out carcasses of a late-fall salmon run. The best place for viewing is an area called Eagle Run, located behind Fergie's Fishing Lodge. During the early winter, this area has the highest eagle count in North America next to the Chilkat River in Alaska. For special photography courses, tours, and information on the annual eagle count each January, call the Brackendale Art Gallery and Cafe at (604) 898-3333.

Farm Animals and Zoos [KIDS] **Vancouver Game Farm** (856-6825) is located in Aldergrove, 48 kilometres (29.8 miles) east of Vancouver off the Trans-Canada Highway at the 264th Street exit. Open year-round, its well-treed, parklike 48 hectares (118.6 acres) are home to 110 species of animals, including tigers, wolves, zebra, rhinoceros, bears, elephant, parrots, flamingo, ostrich, bison, and many others who all roam freely. You can walk, cycle, or drive through the farm, a favourite with kids.

[KIDS] **Maplewood Farm** may be teeming with domestic animals, but this place is still a great hit with kids. A 2-hectare (4.9-acre) municipal park farm, Maplewood's "Rabbitat" and "Goathill" are popular petting areas. Visitors can also take part in daily hand-milking demonstrations. Watch for special family events like the Sheep Fair in May, the Farm Fair in September, and Christmas Carolling in December. From Vancouver via Second Narrows Bridge exit 238 (aka Deep Cove/Mount Seymour exit), turn left at the second traffic light to 405 Seymour River Place, North Vancouver; 929-5610.

[KIDS] [FREE] **Richmond Nature Park** offers everything you always wanted to know about bogs. Interpretative trails and Nature House, complete with salamanders and snakes, make this a hidden gem in the suburban sprawl. ▪ *11851 Westminster Hwy, Richmond; 273-7015.*

Salmon Spawning [KIDS] [FREE] **Capilano Salmon Hatchery**, a federal government fish hatchery set on the Capilano River among majestic red cedars and lush huckleberry bushes, is a family favourite. Meander through the self-guiding facility where information panels describe the life cycles of Pacific salmon. Then watch juvenile salmon in the ponds and returning salmon jumping up a series of chutes (from July to December). This park also boasts some of the tallest trees still standing on the Lower Mainland—the Giant Fir is over 500 years old and 61 metres (200 feet) tall. Open daily. Drive up Capilano Road in North Vancouver, take the first left past the Suspension Bridge onto Capilano Park Road. Proceed approximately 1.5 kilometres (0.9 mile) to the hatchery; 666-1790.

[KIDS] Every four years (1994, 1998, 2002) it's worth taking the six-hour drive to the **Adams River** for the fall sockeye run. This is one of the great life-cycle stories in nature, where salmon that have spent their entire lives in the Pacific Ocean return up the Fraser and Thompson rivers to spawn and die. To reach the Adams River, head west from Salmon Arm on Highway 1 to Squilix, then northeast on the paved highway for 3.8 kilometres (2.4 miles) to the junction just after the Adams River bridge. Contact BC parks, Thompson River district; (604) 828-4494.

Whale Watching For grey whales the best lookout locations are on the west coast of Vancouver Island, a five-hour drive from Vancouver (including ferry). Migrating grey whales can be seen beginning in late November, but are more often seen in March and April, as they travel between their Arctic breeding grounds and Mexican calving lagoons. Many whale-watching boat charters operate out of the West Coast communities

Recreation
▬

▼
Outdoor Sports

Nature Observation

of Tofino, Bamfield, and Ucluelet. There are good land viewpoints in the Long Beach area, all of which have telescopes and are accessible by car. The **Wickaninnish Centre** at Wickaninnish Beach is a prime viewing spot.

Although it's BC's second-largest city, Victoria is one of the best places in the province for spotting killer whales. In fact, you may even see a pod from the BC ferry on the way over to the island. **SeaCoast Expeditions** in Victoria, (604) 477-1818, offers guaranteed sightings of killer whales on its three-hour trips, available by special arrangement June 1 through September 15. Listen to orcas chatting on the hydrophone. SeaCoast also makes two-hour excursions to Race Rocks Ecological Reserve and Lighthouse to view California and Steller's sea lions, harbour seals, porpoises, cormorant colonies, and bald eagle nests.

RIVER RAFTING

For a sheer adrenalin rush, it's hard to beat a day's rafting on one of the province's many stretches of white water, interspersed with a lazy drift through calm patches. Watch for deer nibbling on shoots and leaves near the water's edge, bald eagles whirling on air currents overhead, or even grizzled prospectors panning for gold. River rafting is regulated provincially (for safety reasons) under the Commercial River Rafting Safety Act.

**Outdoor
Sports**

▬

*Nature
Observation*

▲

Chilliwack River   Located 96 kilometres (60 miles) from Vancouver, this river is very popular just after spring run-off (roughly early May to mid-July) for one-day rafting trips. Chilliwack River is also popular with white-water kayakers. ▪ *Hyak Wilderness Adventures; 734-8622.*

Fraser River Most one-day Fraser River excursions are offered from May to the end of August. Customers travel in motorized rafts downriver from Boston Bar to Yale. Raft Scuzzy Rock, China Bar, and Hells Gate with experienced operators. ▪ *Kumsheen Raft Adventures; (800) 663-6667.*

Nahatlatch River The Nahatlatch River, a four-hour drive north of Vancouver, seethes with boiling chutes of white water from May to mid-August. Join the Nahatlatch experts' **REO Rafting Adventures** (684-4438) for a wild ride through ominous-sounding rapids like the Meat Grinder, Lose Your Lunch, and the Big Chill. Free overnight camping is available at REO's private campsite.

Thompson River The emerald-green waters of the Thompson River provide a pleasant mix of casual floating and stomach-churning white water. Rafters follow the Thompson from Spences Bridge to the take-out point at Lytton, where the clear Thompson joins the murky, silt-laden Fraser. The trip includes thrilling rapids like the Devil's Kitchen and the Jaws of Death. ▪ *Hyak Wilderness Adventures; 734-8622.*

Especially at peak periods like lunch hour and after work, there are so many runners on the municipal pathways that visitors to Vancouver might be forgiven for asking, "Is there some kind of race happening today?" Once you include the in-line skaters, mountain bikers, triathletes, and race-walkers, it seems as though the entire city is clad in Lycra tights and carrying water bottles. Exposure to fitness starts early, with jogging moms pushing their infants in specially-constructed strollers, and continues into the golden years, with local masters racers routinely running faster than men and women half their age.

Ambleside Park, West Vancouver As the name implies, this is a great place for a beachside amble or jog. Watch cruise ships, freighters, barges, and even the odd battleship passing underneath the Lion's Gate Bridge into Burrard Inlet. Start at the east end of the park, where the Capilano River enters the ocean, and follow the seawall west. Great views across the First Narrows to Stanley Park.

Central Park The wooded trails of Central Park begin at the boundary between Vancouver and Burnaby, just off of Kingsway. Track athletes use Swanguard Stadium for interval workouts. For runners who wish more diversity, a fitness circuit featuring a variety of exercise options is available nearby.

Outdoor Sports

Kits Beach/Vanier Park A 5-kilometre (3.1-mile) network of flat asphalt and dirt paths skirts Vanier Park on the Kitsilano side of the Burrard Street Bridge. The paths follow the water around Kits Point, and past the Vancouver Museum, the planetarium, the Maritime Museum, and Kits Beach. In the summer, Kits Beach is Vancouver's home of the bronzed and muscle-bound, and there's always a game of beach volleyball or street basketball happening.

Running and Walking

Lost Lagoon, Stanley Park [KIDS] The 1.6-kilometre (1-mile) trail that encircles Lost Lagoon is an easy stroll and a great spot for watching nesting Canada geese in the springtime. The fountain in the centre of the lagoon emits a fine shower of spray at periodic intervals.

Pacific Spirit Regional Park Surrounding the University of British Columbia, this park contains 50 kilometres (31.1 miles) of walking and jogging trails through deciduous and coniferous forests, including Camosun Bog. Trails vary in length; you can enjoy a short stroll or you can take a more vigorous walk all the way from the Fraser River Estuary to Spanish Banks. The Visitor Centre is located on the north side of 16th Avenue, just west of Cleveland Trail.

Stanley Park Seawall The longest seawall in Canada (9 kilometres or 5.6 miles) is a great place to jog or walk. Plaques set in the wall at half-kilometre intervals detail the wall's history. Runners and walkers can also detour into the park. The seawall is a brisk, nonstop two-hour walk.

SAILING

Perhaps no sport quite defines the West Coast lifestyle like sailing. From two-man high-speed catamarans to double-masted schooners, virtually every kind of sailboat can be found in the waters around Vancouver. Some of the best cruising is in the Strait of Georgia, where the land mass of Vancouver Island shelters many tiny bays and inlets that make perfect anchorages. Sailors wishing to charter boats for self-sufficient expeditions must pass tests administered by the Canadian Yachting Association. **Sea Wing Sailing School and Yacht Charters** (669-0840) on Granville Island offers combination learn-to-sail cruises and classroom lectures to develop navigation and other nautical skills.

English Bay During the summer, **Cooper Boating Centre** on Granville Island (687-4110) offers three-hour cruises in English Bay on 6- to 12-metre (19.7- to 39.4-foot) yachts. Cruising in English Bay can also consist of a leisurely sail past all the swank beachfront properties in West Vancouver.

Outdoor Sports

Running and Walking

The Gulf Islands Several sailing schools offer cruise-and-learn, five-day trips around the Gulf Islands. Alternatively, you can rent a yacht, with or without a skipper, to cruise the islands. The Islands offer the solitude of arbutus-lined coves, the charm of neighbourhood pubs and restaurants, and the thrill of watching marine life like harbour seals, whales, porpoises, and sea otters.

Princess Louisa Inlet Princess Louisa Inlet is a saltwater bay carved deep into the Coast Mountains wilderness. Located on the Sunshine Coast north of Sechelt, its calm waters and cascading waterfalls make it an ideal sailing destination. Farther north, the Desolation Sound Marine Park is a favourite summertime objective as well.

SKIING: CROSS-COUNTRY

The moist, mild climate of the south coast means that skiers take their chances on conditions when skiing locally. In Vancouver, cross-country skiing can be as casual as a trip around a golf course or city park during one of the city's infrequent snowfalls, or as extreme as a multi-day expedition into the heart of the Coast Range. Cross-country skiers generally divide along two lines: aerobic-sports enthusiasts, who prefer striding or skating along specially manicured machine-grooved tracks, and backcountry skiers, who blaze their own trails into the pristine wilderness. The former can take classes in everything from skate skiing, waxing, and racing strategy, while the latter will be interested in telemarking, backcountry navigation, avalanche awareness, and winter camping. Both types of skiers should be aware that local weather conditions can change rapidly, and extra food and clothing should always be brought in a day pack.

Cypress Bowl [KIDS] The groomed trails closest to Vancouver are at Cypress Bowl on the North Shore. You'll find 16 kilometres (10 miles) of groomed, track-set trails radiating from historic Hollyburn Lodge. Five kilometres (3.1 miles) of trail are lighted for night skiing. A backcountry trail to the top of Hollyburn Mountain is also navigable, but it is quite steep in places and not suitable for children or inexperienced skiers. Nevertheless, the view over the city and into the Coast Range is unforgettable. Because Cypress is the closest place where Vancouver parents can take their kids for an authentic "winter experience," it's not really a place to get away from it all. Rentals and lessons are available. ▪ *925-2704 for weather and trail information.*

Garibaldi Provincial Park The alpine meadows of Singing Pass, Black Tusk, and Diamond Head, which yield an awesome profusion of wildflowers in the summer, are blanketed with several metres of snow each winter. These three areas are prime backcountry skiing territory, with small huts located close by for protection from the elements. Backcountry skiers travelling in any areas within Garibaldi Park should be entirely self-sufficient and everyone should be trained in avalanche safety. Winter backcountry ski courses are taught through the Federation of Mountain Clubs of British Columbia (737-3053) and through the Alpine Guides Bureau at Whistler, (604) 938-3338. If you're short on experience but still want a winter wilderness adventure, certified alpine guides can also be hired there.

Manning Park Resort Three hours east of Vancouver, Manning Park Resort, (604) 840-8822, offers skiers everything they could ask for: cross-country trails especially designed for skating and classic techniques, hundreds of square kilometres of rugged Coast Range ski touring, and even a challenging little downhill area for perfecting telemark turns. Sigge's Sport Villa (731-8818) in Kitsilano offers bus trips from Vancouver that can include transportation, rentals, and lessons. Manning is a good place to bring kids, and the ticket prices won't break the bank, either. Overnight accommodation is available in wonderful log cabins or at the main lodge.

Mount Seymour Provincial Park Mount Seymour is another local favourite, especially for those with backcountry skiing aspirations. The skiing between First (Pump) Peak and Second Peak can be excellent, especially after a big snowfall. Once you're outside of the downhill ski-area boundary, skiers must

▼

Outdoor Sports

Skiing: Cross-Country

stay close to the wanded trail, especially in foggy weather. It's not uncommon for skiers or snowshoers to become lost in this bluffy, confusing terrain.

Whistler/Lost Lake Trails Although Whistler is known primarily as a downhill ski resort, the nordic facility at Lost Lake is worth checking out. There are 22 kilometres (13.7 miles) of machine-groomed cross-country trails set around Lost Lake and the Chateau Whistler golf course, with 5 kilometres (3.1 miles) lighted for night skiing. These trails are easily accessible from the Village; turn left on Blackcomb Way after entering Village Gate Boulevard and follow the signs for parking at the trailhead. Two warming huts and water stations are provided. Rentals are available at the Village Sports Stop (932-5495) and Sports West (938-7777).

SKIING: DOWNHILL

With the possible exception of Salt Lake City, no city in North America boasts such excellent skiing facilities within a two-hour drive from downtown as does Vancouver. The closest areas are on the North Shore. Cypress Bowl, Grouse Mountain, and Mount Seymour have respectable vertical drops and are ideal places to learn the sport. But ninety minutes north lies the resort municipality of Whistler, North America's largest ski destination, which combines two great skiing mountains: Whistler Mountain and Blackcomb. Both mountains boast fabulous trail networks starting deep on adjacent sides of the Fitzsimmons Creek valley and rising over a vertical mile in elevation, into an alpine wonderland of open bowls, glaciers, and astonishing views. Anchoring both lift complexes is a European-style pedestrian village with an exciting array of restaurants, nightclubs, hotels and shops. There is simply no other mountain town in Canada like Whistler, and the only caveat for visitors is that it can get crowded during peak times and that, as usual, the best does not come cheap. The first-time skier to Whistler and Blackcomb will find its size is so overwhelming that spending one day skiing here will hardly be enough. Each of the two mountains has a distinctive character that makes it worthy of your attention. Which mountain you and your friends will enjoy more will be the endless topic of après-ski debate.

Blackcomb Mountain This is simply the most modern, best-planned, first-class ski resort in North America. Operated by the Intrawest Development Company, no expense has been spared in building high-speed lifts, cutting well-designed fall-line runs, pampering skiers with food far above the norm at most ski resorts, and blanketing the trails with man-made snow when Mother Nature does not cooperate. Blackcomb is shaped like an inverted triangle, with trails spreading out in every direction as you gain altitude. Four runs are "can't miss" on any skier's agenda: south-facing Xhiggy's Meadow, on the Seventh Heaven Express; the fabulous Blackcomb Glacier run, which is one of the longest above-treeline slopes outside of Europe; the aptly named Zig-Zag, a winding cruise run which seems to go on forever; and the vertiginous chutes of Rendezvous Bowl, including the heart-stopping Saudan Couloir. Even lunch at the mountain-top Rendezvous or the spectacular new Glacier Creek restaurant is an experience to be savoured. ■ *From Vancouver, 687-7507; in Whistler, (604) 932-4211. For guest services, ski school programs, and general information, call Whistler Mountain at (604) 932-3434, or Blackcomb Mountain at (604) 932-3141.*

Cypress Bowl For the advanced skier, Cypress Bowl boasts some excellent mogul skiing, especially the Top Gun run underneath the Sky Chair. Cypress is the largest downhill facility on the North Shore, and can be a fantastic place to ski after a big snowstorm. Cars driving the Cypress Bowl road should be equipped with tire-chains or good winter tread tires. ■ *For conditions and weather information, call 926-6007. For ski school programs, call 926-5612.*

Grouse Mountain Closer to Vancouver, the ski runs and lighted trails on Grouse are visible from most parts of the Lower Mainland. Skiers can take the bus from downtown right to the base of the mountain, where you're shuttled to the top on the Skyride, an aerial tram that gives a spectacular view of the city and across the Strait of Georgia to Vancouver Island. Although Grouse's slopes are a fraction of the length of those at Whistler, it's still a great place to go for a quick ski fix. ■ *Snow report phone number, 986-6262; program information, 980-9311.*

Outdoor Sports

Skiing: Downhill

Hemlock Valley Tucked in a side-valley tributary of the Fraser River, Hemlock is one of the least-conspicuous ski areas in the province. Its quaint day-lodge and older, slower lifts make it a throw-back to the days when even downhill skiing was an adventure sport. But that's a good thing, since powder skiing here often lasts longer than it does at more crowded destination resorts. Some slopeside accommodation is available. ■ *797-4444 for reservations; snow phone is 520-6222.*

Mount Seymour [KIDS] This ski area lies within the provincial park of the same name. This is the first ski area many Vancouverites are exposed to because the learn-to-ski programs are inexpensive and often operated in conjunction with the local schools. Even if you don't ski, there's a great tobogganing area at the south end of the parking lot. Seymour's somewhat irregular terrain makes it popular with snowboarders as well. All-season tires or chains are recommended for this road as well. ■ *986-3444 for weather and conditions, 986-2261 for special programs and instruction.*

Whistler Mountain The beauty of skiing Whistler is that its reputation has not been diminished by having such a high-tech, glitzy neighbour to the north. For Whistler has an ambience that cannot quite be described; perhaps it can only be experienced by blasting through a snow-choked glade in waist-deep powder without a soul in sight. It's the kind of place you can ski for days on end and not cross the same trail twice, and which gets better the more you traverse to seek its special charms. The credo of customer-first service starts with the president and goes right down to the parking lot attendant, making Whistler a more intimate, down-home place to ski. The pick of Whistler's litter would include Franz's Run, the original high-speed cruiser that starts near treeline and drops right to the valley floor at the base of Whistler Creek. Harmony Bowl, Symphony Bowl, and the precipitous Glacier Bowl are above-treeline expanses which have cemented the Whistler legend for hard-core thrills, yet even low-skill intermediates can enjoy the bowl skiing on Highway 86 and Burnt Stew Basin. With its banked runs and rocky bluffs, it's also an ideal mountain for snowboarding. Winter recreation at Whistler, however, is not just for skiers. There's heli-flightseeing, ice skating, mountaintop sightseeing, snowshoeing, snowmobiling, and sleigh rides. ▪ *All reservations are handled through the Whistler Resort Association. Their toll-free number is 1-800-WHISTLER. (In BC call 685-3650.) Snow-phone hotline numbers are Whistler Mountain: from Vancouver, 687-6761; in Whistler, 932-4191.*

SNOWSHOEING

Snowshoeing is a tried-and-true way of getting off piste into the backwoods snowy terrain, which is often too uneven for cross-country skiers.

Manning Provincial Park Three hours east of Vancouver, Manning is host to extensive snowshoeing terrain within its vast backcountry. As in any winter backcountry activity, snowshoers should be wary of avalanches and changing weather conditions, and have mountain navigation skills. ▪ *(604)875-7161.*

Mount Seymour Provincial Park Over the Second Narrows Bridge, 16 kilometres (10 miles) north of Vancouver, Mount Seymour offers snowshoe rentals and instruction. Snowshoers can skirt some of the winter cross-country trails, including Goldie Lake Loop, Flower Lake Loop, and Hidden Lake Loop. ▪ *929-1291.*

SWIMMING

[KIDS] Vancouver's 11 sandy beaches are fine for swimming in brisk 21°C temperatures. Lifeguards patrol June, July, and August. Favourite swimming beaches include English Bay (site of the annual New Year's Day Polar Bear Swim), Sunset Beach, Kits Beach (especially after a strenuous session of beach volleyball), Jericho Beach, Locarno Beach, and Spanish Banks (the latter three are popular with cycling and windsurfing crowds).

Kitsilano Pool Kitsilano Beach offers a gigantic (137.5 metres or 150 yards) outdoor saltwater pool adjacent to English Bay. It is heated to 26° C and has graduated depth, making it ideal for both children and strong swimmers. ▪ *Open from Victoria Day (May 24) to Labour Day, seven days a week; 731-0011.*

Newton Wave Pool [KIDS] Because the waters of Vancouver are protected from ocean swells of the Pacific Coast, surfing is not part of the city's aquatic culture. But in the suburb of Surrey, a wave-action leisure pool generates 1-metre (3-foot) waves for body surfing. There are also two water slides, a wading pool, steam room, whirlpool, weight room, and even a licensed lounge. Open seven days a week. ▪ *13730 72nd Ave, Surrey; 594-7873.*

Splashdown Waterpark The owners of Splashdown Waterpark have taken advantage of Tsawwassen's sunny location (less than half the annual rainfall of downtown Vancouver) to construct a giant 2.8-hectare (7-acre) park featuring 11 waterslides. There's a full range of summertime fun to be enjoyed here, from volleyball and basketball courts to a mini-golf course. It's a great place to pack a picnic, and maybe the most reliable spot in the Lower Mainland for getting a suntan. ▪ *4799 Hwy 17, Tsawwassen; 943-2251.*

University of British Columbia Aquatic Centre UBC has Olympic-size indoor and outdoor pools with sauna, steam room, whirlpool, exercise gym, and toddler pool. Open late into the evening for public swimming. ▪ *822-4521 for pool times.*

Vancouver Aquatic Centre In the West End overlooking Sunset Beach, the Vancouver Aquatic Centre features an Olympic-size indoor pool, sauna, whirlpool, and toddler pool. ▪ *1050 Beach Ave; 665-4324.*

TENNIS

Keen tennis players can perfect their topspin lob or two-fisted backhand year-round on Vancouver's 180 public courts, even though the outdoor season officially runs from March to October. Most public courts are free and operate on a first-come, first-served basis.

Stanley Park has 21 courts (17 by the Beach Avenue entrance, and four by Lost Lagoon at the foot of Robson.) From April to September, you can book a Beach Avenue court for a small fee (688-8786). **Queen Elizabeth Park** courts (33rd Avenue at Cambie Street) are centrally located but can be quite hot when there's no breeze. **Kitsilano Beach Park** has 10 courts near the ocean with a concession stand nearby offering a cool drink or french-fries. **Jericho Beach Park**, behind the Jericho Sailing Centre, offers great rugby viewing on the pitch south of the courts while you wait your turn.

WINDSURFING

Although Vancouver is surrounded by water and exposed to breezes from every direction, capricious conditions can test the patience of high-wind sailors looking for waves to jump and steady, consistent winds. But the light winds often found on the beaches of the city's West Side are ideal for learning the sport. **Windsure Windsurfing School** (228-0615) operates from the Jericho Sailing Centre. Their specialty is an intensive six-hour course that guarantees results. At Sunset Beach, **Windmaster Windsurfing School** (685-7245) is more convenient for guests staying in downtown hotels.

For some of the most consistent conditions in North America, you need to drive an hour north to the town of Squamish, actually a native word meaning "place where the wind blows." The Squamish Spit is a man-made dyke that separates the saltwater bay of Howe Sound from the frigid waters of the Squamish River. Skim out on your board within view of the Stawamus Chief, Shannon Falls, and Howe Sound. Conditions are best from May to August, when afternoon thermals generated by warm air temperatures create steady, consistent conditions. The water is very cold, so a thick wetsuit or drysuit is mandatory, especially if you are still developing your jibing and waterstart skills. The **Squamish Windsurfing Society** administers the park, charging a daily fee to pay for rescue boats, washroom maintenance, and liability insurance. To reach the Squamish Spit, turn left at the Cleveland Avenue (McDonald's restaurant) intersection and turn right onto Buckley Avenue. Cross the railways tracks onto Government Road, pass the Squamish Feed Suppliers, and turn left onto the first gravel road. Continue 2 kilometres (1.2 miles) along a dusty, potholed road to the spit. For wind conditions, call 926-WIND.

SPECTATOR SPORTS

See also the Calendar chapter for specific sporting events.

AAA Canadians Baseball On a sunny midsummer afternoon, many member of the city's power elite (and their employees) are out, out, out at the old ball game. Although Vancouver doesn't have a team in The Show yet, the AAA Canadians play at Nat Bailey Stadium on the east side of Queen Elizabeth Park (Ontario and 29th). Believe it or not, the stadium, with its slow, lush field and its beautiful natural setting, probably accounts for the Canadians' continual box-office success. New York Yankee stalwart Roger Maris once called it "the prettiest ballpark I've ever played in." Discount tickets are available through local food chains, but arrive early on sunny days because the 7,000-seat stadium frequently sells out. ▪ *Nat Bailey Stadium; 872-5352.*

BC Lions Football The BC Lions play in the Canadian Football League. A longer, wider field, and only three downs means that the passing game rules, making it a far more exciting game than its American counterpart. Avid fans enjoy home games in the BC Place Stadium downtown from June through late October. ▪ *685-4344.*

Horse Racing From April to October the thoroughbreds race at Exhibition Park (Hastings and Renfrew streets). With the North Shore mountains as a backdrop, serious punters study the horses' form in the paddocks. It's easy to get caught up in the excitement of an afternoon's racing. ▪ *254-1631.*

Vancouver Canucks Hockey Although the National Hockey League has been diluted with the addition of too many new teams and a punishing regular season schedule, a well-played hockey game is still the most spine-tingling spectacle in pro sport. Since winning the Smythe Division in 1992, the Vancouver Canucks have shone in the National Hockey League, ably assisted by the Russian Rocket Pavel Bure. You don't need to know anything about the rules to watch—it's all pretty self-explanatory. Home games are at the Vancouver Coliseum, at Hastings and Renfrew, from September to April. ▪ *254-5141.*

▼

Spectator Sports

▲

ESSENTIALS

Essentials

TRANSPORTATION

AIRPLANES: VANCOUVER INTERNATIONAL AIRPORT

Vancouver International Airport is located south of Vancouver in the city of Richmond, a 20-minute drive from downtown Vancouver. It serves 19 major airlines: Air BC, Air Canada, Air China, Air New Zealand, American Airlines, British Airways, Canadian Airlines, Cathay Pacific, Continental Airlines, Delta Airlines, Horizon Air, Japan Airlines, KLM Royal Dutch Airlines, Korean Air, Lufthansa German Airlines, Qantas Airways, Singapore Airlines, Time Air, and United Airlines.

Perimeter Transportation (261-2299) offers service between the airport and downtown locations, stopping at most major hotels and the bus depot. One way, $8.25; round trip, $14. Average **taxi** fare between the airport and downtown is approximately $25. **BC Transit** provides service to the Vancouver International Airport on the #100 route.

An airport-improvement departure tax of $5 is charged for domestic flights, $10 for US-bound flights, and $15 for international flights.

AIRPLANES: CHARTER

Helijet Airways (273-1414) offers scheduled service between downtown Vancouver and Victoria ($117 one way) and also has service to Victoria from Vancouver International Airport. Flights are aboard spacious 12-passenger Sikorsky S-76 helicopters. **Vancouver Helicopter Tours** (270-1484) has charter jet-powered flights to suit your schedule and desired destination.

BUSES AND LIGHT RAIL

BC Transit (261-5100) makes it easy to get around Vancouver without a car. Bus stops are clearly marked and often list the route numbers serving the stop. Enter by the front door and leave by the rear. Lift-equipped buses that are easily accessible for wheelchairs are identified by a sign on the bus windshield. Deposit exact cash fare ($1.50, one zone; $2.25, two zones; $3.00, three zones) in the fare box and request a transfer if you plan to continue your journey on a second bus or on the SkyTrain or SeaBus. Transfers are good for at least 90 minutes of travel in any direction. A DayPass ($4.50 adults; $2.25 children and seniors) is valid all day weekends and holidays and after 9:30am weekdays. Schedules are available at libraries, community centres, and city hall.

HandyDart (264-5000) is a customized service for passengers with a disability restricting movement who are not on an accessible route or who cannot use the lift-equipped buses. Book at least 48 hours in advance. Depending on the number of zones travelled, cost varies from $1.35 to $2.50.

SkyTrain, Vancouver's advanced light rapid transit system, operates on an elevated guideway between the Vancouver waterfront and Scott Road, Surrey. The four downtown stations are underground and are marked on street level. Fast, efficient, and scenic, the red, white, and blue carriages are computer driven but patrolled by roving attendants. Tickets (same as BC Transit fares) are dispensed from machines in each station and are good for travel on city buses and the SeaBus. Trains run from 5am to 1am.

SeaBus is one of the best services offered by BC Transit ($2.25). Twin-hulled catamarans shuttle up to 400 passengers per sailing between the foot of Lonsdale Avenue on the north shore of the harbour and SkyTrain's Waterfront Station at the foot of Granville Street downtown.

For **West Vancouver** bus schedule call 985-7777.

BUSES: OUT OF TOWN AND CHARTER

Greyhound Lines of Canada (Pacific Centre Station, 1150 Station Street, 662-3222) travels to points across Canada and North America.

Maverick Coach Lines (Pacific Centre Station, 1150 Station Street, 662-8074) serves Nanaimo, the Sunshine Coast, Squamish, and Whistler.

Pacific Coach Lines (Pacific Centre Station, 1150 Station Street, 662-8074) provides scheduled intercity service between downtown Vancouver and downtown Victoria, including Butchart Gardens.

Quick Shuttle Service (244-3744) offers regularly scheduled coach service between Vancouver and Sea-Tac Airport near Seattle, $60 round trip. It also serves Bellingham Airport from Vancouver, $27 round trip.

BC Ferries (669-1211) is a provincial government–operated service that offers a minimum of eight sailings daily from Tsawwassen, about a half-hour drive south of Vancouver, and from Swartz Bay, a similar distance from Victoria. Travel time, city centre to city centre, is about three hours. Car and driver, $27.50 one way; additional passengers, $6 each. Other routes go from Tsawwassen or Horseshoe Bay to Nanaimo, the Gulf Islands, and the Sunshine Coast. The ferries provide a pleasant, stable cruise, with amenities including dining room, snack bar, newsstand, and promenade decks. **Foot passengers**, $6, can either take BC Transit to the terminals or travel via coach. Pacific Coach Lines (662-8074) goes to Victoria; Maverick Coach Lines (662-8051) goes to Nanaimo. Both depart from Pacific Central Station in downtown Vancouver and have priority boarding ferries.

TRAINS

BC Rail (1311 W First Street, North Vancouver, 984-5246) operates a spectacular daily round-trip rail journey to Whistler, Lillooet, the Cariboo region, Prince George, and Quesnel.

VIA Rail (Pacific Centre Station, 1150 Station Street, 669-3050), Canada's national passenger rail network, operates thrice-weekly full-service trains through the Rockies to major destinations in Central and Eastern Canada.

KEYS TO THE CITY

CATERERS

There's nothing lazy about Susan Mendelson, owner of the **Lazy Gourmet** (1595 W Sixth Avenue, 734-2507), Vancouver's best-known caterering operation. Mendelson is the author of seven cookbooks, and her centrally located establishment is open every day, serving unforgettable meals, mouth-watering take-outs, and homemade breads and desserts. Other caterers of note include **Menu Setters** (3655 W 10th Avenue, 732-4218), **Gallery Cafe & Catering** (750 Hornby Street, 688-2233), **Lesley Stowe Fine Foods** (1780 W Third Avenue, 731-3633), and **Major The Gourmet** (102-8828 Heather Street, 322-9211).

CHILD CARE

Most major hotels can arrange for baby-sitters if notified in advance. **Neighborhood Babysitters** (737-2248) brings adult sitters to your door for $10 per hour. Same-day booking. **Over the Rainbow Drop-in Playcare Centre** (1508 Anderson Street, Granville Island, 683-2624) takes children 2 to 5 years old. Open 9:30am-4:30pm, Mon-Fri. Reservations advised.

CITY OF VANCOUVER COMPLAINTS AND QUESTIONS

Vancouver City Hall (453 W 12th Avenue, 873-7011) fields complaints and provides information about the city. An operator will refer you to the department that can best handle the problem.

CONSULATES

Major consulates include **Consulate General of the Federal Republic of Germany** (704-999 Canada Place, 684-8377), **French Consulate General** (1201-736 Granville Street, 681-4345), **British Consulate General** (1111 Melville Street, 683-4421), **Consulate General of Japan** (900-1177 W Hastings Street, 684-5868), **Consulate General of the United States of America** (1095 W Pender Street, 685-4311).

DATING SERVICES

First Impression Singles Network (207-777 W Broadway, 877-1777) offers a video and portfolio library for its exclusive clients, who pay $1,200 per year for the service.

DISCRIMINATION

The **BC Council of Human Rights** (406-815 Hornby Street, 660-6811) assists people who believe they have been the victims of discrimination due to race, age, sex, religion, marital status, political or sexual orientation, disabilities, and so on.

DRY CLEANERS AND TAILORS

The Valetor has built a name for itself over the past 50 years and has seven locations throughout Vancouver: 5405 West Boulevard, 266-7141; Oakridge Shopping Centre, 266-4421; 202-16th Street, West Vancouver, 922-2535; The Bay downtown, 681-6211; 2065 Burrard Street, 732-7817; 5309 Headland Drive, West Vancouver, 925-3900. **Scotty's One Hour Cleaners** (534 Thurlow Street, 685-7732) offers good service and a professional job. **Walker's Professional Wardrobe Care** (704 W 6th Avenue, 879-5454) will pick up and deliver dry cleaning and shoe repairs to home or office. **Georgia's Tailor** (678 Seymour, 684-3426) provides custom tailoring, Mon-Sat.

FOREIGN EXCHANGE

You can exchange US dollars at any major Canadian bank; however, it can be difficult to exchange other foreign currencies. There are also about 35 foreign banks in Vancouver. **American Express** (1040 W Georgia Street, 669-2813) is open Mon-Sat. **Custom House Currency** (375 Water Street, 687-6000) in Gastown is open late seven nights a week. **International Securities Exchange** (1169 Robson Street, 683-9666; and 1036 Robson Street, 683-4686) is open seven days a week, including some evenings. **Thomas Cook Foreign Exchange** (1016 W Georgia Street, 687-6111) is open Mon-Sat.

FOREIGN VISITORS

The **Society of Translators and Interpreters of BC** (684-2940) provides names of accredited translators. The **College of**

Physicians and Surgeons (733-7758) provides a list of doctors who speak second languages.

GROCERY DELIVERY

Safeway (643-6950) stores throughout Vancouver offer delivery via a private contractor. Price varies depending on distance.

INFORMATION

Vancouver Travel InfoCentre (200 Burrard Street, 682-2222) offers a wealth of information about Vancouver. The **Vancouver Public Library** (665-2280) is happy to take your call and refer you to applicable departments within the library.

LEGAL SERVICES

The **Lawyer Referral System** (687-3221) advises people seeking legal representation. The **Law Society of BC** (669-2533), the governing body of lawyers, assists people who have problems with a lawyer. The **Law Students' Legal Advice Program** (822-5791) offers a free consultation service.

LIBRARIES

There are 21 branches of the Vancouver Public Library located throughout the city. In addition to books, they offer readings and lectures. The **Central Library** (750 Burrard Street, 665-2280) is open Monday to Thursday from 10am to 9pm; Friday and Saturday, 10am to 6pm; and Sunday, 1pm to 5pm (October to May). No phone service on Sundays. Many municipalities have their own library systems; next to the Vancouver system, West Vancouver is tops in the province.

LIMOUSINE SERVICES

Star Limousine Service (468 W Seventh Avenue, 875-9466) has been around for more than a dozen years and has a fleet of 26 limousines delivering prompt, reliable service.

LOST CAR

First check to find out if the car was towed. Call 688-5484 if it was parked on a city street or lane and 681-8181 if it was parked in a private lot. If neither of these contract towing companies have your wheels, call 911 and report the missing car to the police.

MEDICAL/DENTAL SERVICES

The**College of Physicians and Surgeons of BC** (1807 W 10th Avenue, 733-7758) has a list of doctors accepting patients. **Denman Medical Centre** (1175 Denman Street, 685-6555) offers a walk-in clinic. The **College of Dental Surgeons of BC** (1765 W Eighth Avenue, 736-3621) has a list of dentists accepting patients.

NEWSPAPERS

The *Vancouver Sun* (732-2111) is published every morning except Sunday. A complete entertainment section is published on

Fridays. The *Province* (732-2222), a tabloid whose mandate appears to be headline-grabbing journalism, is published every morning except Saturday. **Georgia Straight**, a free entertainment weekly that often contains strong features, is published on Thursday.

PET BOARDING

Hugs & Kisses Pet Sitters (731-1948) provides a network of animal lovers who will take pets as temporary guests in their homes. Pick-up and delivery service.

PHARMACIES (LATE NIGHT)

Shopper's Drug Mart (1125 Davie Street, 685-6445) is open 24 hours. The pharmacy in Safeway (2733 W Broadway, 732-5030) is open daily 8am to midnight.

PUBLIC RESTROOMS

Most locals simply stop at any major downtown hotel. You'll also find restrooms in shopping malls and at downtown Sky-Train stations.

SALON CARE

Suki's has three downtown locations (1025 Robson Street, 689-2859; Pan Pacific Hotel, 641-1342; Vancouver Centre Mall, 682-0225) and is open every day. **Avenir Beauty Consultants** (2355 Spruce Street, 731-1798) offers complete makeover service with hair stylists, aestheticians, and the best makeup artist in Vancouver. Open Tuesday to Saturday.

SENIORS SERVICES

Seniors Resources & Research Society (105-2182 W 12th Avenue, 733-2310) provides information about programs and services available to seniors.

SHOE/HANDBAG REPAIR

J. R. Donald has two locations in downtown Vancouver (Bentall Centre, lower level, Dunsmuir Street at Burrard Street, 688-0538; Sinclair Centre, Hastings Street at Granville Street, 662-7505) and makes repairs while you wait. **Express Shoe Repair** (1178 Robson Street, 683-2373) offers while-you-wait services.

SUITCASE REPAIR

Weston Luggage Repair (1111 Homer Street, 685-9749) has a well-established reputation for suitcase repairs. Most repairs completed while you wait.

TELEPHONE NUMBERS

AIDS Hotline...687-2437

Alaska Marine Highway Information ....(206) 676-0212

Alcoholics Anonymous 434-3933

Animal Emergency Clinic 734-5104

BCAA (BC Automotive Association) 293-2222

BC Ferry Corporation 669-1211

BC Government Enquiry Line 660-2421

BC Rail 984-5246

BC Transit 261-5100

Better Business Bureau 682-2711

Birth and Death Records 660-2937

Canada Customs 666-0545

Canadian Coast Guard 666-4302

Chamber of Commerce 681-2111

City Hall General Switchboard 873-7011

City Parks and Recreation Board 681-1141

Consumer and Corporate Affairs 666-5000

Crisis Centre 733-4111

Dentacentre 669-6700

Dial-A-Story 536-6667

Directory Assistance 411

Emergency: police, fire, ambulance 911

Employment & Immigration Canada 681-8253

Immigration Centre 666-2171

Legal Services 687-4680

Medicentre 683-8138

Passports 666-0221

Planned Parenthood 731-4252

Poison Control Centre 631-5050

Postal Code Information 684-9466

Post Office Information 685-2692

Pound 251-1325

Rape Relief 872-8212

Red Cross 431-4200

Road Conditions 525-4997

Royal Canadian Mounted Police 264-3111

Sports Organizations

    BC Lions (football) 583-7747

Essentials

▼

Keys to the City

▲

Vancouver Canadians (baseball) 872-5232

Vancouver Canucks (hockey) 254-5141

Ticketmaster 280-4444

Tourism Vancouver 683-2000

U.S. Customs (Blaine) ....(206) 332-5771

Vancouver City Police 665-3321

Vancouver Health Department 736-2033

VIA Rail ....(800) 561-8630

Weather 664-9010

TOWING

Unitow (1410 Granville Street, 688-5484) provides Vancouver with 24-hour towing. **Buster's** (104 E First Street, 685-8181) provides the same service. If your car was removed from the street for illegal parking, call Unitow; if you were towed from a private lot, call Buster's.

UNIVERSITIES

▼

Keys to the City

▲

Simon Fraser University (Burnaby Mountain, 291-3210) Award-winning architecture set in breathtaking scenery. Student guides lead free tours, starting at the Administration Building. **University of British Columbia** (Point Grey, 822-3131), Canada's third-largest university, is famous for its scenery and attractions, including botanical and Japanese gardens and the Museum of Anthropology. The campus is surrounded by a 763-hectare (1,885-acre) park with kilometres of hiking trails and ocean shoreline. Free campus tours available May to August. Visitors welcome year-round.

VETERINARIANS: EMERGENCY AND WEEKEND SERVICE

Centrally located, the **Animal Emergency Clinic** (1590 W Fourth Avenue, 734-5104) is open 24 hours every day.

ALL-NIGHT SERVICES

COURIERS

Accel Courier Co. (255-4433) will pick up and deliver your package anywhere in the Lower Mainland or to Whistler Mountain 24 hours a day.

SERVICE STATIONS

The 24-hour Chevron Station (1691 W Georgia Street, 681-0028) is centrally located on a busy, well-lit street between downtown and the West End.

SUPERMARKETS

Super Valu (1255 Davie Street, 688-0911) is open 24 hours a day. It provides a delivery service Monday to Saturday, 9am-6pm.

BUSINESS SERVICES

COMPUTER RENTALS

Central Computer Source Rent IBM and peripheral systems for about $150 a month. Delivery and set-up service. Fax machines available. ■ *881 Hamilton St, 684-4545.*

Pacific West Office World Rentals by the day, week, or month, leasing options, rent-to-own, and delivery. IBM compatibles, printers, copiers, office furniture. A complete computer system with printer is about $65 a week. Extremely accommodating and friendly service. Central downtown location. ■ *1134 Homer St, 681-9666.*

CONVENTIONS

Most major hotels and many restaurants offer meeting rooms for rent. The following is a list of other rental facilities appropriate for business meetings, private parties, and receptions. Both the University of British Columbia and Simon Fraser University offer numerous halls, auditoriums, and meeting rooms. Most private and public museums and art galleries also have space available.

ABC Boat Charters A fleet of nine boats (the largest can carry 90 passengers) is available for luncheons, dinners, or private conferences on the water. Catering and entertainment available. ■ *M100-750 Pacific Blvd S, 682-2070.*

BC Place The entire 60,000-seat domed stadium is available for concerts, conventions, sporting events, or just about anything else. There are also private suites, banquet rooms, several meeting rooms with various configurations, and a food court. ■ *777 Pacific Blvd S, 661-3403.*

Centennial Theatre Centre The North Vancouver recreation department rents its 718-seat theatre for meetings and presentations. The department provides twin slide projectors and is equipped to provide light catering. ■ *2300 Lonsdale St, North Vancouver, 984-4484.*

Granville Island Banquet Centre The pleasant setting overlooks the marina on the west side of Granville Island, with two rooms available for meetings, banquets, or conferences. The Granville Island Room seats up to 250 for dinner and dancing, 400 for lectures and seminars. The Marine Lounge offers the best view, seating 120 for dinner, 150 for lectures. ■ *1515 Anderson St, 682-5674.*

Performance Works Used as a rehearsal space for professional performing arts, this venue is also available to the public, accommodating a capacity of 500. The airy building provides a parklike setting with natural light. ■ *1218 Cartwright St (Granville Island), 666-6655.*

Robson Square Conference Centre Part of the Robson Square complex—which includes the law courts, art gallery, and food court—the centre offers two theatres, six meeting rooms, an exhibition hall, two smaller board rooms, and full catering. You can rent all or part of the facilities. ▪ *800 Robson St, 660-2830.*

Vancouver Aquarium How about a board room situated in the killer whale underwater viewing area? Or maybe you'd like the entire aquarium for a standup reception of 1,700 people. From September through June, after business hours until midnight, the Vancouver Aquarium rents its venue for parties, receptions, or formal dinners. Dine with an octopus or sip cocktails in the presence of killer whales. Functions are catered by a number of preselected caterers. There are a board room and theatre available for day use. Prices are competitive. Definitely a best place. ▪ *Stanley Park, 685-3364.*

Vancouver Art Gallery Formerly the provincial courthouse, the neoclassical art gallery is available for receptions and meetings after hours. Rent the entire gallery, the main floor, or the historic board room of the Supreme Court of British Columbia (available for day use). Ideal space accommodates 50 to 500. Open to recommended outside caterers. ▪ *750 Hornby St, 682-4668.*

Vancouver Trade & Convention Centre The centre is housed in a spectacular harbour setting, under the distinctive sails of Canada Place. Three levels and 21 meeting rooms, with one massive ballroom and a lengthy entrance hall. ▪ *Canada Place, Burrard St, 641-1987.*

COPY SERVICES

Copy Time Printing & Copying Service If you need fast, competitively priced copying or printing done at a handy downtown location, this is the place. ▪ *714 W Hastings St, 682-8307; fax 684-7825.*

Kinko's Nobody else offers such a wide range of services, including copying, computer rentals, résumé writing, desktop publishing, and passport photos. Open 24 hours, every day. ▪ *Unit 260-2083 Alma St, 222-1688.*

MESSENGER AND DELIVERY SERVICES
See also All-Night Services: Couriers above.

Federal Express Next-day service to and from anywhere in the world. Two downtown locations. No weight limit. Agents can offer advice about customs requirements. ▪ *(800) 463-3339.*

PDX Courier Fast, reliable delivery service anywhere within Greater Vancouver. ▪ *1-325 Howe St, 684-3336.*

Suite 300 Executive Offices and Secretarial Services Offices
and meeting space with all the required secretarial support in
a professional atmosphere. Just 15 minutes from downtown on
the mountain side of Lion's Gate Bridge, two blocks from West
Vancouver's waterfront. ■ *400-850 W Hastings St, 687-5516.*

CALENDAR

Calendar

JANUARY

Average daily maximum and minimum temperatures: 5°, 4°C (41°, 39°F). Average rainfall: 201 millimetres (8 inches).

Chinese New Year [FREE] In late January or early February (depending on the lunar calendar), Chinatown greets the Chinese New Year with a fanfare of fireworks, displays, and a lively parade featuring lion dancers. ▪ *Chinatown; 671-6303.*

Polar Bear Swim [FREE] Start the new year by plunging into the cold Pacific with several hundred others, urged on by thousands of noisy supporters. ▪ *English Bay; 732-2111.*

Women In View Festival During the doldrums of the post-holiday season, there is at least one reason for celebration. Each January, the Women In View Festival, whose mandate is to showcase work initiated by women, presents a variety of performances, workshops, and networking sessions. From solo performers to choirs, from the traditional to the cutting edge, the festival roster highlights the creative achievements of women in music, theatre, dance, storytelling, and other art forms. Performances are held in various venues around Vancouver, attracting a mix of viewers. ▪ *685-6684.*

FEBRUARY

Average daily maximum and minimum temperatures: 8°, 3°C (46°, 37°F). Average rainfall: 161 millimetres (6.3 inches).

Spring Home Show If you're looking for contemporary West Coast ideas for decorating, this is the place. The largest home show in Western Canada. ▪ *BC Place Stadium; 433-5121.*

MARCH

Average daily maximum and minimum temperatures: 9°, 4°C (48°, 39°F). Average rainfall: 151 millimetres (6 inches).

BC Great Outdoors Show Ideas galore for the great outdoors. Where to go and what to take. All the newest gadgets with plenty of time-tested wisdom. ▪ *BC Place Stadium; 291-6651.*

Pacific Rim Whale Festival Migrating gray whales can be observed during March and April just off the shores of the Long Beach section of Pacific Rim National Park. Numerous charter boats and a seaplane company offer close-up looks at the pods. The actual festival, including dances and education programs, begins the last week in March. ▪ *Tofino, BC; (604) 725-3414.*

Vancouver Storytelling Festival Few events underline Vancouver's ethnic mix as well as the storytelling festival, held for three days each March at various West End locations. More than 20 participants, including First Nations storytellers and tellers spinning tales in five different languages (translators come too), hold audiences spellbound. ▪ *228-1274.*

APRIL

Average daily maximum and minimum temperatures: 13°, 6°C (55°, 43°F). Average rainfall: 91 millimetres (3.5 inches).

Brant Festival The annual Brant Festival celebrates the stopover of the brant (a species of geese) on their migration from Mexico to northern Canada. Staging areas provide fine opportunities to view the geese, once nearly extinct, as they feed. Wildlife art, photography exhibits, and carving competitions too. ▪ *Parksville, BC; (604) 284-4117.*

Vancouver Playhouse International Wine Festival Reputed to be the largest and most prestigious consumer wine event in North America, attracting more than 115 wineries from over 15 countries. ▪ *Vancouver Trade and Convention Centre; 872-6622.*

MAY

Average daily maximum and minimum temperatures: 16°, 9°C (61°, 48°F). Average rainfall: 76 millimetres (3 inches).

Cloverdale Rodeo The Lower Fraser Valley Exhibition Grounds attracts competitors from around the world for one of this continent's largest rodeos. ▪ *6050-176th St, Cloverdale; 576-9461.*

Hyack Festival The Hyack Anvil Battery, which has fired a "21 gun anvil" salute to the memory of Queen Victoria since 1871 (when cannons were not available), gave today's festival its name. Hyack is a Chinook word meaning "hurry up." High-

lights of the nine-day New Westminster festival include the
May Day celebration, an international parade, sporting events,
and fireworks. ▪ *New Westminster, BC; 522-6894.*

Vancouver International Children's Festival International theatre, music, dance, storytelling, and comedy for youngsters.
Lots of hands-on activities, roving performers, games, and arts
and crafts. Big-top tents on the lawns of Vanier Park at the entrance to False Creek. For kids, it's a winner. Tickets to main-
stage shows $3.50 to $6.50. ▪ *Vanier Park; 687-7697.*

Vancouver International Marathon An international field of
runners sets out from the Plaza of Nations on the first Sunday
in May for a 42-kilometre (26.2 mile) race that takes over 4,000
runners through Stanley Park, across the Lions Gate Bridge,
along the North Shore, back across the Second Narrows
Bridge, and through East Vancouver to the finish line. A half
marathon and the Health and Fitness Expo take place in conjunction with the marathon. ▪ *672-2928.*

JUNE

*Average daily maximum and minimum temperatures: 19°, 11°C
(66°, 52°F). Average rainfall: 63 millimetres (2.5 inches).*

Bard on the Beach From June through September, Bard on
the Beach presents Shakespeare under a tent at Vanier Park.
The company presents 78 performances with renowned actors
in two plays each summer. Tickets are $12 and go on sale April
1. ▪ *280-3311.*

Canadian International Dragon Boat Festival Vancouver's
premier multicultural festival features dragon boat racing,
entertainment, and food from around the world. ▪ *Plaza of
Nations; 683-4448.*

du Maurier International Jazz Festival Hundreds of jazz and
blues artists from five continents perform during the two-week
festival, presenting a full spectrum of traditional and contemporary jazz at various locations. ▪ *Downtown Area; 682-0706.*

Salmon Festival British Columbia is famous for its salmon,
and Steveston, a traditional fishing village, is famous for its
salmon festival. It's worth the 45-minute drive out of town to
feast on barbecued salmon, clam chowder, and other treats.
Now in its 45th year, the Salmon Festival is the finale of special events held throughout June. ▪ *Steveston; 277-6812.*

JULY

*Average daily maximum and minimum temperatures: 22°, 13°C
(72°, 55°F). Average rainfall: 50 millimetres (2 inches).*

Benson and Hedges Symphony of Fire Pyrotechnicians from

around the world compete in an extravaganza of fireworks set off from a barge on English Bay before thousands of people. On four nonconsecutive nights beginning the last Saturday in July. ■ *English Bay; 688-1992.*

The Gastown Gran Prix The major bike racing event of the year, the Gastown Gran Prix is held on the weekend closest to Canada Day (July 1). Racers complete 65 short laps over the bumpy, treacherous cobblestone streets of Gastown. Sharp corners, narrow streets, and tightly bunched riders can result in spectacular crashes. A fantastic spectator sport, even if you don't pedal. ■

Harrison Festival of the Arts During this nine-day event, over 35,000 people visit Harrison Hot Springs to celebrate the musical, visual, and performing arts of a different set of countries each year. Theatres, lectures, workshops, and live entertainment give visitiors many activities from which to choose. ■ *Harrison Hot Springs, BC; (604) 796-3664.*

Italian Week The Italian community offers pasta, parades, marvellous coffee, games, and many more activities for one week in early July. The city's Italian area is famous for its cosmopolitan flavour and great food. ■ *Commercial Dr; 430-3337.*

Vancouver Chamber Music Festival Leila Getz's tradition of presenting the best of young, budding artists during the summer months has made the Chamber Music Festival one of the hottest tickets in town. In a relaxed, casual setting, concerts are held during the last week of July and the first week of August. Each of the six concerts features a cast of superb soloists, who combine their talents to offer a wonderful menu of chamber music. ■ *Crofton House School for Girls; 3200 W 41st Ave; 263-3255.*

Vancouver Early Music Festival Running from mid-July to mid-August, the concert series features music from the Middle Ages to the classical era performed on period instruments. ■ *UBC Recital Hall; 732-1610.*

Vancouver Folk Music Festival [KIDS] Travel around the world in 2½ days, aurally. The third weekend in July, the United Nations of the folk music world gathers at Jericho Beach Park, a spectacular setting for a spectacular celebration of music, heritage, and folklore. Over the festival's 16-year history, an amazing diversity of performers have made this event one of the best music festivals anywhere. The heart and soul of the festival are the various themed workshops held on six separate stages throughout the day. Evenings are devoted to music making, with one main stage holding the limelight. An alcohol-free event, the festival also stages a little-folks' festival that includes water play, face painting, crafts, and great food. Throughout the year, the festival's organization also hosts independent concerts at the Vancouver East Cultural Centre and the Commodore Ballroom. ■ *Jericho Beach Park; 879-2931.*

Vancouver International Comedy Festival Featuring an eclectic and diverse mixture of comic artists, the festival stretches over nearly two full weeks, from the end of July to early August. ■ *Granville Island; 683-0883.*

Vancouver Sea Festival A celebration of Vancouver's glorious waterfront, held on the edge of the city's high-rise West End. The size and format of the festival have continually changed over the years, but it now seems to have settled into an event geared toward family fun. Spectacular fireworks and a bathtub race from Nanaimo on Vancouver Island are two of the highlights. ■ *English Bay; 684-3378.*

Victoria International Festival Artists from the Northwest gather at various Victoria venues to give classical music concerts, recitals, and ballet performances throughout the months of July and August. Ticket prices top out at $21 per performance. ■ *Victoria, BC; (604) 736-2119.*

AUGUST

Average daily maximum and minimum temperatures: 22°, 14°C (72°, 57°F). Average rainfall: 48 millimetres (2 inches).

Abbotsford International Airshow/Airshow Canada Want to see a Russian MIG up close or watch wing-walkers defy gravity? How about the aerobatics of the U.S. Thunderbirds and the Canadian Snowbirds? Abbotsford's International Airshow has it all and more. Airshow Canada is a trade show that happens in odd-numbered years. ■ *Abbotsford Airport, BC; (604) 852-8511.*

Fine Arts Show Residents of southern Vancouver Island display their paintings and sculptures in the largest juried art show and sale in BC. A $6 admission is good for the entire 10-day event. ■ *Sooke Region Museum, Sooke, BC; (604) 642-6351.*

Pacific National Exhibition The second-largest exhibition in Canada. It features big-name musical entertainment, livestock displays, equestrian events, arts and crafts, and amusement rides. ■ *Hastings St at Renfrew St; 253-2311.*

Powell Street Festival This is the city's largest ethnic festival, held every year in early August. A celebration of Asian history, arts, and cultural events, the festival provides a fascinating range of events and experiences including sumo wrestling, exotic foods, martial arts, theatre, and dancers performing traditional dances in delightful costumes. ■ *Oppenheimer Park, Powell St; 682-4335.*

Vancouver Fringe Festival An 11-day theatre festival featuring close to 100 productions of original works and classics by local, national, and international artists. ▪ *Mount Pleasant Area; 873-3646.*

SEPTEMBER

Average daily maximum and minimum temperatures: 18°, 8°C (64°, 46°F). Average rainfall: 69 millimetres (2.7 inches).

Dancing on the Edge A ten-day celebration of dance held at various locations, including Granville Island, coinciding with the Fringe Festival. ▪ *Downtown Area; 689-0691.*

Molson Indy Vancouver For three action-packed days on Labour Day weekend, a world-class field of racing superstars thunder through the streets of Vancouver in wheel-to-wheel combat to decide who is Indy Car's best on the challenging 2.6 kilometre (1.6 mile) circuit. ▪ *Pacific Place; 684-4639.*

The Terry Fox Run Every September hundreds of thousands walk, run, bike, and blade 1-10 kilometres (0.6-6.2 miles) to raise funds for cancer in the memory of Terry Fox. He began his Marathon of Hope Run across Canada in 1980, but had to stop after cancer spread to his lungs. ▪ *The Terry Fox Foundation; 688-4611.*

The Vancouver Playhouse Theatre Company Stretching from late September to June, the Vancouver Playhouse Theatre's season features six different performances that run approximately four weeks each. ▪ *Hamilton St at Dunsmuir St; 873-3311.*

Vancouver Recital Society Internationally celebrated artists perform on various dates throughout the September to May season. ▪ *Orpheum Theatre; 736-6034.*

World Championship Sand Sculpture Competition Every second weekend in September, 30 master sculptors build 150 sand creations on the Main Beach at Harrison Hot Springs. As many as 25,000 spectators show up to view the masterpieces and see who will win $20,000 worth of prize money. ▪ *Main Beach, Harrison Hot Springs, BC; (604) 796-3425.*

OCTOBER

Average daily maximum and minimum temperatures: 14°, 4°C (57°, 39°F). Average rainfall: 158 millimetres (6 inches).

International Writer's and Reader's Festival This five-day event during the third week of October brings together more than 50 Canadian and international authors, playwrights, and poets from diverse cultural backgrounds, life experiences and places of origin, writing in every conceivable genre. Readings, interviews, and a poetry bash are informative, challenging and entertaining. ▪ *Granville Island; 681-6330.*

Masterpiece Chamber Music A season of romantic masterpieces is presented from October to April. Call for performance dates. ■ *Vancouver East Cultural Centre; 254-9578.*

Vancouver Canucks Hockey The NHL team season runs from October to April and potentially into June if the team makes the Stanley Cup finals. ■ *Pacific Coliseum; 280-4400.*

Vancouver International Film Festival More than 150 films from upwards of 40 countries are screened at six locations around town over a 17-day period. Tickets are sometimes available at the door a half hour before show time. A major event for international filmmakers. ■ *Downtown Area; 685-0260.*

Vancouver Opera The season runs from October to June, with five different performances offering extraordinary melodies, captivating drama, and magnificent sets and costumes. Call for performance dates. ■ *Queen Elizabeth Theatre; 683-0222.*

Vancouver Symphony Orchestra The varied and exciting season of the VSO runs from October to June. Call for performance dates. ■ *Orpheum; 876-3434.*

NOVEMBER

Average daily maximum and minimum temperatures: 9°, 2°C (48°, 36°F). Average rainfall: 235 millimetres (9 inches).

Vancouver Cantata Singers The four-concert season offers performance dates in November, December, March, and May. ■ *Orpheum; 921-8588.*

Vancouver Classic Jazz Band Ball An annual three-day classic jazz and swing festival in downtown Vancouver held the first weekend in November. ■ *Downtown Area; 732-8411.*

DECEMBER

Average daily maximum and minimum temperatures: 7°, 4°C (45°, 39°F). Average rainfall: 243 millimetres (9.5 inches).

Christmas Carol Ship Parade Carollers sail around the harbour on brightly lit boats accompanied by a flotilla of charter vessels carrying holiday revellers. ■ *Vancouver Harbour; 682-2007.*

Eagle Watching (Qualicum Beach) Bald eagles converge on these rivers from December through February. The scavengers are best seen before noon, when they're hunting spawning salmon. Bring binoculars and wear rain gear. ■ *Big and Little Qualicum rivers near Nanaimo, BC; (604) 752-9532.*

VanDusen Garden's Festival of Lights At Christmastime the gardens are transformed into a twinkling fairyland with 15,000 lights. There are also holiday events and special displays to help set the seasonal mood. ■ *37th and Oak St; 266-7194.*

Index

F

Fabrics, 158
Fairview, 86
Famous Foods, 170
Farm animals, 240
Fashion accessories, 159
Federal Express, 264
Federation Gallery, 102
Ferragamo, 154
Ferries, 257
Fiasco, 27, 89
Fiesta's, 87
Film, 106
Fine Finds, 157
Finlandia Pharmacy, 163
Firehall Arts Centre, 105
Fish House at Stanley
    Park, 27
Fishing, 232
    Horseshoe Bay/
        Hole in the Wall, 233
    Rice Lake, 233
    Salmon Lake Resort,
        233
    Spences Bridge, 233
Five Sails (Pan Pacific
    Hotel), 28
Flag Shop, 165
Floata ChiuChow
    Restaurant, 28
Florists, 159
Flower Show, 159
Flutterby's Lingerie &
    Hosiery, 164
Flying Wedge, 28
Folkart Antiques, 147
Football, BC Lions, 251
Foreign exchange, 258
Foreign visitors, 258
Form & Function, 160
Forster's Fine Cheeses,
    170
Fortune House, 29
Foto Base Gallery, 102
Four Seasons, 178
Frank's Place, 80
Fraser River Park, 135
Fraser River Tours, 141
Fraser Valley, 191
Friends of Chamber
    Music, 115
Fringe Festival, 109
Frisco's, 80
Fujiya, 170
Furniture, 160
Future Shop, 150

G

Gaia Garden Herbal
    Apothecary, 163
Galleries, 101
Gallery Cafe, 18
Gallery of BC Ceramics,
    104
Gallery of Tribal Art, 103
Galloway's, 170
Garden Lounge, 89
Garden Rooms, 159
Garden shops, 159
Gardens, 138
Garibaldi Provincial Park,
    245
Garry Point Park, 135
Gastown, 122
Gastown Garden Tea
    Room, 93
Gehringer Brothers Estate
    Winery, 209
Geology Museum-
    University of British
    Columbia, 112
Georg Jensen, 161
Georgian Court Hotel, 178
Gerard Lounge (Le
    Meridien Hotel), 89
Gibsons, 193
Gifts, 160
Giraffe, 29
Golden Age Collectables,
    165
Golfing, 233
    Fraserview Golf Course,
        234
    Mayfair Lakes, 234
    Peace Portal Golf Course,
        234
    Queen Elizabeth Pitch
        and Putt, 234
    University Golf Club, 234
Graceland, 81
Grand King Seafood
    Restaurant, 29
Grand View Restaurant, 30
Granville Book Company,
    149
Granville Island, 123
Granville Island Banquet
    Centre, 263
Gray Line, 142
Gray Monk Estate Winery,
    207
Griffins, 30
Grocery delivery, 259
Grouse Mountain, 125, 247

H

Hainle Estate Vineyards,
    208
Hair care products, 168
Hamburger Mary's, 31
Handbag repair, 260
Hanson's Fishing
    Outfitters, 172
Harbour Air, 142
Harbour Centre Tower, 125
Hardware, 162
Harrison Hot Springs, 191
Harry Rosen, 152
Hastings Mill Store
    Museum, 112
Health food, 162
Hearts Natural Foods, 163
Heffel Gallery, 102
Helicopter tours, 142
Hemlock Valley, 247
Hermitage, 31
Herons (Waterfront
    Centre Hotel), 31
Hewer Home Hardware,
    162
Highlife Records and
    Music, 166
Hiking, 234
    Garibaldi Provincial Park,
        234
    Golden Ears Provincial
        Park, 235
    Howe Sound Crest Trail,
        235
    Lighthouse Park, 235
    Manning Provincial Park,
        235
    Pitt River Dykes, 236
Hill's Indian Crafts, 164
Hill's of Kerrisdale, 152
Hockey, Vancouver
    Canucks, 251
Hogan's Alley, 90
Holliday's Funwear, 155
Hon's Wun Tun House, 32
Horizons on Burnaby
    Mountain, 32
Hornby Island, 205
Horse racing, 251
Horseback riding, 236
    Campbell Valley Regional
        Park, 236
    Golden Ears Provincial
        Park, 236
    Manning Provincial Park,
        236
    Whitbread Stables II, 236

World, 85
World Wide Books and
    Maps, 150
Wreck Beach, 138
Write Place, 172

Y
Yale, 88
Yaohan Supermarket and
    Shopping Centre, 71
Yerushalem Imports, 162
Yuk Yuk's, 85

Z
Zefferelli's, 72
Zeppo's Trattoria, 72
Zig Zag Boutique, 156
Zonda Nellis, 156
Zoos, 240
Zulu Records, 167
Zuni Cafe, 72

VANCOUVER BEST PLACES REPORT FORM

Based on my personal experience I wish to nominate/confirm/disapprove for listing the following restaurant, place of lodging, shop, nightspot, sight, or other:

_____

_____

_____

_____

(Please include address and telephone number of establishment, if convenient.)

Report:

(Please describe food, service, style, comfort, value, date of visit, and other aspects of your visit; continue on overleaf if necessary.)

_____

_____

_____

_____

_____

_____

_____

_____

_____

_____

_____

_____

_____

_____

I am not concerned, directly or indirectly, with the management or ownership of this establishment.

Signed _____

Address_____

Phone Number_____

Date_____

Send to: _Vancouver Best Places_
1008 Western Avenue, Suite 300
Seattle, WA 98104

VANCOUVER BEST PLACES REPORT FORM

Based on my personal experience I wish to nominate/confirm/disapprove for listing the following restaurant, place of lodging, shop, nightspot, sight, or other:

_____

_____

_____

(Please include address and telephone number of establishment, if convenient.)

Report:

(Please describe food, service, style, comfort, value, date of visit, and other aspects of your visit; continue on overleaf if necessary.)

_____

_____

_____

_____

_____

_____

_____

_____

_____

_____

_____

_____

_____

_____

I am not concerned, directly or indirectly, with the management or ownership of this establishment.

Signed _____

Address _____

Phone Number _____

Date _____

Send to: *Vancouver Best Places*
1008 Western Avenue, Suite 300
Seattle, WA 98104

Did you enjoy this book?

Sasquatch Books publishes high-quality books and guides related to the Pacific Northwest. Our books are available at bookstores and other retail outlets throughout the region. Here is a partial list of our current titles:

GUIDEBOOKS

Northwest Best Places
The Definitive Guide to Restaurants, Lodgings, and Touring in Oregon, Washington, and British Columbia
Edited by David Brewster and Stephanie Irving

Northern California Best Places
The Definitive Guide to Restaurants, Lodgings, and Touring in Northern California
Edited by Laura Hagar and Stephanie Irving

Seattle Best Places
The Most Discriminating Guide to Seattle's Restaurants, Shops, Hotels, Nightlife, Arts, Sights, and Outings
Edited by Stephanie Irving

Portland Best Places
The Most Discriminating Guide to Portland's Restaurants, Shops, Hotels, Nightlife, Arts, Sights, and Outings
Edited by Kim Carlson and Stephanie Irving

Northwest Cheap Sleeps
Great Lodgings for Under $50 and Hundreds of Travel Ideas for the Adventurous Road Tripper in OR, WA, and BC
Edited by Stephanie Irving

Back Roads of Washington
74 Trips on Washington's Scenic Byways
Earl Thollander

Back Roads of Oregon
82 Trips on Oregon's Scenic Byways
Earl Thollander

**Earl Thollander's
Back Roads of California**
65 Trips on California's Scenic Byways

Earl Thollander's San Francisco
30 Walking and Driving Tours from the Embarcadero to the Golden Gate

FIELD GUIDES

Field Guide to the Bald Eagle
Field Guide to the Gray Whale
Field Guide to the Grizzly Bear
Field Guide to the Humpback Whale
Field Guide to the Orca
Field Guide to the Pacific Salmon
Field Guide to the Sasquatch
Field Guide to the Slug

GARDENING

The Cascadia Gardening Series:
  Growing Herbs
  North Coast Roses
  Water-Wise Vegetables
  Winter Ornamentals

The Year In Bloom
Gardening for All Seasons in the Pacific Northwest
Ann Lovejoy

FOOD AND COOKING

The Encyclopedia of Country Living
An Old Fashioned Recipe Book
Carla Emery

Breakfast In Bed
The Best B&B Recipes from Northern California, Oregon, Washington, and British Columbia
Carol Frieberg

Pike Place Market Cookbook
Recipes, Anecdotes, and Personalities from Seattle's Renowned Public Market
Braiden Rex-Johnson

Eight Items or Less Cookbook
Fine Food in a Hurry
Ann Lovejoy

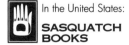

In the United States:
SASQUATCH BOOKS
1008 Western Avenue, Suite 300
Seattle, WA 98104
(206) 467-4300   1-800-775-0817

RAINCOAST BOOKS
112 East Third Avenue
Vancouver, BC V5T 1C8
(604) 873-6581   1-800-663-5714

WE STAND BY OUR REVIEWS

Sasquatch Books is proud of *Vancouver Best Places*. Our editors and contributors take great pain and expense to see that all of the restaurant and lodging reviews are as accurate, up-to-date, and honest as possible. If we have misled you, please accept our apologies; however, if this edition of *Vancouver Best Places* has seriously disappointed you, Sasquatch Books would like to refund your purchase price. To receive your refund:

1) Tell us where you purchased your book and return the book to: Satisfaction Guaranteed, Sasquatch Books, 1008 Western Avenue, Suite 300, Seattle, WA 98104.

2) Enclose the original hotel or restaurant receipt from the establishment in question, including date of visit.

3) Write a full explanation of your stay or meal and how *Vancouver Best Places* misled you.

4) Include your name, address, and phone number.

Refund is valid only while this edition of *Vancouver Best Places* is in print. If the ownership has changed since publication, Sasquatch Books cannot be held responsible. Postage on the returned book is your responsibility. Please allow four weeks for processing.